LEGAL RISK IN THE
FINANCIAL MARKETS

LEGAL RISK IN THE FINANCIAL MARKETS

ROGER MCCORMICK

OXFORD

UNIVERSITY PRESS

OXFORD
UNIVERSITY PRESS

Great Clarendon Street, Oxford OX2 6DP

Oxford University Press is a department of the University of Oxford.
It furthers the University's objective of excellence in research, scholarship,
and education by publishing worldwide in

Oxford New York

Auckland Cape Town Dar es Salaam Hong Kong Karachi
Kuala Lumpur Madrid Melbourne Mexico City Nairobi
New Delhi Shanghai Taipei Toronto

With offices in

Argentina Austria Brazil Chile Czech Republic France Greece
Guatemala Hungary Italy Japan Poland Portugal Singapore
South Korea Switzerland Thailand Turkey Ukraine Vietnam

Oxford is a registered trade mark of Oxford University Press
in the UK and in certain other countries

Published in the United States
by Oxford University Press Inc., New York

British Library Cataloguing in Publication Data

Data available

Library of Congress Cataloging-in-Publication Data

McCormick, Roger.
Legal risk in the financial markets / Roger McCormick.
p. cm.
Includes index.
ISBN–13: 978–0–19–928191–6 (alk. paper)
ISBN–10: 0–19–928191–2 (alk. paper)
1. Financial services industry—Law and legislation—China—Hong Kong.
2. Corporate governance—Law and legislation—China—Hong Kong. 3.
Securities—China—Hong Kong. I. Title.
KNQ9323.6.M43 2006
346.5125'082—dc22   2006002074

Typeset by RefineCatch Limited, Bungay, Suffolk
Printed in Great Britain
on acid-free paper by
Biddles Ltd., King's Lynn

ISBN 0–19–928191–2 978–0–19–928191–6

1 3 5 7 9 10 8 6 4 2

FOREWORD

Legal risk is a subject that has gained increasing attention from banks and other financial institutions over the past fifteen years. Legal risk takes many forms but they may be broadly divided into two groups: transactional risk, where because of legal doubts or difficulties a financial institution may be exposed to liability on a dealing or be unable to enforce a contract or security; and regulatory risk, which exposes the institution to restrictions, penalties, or criminal sanctions for breach of regulatory rules that may be complex or unclear. Central to both forms of risk is uncertainty: uncertainty as to the way a transaction will be characterized or as to whether a particular mode of business is or is not legally permissible or as to the law to be applied to determine the rights and duties of the parties. The perceived predictability of English law and, more particularly, of decision-making by English judges, is one of the reasons why English law is so regularly selected as the governing law in transactions which have little or no connection with this country. Yet every now and then uncertainty is created by new instruments or by unexpected judicial decisions, of which the most regrettable was that of the House of Lords in *Hazell v Hammersmith and Fulham London Borough Council* [1992] 2 AC 1, overturning an eminently sensible and realistic ruling by the Court of Appeal.

This new book by Roger McCormick provides a clear and up-to-date analysis of the nature of legal risk, the different forms it can take, the various initiatives that have been taken to identify and manage legal risk, and the lawyers' responsibility for risk management. As co-chair of the International Bar Association's Working Party on Legal Risk, Roger McCormick is particularly well placed to offer guidance on this complex topic and his measured approach and lightness of touch combine to make this book not only informative but a good read. Characterization deservedly receives a good deal of his attention, whether it relates to set-off (as in the *British Eagle* case), the distinction between a sale and a security interest (as in the *Welsh Developmment Agency* case), or between a fixed and a floating charge (as in *Spectrum*), the legal effect of a charge-back (as in *Re Charge Card Services Ltd*, and the subsequent *BCCI* case), or the nature of an investor's interest in securities held through an account with an intermediary. The last part of the book focuses on the management of legal risk, including the role of legal opinions and the range of issues which a well-drawn opinion can be expected to cover in relation to financial transactions, with particular reference to the legal efficacy of close-out netting agreements.

I have no doubt that this new book will be widely welcomed by the practising profession as well as by scholars having an interest in this field. It is impossible for those engaged in business to avoid legal risk; the best that can be done is to take reasonable steps to manage it. *Legal Risk in the Financial Markets* shows how this might be done.

Roy Goode
Oxford
August 2005

PREFACE

This book has been brewing for some time. The idea of writing it was first put to me while I was still in full-time legal practice. Naturally, I gave it very serious consideration; it seemed to have some merit, fitting well with my areas of professional interest. So I did absolutely nothing about it for the best part of a year. I did not get around to putting pen to paper with any serious intent until the period of transition (for me) had started, which now finds me largely (but not entirely) free of commitments to clients and engaged much more in academic activities.

At first, I was far from certain that legal risk (and our perception of it) was anything more than the manifestation of an ephemeral preoccupation that had been spawned by modern society's fear and dread of risk of any kind. Our obsession with risk seems to go hand-in-hand with the so-called compensation culture (and its close companion, the blame culture) that dominates public life, at least as it is reported, day in and day out, by the 24-hour news 'media'. This scepticism is still with me up to a point, and is partly reflected in the book. However, I did (as the production of this book shows) eventually come to the conclusion that there is in fact a relatively modern phenomenon—represented by the notion of legal risk—that is likely to be with us for the foreseeable future and merits some attempt at analysis and comment. I decided to take the plunge.

The writing of the book took place, for the most part, between October 2004 and August 2005. Much of the data extracted from media commentary originates in that period. However, legal risk does have a 'history' and the first part of the book therefore looks at how the idea first came to be a talking point in the financial markets and how it led, in time, to the formation of the Legal Risk Review Committee. An account (which happens to be closely linked to my own experience as a practitioner) is also provided of the development, through case law and legislation, of the issues (which, in my view, comprise some of the most interesting legal issues that have confronted City lawyers in the past twenty years) that were of primary concern at the time legal risk first surfaced and was perceived to be something to be taken seriously. The later parts of the book are concerned with what legal risk is now thought to signify, where the pressure points are currently felt most keenly, and, inevitably, how we might set about managing the various aspects of legal risk. The net result is something that is partly a law book, partly social commentary, and partly a guide to risk management.

Any period of transition involves doubts and uncertainties and the time of my own move away from City legal practice proved to be no exception. This book would not have been written without the support and encouragement of a great many friends and colleagues. It is not possible to name them all. However, the following (no doubt to their great embarrassment) deserve special mention for the assistance (which took many forms) they have given me along the way: Hugh Pigott, Joanna Benjamin, Michael Crystal QC, Colin Bamford, Paul Watchman, Hugh Bryant, Philip Wood, Nigel Asprey, William Elliott, Adrian Marsh, Martin Thomas, Mark Harding, Penny Curtis, Bill Parker, Alan Redfern, Ian Hewitt, Guy Morton, Peter Bloxham, Richard Drummond, Michael Allen, Sebastian Hofert, John Thirlwell, Mark Johnson, Mike Power, Andrew Whittaker, Richard Rosenfeld, Gavin Watson, and John Heath. They are not, of course, to be blamed for any of the content!

I would also like to thank Grant Sullivan for his unfailing and timely help with my computer, which on more than one occasion pushed me to the brink of nervous breakdown. (Can't live with it; can't live without it.)

Finally, and most important of all, my eternal gratitude goes to my wife, Sophie, and my daughter, Lucy, for their patience and understanding, as well as a good deal of very practical help and advice. Without them, none of this would have seen the light of day.

The law and general position is stated as at 31 August 2005.

Roger McCormick
31 August 2005

ACKNOWLEDGEMENTS

Grateful acknowledgement is made to all the authors and publishers of copyright material which appears in this book, and in particular to the following for permission to reprint material from the sources indicated:

Turnbull guidance is reproduced by kind permission of the Financial Reporting Council.

The Code of Market Conduct is reproduced with the kind permission of the Financial Services Authority (FSA), which holds the copyright. Use of FSA material does not indicate any endorsement by the FSA of this publication, or the material or views contained within it.

Extract from *The View from No. 11: Memoirs of a Tory Radical* by Nigel Lawson (Copyright © Nigel Lawson, 1992) is reproduced with permission of PFD (www.pfd.co.uk) on behalf of Lord Lawson of Blaby.

The C&I Group Corporate Governance Committee & Wragge & Co jointly wrote and produced the C&I Group Corporate Governance Guidelines for In-House Lawyers.

The Basel principles are reproduced with the kind permission from the Basel Committee or Banking Supervisor. All original texts are available free of charge from their website (www.BIS.org).

Financial Law Panel (FLP) extracts are kindly reproduced with the permission of the Financial Markets Law Committee (FMLC).

CONTENTS—SUMMARY

CONTENTS

III EXAMPLES

TABLE OF CASES

TABLES OF LEGISLATION

LIST OF ABBREVIATIONS

General

ACLA	Australian Corporate Lawyers Association
Andersen Amicus Briefs	The briefs of 'amicus curiae' dated February 2005, presented by the National Association of Criminal Defense Lawyers and by the Washington Legal Foundation and Chamber of Commerce of the United States in the case of *Arthur Andersen v United States of America* (No 04–368)
BCBS	Basel Committee on Banking Supervision
BCBS Operational Risk Paper	The paper published by BCBS in February 2003 on 'Sound Practices for the Management and Supervision of Operational Risk'
BCBS Principles	The principles set out in para 10 of the BCBS Operational Risk Paper, as set out in Appendix 3 Part 1
BCCI	Bank of Credit and Commerce International SA
BIS	Bank for International Settlements
CDOs	collateralized debt obligations
CEDR	Centre for Effective Dispute Resolution
CHAPS	Clearing House Automated Payment System
CLANZ	Corporate Lawyers Association of New Zealand
Collateral Directive	Directive 2002/47/EC of the European Parliament and of the Council of 6 June 2002 on financial collateral arrangements
CSFI	Centre for the Study of Financial Innovation
EFMLG	European Financial Market Lawyers Group
FCA(2)	Financial Collateral Arrangements (No 2) Regulations 2003
First Giovannini Clearing and Settlement Report	The first report, published by the Giovannini Group, on Clearing and Settlement Systems (November 2001)
FLP	Financial Law Panel
FMLC	Financial Markets Law Committee
FRC	Financial Reporting Council
FSA	Financial Services Authority
FSA 1986	Financial Services Act 1986
FSA Principles	The eleven principles for banks referred to Dr Huertas' speech of 8 February 2005
FSMA 2000	Financial Services and Markets Act 2000
Giovannini Group	The expert group of financial market participants, chaired by Alberto Giovannini, advising the EU Commission on financial market issues
IBA	International Bar Association

IBA legal risk symposium	The International Bar Association Symposium on Legal Risk, October 2003
ICAEW	Institute of Chartered Accountants in England and Wales
ICSD	International Central Securities Depositaries
IOSCO	International Organization of Securities Commissions
ISDA	International Securities Dealers Association
ISLA	International Securities Lending Association
Joint Forum	The BCBS, IOSCO, and The International Association of Insurance Supervisors
LRRC	Legal Risk Review Committee
NCIS	National Criminal Intelligence Service
PFI	The Private Finance Initiative (as implemented in the UK)
POCA 2002	Proceeds of Crime Act 2002
PPP	Public Private Partnership
Proposed Interagency Statement	The 'Proposed Statement on Sound Practices Concerning the Complex Structured Finance Activities of Financial Institutions' issued on 13 May 2003 by the Securities and Exchange Commission and various other US regulatory agencies
Rule 4.90	Rule 4.90 of the Insolvency Rules 1986 (see Appendix 1)
SEC	Securities and Exchange Commission (US)
Second Giovannini Clearing and Settlement Report	The second report, published by the Giovannini Group, on clearing and settlement issues (April 2003)
Settlement Finality Directive	Directive 98/26/EC of the European Parliament and of the Council of 19 May 1998 on settlement finality in payment and securities settlement systems
SIB	Securities and Investments Board
SOCPA 2005	Serious Organised Crime and Police Act 2005
Turnbull Report	'Internal Control: Guidance for Directors on The Combined Code', published by the Internal Control Working Party of the Institute of Chartered Accountants in England and Wales (now embodied in the FRC's Combined Code on Corporate Governance)
UNIDROIT	International Institute for the Unification of Private Law

Journals

BLI	*Business Law International*
IFLR	*International Financial Law Review*
JIBFL	*Journal of International Banking and Financial Law*
LQR	*Law Quarterly Review*
LS Gaz	*Law Society's Gazette*

INTRODUCTION

British insurance companies, banks and other financial institutions achieved net exports of £19bn . . . in 2004, almost three times higher than their contribution to the UK's balance of payments a decade ago. No other advanced country has enjoyed Britain's success in deriving a large increase in export earnings from its financial sector . . . The surge has been driven principally by increased business in the City of London.[1]

. . . the market is entitled to expect the law:
* to be accessible; . . .
* to facilitate the efficiency and stability of the market and reduce systemic risk;
* to be sufficiently responsive to the legitimate needs of investors, intermediaries and collateral takers to encourage them to select English law as the governing law and avoid a situation in which . . . English law is seen as the weak link in the chain . . .[2]

A. Risk and the Financial Sector

No one who leads a normal life can avoid taking risks. They are part of the human condition, infinite in variety, both as to nature and as to seriousness. Everyday life involves taking risks on commonplace things such as the weather or the punctuality of trains as well as on more weighty matters such as the financial performance of investments or whether or not to change jobs or move house. We take risks from time to time on matters that might affect our health and physical well-being. We may risk our fortune or our reputation. Sometimes, albeit unwillingly, we may even have to take decisions that have life or death implications for ourselves or others. **Intro 1.01**

How do individuals deal with everyday risks? If we are faced with a risk that we do not feel we should take, we might change our plans in order to avoid it or we might insure against it, so that our insurer bears the financial consequences. To be able to take a decision like that, we need to be alert to the risk in the **Intro 1.02**

---

[1] From the *Financial Times*, 19 July 2005.
[2] From the Financial Markets Law Committee's paper 'Property Interests in Investment Securities' (analysis of the need for and nature of legislation relating to property interests in indirectly held investment securities, etc), July 2004, p 8, para 4.1.

first place and have some idea of its seriousness—by which we usually mean: how likely is this to happen and how badly would it affect things if it did happen? We also need to judge whether the benefit gained by transferring some or part of the risk to an insurance company is worth the cost (ie the premium). Not all these decisions are easy and we sometimes make mistakes. Sometimes they can be expensive mistakes. Unless we are content to rely purely on chance or luck, it is important that the decisions are informed decisions. Most of us seek a happy balance, not wishing to be overburdened with worry about relative trivia. But there are times when it obviously pays to be cautious and not to rush decisions before all the implications have been taken into account. The same rules that apply to our personal lives apply, broadly, to business life. The main differences stem from the fact that business life involves third parties with commercial expectations and, all too often, legal rights to have those expectations met, as well as, generally, a more legally (and politically) intrusive regime than applies to the everyday life of an individual.

Intro 1.03 This book is about risks that are commonly called legal risks. More specifically, it is about legal risks arising in the day-to-day operation and practices of the financial markets. These are the risks that are inherent in the operations of banks and other financial institutions, affecting the lives of the people who work there and customers of all kinds who put their trust in them. The more serious risks also affect, in some cases, the financial stability of modern economic life. It is in our collective interest that the banking system and the financial markets are reasonably secure. This is not the same as guaranteeing bankers' profits, although it is certainly the case that the financial sector in the UK is remarkably successful, the City of London having achieved an enviable pre-eminence in the world's international financial markets. The desire for stability is stimulated more by the need to ensure as far as possible that, to put it rather crudely, our money is 'safe' to the extent it is placed in the hands of banks and financial institutions for non-speculative purposes.

Intro 1.04 The City of London's success (and the stability of our financial system) is built upon an enduring, sound relationship between the market participants, those who regulate them, and those responsible for the laws that apply to market transactions. A vibrant and confident marketplace needs more, of course, than just a reliable legal system for its well-being. But if it does not have that as a foundation, it will not last for very long. Bad laws, which may threaten the reliability of bargains entered into in good faith or expose honest businesses to unacceptable hazards, cause risks to arise (these days, often termed 'legal risks') which, ultimately, can drive markets away. Although, as we shall see, the financial markets will tolerate a degree of legal risk (risk-taking, of all kinds, is, after all, what financial business is all about) legal risk is rarely welcomed and generally only accepted, grudgingly, if it is unavoidable.

Some legal risks are quite easy to understand and some are much more complex. **Intro 1.05**
However, they are all of concern to all of us, and their importance has increased
markedly over the last twenty years. The concern extends not only to the risks
themselves but also the cost of managing them and the impact of that cost on
running a financial services business, which is subject to what some commentators now regard as 'over-regulation'.[3] Let us take, as an example of legal risk, the
risk for a bank or insurance company of falling foul of laws or regulations, and
the consequent risk of being heavily fined. This kind of risk is not new but it
seems to have become perceived as a much more serious threat in recent years.
One reads of substantial fines being imposed on regulated entities more and
more often. Are they behaving more badly than before or have we become
stricter about what they are allowed to do?

The financial markets in the modern era are, perhaps more than ever before, a **Intro 1.06**
heavily regulated sector. The regulator in the UK is the Financial Services
Authority (FSA),[4] which covers banking, mortgage lending and advice, all kinds
of insurance, and investment business. The cost of administering the regulatory
regime, monitoring compliance with it, and enforcing that compliance (a cost
which is ultimately passed to the consumer) is very high and rising rapidly. (The
international bank, HSBC, recently estimated that its compliance costs for the
many countries in which it operates were £400 million a year. 'Compliance
staff' are estimated to represent about 5 per cent of all financial services recruit-
ment in the current market in the UK).[5] Concern is increasing as to whether the
cost is worth the benefits.

Should the complaints about over-regulation be taken seriously? One would **Intro 1.07**
not, after all, expect the regulated to go out of their way to shower their

---

[3] Many examples of industry concerns about over-regulation could be cited. A recent joint
report on behalf of the Corporation of London and the Investment Management Association
(May 2005) stated that one in four respondents regarded the UK tax and regulatory regime as
the single greatest disadvantage of having a business located in the UK. See also Pigott, 'Banana
Skins 2005: The CSFI's Annual Survey of the Risks Facing Banks' (2005) 05 JIBFL 165, where
Andrew Hilton, the director of the Centre for the Study of Financial Innovation, is quoted as
saying: 'There is a feeling that a regulatory tide is sweeping all before it—and that it could well
drown some of the industry's smaller players. The cost is enormous: it jacks up the price of
even the simplest products, it deters innovation, it undermines the principle that investors should
take responsibility for their own actions, and it makes it harder for new entrants to join the
market.'

[4] The FSA is an independent non-governmental body with statutory powers under the
Financial Services and Markets Act 2000. Its board is appointed by HM Treasury and it is
accountable to Treasury Ministers and, through them, to Parliament. See generally website at
http://www.fsa.gov.uk.

[5] See *The Sunday Times*, 24 October 2004, p. 3.6. See also the FSA press release of 2 December
2004, in which it is acknowledged that: 'A key question for us is: what can we do to reduce the
FSA's contribution to the cost of regulation?' The FSA, which has become keenly aware of
complaints of this kind, is currently examining whether it can do more to cut such costs.

regulator with praise. Some of the criticism needs to be taken with a pinch of salt. There does, however, seem to be some substance to the growing clamour of complaint. The regulated, after all, are not merely governed by laws (as we all are). They are also bound by 'rules' (some of which are expressed as very broad principles), told what to do by 'directions' and 'requirements', expected to be steered by 'guidance', protected by 'safe harbours' (but potentially damned by other 'evidential provisions'), and required to comply with an ever-increasing number of codes of conduct.[6] And that is just in the UK. The appropriate multiplier can be applied, depending on the number of jurisdictions in which a regulated business has activities. Managing the risks associated with this costs a great deal. Does the expense justify the extra protection we get from, say, being 'mis-sold' an insurance policy that is ill-suited to our needs or having more accessible complaint procedures? Why are we now so much more concerned about such risks? Are we more likely to be 'victims' of mis-selling than before? Have the products on offer become more difficult to understand or have we only recently woken up to their inherent risks?[7] Or have we become reluctant to accept responsibility for our own investment decisions?

Intro 1.08 The cost and extent of regulation (and the risk of being sued or fined) is a major issue, but legal risk for banks and other financial institutions involves other hazards affecting, for example, the recoverability of money lent or invested or the effectiveness of security for loans. There are also more technical, but crucially important,[8] risks associated with whether or not claims and liabilities amongst financial market participants (and their customers) should be measured on a gross or net basis (so that, in the latter case, a bank's liability to X is deemed to be reduced by the amount that X owes to that bank) and whether the legal analysis of the contracts that have been entered into, including property rights as well as the position on a party's insolvency, supports the practice of the market.[9] The management of these risks is a big business in itself and a major concern of regulators. Such risks have, in the last few years, prompted a number of important EU directives (some of which are still in the pipeline) as well as

---

[6] See para 5.56.

[7] It should be noted that accusations of mis-selling are not confined to sales to consumers. In late 2004, HSH Nordbank claimed that Barclays Bank had mis-sold it derivative products known as Collateralized Debt Obligations (CDOs) worth US$151m. That claim was settled. In February 2005, it was reported that Banca Popolare di Intra was claiming compensation from Bank of America for a sale of CDOs worth US$80m. See the *Financial Times*, 15 February 2005.

[8] The ability to enter into legally secure agreements that allow for liabilities to be netted against each other can result in enormous reductions in a bank's market exposure. See further, Ch 3 below, and also Henderson, 'Master Agreements, Bridges and Delays in Enforcement Part 1' (2004) 10 JIBFL 394.

[9] See Chs 3 and 7 below.

legal reforms all over the world in countries that host significant financial markets.

Why is legal risk important to the financial markets? Is it more important now than it used to be? What exactly is it? How is it to be managed? By the private sector or the public sector? Is it in fact possible to manage it (and what do we really mean by 'management')? These are important questions that need to be considered in their social, political, and historical context as well as the context of current laws and regulatory regimes. In this book, we shall look at how our perception of legal risk has evolved and changed over the years, what we currently understand by the expression, how and why legal risk arises, current examples of it, and how we can best manage it. **Intro 1.09**

Banks and financial institutions trade, for the most part, in products that are 'creatures' of the law rather than tangible goods. Commercial banks, for example, are regulated because they accept deposits from the public. Their business is the creation of, and trade in, 'intangibles', such as debts and similar obligations, of varying degrees of complexity. These intangibles (unlike tangible property such as land, ships, or aircraft) exist, in law, as 'things' (or 'choses in action', to use a legal term)[10] capable of being owned as property only because we, through our financial dealings with each other, bring them into existence. Trade in goods and other physical 'things' frequently involves credit, and so the ordinary trade transaction, which is primarily about something that we can touch and see, also gives rise to things that we cannot touch or see—'invisibles' and 'intangibles', such as debts and various other kinds of claim. Things that fall into this latter category, which may themselves be owned and traded, owe their existence (and value) to the legal infrastructure that recognizes the intellectual concepts that underpin them. They are the lifeblood of banking business. For a bank, therefore, legal risk, when it threatens the legal validity of an 'intangible' asset owned by it or exposes the bank to large claims, is somewhat akin to, say, engineering risk for an aircraft manufacturer, maintenance risk for a railway operator, or fire and earthquake risk for an owner of valuable real estate. In the worst case, the bank may lose a great deal of money, its reputation, and/or the ability to continue in business. And a major loss for a bank, if it threatens a bank's financial survival, frequently causes reverberations around society as a whole. **Intro 1.10**

The recent history of the financial markets, from around the time of the first major UK privatization share issues of the 1980s, has featured a number of significant developments that have tended to bring concern about legal risk, albeit in specific contexts, to the fore. These include the growth of global **Intro 1.11**

---

[10] Sometimes also referred to as 'things in action'.

markets, the arrival of 'universal' banks (whose business involves much more than banking, as traditionally understood), and the huge expansion of markets in instruments commonly known as 'derivatives' and other highly structured financial products. Such developments have brought great benefits but they have also added greatly to the complexity of financial activity. This complexity has in turn led to increased risks and an increased awareness of legal risk.

Intro 1.12   However, legal risk is not a new phenomenon for banks to deal with. In the 1960s, for example, the English courts were still grappling with questions such as the appropriate definition of a 'bank' (the penalty for lending money if you were not a bank being that the loan transaction was unenforceable) and even invented a new tort (of negligent misstatement) that, in the case in question, had specific application to an unreliable banker's reference.[11] These were basic, fundamental issues. It is hard to imagine that the English courts would have to decide today questions as basic as 'what is a bank?'[12] Nevertheless, even as late as the 1980s, case law on questions such as the validity of corporate guarantees was still developing,[13] with resultant uncertainty for lending banks. Case law developments on some fairly fundamental issues associated with the kind of security that banks can take for loans to customers continues to this day.[14]

Intro 1.13   The earlier cases involved and, arguably, exacerbated legal risks for financial institutions, but they did not produce a reaction that compared with the extremely hostile response of the markets to various, more recent, case law developments in the English courts in the late 1980s and early 1990s. What caused the markets to become so much more sensitive about what we started to describe as 'legal risk' at that time? Was the reaction caused by the nature of the issues decided by the courts or had something changed in the markets themselves? Was this when we suddenly 'woke up' to legal risk? Should we still be worried about it?

Intro 1.14   One reaction to the more recent case law, and perhaps the most significant, came from the Bank of England. This was the formation (in April 1991) of a committee, called the Legal Risk Review Committee (LLRC), which, amongst other things, considered whether the state of the law at that time involved too

---

[11] See *United Dominions Trust Ltd v Kirkwood* [1966] 2 QB 431 and *Hedley Byrne & Co Ltd v Heller & Partners Ltd* [1964] AC 465.

[12] The courts have, however, recently had to consider the meaning of 'financial institution'; see *The Argo Fund Ltd v Essar Steel Ltd* [2005] EWHC 600 (Comm).

[13] See, eg, *Rolled Steel Products (Holdings) Ltd v British Steel Corp* [1986] Ch 246. In the 1970s case law was also still developing on the nature of foreign currency (whether or not it was a commodity). See *Miliangos v George Frank (Textiles) Ltd* [1976] AC 443 and *Barclays Bank International Ltd v Levin* [1977] 1 Lloyd's Rep 51.

[14] See *National Westminster Bank plc v Spectrum Plus Ltd* [2005] UKHL 41 (considered in more detail in Ch 9 below) for a famous recent example.

much 'legal uncertainty'. This short phrase (which is now in common use whenever legal risk is a topic of discussion) related to concerns in the markets which could hardly be more fundamental, ie 'uncertainty over whether financial transactions freely entered into in the wholesale financial markets might suddenly turn out to be based on shifting legal foundations'.[15] Some of the language used in the LRRC's Final Report[16] shows the depth of these concerns. One recent case, for example, was described as being 'of real practical concern to the markets'[17] and the *ultra vires* doctrine (which had featured in another case involving 'swap' transactions with a local authority, considered at more length in Chapter 1 below) was described as leading 'to a denial of legitimate expectations that bargains will be enforced' and, as a result, 'damaging to the market'.[18] In reviewing the impact of a number of recent cases involving swaps with local authorities, the LRRC was trenchant in its views: 'There is no doubt that the swaps saga has damaged the reputation of English law. One way or another, it is important to ensure that it does not happen again.'[19]

Apart from specific law reform proposals, the LRRC felt that one way of achieving this objective, and ensuring that in the future the interests of the markets were more appropriately taken into account by all concerned, was to set up a new body 'without precedent either in this country or, as far as we are aware, any other', under the aegis of the Bank of England, to be a 'central forum' for the discussion and resolution of issues of legal uncertainty affecting the wholesale financial markets and services in the UK.[20] This recommendation was swiftly implemented, and the body was set up as the Financial Law Panel (FLP). **Intro 1.15**

The LRRC (and later the FLP) was composed of some of the most senior and respected lawyers and bankers in the land. There can be no doubt that its views were representative of the vast majority of City of London practitioners. The concern about legal risk at the beginning of the 1990s was real and widely felt. A decade later, legal risk was still providing much food for thought. For example, in July 2001, the FLP launched a new project 'to try to bring clarity and consistency to this topic'.[21] This initiative took place against a background of growing acceptance of the need for more sophisticated risk management techniques in the management of commercial enterprises. This was evidenced in the UK by requirements such as those of the Combined Code on Corporate Governance, which applies to all listed companies, and involves an annual **Intro 1.16**

---

[15] See LRRC Final Report, October 1992, para 2.1. [16] Published in October 1992.
[17] See LRRC Final Report, para 4.2.7. [18] See LRRC Final Report, App 1, para 1.4.
[19] See LRRC Final Report, App 1, para 2.6.
[20] See LRRC Final Report, paras 4.1.2 and 5.
[21] See FLP paper, 'Legal Risk Assessment', July 2001. This is now available on the FMLC's website at <http://www.fmlc.org>.

review by directors of systems of 'internal control'.[22] Throughout the preceding decade, the FLP had issued numerous papers on issues concerned with legal risk, and that work still continues with the activities of its successor body,[23] the Financial Markets Law Committee (FMLC). The FSA is also actively involved in this area, particularly with regard to risk management. In a recent letter[24] issued by the FSA to chief executives of life insurance firms and friendly societies, concern is expressed that such firms 'may not be exercising sufficient management control over legal risk' and they are urged to 'look again at their procedures for managing legal risk'.

Intro 1.17 Concerns about legal risk in the context of the reliability and 'user-friendliness' of English commercial law are not as great now as they were at the time of the formation of the LRRC[25] but the general topic of legal risk, which is multi-faceted, is still very high on the agenda for many financial market participants and regulators in the UK, the EU, and the US, as well as elsewhere. Even in areas where uncertainties or other problems are perhaps more imagined than real it remains important that unfounded doubts or anxieties do not take hold in a way that adversely affects normal market activity. Perceptions of problems, even if misconceived, can sometimes be almost as damaging as the problems themselves.

B. Sensitivities of the Financial Sector

Intro 1.18 Of course, all commercial enterprises take risks. The word 'enterprise' implies risk-taking—with a view to profit. Entrepreneurs, as individuals, have an appetite for risk and that appetite is reflected in every kind of business enterprise, large or small, whether run as a corporation, partnership, or otherwise. Investors in such enterprises are expected to accept the risk that is inherent in the arrangement, although there are a great many laws and regulations to

---

[22] See the Turnbull Report published by the Institute of Chartered Accountants in England and Wales (ICAEW).

[23] The FMLC effectively replaced the FLP in 2002. To the surprise, indeed consternation, of some, the FLP apparently had to cease activities because its voluntary funding sources were drying up. Whereas the FLP was set up as an independent body (technically, it was a company limited by guarantee and a subsidiary of the Bank of England), the FMLC is a committee of the Bank of England. The Bank provides facilities for the FMLC to meet and its Secretariat. However, the Bank is keen that it should be independent and that any views it expresses should be understood as its own, and not necessarily those of the Bank.

[24] Dated 24 August 2004. In a subsequent letter (17 September 2004) to senior officers of banks the FSA wrote a 'reminder' of 'responsibility to implement appropriate processes and procedures for the effective risk management of conflicts of interest and risks arising from financing transactions'. See further Ch 10 below.

[25] Even in October 1992, the LRRC was able to conclude in its Final Report that English law was as user-friendly to the markets as any other, and better than most.

protect investors against the unscrupulous and, up to a point, the negligent. The activities of banks and other financial services enterprises, however, give rise to special considerations because they may attract funds not only from individuals as risk-taking investors but also from individuals (and others) who have either no appetite for risk (such as an account-holder with a high street bank) or a much more conservative attitude to risk (such as the holder of, say, a 'with-profits' insurance policy). The inter-connection of financial institutions in the wholesale financial markets, where they enter into transactions with each other involving enormous sums of money on a daily basis, also means that if one institution gets into financial difficulty there is a serious risk that the problem may spread rapidly to other financial institutions (who have credit exposures to the one in trouble) and cause serious financial instability, damaging economic activity across the board.

These special considerations require a degree of regulation and supervision which would not normally be necessary for commercial enterprises in non-financial sectors. As mentioned above, it is vitally important that 'the financial system' works properly (if not always perfectly) and that the public have confidence in it. Banks, more than most commercial enterprises, carry on business using 'other people's money'. We do not generally wish to place our life savings with someone who will take rash decisions that may affect the chances of our seeing our money again. Consequently, the risks taken by banks and other financial institutions are a matter of concern to everyone and that is why the regulatory regime requires, amongst other things, that banks set aside an appropriate amount of capital so that there is a reasonable chance that any adverse consequences of risk can be absorbed. This concept is known as 'capital adequacy'. Most regulatory systems determine what is 'adequate' capital for an institution by reference, mainly, to the risks undertaken by it.[26] In this

Intro 1.19

---

[26] Rule 3.3.13R of the FSA *Interim Prudential Sourcebook: Banks* (January 2005 version) requires that a bank 'must maintain capital resources which are commensurate with the nature and scale of its business *and the risks inherent in that business*' (emphasis added). The link between capital and risk is illustrated by a recent *Financial Times* article (the 'Lex' column of 13 December 2004) which (commenting on the Bank of England's 'Financial Stability Review', published the same day) makes the following observations:

> . . . the British financial industry, like its US counterpart, has enjoyed extraordinarily benign conditions this year, with small credit losses, declining provisioning and no market shocks. However, the ensuing sense of calm is now creating its own dangers. One problem is that consumers . . . keep increasing debt. Another is that institutional investors are raising their exposure to market risk . . . The consequence is an explosion in structured credit products, energy and commodity trading and prime brokerage services for hedge funds. The good news is that British banks currently seem able to handle this risk. Tier 1 capital for UK banks is at a very healthy 9 per cent, up from 8 per cent last year, and liquidity levels are high . . . Most banks have revamped their risk modelling practices after the 1998 Long Term Capital Management crisis, and claim they are less vulnerable to a repeat of that debacle.

context, capital means equity capital or capital that has the principal legal and economic features of equity (such as certain kinds of heavily subordinated debt). From the perspective of the institution, such capital is 'expensive' in that it demands a higher return than debt capital (because it takes higher risks). So the determination of what is 'adequate' by the regulator is a highly sensitive matter.

C. The Basic Concept of Legal Risk

Intro 1.20 Legal risk is a particular kind of risk. It is commonly understood to relate to the risk of being sued or being the subject of a claim or proceedings due to some infringement of laws or regulations, or the commission of a tort such as negligence or some other act giving rise to civil liability (referred to as 'Type 1 risks' in this book). However, in the context of the financial markets, the phrase is also frequently used to mean the risk of technical defects in the manner in which a transaction is carried out, resulting in loss, sometimes very serious financial loss, for those that put money at risk in the transaction. (We shall call that kind of risk a 'Type 2 risk'.) In more extreme situations, as indicated above, legal risks can have a 'domino' effect in the market, either because the financial failure of one major institution may trigger failures in other institutions that have funds at risk with it or because the market as a whole has misunderstood the legal position on a point which is of particular importance to the recoverability of funds thought to be safely (or relatively safely) invested. This is sometimes referred to as 'systemic risk'.

Intro 1.21 Systemic risk is the most serious kind of risk that, from time to time, threatens the financial markets. Concern about it has triggered a great deal of debate and legislative reform in recent years. For example, as the FMLC recently noted,[27] concerns about systemic risk underlie recent EU directives on settlement finality

---

However, the bad news is that these new quantitative risk modelling practices have generally not been tested by any 'real life' market shock yet, making it hard to judge whether banks are really less exposed.

(Tier 1 capital is the form of capital that, from the regulatory perspective, is the 'most reliable' in the sense that, if a bank gets into financial trouble that capital should 'be there' to absorb at least some of the losses while allowing a bank to continue to trade. There are detailed requirements as to the criteria to be satisfied for capital to 'count' for Tier 1, especially 'Core Tier 1' (essentially, fully paid ordinary shares, certain kinds of preference shares, and retained earnings) (see FSA Policy Statement 155). Consequently, the more Tier 1 capital a bank has, the more financially stable it should, in principle, be. However, a sound capital structure is not, of course, a guarantee of stability, especially if risk is poorly managed).

[27] See FMLC paper of July 2004 'Property Interests in Investment Securities'.

and financial collateral[28] which 'are specifically directed to market stability and reduction of systemic risk'. The fear of a collapse of a bank triggering other collapses elsewhere, with financial panic spreading like a contagion around highly sensitive and suggestible markets, is a fear that regulators have lived with from the late nineteenth century but there are a number of characteristics of the modern, globalized financial markets that have given rise to increased cause for concern in this area. There are also particular features of legal risk that can trigger a systemic reaction, quite independently of any one institution's financial failure. As the international law reform organization, UNIDROIT[29] observed in a recent paper:

> . . . legal risk may become systemic in a less destructive sense. Consider, for example, the scenario in which an entire market suddenly changes its behaviour because the participants become aware of a major legal problem inherent in a specific kind of transaction unsuspected until then. In order to avoid this risk, the market participants avoid entering into this type of transaction as long as the legal problem remains unsolved. Such a mass reaction, if not properly restrained, could seriously damage the market.[30]

D. Increasing Concerns over Operational Risk—'Basel II'

Over the last few years, concerns about risk in the financial markets have grown. **Intro 1.22** The financial collapse of major companies and financial institutions (and the well-known difficulties of BCCI, Baring Brothers, Enron,[31] and Parmalat are just four from a distressingly long list) carries with it not only enormous losses for investors, creditors and, possibly, employees and pension-holders, but also potential liabilities for individuals such as directors (including non-executive directors) and professional advisers, as well as the company's auditors.[32] The

---

[28] See European Parliament and Council Directive of 19 May 1988 on Settlement Finality in Payment and Securities Settlement Systems (98/26/EC) and European Parliament and Council Directive of 6 June 2002 on Financial Collateral Arrangements (2002/47/EC).

[29] International Institute for the Unification Of Private Law.

[30] See UNIDROIT's Explanatory Notes to the Preliminary Draft Convention on Harmonised Substantive Rules Regarding Securities held with an Intermediary, December 2004; considered further in Ch 7 below.

[31] According to the *Financial Times*, 20 June 2005, Citigroup and J P Morgan have between them paid US$4.2bn to settle class action claims by Enron investors. 'Eight other banks have yet to fold. But estimates of total proceeds are $7bn–$15bn.' A later report in the same newspaper (3 August 2005) records Canadian Imperial Bank of Commerce paying $2.4bn to settle Enron-related litigation.

[32] The reputational issues associated with the collapse of Enron (especially allegations of shredding documents) ultimately led to the collapse of its auditor, Arthur Andersen. Robert Herz, the chairman of the Financial Accounting Standards Board, has recently expressed the view that, in the increasingly litigious climate (especially after the Enron failure) auditors (and audit

liabilities can be so large that, in some cases, they are virtually uninsurable and, for this reason, there have been calls for the law to be changed in order to limit liability, in certain contexts, to a 'reasonable' level. This raises difficult policy issues,[33] but also raises the question as to how the law could have developed to the point where, apparently, there is now a shortage of individuals who are willing to take on roles that might expose them to such liabilities (which may arise even where they have acted in good faith).[34] The deterrent effect of the risk is partly due to the fact that legal risk is not confined to the risk of being found culpable, but also embraces the risks associated with defending major law suits whether or not one is legally culpable. (Within days of the collapse of MG Rover in April 2005, at least one Sunday newspaper was calling for its auditors to return various fees earned, not because of any alleged breach of duty on their part, but simply because certain payments from the company to its directors (of which the newspaper disapproved) had been made 'on their watch'.)

Intro 1.23 These risks are not only financial (for example, the need to pay advisers' fees) but also personal and health-related because of the extraordinary stress and time commitment that litigation (and attendant media coverage) can involve for individuals. Further, the management time taken up can severely disrupt the running of the business involved in the litigation. Contingency-fee fuelled, deep-pocket seeking litigation is a concern for all kinds of business, and the management of this kind of risk, in what is now widely regarded as a 'compensation culture', has become increasingly important for banks as well as others. Apart from government and regulatory agencies, firms of accountants (mainly because of the audit function), banks, and insurance companies are probably

---

committees in companies) have become reluctant to make judgments, preferring a reporting regime based on 'rules' rather than 'principles'. He says: 'There seems to be a reluctance to exercise more judgment. If anything, we have perceived people are requesting more rules because they want clarity and defences against being second guessed' (*Financial Times*, 24 January 2005).

[33] At the time of writing, it appears that a forthcoming Companies Act will contain provisions enabling auditors to limit their liability.

[34] In an article, 'What possesses somebody to be a director of a public listed company these days?', *Financial Times*, 18 April 2005, Tucker points out that: 'For executive management, the risk–reward ratio has changed for the worse since a spate of corporate scandals forced regulators and shareholders to assert their rights. It is now common for investors, both in the US and Europe, to turn to the courts for financial redress when businesses falter—and aim their fire at the executive management . . . On average, every year more than 200 lawsuits are filed by investors in the US alone, most of which target the boardroom.' The article also notes that of the 234 such (class action) lawsuits brought last year, 33 were against non-US domiciled companies, including Shell, Parmalat, Deutsche Bank, and Astra Zeneca. The theme was reprised in the same newspaper in an article of 22 June 2005, Dickson, 'The sweet siren's song that calls a little louder': 'Is the accumulated weight of governance rules, government meddling, a hostile press and legal risk driving talented executives off the boards of quoted companies into less exposed and more profitable private equity?'

the favourite deep-pocket target. Lawyers themselves are probably not far behind.

Not surprisingly, institutions active in the financial markets, and those who regulate them, are concerned that risks such as legal risk are identified and managed as efficiently and effectively as possible—if they are not, the consequences will include the regulators requiring greater capital reserves than would otherwise be necessary, with consequent inefficiencies for everyone. The focus of market participants on legal risk has recently been sharpened, to some extent, by the publication, in June 2004, of the Basel Committee on Banking Supervision's report 'International Convergence of Capital Measurement and Capital Standards'. This is the report, following on from, and replacing, the Basel Accord of 1988 (which has the same title as the 2004 document) which is commonly known as 'Basel II'.[35] The work of the BCBS demonstrates, and is driven by, the importance of these issues for the financial markets internationally. Basel II is of enormous importance to banking regulation but is also of specific importance to consideration of legal risk because of the new emphasis it places upon operational risk[36] (which, under Basel II, specifically includes legal risk) and the desire of BCBS to 'engage the banking industry in a discussion of prevailing risk management practices'. 'Stronger risk management practices' are a key objective of Basel II, much of which is clearly influenced by the recent spate of serious operational problems experienced by international financial institutions, many of them involving fraud and some of them leading to the financial collapse of the entire institution.

Intro 1.24

Concerns have been expressed about whether the 'architecture' of the international financial system is sufficiently robust.[37] Such concerns and the perceived relationship between operational failures and the expansion of activities of banks into a wide range of financial product areas (especially in the derivative markets), which bear little, if any, resemblance to the commercial banking activities that were the subject of more traditional regulation methods, is an evident stimulus of the regulators' new determination to require a more focused

Intro 1.25

---

[35] That terminology is used throughout in this book (and the Basel Committee on Banking Supervision is referred to as 'BCBS').

[36] Basel II defines operational risk as 'the risk of loss resulting from inadequate or failed internal processes, people and systems or from external events. This definition includes legal risk but excludes strategic and reputational risk.' Operational risk is thus something of a miscellany. It is contrasted, chiefly, with credit risk and market risk. The reference to legal risk was broadened when the final version of Basel II was published in June 2004. A footnote now states: 'Legal risk includes, but is not limited to, exposure to fines, penalties, or punitive damages resulting from supervisory actions, as well as private settlements.'

[37] See, eg Attanasio and Norton (eds) 'A New International Financial Architecture: A Viable Approach', British Institute of International and Comparative Law, Sir Joseph Gold Memorial Series vol 3, 2001.

approach to operational risk management. It is, of course, an inevitable consequence of this expanded range of financial activities, the rapidity with which new financial 'products' are developed and deployed, and the increased potential for conflict of interest which results from the new multiplicity of roles of financial institutions that the legal risks involved in the financial markets have become more complex and, potentially, more serious. The regulators are therefore seeking the establishment of, and are prepared to offer significant financial incentives for, a more pro-active risk management function within financial institutions. It is thought that this might in turn lead to an enhanced appreciation of the need for sound corporate governance across the board. However good the laws and legal system may be (and however vigilant a bank's lawyers may be), if corporate behaviour is bad, legal risks will follow. The new philosophy places less reliance upon 'backward-looking evaluations' of performance and instead involves much more analysis of what financial institutions themselves regard as significant risks and the appropriate measures to be taken to mitigate and manage them. Commentators have noted that Basel II moves away from 'over reliance on capital adequacy as a signal of bank soundness. The problems of the Japanese banks and of those in many emerging economies have shown this measure in isolation is insufficient and that good risk management processes are at least, if not more, important than attaining an arbitrary capital ratio'.[38]

Intro 1.26 Basel II operates at a high level in that it does not itself constitute law in any particular country. Instead, it operates as an authoritative set of principles and standards which are designed to 'secure international convergence on revisions to supervisory regulations governing the capital adequacy of internationally active banks'. Insofar as standards are laid down, they are intended to be minimum standards. The BCBS itself is not a legislator; it is a committee established by the Central Bank Governors of the 'Group of Ten' countries in 1975 and its members include senior banking supervisors from Belgium, Canada, France, Germany, Italy, Japan, Luxembourg, the Netherlands, Spain, Sweden, Switzerland, the UK and the US. It can be expected, therefore, that Basel II will be implemented as a banking regulatory measure, in one form or another, in at least these countries[39] (the current timetable expects implementation at national level by the end of 2007).

---

[38] Pigott and Anderson, 'The Achilles' Heel of the International Financial System' (1998) 7 JIBFL 271.

[39] The 1988 Accord was adopted by more than a hundred countries, although Basel II has, initially at least, met a certain amount of resistance. For an excellent summary of the origins and purpose of Basel II, see Taylor, 'What is Basel II and why has it got three pillars?' (2004) 4 JIBFL 123. In the EU, the new Capital Requirements Directive (published as a proposal on 14 July 2004) will implement Basel II. In the UK, this Directive will, in turn, be reflected by rules of the FSA (Parliament has delegated extensive rule-making powers to the FSA). Hector Sants (the FSA's Managing Director, Wholesale and Institutional Markets) pointed out in a speech to the

E. Legal Risk in the London Markets

Analysis of legal risk, however, involves much more than a commentary on Basel II (which, in any event, addresses many other issues apart from legal risk). Concerns over legal risk in the financial markets pre-date Basel II by many years. Further, although Basel II is of international application, consideration of the practical issues associated with the phenomena that give rise to legal risk, as well as risk identification and management, needs to be tied in some way (albeit not exclusively) to a specific jurisdiction or jurisdictions. It is not possible, in a work of this kind, to examine every jurisdiction in the world. Our analysis is, therefore, centred on the laws of England with priority being given to legal risk issues affecting the financial markets in the context of English law and financial market practice as followed in the City of London.

Intro 1.27

All jurisdictions, of course, present their own distinct legal risk issues but English law, as one of the favoured 'governing laws' for financial market documentation and the 'home law' for the City of London, is worthy of analysis in its own right in the context of legal risk management. Such analysis is far from a parochial exercise.[40] Many of the issues considered in the English courts and the London market have parallels elsewhere. Indeed, it is a feature of the markets that phenomena such as the imposition of sanctions or penalties for various forms of market abuse frequently arise with near-simultaneity on both sides of the Atlantic. Further, legal issues affecting the wholesale financial markets in London usually affect the markets in the EU as a whole (and vice versa), depending, to some extent, on the degree of 'harmonization' achieved. It is notable, in this context, that legal projects undertaken by bodies such as the FMLC have often taken place at the same time as parallel projects in other countries.[41]

Intro 1.28

In reviewing how the City of London and the English courts have dealt with legal risk issues, we shall see that the establishment, and activities, of the Legal

Intro 1.29

FSA's annual public meeting on 15 July 2004 that the CRD 'implements Basel II but also goes a lot further', eg it does not only apply (like Basel II) to internationally active banks but to all regulated financial firms other than insurance companies. It thus embraces building societies as well as banks and, with some exceptions and exemptions, investment banks and firms.

[40] As Wood points out, '. . . England is only 0.33% of the world's jurisdictions. It occupies less than 0.01% of the planet's land mass and has less than 0.75% of the global population. Nevertheless, if we take the world's most important and biggest international contracts—which are syndicated credits, bond issues and to a lesser extent ISDA master agreements—it may be that somewhere between 40% and 70% of international bond issues are governed by English law and the proportion of international syndicated credits may be the same . . . English law is the workhorse of international contracts' ('English law and legal leadership in the global economy'—a paper given to the Chancery Bar Association, 23 June 2003).

[41] See, eg the issues considered in Ch 7 below.

Risk Review Committee, the Financial Law Panel, and the Financial Markets Law Committee have been of crucial importance. Bodies like this are now rightly seen as part of the 'legal infrastructure' of the wholesale financial markets. Also of great, and growing, significance are the rules, policies, and practices of the Financial Services Authority (whose compliance Handbook, at the last count, ran to over 8,000 pages). The interaction of law, regulation, and the financial markets at various levels, set against the background of the rapid development of globalized markets, provides a vital social context to the many technical legal developments. As Jaime Caruana, the Chairman of BCBS, has pointed out, 'the legal and judicial system must make the rights and responsibilities of both banks and their counterparties clear and enforceable so that banks and borrowers can make the most effective use of collateral, guarantees and other measures to secure credit'.[42]

Intro 1.30 The mutual interdependence of the legal profession (including commercial court judges) and those who wish to preserve London's position as one of the leading international financial centres is one of the dominant themes to emerge from this exercise. The financial marketplace can only function properly in an environment which provides a satisfactory level of legal certainty. Although the English courts are not enslaved by the need for commercial efficacy, the development of English case law over more than a hundred years has taken place against a background of consistent judicial awareness of a policy objective that, as far as possible, commercial bargains should be enforceable in accordance with their terms and that a successful marketplace does not welcome legal (or regulatory) 'surprises'. Even in the (somewhat notorious) case of *Hazell v Hammersmith and Fulham London Borough Council*,[43] the Court of Appeal noted that 'fundamental fairness and pragmatic good sense . . . are boasted to infuse' the common law of England and, more recently, in the course of a judgment which appeared (at least in part) to be intended to address market anxieties about the celebrated dictum of Millett J in *Re Charge Card Services Ltd*,[44] Lord Hoffmann noted that 'law is fashioned to suit the practicalities of life'.[45] This judicial awareness of market pressure has only increased as the

---

[42] Caruana, 'Making diligent preparations for Basel II', 22 September 2004, speech delivered to 13th International Conference of Banking Supervisors.

[43] [1990] 3 All ER 33; see generally Ch 1 below.

[44] [1987] Ch 150. The dictum was believed to cast doubt on the ability of a bank to take a charge over money deposited with it; see further Ch 2 below.

[45] *Morris and ors v Rayners Enterprises Inc, Morris and ors v Agrichemicals Ltd (BCCI No 8)* [1998] AC 214 (this case is referred to below as '*BCCI No 8*'). In the same case the Court of Appeal was clearly mindful of the potential 'market impact' of its decision. In looking at the *Charge Card* case, the Court noted: 'It is important that . . . routine financing arrangements should not be put at risk. If the reasoning in re Charge Card Services Ltd. led to the conclusion that

City of London has become more open to international competition for its pre-eminent role as a leading financial centre. As Goode notes:

> In a world financial centre such as London it would be surprising indeed if the courts were insensitive to the need to uphold reasonable business practice where not otherwise constrained by rules of positive law. In a major market the consequences of a refusal to accept the market's perception of the legal nature and incidents of contracts and financial instruments in widespread use could be severe; indeed, in some cases confidence could be seriously undermined ... There is therefore considerable scope for the business community to establish law through practice and thus, as it were, pull itself up by its own legal bootstraps.[46]

Our analysis will provide a number of examples of law being established through practice in recent years. Mercantile usage or custom has, in any event, always been an important source for English commercial law. An example of the practicality and flexibility that results from this, which is of enormous importance to bankers, can be found in the law relating to negotiable instruments, which expressly recognizes that, although instruments such as bills of exchange, cheques, and promissory notes are conferred by statute with the important beneficial characteristics of negotiability, the categories of negotiable instruments are not closed and new instruments can be added to the list which, in a sense, updates itself in line with the custom and practice of the market.[47] The law follows, and automatically adjusts to, market practice. Another example can be found in the law relating to the duties of paying banks in connection with letters of credit. The duty of care relating to the inspection of shipping documents is such that although a bank may refuse to pay in the absence of strict compliance, it is protected against claims from its customer as long as it acts reasonably, a test which turns substantially on market practice.[48]

Intro 1.31

Bodies like the FMLC (and its predecessors) are clearly very conscious of the need to act as 'a bridge to the judiciary to help UK courts remain up to date with developments in financial markets practice'.[49] The FMLC, in performing what it describes as its 'radar' function, consults regularly and widely with market participants to ensure that it is aware, on a current basis, of any legal

Intro 1.32

---

charge-backs were invalid or ineffective to give security in the event of that chargor's insolvency, then that reasoning would be suspect; and if it could not be faulted *we would be willing to sacrifice doctrinal purity on the altar of commercial necessity*' (emphasis added). See further, Ch 2 below.

[46] Goode, *Commercial Law* (3rd edn) 159.

[47] Examples of instruments that are negotiable as a result of mercantile usage include treasury bills, bearer bonds, share warrants, and negotiable certificates of deposit: see Goode, *Commercial Law* (3rd edn) 477.

[48] See, eg *Edward Owen Engineering v Barclays Bank International Ltd* [1978] QB 159.

[49] See FMLC website: http://www.fmlc.org.

issues that are perceived to be adverse to the orderly functioning of the markets. The virtues of English commercial law are seen to be part and parcel of the general 'invisible export' effort. They give London a significant 'edge' because of the 'certainty' qualities of the common law system. In a letter, dated 1 September 2003, addressed to Lord Woolmer (the Chairman of a House of Lords Subcommittee concerned, amongst other things, with the European Commission's 'Financial Services Action Plan')[50] Lord Browne-Wilkinson (the Chairman of the FMLC, and, prior to his retirement, the UK's senior law lord) observed that 'wholesale financial markets require, and by their regulators are required to exhibit, an unusually high level of "to-the-minute" and "to-the-penny" legal certainty. In English law, business dealings are governed by that part of the common law known as commercial law. English commercial law offers its users the opportunity to achieve a level of legal certainty greater than in almost any other walk of life.' Similar remarks can be found in an earlier letter[51] from Lord Browne-Wilkinson (again, in his capacity as Chairman of the FMLC) to Sir Roger Toulson, the Chairman of the Law Commission, resisting proposals that laws invalidating 'unfair' contract terms should be extended (beyond consumer contracts) to, amongst other things, 'the type of contract which arises in the wholesale financial markets'. Expressing the view that 'legal certainty is even more important in a commercial environment than fairness', Lord Browne-Wilkinson drew attention to why the LRRC had been set up in 1991 and its conclusions on the importance of legal certainty, including the following points with regard to the financial markets:

- these markets are an important contributor to the UK's GNP and foreign earnings;
- they involve huge sums, so that unpredictable legal results could produce huge unexpected losses, leading to market instability;
- the markets are international—they are not locked into the English legal system but are free to choose another, if English law is considered to be unsafe;
- its participants assume that transactions freely entered into will be upheld as legally valid, unless there is a compelling reason to the contrary which would be reasonably apparent to a prudent and sophisticated person taking whatever advice is appropriate to the transaction in question;
- Markets depend on certainty (including legal certainty). Lack of certainty undermines confidence and the damage can spread far beyond its original cause.

---

[50] This plan was launched by the EU in 1999 (following the introduction of the euro) as part of a drive to create a single European financial market. It has, however, met with a number of difficulties in implementation and there remain many areas where there is a distinct lack of harmonization. The new commissioner in charge of the EU internal market, Charles McCreevy, is reported as being 'convinced by the argument of regulatory fatigue' and has acknowledged that the plan has produced a 'mountain of legislation', see *Financial Times*, 17 January 2005.

[51] Dated 20 June 2003.

Comparable sentiments are frequently echoed in the language used by the judges themselves. For example, in the case of *Scandinavian Trading Tanker Co AB v Flota Petrola Ecuatoriana*[52] Goff LJ noted:

> It is of the utmost importance in commercial transactions that, if any particular event occurs, which may affect the parties' respective rights under a commercial contract, they should know where they stand. The court should so far as possible desist from placing obstacles in the way of either party in ascertaining his legal position, if necessary with the aid of advice from a qualified lawyer, because it may be commercially desirable for action to be taken without delay, action which may be irrevocable and which may have far-reaching consequences. It is for this reason of course that the English courts have time and again asserted the need for certainty in commercial transactions—for the simple reason that the parties to such transactions are entitled to know where they stand, and to act accordingly.

Intro 1.33

However, as Hart has famously observed,[53] 'all rules have a penumbra of uncertainty where the judge must choose between alternatives'. Judges are not mere fact-finders, applying immutable legal rules to the facts that present themselves. They make law on occasions as well. This has considerable advantages as long as the 'bridge' between the market and the judges remains strong, not least because commercial courts can sometimes take the opportunity to 'clear up' uncertain areas of the law which cannot get the attention of the legislature. But the corollary is that, from time to time, there will be legal uncertainties (for example, pending the hearing of an appeal from a controversial decision) and the resultant risk has to be managed.[54]

Intro 1.34

Although English commercial law can rightly be seen as a success story in providing a rules and principles system that works very well for rapidly evolving financial and commercial practice, it is important that we do not become complacent. The financial markets are volatile, mobile, and hyper-sensitive to risk and uncertainty. Legal risk is more likely to be successfully managed if we maintain an effective dialogue amongst legislators, judges, and lawyers in

Intro 1.35

---

[52] [1983] QB 529, 540.

[53] H L A Hart, *The Concept of Law* (2nd edn) 12. This statement, by a leading academic and barrister, was echoed by the reference by Hoffmann J (as he then was) in *Re Brightlife Ltd* [1987] Ch 200 to 'penumbral cases' when it is difficult to determine whether a security interest is or is not a floating charge (which Hoffmann J did not think could be defined precisely), a question which may turn on 'whether the degree of deviation from the standard case is enough to make it appropriate to use such a term'.

[54] In his Chief Executive's report, set out in the FLP's first Annual Report, of October 1994, Colin Bamford points out that: 'Legal uncertainty can take a number of forms: the law itself may be unsettled; the law may be settled, but of such complexity that it is not generally understood by non-specialist lawyers; or the law, although in itself quite clear, may have consequences and practical effects which are not easy to quantify or evaluate.' As to sources of legal risk generally, see Ch 5 below.

private practice. As we shall see, the management of legal risk is not exclusively a function and responsibility of either the public sector or the private sector acting alone, and open communication amongst all those involved (sometimes on an international basis) is vital if management efforts are to be successful. The importance of effective dialogue has only been reinforced by the advent of globalization, which has accentuated the need for London to compete effectively with other actual and potential financial centres. As the FSA says (in describing itself) 'Ultimately, the FSA is all about maintaining confidence in the UK's financial marketplace for the benefit of everyone.' That confidence can only be maintained if a solid legal foundation is preserved and kept up to date.

F. The Global Context

Intro 1.36 We cannot, however, look at English law issues to the complete exclusion of what may be happening in other countries. Recent developments of law and policy, especially in the financial sector, have been enormously influenced by the impact of globalization. To the extent that law is intended to serve the interests of those carrying on a legitimate business, and the customers and employees of that business, it must recognize that, for many market participants, national boundaries are of no particular relevance and that 'once the market becomes international and the players are operating globally, distinctions between national laws become a technical issue'.[55] Increasingly, policy-makers and those who may influence policy and the need for changes to the law, such as the Law Commission, look at the comparative position in other similar countries and seek to address the need for English law to remain in step with international developments that assist with the efficient functioning of a financial market wishing to attract international financial institutions and their clients. Further, legal risk management for, say, a London-based bank must involve an appreciation of the 'foreign' legal risks that arise in what are now commonplace cross-border transactions.

Intro 1.37 The requirements of the directives and laws of the EU (and associated harmonization requirements) must also be taken into account. EU directives are now the single largest source of regulatory change in the London financial markets.[56] And the process of harmonization gives rise to legal risk in its own right. As Lord Browne-Wilkinson notes in the first of the two letters referred to

---

[55] See Pedrazzini and Simpson, 'The Legal Framework for Secured Credit: A Suitable Case for Treatment' (1999) 1 BLI 127.

[56] See the FSA's 'Financial Risk Outlook' 2004, 80.

above,[57] Community legislation sometimes seems to fall short of the certainty standards required in the financial markets because of 'the purposive, teleological approach to the interpretation that applies to Community legislation'. The continental European legal tradition, rooted in civil law concepts, is very different to the English common law in many important respects. The implementation across the Community of a concept that is intended to have the same effect in each country is, technically, a very difficult exercise when the subject matter includes the many intellectual constructs involved in financial transactions, as opposed to, say, the regulation of weights and measures and other, more 'tangible' matters. But the development of a single financial market in the EU is a political imperative and, as Whittaker has pointed out,[58] law is in fact the main tool being used for the purpose of achieving the objective. As can be seen from the case law and legislative changes considered in Chapter 3 below, UK legal developments in important areas such as set-off and netting, have, as time has gone by, gradually started to influence, and be influenced by, legal policy in the EU as a whole. Within the institutions of the EU itself, legal risk and legal certainty have, over the years, steadily climbed the agenda, as evidenced, for example, by the Giovannini Reports and the establishment recently of the 'Legal Certainty Group' to look into problems of legal uncertainty in connection with clearing and settlement procedures in the EU.[59] So the maintenance and development of sound financial law in the UK has to be undertaken, to a very large extent, in tandem with the maintenance and development of sound financial law for the EU.

However, notwithstanding the need for a harmonized system in the EU, it has **Intro 1.38** to be recognized that having a sound financial legal system, rather like having sensible taxation and fiscal policies, has become a competitive exercise amongst states. If, for example, countries such as Belgium and Luxembourg adopt laws which meet reasonable market expectations in the context of the treatment of indirectly held securities upon insolvency, it is important that the UK considers whether it should do likewise, if our laws involve risks and uncertainties which compare unfavourably.[60] If we fail to act, we take the risk that business is driven elsewhere. We cannot afford the luxury of laws that are perceived to be 'unfriendly' to the modern, globalized financial system. For the same reason, it is now extremely difficult for any one state to 'regulate away' the risks involved in certain kinds of market transaction by simply banning them (except, to an extent, in the context of consumer markets). In a sense, globalization has

---

[57] See para Intro 1.32   [58] 'Confronting the Regulatory Challenge' (2005) 3 JIBFL 98.
[59] The Legal Certainty Group held its first meeting on 31 January 2005 and minutes of its meetings are available on the internet. See further, Ch 7 below.
[60] See Ch 7 below.

allowed the genie out of the bottle. Instead, the approach has to depend much more on highlighting the risks, and requiring 'risk management'.

Intro 1.39   Finally, it should be remembered that, for developing economies, the reduction of legal risk can act as a stimulus to inward investment and lower the cost of borrowing. The policies and activities of many international institutions are directed towards achieving this end.[60a]

G. The Law-maker and the Regulator

Intro 1.40   There is no perfect commercial legal system and even an advanced and finely tuned body of laws requires 'repairs and maintenance' on a continuous basis. (This is one of the arguments against calls for more codification of the common law.) It is not realistic to expect all the necessary changes to come about as a result of case law. The legislature (Parliament) is the principal source of new law (other than 'soft law',[61] which emanates from regulatory authorities and elsewhere at an alarming rate). Legislative changes do not come without risk and they very frequently introduce an element of uncertainty, at least for an initial period until the markets have adjusted to the change and some degree of stability of interpretation has been achieved. However, the imperative for London is for the law to 'keep up'. We need to avoid the creation of 'a mismatch between the expectation of the law and modern commercial reality'.[62] The law-maker's job is never finished or complete. If one of the objectives of law is to serve the interests of society, this objective will always be a moving target. The particular section of society which is principally affected by what we loosely call 'financial law' appears to be in a state of virtually constant change and so its demands of the legal system are also constantly changing.

Intro 1.41   Regulators such as the FSA also have a key role in developing enforceable rules and standards. The regulator's job appears, at times, to be a truly thankless task. There is a probability, not a possibility, that any financial misdemeanour by a regulated body will be blamed on the regulator. On the other hand, we seem to be very quick to criticize regulators for being over-zealous if they impose fines or other penalties when shortcomings are detected. And of course the responsibility for the 'red tape' and general cost of 'bureaucracy' associated with

---

[60a]   See para 10.38.

[61]   See para 5.50.

[62]   See Bamford (former Chief Executive of Financial Law Panel), 'The Banker/Customer Relationship Fiduciary Duties and Conflict of Interest' (paper presented to International Bar Association Committee, Berlin Conference, 24 October 1996). This paper does in fact conclude that in relation to conflict of interest and fiduciary duties 'the courts are themselves adapting the requirements to market expectations and circumstances'.

compliance is laid at the regulators' door as well. We seem, recently, to have made a habit of changing our regulatory bodies, and their powers and scope of activities, with every perceived 'failure' of any significance. They are an easy target for politicians who wish to distance themselves from responsibility for such failures and for a financial press that will always lean in favour of taking a knock at those perceived to be in a position of authority. Sometimes it seems that they cannot win.[63]

H. Some Current Preoccupations

Legal risk will always be present in the financial markets. It can be controlled and managed, but it cannot be eradicated (although certain specific legal risks can sometimes be removed, for example, by legislation or by contractual restructuring). Each year, the Centre for Study of Financial Innovation publishes a survey of 'Banana Skins', which ranks banking risks by their perceived severity. In the 2005 Survey, legal risk entered the 'top 30' for the first time, at number 17. Hardly a week goes by without there being some mention of legal risk (whether or not by name) in the financial pages of the press. One issue of the *Financial Times* chosen at random recently[64] contained articles on the following: **Intro 1.42**

(1) Sir Peter Middleton, formerly the Chairman of Barclays Bank, was interviewed in connection with his new role as the Chairman for the Centre for Effective Dispute Resolution. In the course of the interview he described some of the advantages of mediation over traditional litigation:

> it's a lot cheaper . . . the hidden costs of litigation are much greater than you think, particularly the amount of management time it takes up. If you invite a QC along to give you his view of a case, it takes up half a day. The courts give you an answer, but it's a long, tortuous process and lacks flexibility. The other thing that's hugely important is the confidentiality of the process. In a court case you never know what is going to come out that had nothing to do with the case.

---

[63] However, as the *Financial Times* 'Lombard' column noted, on 2 December 2004, HM Treasury's two-year review of the FSMA 2000 (which set up the FSA) gave the FSA 'a broadly clean bill of health'. It is (somewhat grudgingly) acknowledged that the regulator 'has not lived up to the worst fears of the City'. See, however, press comment on the *Legal & General* case, considered at para Intro 1.42 n. 65 below.

[64] Dated 13 September 2004. The same issue also contains articles on the desire of the accountancy firms for legal limits to their liability for negligent audit work and on the European Commission's desire to see 'more private law suits brought against companies accused of breaching anti-trust rules, bringing Europe's competition regime more into line with the US system'. As regards the position of accountants, the collapse of the Italian company, Parmalat has given rise, amongst other things, to a US$10bn claim (in the US) by the company's administrator against the company's auditors.

(2) The FSA was being challenged by Legal & General (the insurance company) in relation to a £1.1 million fine levied on it for 'alleged endowment mis-selling'. The hearing was expected to take six weeks, before the Financial Services and Markets Tribunal (and there may be appeals thereafter). In a summary of the case, the FSA alleged that endowment policies known as 'with profits flexible mortgage plans' were 'sold to customers for whom they were not suitable, either because they were not prepared to take the risk of a shortfall at maturity or because they did not properly understand that risk'. These allegations were denied by Legal & General.[65]

(3) A US lawyer was reported as representing clients 'who suffered under the brutal apartheid regime' in South Africa and bringing claims on their behalf under the eighteenth-century US law known as the Alien Tort Claims Act. The article reported that this legislation is now 'increasingly used as a means of holding multi-nationals to account in the U.S. courts for human rights abuses committed abroad'. The defendants were reported as including UK banks, NatWest, Barclays, and Standard Chartered.

Intro 1.43 The above three articles feature three different facets of legal risk. The first relates to some of the more obvious problems associated with litigation, including the amount of time it takes and the possibility of unwelcome 'surprises' emerging from the proceedings and consequent unflattering (and possibly damaging) media coverage. The second relates to the hazards of selling (or 'mis-selling') complex (or relatively complex) products in the consumer market, and the third relates to the growing unease associated with certain kinds of

---

[65] The tribunal later upheld the FSA's claim that there were defects in certain sales procedures but also criticized the FSA for over-reliance on relatively slender evidence as to the degree of mis-selling. In a further ruling on 26 May 2005 the tribunal cut the original fine imposed on L&G from £1.1m to £575,000, but did not allow L&G costs (which would almost certainly have been more than the fine). The tribunal also, according to the *Financial Times* of 27 May 2005, described the FSA investigators as having been 'more concerned with identifying reasons for maintaining sanctions than objectively evaluating the evidence'. And it noted that the FSA's refusal to disclose to firms what goes into its 'case review papers'—which the Regulatory Decisions Committee sees—is 'open to inadvertent abuse and an enemy of transparency'. Criticism in the same vein has come from the Association of British Insurers (press release of 21 April 2005) which comments that 'The FSA must be fair, and be seen to be fair. It must demonstrate more openly that the work of the Regulatory Decisions Committee (RDC) is "independent, fair and robust". In particular, the ABI argues that firms being investigated are entitled to know precisely what evidence has been presented about them to the RDC by FSA officials and given adequate opportunities to respond.' The *Daily Telegraph*, 28 May 2005, was particularly virulent in its criticism of the FSA, commenting, 'It's no exaggeration to say the whole of the financial services industry was willing L&G on. Companies large and small are heartily sick of the way the FSA works, churning out more directives than the human brain can comprehend and imposing fines for laughably trivial beaches of the money-laundering rules.' The FSA appears to have addressed the criticisms of the procedures of its RDC by making various procedural changes, announced on 19 July 2005.

US class actions which, apparently, may have little if anything to do with the US itself but nevertheless expose international companies (including banks) to very large financial claims which some may feel are of a somewhat nebulous nature.

Another, randomly selected (but more recent) issue of a US newspaper[66] featured articles on the following: **Intro 1.44**

- The firm of accountants, KPMG LLP, 'agreed to pay $22.5 million to settle charges brought by the Securities and Exchange Commission in connection with the . . . audits of Xerox Corp. from 1997 through 2000'. The SEC said this was the largest ever payment they had received from an audit firm. According to the SEC, Xerox had been overstating its results in order to bolster its share price. (Xerox itself and six of its former senior executives had also paid penalties and/or disgorged profits totalling around US$32 million). According to the newspaper: 'The SEC said that KPMG "wilfully aided and abetted Xerox's violations of the anti-fraud, reporting, record-keeping and internal controls provisions of the federal securities laws". Among other things, the SEC noted that KPMG removed its audit partner after Xerox complained about his actions in the 1999 audit; ignored warnings from international KPMG officers about Xerox's accounting practices; and failed to inform Xerox's board or audit committee of concerns KPMG partners had about the company's accounting.' As part of the settlement, KPMG agreed to take certain remedial measures, including reviewing any change in assignment of an audit partner, establishing whistle-blower channels within the firm and retaining a consultant to check its policies and certify to the SEC in two years' time as to the changes still being in effect.

- The US Supreme Court 'reined in' securities fraud class action litigation with a ruling that plaintiffs alleging losses (due to falls in share prices) because of misrepresentation by a company's management 'must show that the lies were to blame'. Justice Stephen Breyer delivered an opinion which, although it accepted that 'The securities statutes seek to maintain public confidence in the marketplace . . . by deterring fraud' partly by enabling private civil actions, did not accept that such laws were intended 'to provide investors with broad insurance against market losses'. It would be necessary to show economic loss 'that misrepresentations actually cause'. One commentator observed: 'The Fantasyland damage numbers that plaintiffs are thinking about are now out the windows and plaintiffs are going to have to be much more realistic even where there is a stock decline.'

---

[66] The *Wall Street Journal*, 20 April 2005.

- Mr Ronald Perelman was reported to be suing the investment bank, Morgan Stanley, in connection with a transaction where the bank had advised a company (Sunbeam) to whom Mr Perelman sold his interest in a company called Coleman Inc (partly in consideration for shares in Sunbeam). Although Morgan Stanley had advised Mr Perelman on earlier deals and Mr Perelman apparently had great confidence in them (seeing their 'stamp of approval' on Sunbeam as significant) Mr Perelman was not the bank's client in the Sunbeam deal. Not long after the transaction was completed: 'Sunbeam became engulfed in an accounting scandal, driving down the value of Mr. Perelman's stock. His suit cuts to the heart of a key issue facing Wall Street: What is the responsibility of an investment banker in identifying problems at a client, and to whom is the underwriter responsible.' Morgan Stanley had, it was reported, set aside US$360 million to cover the potential costs of the court action.[67]

Intro 1.45 These reports focus, not surprisingly, on litigation (Type 1 risk). They feature issues which are recurrent themes in both the US and the UK, such as the liability of auditors, the level of fines (and on whom they are imposed), the responsibilities of advisers (especially in relation to conflicts of interest, real or imagined), and, more generally, the legal consequences of corporate fraud for parties other than the primary actors themselves. Class actions are, to date, a concern that is peculiar to the US, although, as indicated in one of the articles mentioned earlier, it seems that the effect of US class actions can certainly be felt beyond US borders and are of increasing concern to banks in London.

Intro 1.46 It is important for the risk management function to develop and maintain a keen sense of when legal risk is likely to be present. This needs to be coupled with an awareness of when the risk is likely to be material. Andrew Whittaker, the General Counsel of the FSA, in a recent paper identified four circumstances when legal risk 'is particularly likely to be high'.[68] These are:

(1) where the legal risk challenges the firm's business model or business practices;
(2) where it leads to large or uncertain liabilities;

---

[67] According to the *Financial Times* of 16 and 18 May 2005, Morgan Stanley have, since the date of the above article, been ordered by the Florida court to pay $604.3m in 'compensatory' damages and $850m in punitive damages to Mr Perelman. The judge in the case, having found evidence of 'bad faith' in respect of certain aspects of the bank's handling of the case, ordered the jury to assume that Morgan Stanley 'had aided and abetted Sunbeam to defraud Mr. Perelman'. The jury are now to decide whether or not to award punitive damages. (Mr Perelman claimed $2.7bn in actual and punitive damages.) At the time of writing, the bank is expected to appeal.

[68] 'Legal Risks and the Basle Capital Accord', presentation to International Bar Association Financial Law Seminar, Munich, 22 May 2003.

(3) where it impacts across the industry as a whole rather than being confined to a single institution; and

(4) where it crystallizes rapidly.

But are we becoming obsessive about risk? Observers have commented that we seem to have become more preoccupied with risk, and risk management, than might be good for us.[69] At government level, for example, public procurement policy is now dominated by the Private Finance Initiative,[70] which is in turn justified in very large part by its perceived effect of 'transferring risk' from public to private sector. The FSA itself frequently refers to its 'risk-based' approach to regulation[71] and, apart from its annual business plan, also produces a 'Financial Risk Outlook' each year. At the level of private enterprise, we see that many companies now have a 'Chief Risk Officer' as well as a Chief Financial Officer, Chief Executive Officer, etc.

The preoccupation affects all walks of life (and seems to go hand-in-hand with the 'compensation culture'). For example, in the context of running a school, head teachers find that they are now severely constrained in relation to activities such as field trips, which require detailed risk assessments to be carried out beforehand. One senses that there is a great deal of second guessing and wisdom after the event involved if, heaven forbid, any accident should occur. One head teacher recently complained that 'so far as organising trips is concerned, our increasingly risk-averse, bureaucratic and lawyer-plagued culture means that many children are already being deprived of opportunities'.[72]

Intro 1.47

---

[69] See especially Michael Power, 'The Risk Management of Everything', paper published by Demos (2004) (http://www.demos.co.uk): '. . . the story of operational risk characterises a new risk management in which the imperative is to make visible and manageable essentially unknowable and incalculable risks. New categories are a part of the appearance of manageability, a conceptual "mopping-up" exercise involving definitions and formalisations . . .' Power also observes that 'the implementation process under the Basel 2 proposals remains controversial. Much discussion has taken place about what constitutes an operational risk "event" (actual loss, possible loss, a near miss?). Furthermore the case of Barings suggests that significant operational risk events . . . by their very nature . . . lack rich historical data sets and exist at the limits of manageability. However, a great deal of operational risk management activity in financial institutions in fact focuses on routine systems errors and malfunctions. In many cases it is as if organisational agents, faced with the task of inventing a management practice, have chosen a pragmatic path of collecting data which is collectable, rather than that which is necessarily relevant. In this way, operational risk management in reality is a kind of displacement. The burden of managing unknowable risks, a Nick Leeson, is replaced by an easier task which can be successfully reported to seniors.'

[70] Now frequently referred to as 'Public Private Partnership'.

[71] This terminology has also been adopted recently by the Chancellor of the Exchequer in connection with non-financial regulation as well as financial regulation: see HM Treasury announcement of 24 May 2005, launching the 'Better Regulation Action Plan' (which will feature a Better Regulation Bill as well as a Deregulation Bill to be presented to Parliament).

[72] See Lenton, 'Litigation, Litigation, Litigation', *The Spectator*, 18 September 2004. See also speech given on 2 May 2005 (to the National Association of Headteachers) by Sir Digby Jones

Intro 1.48   Concern about the perception that there is 'for every injury someone to blame' prompted the Lord Chancellor, Lord Falconer, to issue a statement on 10 November 2004, which was very widely (and sympathetically) reported, decrying the growth of highly speculative litigation and the misuse of 'Conditional Fee Arrangements' and demanding that 'we must break the cycle'. The statement (which was largely concerned with personal injury claims but is nevertheless clear evidence of the extremely litigious climate that now affects all businesses) was accompanied by the threat that 'if the claims management sector does not put its own house in order we will consider how new formal regulation could be introduced'. The theme was taken up by the Prime Minister in a speech reported by *The Times* on 27 May 2005:

> The Prime Minister called for new laws yesterday to demolish the myth of the compensation culture and rein in ambulance-chasing companies.
>
> Britain was in danger of developing a disproportionate concern about risks, Tony Blair said . . . The perception of the 'so-called compensation culture' had the adverse effect, causing public bodies and others to act in 'highly risk-averse ways', he said. Too often the knee-jerk response from public bodies was to do everything to avoid blame in a 'something must be done' culture. 'In the end, risk is inescapable,' Mr. Blair said. 'Government cannot eliminate all risk. But too often our reflex as a society is to regulate and to introduce new rules . . . If we start to believe that every possible problem must be avoided at all costs we end up with a mind set that says that nothing good should happen in case it leads to something bad. Irrational decisions should not be made through fear of litigation. Rather, there should be a commonsense culture, not a compensation culture.[73]

Intro 1.49   Most would agree with the Prime Minister's sentiments. But until the changes he advocates arrive (by changes in law, changes in social attitudes, or some combination of the two) there is a problem to be dealt with. If entrepreneurs (including banks) are to maintain their appetite for risk, how are they to cope with this claims (or, as described by the Lord Chancellor, 'have a go') culture which, for obvious reasons, walks hand-in-hand with a general risk-averse mentality? The regulators must obviously allow that entrepreneurs can take risks;

(the Director-General of the Confederation of British Industry) in which he said: 'We, and especially politicians and the media, are all taking part in something of a deceit because we are teaching the next generation that risk doesn't exist . . . Don't play conkers in the playground, you might get hurt. Don't do backstroke in the swimming pool, you might bump into somebody. Don't take kids canoeing on a Saturday, they might put you in the slammer . . . Unless we educate children about risk, get them to understand it, embrace it and exploit it, then we will fail as a nation.'

[73] The Prime Minister also made some remarks in this speech which appeared to be critical of the FSA. The language used was cautiously worded; ie the FSA was 'seen as' being 'hugely' inhibiting to efficient business. The FSA has responded by asking the Prime Minister to substantiate his remarks. Both *The Times* and the *Financial Times* have roundly condemned the Prime Minister's comments about the FSA.

but they must 'manage' them. There is perhaps an unfortunate tendency to assume that if, notwithstanding sensible and reasonable efforts, the risk actually materializes then there must have been something wrong with the risk management. (Someone must be found to take the blame.) The spotlight on risk management procedures grows more and more intense. As Nugee and Persaud point out:[74] 'Risk management is a great business. But it almost seems that the more vigilant we are and the more safeguards we build into accounting rules, bank stress tests and contingency reserve funds the more new risks emerge. There is evidence that the adoption of risk management practices in institutional investment in the 1990s has increased, not reduced, volatility in financial markets.'

Some feel that risk management is something of a passing fashion or fad. A degree of scepticism may indeed be healthy but, as Callum McCarthy, the Chairman of the FSA, points out, those who make the argument that: **Intro 1.50**

> . . . regulatory concern for consumer protection purposes is overdone . . . tend to forget the scale of past problems: pensions mis-selling has involved compensation payments of £11.5 billion; the losses associated with split capital trusts— depending on how they are calculated—are variously estimated to amount to between £650–£900 million for the zero dividend preference share holders; precipice bonds mis-selling—a recent event—has so far involved compensation of over £150 million and is very far from finished.[75]

(It is not immediately obvious, however, why the fact that very large sums have been paid in compensation is a complete answer to the suggestion that perhaps we are making it too easy to make allegations and claims that lead to such a result.)

Whether or not the problems associated with operational risk are exaggerated, legal risk, as a component of operational risk, has played a very significant role in this context. The extreme difficulties of the Equitable Life Assurance Society[76] were largely sparked off by litigation that went to the House of Lords and the case of *Hazell v Hammersmith and Fulham London Borough Council*[77] gave rise to widespread concern as to the validity of, and the recoverability of moneys paid, in the 'swap' transactions sector of the derivatives market involving local government (and to some extent, building societies). As these cases show, legal risk, like many other kinds of operational risk, is one of the most difficult to deal with because it tends to be 'low probability/high impact'. In **Intro 1.51**

---

[74] *Financial Times*, 17 September 2004, 19.
[75] Mansion House speech, 21 September 2004.
[76] This is the world's oldest mutual insurance company; the adverse court ruling ultimately forced it to close its doors to new business. See further, the Penrose Report, March 2004, HC 290.
[77] [1992] 2 AC 1; see generally Ch 1 below.

other words, situations triggered by legal risk do not generally happen very frequently (and historical data are not very illuminating), but when they do they can cause extremely serious problems. The Giovannini Group has observed that, 'experience suggests that financial institutions often fail to manage adequately very low probability risks of catastrophic events, which may have the nature of externalities'.[78] Legal risk, and related questions such as how and why it arises and what it actually is, needs to be taken seriously.

Intro 1.52 The analytical exercise involved in describing precisely what we mean by legal risk is a complex one. As with the definition of law itself, most definitions of legal risk tend to have 'fuzzy edges'. Definitional issues and the general characteristics of legal risk are considered in some detail in Part II of this book. Finding an appropriate definition is not an academic exercise. It is important for financial institutions to have a clear understanding, reflected in established procedures, of who is responsible for the management of different kinds of operational risk. Let us say, for example, that a bank determines that its own legal department should have some responsibility for managing legal risk but not for other kinds of operational risk. Where is the line to be drawn? Taking risks often involves legal consequences (for example, being subject to claims for damages or fines). It does not follow, however, that the risks inherent in all actions which could give rise to litigation must be classified as 'legal risks'. The possibility that an employee of the bank might behave in a fraudulent manner is an operational risk, and can be a very serious risk, but it does not generally have the necessary attributes to qualify as a legal risk. There may also be borderline definitional problems with risks which are commonly thought of as political risk. If a bank's assets in a particular country are confiscated by the dictatorship which has assumed political control there, that is primarily a political problem even though the means by which the confiscation is effected may involve the passing of laws and legal enforcement measures. Further, the materialization of a legal risk may exacerbate a credit risk, for example, where the security taken for a loan to a borrower which is heavily indebted to other creditors turns out to be defective.

Intro 1.53 It is not practical or sensible to consider legal risk in isolation from other kinds of risk. However, the new regulatory approach will require some degree of precision. Analysis of where the line is to be drawn is important not only for allocation of responsibility within an institution but also for developing appropriate risk management procedures. The handling of a court case in England involving, say, a claim that a spouse's guarantee of a customer's loan is invalid is likely to involve different procedures to those that may be relevant for handling

---

[78] See the Second Giovannini Clearing and Settlement Report, 29.

an assertion that a bank's loan or security documentation in a country where it does very little business does not conform to the local legal requirements in that country unless and until a relatively insignificant stamp tax has been paid. Certain kinds of legal claim may have precedent-setting implications for a broad range of the bank's business whereas other legal problems may be capable of being ring-fenced to a particular country or perhaps a particular customer. Nevertheless, although there may be differences in procedure, the underlying rationale for analysis and management will be more effective if it is consistent with a coherent model which explains and identifies legal risk as a whole and contains a proven and accepted methodology for its assessment and mitigation, including a system of reporting, assessment, decision-making, and recording. Those who are faced with difficulties of the kind described in the *Financial Times* and *Wall Street Journal* articles referred to above will no doubt accept that, whatever the parameters of the legal risk concept may be, you tend to know it when you see it. The problem is: you can't always see it coming.

PART I

HISTORY

1

A LANDMARK CASE AND ITS AFTERMATH

It appears therefore at the time when the transactions in the present case were entered into there was a general understanding, which was shared by banks and local authorities as regular participants in the money markets, that interest rate swap contracts were within the borrowing and lending powers of local authorities. This understanding appears to have been based upon commercial assumptions which developed within the money markets, not as a result of initiatives taken on legal advice by either party in the transactions.[1]

A. A Shock to the Markets—a Legal Debacle

The case that no one saw coming was *Hazell v Hammersmith and Fulham* **1.01** *London Borough Council*.[2] This was a House of Lords decision on an *ultra vires* point—specifically, the power of the council in question to enter into 'swap' transactions. The case arose because this power was challenged by the auditor appointed by the Audit Commission. Although it was undoubtedly of some interest as regards the legal point that was decided, the technical significance of the case was completely overshadowed by the reaction that it caused in the financial markets. Its place in history is earned not by its legal, but by its political, significance. The surrounding circumstances, and the unprecedented manner in which the City of London responded to the case, provide both the classic case study and a historical explanation of why legal risk is seen to be so important and how seriously it is taken by those concerned with orderly

---

[1] From the judgment of Lord Hope in *Kleinwort Benson v Lincoln City Council* [1999] 2 AC 349, 404.

[2] [1992] 2 AC 1. This was one of many cases concerned with the restitutions of moneys paid over in swap transactions which, following the *Hammersmith and Fulham* case were determined to be null and void. (By and large, the banks got most of their money back but made no profit.)

financial markets. Because of its impact on how we now see and deal with legal risk, the case is a turning point in the City of London's legal and regulatory evolution.

1.02   There is a wealth of commentary describing the furore that the case caused but perhaps the most succinct description of its effect can be found in the judgment of Lord Goff of Chieveley in the later House of Lords decision in *Westdeutsche Landesbank Giro Zentrale v Islington London Borough Council*.[3] Lord Goff records that the *Hammersmith and Fulham* case 'caused grave concern amongst financial institutions, and especially foreign banks, which had entered into . . . transactions with local authorities in good faith, with no idea that a rule as technical as the ultra vires doctrine might undermine what they saw as a perfectly legitimate commercial transaction'. The emphasis on foreign banks, good faith, and the rule being 'technical' is important. The City was entering the new world of global financial markets, with justifiable ambitions to be a leading centre for international financial markets and their participants. It could not afford to be seen as a place that 'foreigners' could not trust because of out-of-date technicalities in the law which could undermine confidence in the predict-ability of the legal process and the ability to conclude deals that would be respected by courts in comparable (and competing) market jurisdictions—especially where the entity that would benefit from the technical defect would be a public sector entity.

1.03   As mentioned above, the case concerned interest rate swap transactions. Again, Lord Goff's judgment in the *Westdeutsche* case provides a succinct summary of the nature of an interest rate swap:

> Under such a transaction, one party (the fixed rate payer) agrees to pay the other over a certain period interest at a fixed rate on a notional capital sum; and the other party (the floating rate payer) agrees to pay to the former over the same period interest on the same notional sum at a market rate determined in accordance with a certain formula. Interest rate swaps can fulfil many purposes, ranging from pure speculation to more useful purposes such as the hedging of liabilities.

1.04   The judgment of the House of Lords in the *Hammersmith and Fulham* case determined that a local authority had no power whatsoever to enter into a swap transaction, or a related transaction, in any circumstances whatsoever. As Revell and Jakeways pointed out in a near-contemporaneous article:

> This decision was reached on the basis that the only source of power a local authority had to enter into such transactions was under Section 111 of the Local Government Act 1972 (which gives local authorities a general power to do

---

[3] [1996] AC 669; see also the reaction of the LRRC described at Intro 1.14 above.

anything which is 'calculated to facilitate, or is conducive or incidental to,' the discharge of any of their functions).[4]

The House concluded that the entry into swap and similar transactions could not be said to 'facilitate' or be 'conducive' or 'incidental' to the discharge of any local authority function. Revell and Jakeways went on to comment that the case 'led to unexpected losses which at least in some instances were a complete surprise and are viewed with outrage by the banks involved'. **1.05**

As noted by Lord Goff (and others), the reaction of foreign banks was particularly severe. Local authorities were, after all, seen as a form of UK sovereign credit by many of them. How could it be that another arm of 'government' (the judiciary) would allow them to walk away from obligations freely and openly entered into on the (perceived) pretext of a technicality? Within a few months of the decision (in April 1991), the Bank of England (which was reported to be advocating retrospective validation of the swap contracts by legislation in order to 'preserve the good name of the London markets') reacted to the *Hammersmith and Fulham* case by arranging for the formation of the Legal Risk Review Committee (LRRC), whose terms of reference included: **1.06**

- reviewing existing law in the light of current practice (domestic and international) in the financial markets and identifying areas of obscurity and uncertainty;
- examining the options in relation to such areas and proposing solutions;
- considering means by which legal certainty can be speedily and effectively established; and
- considering means by which changes and developments in financial market practice and future legislation can be reviewed regularly to identify prospective problems and propose appropriate remedies in good time.

The official announcement of the establishment of this committee stated that it followed 'a controversial Law Lords ruling which concerned the power of a local authority (Hammersmith and Fulham) to enter into interest rate swap transactions. The ruling cast into doubt the legality of other similar financial transactions, and uncovered many areas of legal uncertainty in city operations.' **1.07**

The legal atmosphere in the City was charged. Something had to be done. One of the earliest recommendations of the committee was to recommend the abolition of the doctrine of *ultra vires*. (To date, the doctrine remains as part of English law, although the practical difficulties associated with local authorities **1.08**

---

[4] (1991) 06 JIBFL 291.

have been eased by statutes such as the Local Government (Contracts) Act 1997 and, in practice, the doctrine is now of limited relevance to companies as well.)

1.09   Elsewhere, Hong Kong introduced legislation along the lines apparently advocated by the Bank of England, which had the effect of validating swap transactions retrospectively that had been entered into by the Kowloon-Canton Railway Corporation and the Mass Transit Railway Corporation.

1.10   The *Hammersmith and Fulham* case drew the fire of all those who, like Colin Bamford (who became the Chief Executive of the Financial Law Panel) observed that:

> . . . at the end of the 1980's and into the beginning of the 1990's, there was a growing feeling in the financial markets that the pace of development of concepts and products was much greater than that of development in the legal system. The concern that legal concepts and procedures were no longer able to cope was confirmed, as far as many market practitioners were concerned, by the decision in the *Hammersmith & Fulham* case.[5]

1.11   The Chairman of the Financial Law Panel, Lord Donaldson of Lymington, looking back at the case some years later, referred to the LRRC being set up 'in the wake of the *Hammersmith and Fulham* swaps debacle'.

1.12   So what exactly was it that caused all the fuss? The *ultra vires* doctrine is hardly the stuff of legal novelty. Banks would, for example, have been well aware of important, and recently decided, cases on *ultra vires* questions in company law, as applied in the context of the power of companies to give guarantees[6] and, notwithstanding the fact that different considerations arose with regard to public bodies such as the Hammersmith and Fulham council, the possibility of there being 'an *ultra vires* point' would surely have surfaced in any legal appraisal of the issues that the transactions might involve. One would have expected any financial institution entering into significant transactions with counterparties such as local authorities (who were known to have unusual constitutions) to have obtained very careful legal advice on the powers of those authorities to enter into such transactions. So why did the *Hammersmith and Fulham* case come as such a great surprise and why did it cause such consternation? To understand the reaction of the markets it is necessary, first, to examine the decision in more detail and then to consider its social and political context.

---

[5] 'The Financial Law Panel: A Review of its First Year' (1994) 10 JIBFL 475.
[6] See, eg *Rolled Steel Products (Holdings) Ltd v British Steel Corp* [1986] Ch 246.

B. The Points of Law Decided in *Hammersmith and Fulham*

The legal point decided by the House of Lords was relatively narrow. It was **1.13** contended by the banks that were parties to the swaps that the Hammersmith and Fulham London Borough Council had power to borrow money and that the borrowing of money was a 'function' within the meaning of section 111(1) of the Local Government Act 1972. Further, the banks contended that swaps transactions which were entered into for the purpose of either 'replacing' the interest payable under an actual borrowing or for the purpose of 're-profiling' existing interest obligations could be said to be 'calculated to facilitate', 'conducive to', or 'incidental to' the discharge by the council of its borrowing function (or an alleged function of 'debt management'). It was decided by the House of Lords that, in this context, the borrowing of money by the council was a 'function'. However, their Lordships did not accept that swap transactions could be said to facilitate borrowing or be conducive to it or incidental to it. That approach was regarded as impermissible because (amongst other things) 'a local authority when considering expenditure must carefully consider the amount required to be borrowed and the resources available for payment of interest and capital. A local authority which borrowed in reliance on future successful swap operations would be failing in its duty to act prudently in the interests of the rate payers.'

Their Lordships also observed that 'local authorities should not be encouraged **1.14** to borrow by the prospect of swap transactions' and that 'a power is not incidental merely because it is convenient or desirable or profitable'. The speculative nature of swap transactions weighed heavily on their Lordships' minds. The following passage is particularly telling: 'Individual trading corporations and others may speculate as much as they please or consider prudent. But a local authority is not a trading or currency or commercial operator with no limit on the method or extent of its borrowing or with powers to speculate. The local authority is a public authority dealing with public moneys . . .'

Their Lordships gave short shrift to the argument that 'debt management' **1.15** should be considered an independent function:

> Debt management is a phrase which has been coined in this case to describe the activities of a person who enters the swap market for the purpose of making profits . . . Debt management is a phrase which describes prudent and lawful activities on the part of the local authority. If swap transactions were lawful, a local authority would be under a duty to consider entering into swap transactions as part of its duty of debt management, but if a swap transaction is not lawful, then it cannot be lawful for a local authority to carry out a swap transaction under the guise of debt management.

1.16 The points of law were complex, and of great interest at the time. However, the case's ongoing significance—the first *cause célèbre* of legal risk in the London financial markets—emerges more clearly when it is seen in the context of the activities and behaviour of the principal institutions involved in it, events in, and the evolution of, the financial markets in the period leading up to it and the enormous legal, economic, and political changes that had taken place in the preceding decade.

C. Background Facts

1.17 In the context of the case itself, a great deal of data emerges from the facts cited in the judgments of the three courts who considered the case. Much of this merits study simply as a factual scenario depicting how serious legal risks can arise. The facts are also instructive for those concerned with the management of legal risk today.[7] With the benefit of hindsight, one can see that a number of significant mistakes were made by several of the parties involved, which, one might hope, would probably not be repeated now. The following points all emerge from the judgment of Lord Templeman in the House of Lords:

(1) The relatively new phenomenon of a 'swap market' began to be established 'in the world of international finance' around 1981.

(2) Their Lordships were well aware of the perfectly legitimate commercial reasons why commercial enterprises might enter into swap transactions and cited an article on the subject that had been published in the *Bank of England Quarterly Bulletin* of February 1987. Their Lordships even noted that in most cases the reason for entering into such a transaction is the 'elimination of speculation and uncertainty' rather than the making of profits by speculation.

(3) Evidence was produced that seventy-seven local authorities (out of 450) entered into about 400 swap transactions, nearly all between 1987 and 1989. Only ten of those authorities (apart from Hammersmith and Fulham) entered into more than ten swaps and only eighteen (other than Hammersmith and Fulham) entered into more than five. However, Hammersmith and Fulham had entered into no fewer than 592 swap transactions by 31 March 1989 and, as at that date, 297 were still outstanding. The council's actual borrowings at that date were only £390 million, whereas the notional principal amount of the swaps was £2,996 million (although it was acknowledged that the latter figure was distorted to an

---

[7] See Chs 10 and 11 below.

extent because some swap transactions were hedged against others). The activities of this particular customer were therefore noteworthy, from the perspective of risk management, if only because of the very high volume of transactions.

(4) The banks involved in the case conceded that the swap transactions entered into by the council between April 1987 and July 1988 were unlawful because they were acknowledged to be purely speculative (ie the argument that they were in some sense associated with the function of borrowing could not be applied to those transactions). The case was in fact only concerned with certain transactions carried out after July 1988.

(5) It was noted that the functions of bodies like the council, having regard to its normal range of activities, generally tend to extend to public health, housing, planning, and highways and other environmental matters and to education, housing, and social welfare services, including the care and protection of children, the sick, and the elderly. They are not of course financial institutions. However, because of the timing mismatch of receipt of revenue (rates, community charges, etc) and the payment of expenditure, Parliament (pursuant to the legislation mentioned) gives local authorities 'controlled power' to borrow on both a short-term and long-term basis.

Other background data emerge from the judgments of the lower courts, at **1.18** Divisional Court and Court of Appeal level. For example:

(1) If the transactions under consideration had been enforceable, the council could have lost in excess of £100 million. (In effect, the council had taken a position that would benefit it if interest rates fell; however, during the relevant period rates rose substantially.)

(2) There was a breakdown in communication inside the council. According to the Divisional Court: 'The council's activities in relation to the transactions were initiated and substantially expanded without any report to the members of the council describing what was happening or the members considering the advantages and disadvantages or legality of the transactions and without any authorisation from the council, its committees or sub-committees.' The auditor contended (and the Divisional Court agreed with him) that 'the information as supplied to the council, its committees and sub-committees in the reports in 1988 and 1989 was in my view inadequate to enable members of them to consider properly the legality, reasonableness and prudence of the activities in the London Money/Capital Market'.

(3) Although the Audit Commission obtained various legal opinions (in mid-July 1988) about the transactions (which clearly raised significant doubts about their legality) it seems that 'no legal advice had been obtained from within or on behalf of the council about the legality of the transactions'—as

at July 1988. Whatever advice the banks may have obtained, the council did not get legal advice itself before entering into 'its capital market activity'. The council eventually obtained an opinion from leading counsel in December 1988. This opinion, which was based on a number of factual assumptions, was broadly favourable to the council. However, a further opinion, provided in February 1989, stated: 'I can say that in my opinion the council have been engaged in various types of interest swap transactions which as a whole are on a scale outside the parameters I explained in (my earlier) written opinion and that therefore looking at the totality of the transactions it is not possible to say that these transactions were part and parcel of debt management so as to be lawful.'

(4) Whatever the formalities as to who obtained what legal advice, the Audit Commission was broadly aware of the fact that local authorities were active in the swap market and appeared to approve. For example, in its annual report for 1986–7 the Commission accepted that it was 'right that local authorities should take advantage of the opportunities to reduce borrowing costs offered by new types of financial instrument'. As the Court of Appeal observed: 'If, until the auditor's intervention, the council and the banks dealing with it believed transactions of this kind to be lawful if genuinely used for the purposes of debt or asset management, they were not alone.' Anecdotal evidence even suggests that some banks thought that the UK government would 'stand behind' the local authorities as a matter of credit risk.

1.19 Ideally, the requirements of sound policy and achieving the 'correct' legal result usually coincide. However, in many of the harder cases that come before the courts some relatively innocent party, perhaps even a completely innocent party, has to lose. It is arguable that the banks were misled by the apparent endorsement of the activities of local authorities in the swap markets that could be detected in certain 'official' circles. It is also arguable that rigorous legal checks would have alerted them to the dangers. It is certainly true that the residents of Hammersmith and Fulham were entitled to protection against the proceeds of local taxes being spent in an unauthorized manner. These are not just legal questions. They are political and economic as well. Throughout the twentieth century there were a number of instances of local authorities adopting policies, which required funding, that reflected a political stance that did not necessarily command the wholehearted support of the local population and were susceptible to legal challenge on the grounds of *ultra vires*. The cases on what Wade and Forsyth[8] call 'misplaced philanthropy' show that the courts are, as they say,

---

[8] *Administrative Law* (9th edn) 398.

'in general hostile to the use of public funds ... for new social experiments'. Why should one expect them to be less hostile to using such funds for what many regarded as pure speculation on the financial markets? To examine this question further, and fully understand the markets' response to the *Hammersmith and Fulham* case, we need to look at some of the events in the financial markets and across the wider political spectrum that led up to it.

D. The Wider Context of the Case

The *Hammersmith and Fulham* case was decided early in 1991. The previous **1.20** decade had seen enormous changes in the financial markets and in the legal and regulatory environment that applied to them. Of huge significance, for example, was the abolition of exchange control in 1979. This made capital (whether owned by individuals or companies) mobile. As a result it became much more difficult to regulate how capital should be deployed. (Capital that did not care for the UK's laws and regulations could now simply go elsewhere.) A few years later, the Financial Services Act, enacted in November 1986 (largely in response to Professor Gower's Review of Investor Protection, published in two parts in 1984 and 1985, and also in response to EU (then, EEC) requirements for harmonized rules for listed securities), introduced a completely new regulatory regime for all kinds of 'investment business'. The new system relied on the use of various, largely new, 'self regulating organisations' and the overseeing function of the completely new Securities and Investments Board (SIB) (which latter body was, several years later, under the Labour government elected in 1997, replaced by the FSA). Much of the legislation concerned with regulation in this area, and with associated matters such as the issuance and content of prospectuses, was repealed and replaced as part of a general drive towards 'deregulation' and European harmonization. However, at this stage, commercial banking, as opposed to merchant or investment banking, remained under the supervision of the Bank of England, pursuant to the Banking Act 1979, as replaced by the Banking Act 1987.

With the repeal of old laws, such as the Prevention of Fraud (Investments) Act **1.21** 1958 (even the name evokes a more conservative era), many of the more traditional market practices that had prevailed before the wave of privatization issues in the 1980s gradually disappeared. Changes in market practice were accelerated to a significant extent by the abolition of various restrictions which had previously affected securities business. The most significant of these was popularly known as the 'Big Bang'. Big Bang (which ran alongside the new laws, but was not itself a part of them) was largely triggered by pressure from the Office of Fair Trading, which had been scrutinizing many of the traditional practices of the

London Stock Exchange, and had not been satisfied that the numerous restrictive elements could be justified in the newly competitive, market-driven age being ushered in by Margaret Thatcher's Conservative government. Fixed commission structures and restrictions on membership had to go and 'dual capacity' (enabling the same firm to be a market-maker or 'jobber' in stocks and shares as well as a broker) became possible. Member firms could now be owned by banks, even foreign banks. As a result, market participants could benefit from much-needed injections of new capital. Many stockbrokers 'of the old school' were able to reap substantial personal rewards as their firms were sold off and many, notwithstanding supposed 'golden handcuff' arrangements, were able to retire rich (or even richer). At the same time, international banks (and the UK's own high street banks) could begin to spread their activities well beyond the scope of traditional deposit taking and lending, into all kinds of securities business and 'investment banking'. The character, and culture, of life in the financial markets started to change, and so did the risk profile of the businesses carried on by banks.[9]

1.22 Investors, who had been accustomed to reading about new share issues only in the financial pages of the broadsheet press, now found that shares in newly privatized companies, such as British Telecom and British Gas, were being advertised on television and radio. They even featured on billboard advertisements in the high street. The detailed, cautiously compiled, financial

---

[9] The Review Committee on Banking Services Law (under the Chairmanship of Professor R B Jack CBE) reporting in December 1988, commented on a number of the changes being experienced by banks and their customers at that time, eg (at para 2.25): 'In the 1980's too, the global aspect of banking has become much more apparent, thus accelerating a trend which began in the 1970's. Banking transactions of all kinds across international frontiers have been greatly facilitated by the speed of new technology. There are important benefits in this, but also magnified risks. The global nature of banking, for example, again offers scope for fraud on an enhanced scale. The possibility, albeit remote, of the sudden insolvency of an overseas partner in a banking transaction puts a new focus of interest on the precise timing of payment processes' and (at para 2.26) 'both deregulation and regulation, in the domestic market, are significantly changing the shape of the playing field for banking operations. The beginning of deregulation in the early 1970's signalled a general move by banks to diversify into new and hitherto unfamiliar markets, ranging from leasing and unit trusts to estate agencies, insurance, travel and mortgage lending; and, since "Big Bang" in 1986, to a more direct involvement in the securities industry.' Observations on the changes to the banker–customer relationship are also relevant to the evolution of legal risk for banks in the new era (at para 2.31): 'banks have inevitably become more sharply commercial in their outlook towards customers. The bank manager has perforce moved away from his role as the trusted financial adviser, the "man of business", to that of the salesman of a whole range of products and services. Automation has further depersonalised the relationship, putting it on a more formal basis of contract. While high standards of service are generally maintained—despite occasional complaints of falling standards in certain areas—customers could be said to have found a new, less patient, attitude taking over from the "friendly paternalism" of the past; increasingly, they have become parties to a business relationship little different from any other. For the private bank customer, the halcyon simplicity of the pre war era may be thought to have gone forever—a lost Eden.'

information was still there, for those who looked for it, but many looked no further than catchy slogans such as that used for the British Gas flotation: 'Don't forget to tell Sid.' Most privatization issues traded at a profit immediately following flotation and, not surprisingly, they proved to be extremely popular with the public at large, both in the UK and elsewhere. Many of these privatization issues were of such an enormous scale that the shares were offered on several different markets around the world at the same time.[10] This is commonly done now but it was very new then. Privatization in the UK made a notable contribution to the globalization of the markets. Naturally, all this activity generated a great deal of fee income for all those involved. Everyone seemed to win and most seemed happy. The City of London experienced boom times, a new generation of 'yuppie' securities dealers and traders swelled the sales of Porsches and BMWs and the profits of champagne bars, and when Gordon Gekko, a fictional character in the film 'Wall Street', pronounced that 'greed is good', many seemed to agree with him.

The mood of the times was caught by the Conservative Party's election manifesto of 1987:   **1.23**

> The City of London is the world's leading market place in foreign exchange, international bank lending and international insurance. It is a major source of funds for British companies. The financial services sector as a whole accounts for nearly 6% of our national income, generates a net £7 billion per year to our balance of payments and employs over one million people.
>
> Like other sections of British industry, however, the City was held back by restrictive practices, until they were swept away in last year's 'big bang'. This has brought nearer the day when shares can be bought and sold over the counter in every high street. We have also given building societies greater freedom to make a wider range of financial services available to the average family.
>
> At the same time, the Conservative Government has introduced a legal framework to protect investors and consumers:
>
> The Companies Acts of 1980 and 1981 strengthened the powers of investigators and increased the courts' power to disqualify directors for misconduct in the City as elsewhere. The Insolvency Act of 1985 made it easier to disqualify directors who had been guilty of unlawful trading.

---

[10] The British Telecom share issue in 1984 (of half the company) was valued at £4bn, 'some seven times bigger than any previous UK issue and some four times bigger than any issue attempted anywhere in the world. It represented approximately the amount which the big UK investment institutions, the pension funds, and insurance companies had put into the equity market over a two-year period. Against this background, it was always clear that to achieve success for an issue the size of British Telecom as well as British Gas, which was bigger still, it would be necessary to achieve the widest possible pool of potential demand and that this would involve an extensive selling campaign in different markets'—see remarks by Henderson reported in 'The Developing Securities Market' (proceedings of IBA Conference, 4–5 May 1987, edited by Neate) 58.

And now the Financial Services Act of 1986 provides the first comprehensive system of investor protection we have had in this country. It also contains stringent new powers to investigate insider dealing which was first made a criminal offence by the Conservative Government in 1980.

1.24 This was 'popular capitalism', a 'capital-owning democracy'. According to the manifesto, share ownership had trebled and 'almost one in five of the adult population now own shares directly'. Of that total, most were first-time shareholders and most owned shares either in the privatized companies or the recently floated TSB group (previously the Trustee Savings Bank). One in five British adults now owned shares, compared with one in ten Frenchmen and one in twenty Japanese.

1.25 Nearly ten years later, in September 1996, the then Conservative Chancellor of the Exchequer, Kenneth Clarke boasted that:

Ten years ago we had launched BT down the slipway of privatisation, British Airways was just taxiing down the runway, Sid was about to be told about British Gas—but water, electricity and steel were still in the public sector.

50 major businesses have now been privatised and about a million employees transferred to the private sector . . . 10 years ago the City was on the threshold of Big Bang. The financial services revolution of the mid-80's swept away the cobwebs, and created the conditions which have allowed the City to prosper and to become the world international financial centre. Last year the net overseas earnings of the UK financial sector were over £20 billion (3% of GDP).[11]

1.26 Another Conservative Chancellor, Nigel Lawson, summarized the financial deregulation policies of the 1980s as follows:

Although financial deregulation is a somewhat imprecise term, it is possible to identify at least ten specific events, of varying degrees of importance, that qualify as acts of financial deregulation, most of which occurred during the early part of the Government's term of office. In chronological order, these were:

1. The unannounced ending, virtually as soon as the new Government took office in May 1979, of the restrictive guidelines on building society lending.
2. The abolition of exchange controls in October 1979.
3. The abolition of the so-called 'corset', the Supplementary Special Deposits Scheme designed to curb bank lending, in June 1980.
4. The abolition of the Reserve Assets Ratio requirement, under which banks had to hold at least 12.5% of their deposits in a specified range of liquid assets, in August 1981.
5. The abolition of hire-purchase restrictions in July 1982.
6. The collapse of the Building Societies' cartel in October 1983.
7. Some aspects of the Building Societies Act, 1986.

---

[11] From speech by Kenneth Clarke given to London School of Economics on 16 September 1996.

8. The ending of the restrictive practices of the stock exchange in the so-called 'Big Bang' of October 1986.
9. The withdrawal of mortgage lending 'guidance' in December 1986.
10. The effective abolition of the Control of Borrowing Order in March 1989.

Two of these events stand out as being of particular importance. The first, and most important of all, was the abolition of exchange control. At the time a radical and highly controversial act, it became the norm throughout the major industrial nations of the world—partly because of a genuine belief in freedom and deregulation, partly because the information technology revolution made controls on capital movements increasingly difficult to police. As a result we were returning to a degree of economic freedom last seen in the early years of this century, before the First World War—*but with international capital flows on a much larger scale.*[12]

The consequences of this for the conduct of economic policy were considerable. In the first place it transformed the foreign exchange markets. Whereas for over half a century the movement of currency across the exchanges had been largely associated with trade flows, and the external values of currencies largely determined by the state of the balance of payments on current account, this ceased to be the case in the 1980s. But in the second place, and of greater relevance to the events considered in this chapter,[13] the ending of exchange control rendered ineffective any form of direct national controls on credit. For in a world in which capital can flow freely across the exchanges, the effect of such controls would merely be to drive lending offshore.[14]

The financial world had experienced, and enjoyed, a very significant loosening **1.27** of controls. The City was more open than ever to international players, who were of course greatly attracted by the opportunities that came with these changes. Inventiveness in devising new 'products' for the financial markets (and the employment of financial 'rocket scientists' for the purpose) was entirely in keeping with the spirit of the times. Taking risks simply on lending to customers suddenly seemed old-fashioned. A whole new world of 'capital markets' was being born. As the technicians devised new products, the bankers became 'salesmen' for an increasingly complex range of transaction structures designed primarily to hedge risks (of, say, currency or interest rate fluctuations) but which could be used, if the customer chose, for pure speculation. The Financial Services Act 1986 even contained a provision which, in removing various legal doubts about 'wagering', actually promoted the swaps market. From the outset, lawyers advising on these transactions had had concerns about whether purely speculative swaps, which were not linked to any underlying borrowings but were no more than 'contracts for differences', might be regarded by the courts as mere 'wagers' and, consequently, null and void. However, section 63 of the Financial Services Act 1986[15] provided that wagering contracts would not be unenforceable as such if they were entered into 'by way of business'. The

---

[12] Emphasis added.   [13] Deregulation and the 'credit boom' of the 1980s.
[14] Lawson, *The View From No. 11*, 626.   [15] See now FSMA 2000, s 412.

law-makers thus seemed to be on the same side as the fast-burgeoning derivatives market. It did not seem likely that legal technicalities would be allowed to stand in the way of its growth. In any event, as we have seen, everyone in any position of authority knew what was going on in the local authority swaps market and seemed to approve.

1.28 The 1980s were brash and greedy. Not everyone remembers them with great affection. But this was a confident, can-do society for those who were fortunate enough to remain in work and ride the wave. Most of those who worked in the City of London were in that category. None more so than those who worked in the more innovative sectors of the financial markets. For the most part they were highly paid, clever, used to taking risks, and used to getting their way. And then, just as an economic recession was beginning to bite (even in the City) in the early 1990s, along comes the *Hammersmith and Fulham* case to tell them, in relation to a kind of transaction that they had become used to regarding as routine: 'You can't do that.' The judicial pronouncement appeared to many as if it had come from another planet, from people who were not sufficiently 'tuned in' to what had been happening in the previous ten years. Few cases on, essentially, highly technical questions of capacity to contract can have provoked as much hostility as this one did.

1.29 The impact of the *Hammersmith and Fulham* case was felt throughout 1991 and 1992 (with the LRRC delivering its Final Report in October 1992) and for several years afterwards. This was a tumultuous period for the City of London. BCCI had been closed down in 1991, amidst allegations of fraud on a massive scale, and the banking regulatory system (especially the Bank of England, which at that time was responsible for the supervision of banks) was still reeling from the shock. The European 'Single Market' (establishing free movement of goods, people, services, and capital throughout the EU) was due to come into force in January 1993. The world at large was still trying to come to terms with the collapse of communist regimes in Eastern Europe and, in celebrating the pre-eminence of liberal democracies, one well-respected author was proclaiming 'the end of history'.[16] The Conservative Party, led by John Major, won a surprise victory in a General Election in May 1992. But the euphoria quickly evaporated with 'Black Wednesday' of 16 September 1992, when sterling was forcibly ejected from the European Exchange Rate Mechanism. The government's reputation for financial competence (whether or not you agreed with it) was ruined as a result of this. For a while it seemed as though the country was as

---

[16] Francis Fukuyama, *The End of History and the Last Man*, which was published in 1992, expanding on an article published in 1989. The principal argument was that 'the ideal of liberal democracy could not be improved on'. 'Liberal principles in economics—the "free market"—have spread, and have succeeded in producing unprecedented levels of material prosperity . . .'

well.[17] As one commentator put it: 'At the time, it seemed that after Black Wednesday, Britain was sailing into the unknown.'[18] There was more than enough uncertainty around. The last thing the City wanted was a dose of legal uncertainty on top of everything else. But that was precisely what the *Hammersmith and Fulham* decision was perceived to have delivered.

As stated above,[19] the case led directly to the formation by the Bank of England **1.30** of the Legal Risk Review Committee, chaired by Lord Alexander, with a remit to look at legal uncertainties affecting wholesale financial markets (it was essentially concerned with Type 2 risks). The *Hammersmith and Fulham* case had a major impact on how the City of London thought about, and dealt with, legal risk, especially risk that resulted from what the markets perceived to be 'legal uncertainty'. Insofar as it led to the establishment of learned committees and regular pronouncements by them on 'grey areas' in the law (which activity in turn has led, with beneficial results, to a heightened awareness of legal risk) it was, in a sense, aided and abetted by a slightly earlier case. *Re Charge Card Services Ltd.,*[20] decided at first instance in 1986, by Millett J, gave rise to enormous controversy, not because it invalidated transactions leading to loss (or potential loss) of money by banks, but because the judgment contained remarks which threw doubt on the precise legal nature of one of the oldest (and, one might have thought, simplest) forms of security that a bank can take from its customer, ie a deposit of cash. The implications of that case are considered in the next chapter.

---

[17] Although it has been noted many times since, that Black Wednesday in fact seemed to mark the beginning of a sustained economic recovery for the UK.

[18] Evan Davis (BBC Economics Editor), 15 September 2002.

[19] See Intro 1.14 above.   [20] [1989] Ch 497.

2

A CASE OF CONCEPTUAL IMPOSSIBILITY

I think that the courts should be very slow to declare a practice of the commercial community to be conceptually impossible.[1]

A. 'Charge-backs' and Legal Logic

The case of *Re Charge Card Services Ltd*[2] concerned the relationship between a **2.01** company and a finance house which had provided funds to it, pursuant to an invoice discounting agreement, by purchasing trade debts of the company. Under certain circumstances the company was obliged to repurchase trade debts, which, in any event, it guaranteed would be paid. The accounting and payment system operating between the parties gave the finance house various rights to hold on to moneys, make deductions from payments, and exercise set-offs. When the company went into liquidation it was contended that certain rights of the finance house were void as against the liquidator because they constituted charges over book debts and they had not been registered as required under the Companies Act 1948. However, Millett J decided that the arrangements could not be a charge because it is 'conceptually impossible' for a debtor to take a charge (securing a claim he has against a counterparty) over a debt that he himself owes to that counterparty. Instead the debtor has, and should rely upon, a right of set-off (which Millett J evidently thought would be just as good as a charge for all practical purposes).

The point at issue in the *Charge Card* case is often illustrated by contrasting the **2.02** two-party situation (considered by Millett J) with the situation involving three parties, where A assigns (or charges) to B a debt owed to him by C (which

---

[1] From the judgment of Lord Hoffmann in *BCCI (No 8)* [1998] AC 214.
[2] [1986] 3 All ER 289; [1989] Ch 497 (CA) 242.

51

clearly *is* conceptually possible). In the two-party (or bilateral) situation, where A purports to assign (or charge) to B the debt that B owes to A there is, at first sight at least, something that does not seem altogether logical. This arises simply because the object of the transaction, the debt, is the very debt owed by the person acquiring (or expressed to acquire) an interest in it. You cannot sensibly be said to own a debt that you yourself owe, so how, logically, can you own a chargee's interest in such a debt? Unfortunately, this point of legal logic (which had worried lawyers in practice well before the *Charge Card* decision) became a matter of great controversy, even notoriety, when considered in the context of certain transactions. The situation that most worried the markets (or at least the lawyers in the markets) arose where, in the bilateral situation, B is a bank and A is its customer and the subject of a purported charge (in this context, sometimes referred to as a 'charge-back') is a deposit that A holds with B. (The deposit is of course, in law, a debt owed by the bank to its customer.) There was no question that A could charge the deposit to, say, a third bank, C. Was the *Charge Card* decision suggesting that A could not charge the deposit to B? Apparently, it was indeed saying just that. But did it matter?

2.03 Perhaps the most important point to bear in mind when considering the *Charge Card* case is that, in contrast to *Hammersmith and Fulham*, there is no evidence that anyone lost any money or was even threatened with losing money as a result of it.[3] Much of the debate in fact turned not so much on the principal question (whether so-called 'charge-backs' should be regarded as conceptually impossible) but on the (perhaps rather more important) secondary question of whether the alternative security (which a perfectionist might categorise as 'quasi-security') of set-off (which clearly was both 'conceptually possible' and available in virtually all situations likely to arise in practice) was just as good, in the 'bilateral' context, as a charge. Although the case has now lost much of its legal significance in view of Lord Hoffmann's pronouncement in *BCCI (No. 8)*[4] that charge-backs are in fact possible (and recent proposals from the Law Commission would give statutory authority to this proposition, if they become law),[5] it remains of great interest (one commentator describes the point at issue

---

[3] The LRRC described the effect of the case as creating 'pin-pricks in daily business dealings which have increased documentary expenses, required highly specialist advice and cumulatively damaged the perception which the layman has of the law' (see LRRC Final Report, Appendix 2, para 6.2)

[4] [1998] AC 214.

[5] At the time of writing, a draft Statutory Instrument (The Company Security Regulations 2006) is in circulation (for comment) which, amongst other things, would provide that 'A person who owes receivables . . . may take a charge over the receivables' and that 'A cash debtor may take a charge over the cash it owes.'

as a 'hardy perennial')[6] because of its historical role in raising the profile of legal risk as that term is currently understood in the financial markets and, also, as an example of how markets, regulators, law-makers, and judges, as well as other academic and practising lawyers, respond to technical legal issues that might, if unresolved, threaten the orderly functioning of the markets and the UK's competitive position. The case also remains in the collective legal consciousness of the City of London, mainly because of the continuing importance of set-off in insolvency generally and its 'close relative', netting.[7]

Although the debate is, for practical purposes, now almost certainly closed, **2.04** we should not leave the case without looking more closely at the basic point of legal logic that underlay Millett J's view on the conceptual impossibility point. Although some commentators have, rather unfairly, accused Millett J of indulging in 'metaphysics', the point at issue was fairly simple: a debt is an item of property (a right, or chose in action) and, as such, it can be bought and sold (by means of assignment) and it can be charged as security. However, it does not require any specialist legal training to see that it does not make sense to attempt to sell a debt to the person who actually owes it (since he cannot exercise the right that constitutes the property against himself). You could agree with the debtor to forgive the debt, thus extinguishing it (wholly or in part) but you cannot make the debtor the *owner* of his own debt. Everyone seemed to be in agreement on this. The majority of opinion, at least amongst lawyers practising in the City, did not, however, want to go to the next step, ie to accept that the debtor could not take a 'charge-back' over his own debt, notwithstanding that the very old-established right of set-off (with suitable contractual embellishment) seemed to be a good alternative.

The arguments for and against the proposition have been very well developed **2.05** and are fully documented elsewhere. In summary, there was persuasive case law[8] supporting the 'Millett view' and, in addition, highly respected academic opinion came out on his side.[9] Further, the 'alternative' protection offered by set-off,

---

[6] See Cranston, *Principles of Banking Law* (2nd edn) 406. The FLP, in its first Annual Report (October 1994), described the issue as 'one of the most technical and irksome of legal problems to affect the financial markets in recent years'.

[7] See Ch 3 below.

[8] Notably, the House of Lords decision in *Halesowen Presswork & Assemblies v National Westminster Ltd* [1971] AC 785, where Lord Cross remarked that 'a debtor cannot sensibly be said to have a lien on his own indebtedness to his creditor'; see also the Australian case *Broad v Commissioner of Stamp Duties* [1980] 2 NSWLR 40.

[9] See Goode, *Legal Problems of Credit and Security* (3rd edn) 94 and 'Charge-backs and Legal Fictions' (1998) 114 LQR 178. The case law supporting the 'pro charge-back' view was somewhat patchy (although Wood marshalled an impressive range of 19th-century authorities to support charge-backs in his article, P Wood, 'Charge Card revisited' (February 1998) IFLR 26; the argument in favour of charge-backs was ultimately more persuasive because of business efficacy.

especially when coupled with provisions that relieved a depositee bank from any obligation to repay until its customer's debt was satisfied (generally known as 'flawed asset' provisions), did seem to meet the requirements of the vast majority of transactions. (Many lawyers, both before and after the case, documented transactions in the bilateral situation using the so-called 'triple cocktail' of (1) a purported charge, (2) an express right of set-off, and (3) a 'flawed asset' provision; this practice in itself was evidence that there was a lack of confidence about the correct legal analysis of charge-backs long before the *Charge Card* case was decided.) On the other hand, there was disquiet at many levels in the City that we might perhaps have scored an 'own goal' in allowing it to be put about in a competitive international market place that, in the UK, a bank 'can't even take a charge over its own customer's deposits', however misleading that statement may have been.

B. Pressure from Other Jurisdictions

2.06 The fact that a number of Commonwealth jurisdictions decided to change (or clarify) their own laws for the sole purpose of stating that 'charge-backs' could be done in their country did not help matters, from a UK perspective. The Legal Risk Review Committee (LRRC), whose members included Lord Hoffman, were clearly disturbed by the decision and recommended legislation to reverse it.[10]

2.07 Lord Hoffmann's judgment in *BCCI (No 8)* records not only the 'competitive' position in other jurisdictions but also the somewhat 'black and white' nature of the debate. The Court of Appeal (of which Millett LJ was a member) had held to the 'conceptual impossibility' line and was not persuaded that charge-backs were possible. Lord Hoffmann flatly disagreed:

> The Court of Appeal said that the bank could obtain effective security in other ways. If the deposit was made by the principal debtor, it could rely upon contractual rights of set-off under provisions such as r.4.90.[11] If the deposit was made

---

[10] Interestingly, the FLP's Practice Recommendations on how to provide effective security over cash deposits if one proceeded on the 'prudent assumption' that the Millett view was correct (before the House of Lords decision in *BCCI (No 8)* were much more sanguine. The FLP noted that 'however their views on legal theory diverge, lawyers practising in this field are agreed that mechanisms exist to allow transactions to be carried out without the use of a charge. Uncertainty in the market stems from the lack of uniformity in the practical approaches which advisers take. Save in exceptional circumstances, properly drawn contractual set-off terms will provide satisfactory security to a bank or other institution over a debt which it owes.' After a slight revision to its recommendations (following the Court of Appeal Decision in *BCCI (No. 8)* the FLP in essence endorsed the use of the 'triple cocktail'.

[11] See App 1 below.

by a third party, it could enter into contractual arrangements such as the limitation on the right to withdraw the deposit in this case, thereby making the deposit a 'flawed asset'. All this is true. It may well be that the security provided in these ways will in most cases be just as good as that provided by a proprietary interest. But that seems to me no reason for preventing banks and their customers from creating charges over deposits if, for reasons of their own, they want to do so. The submissions to the Legal Risk Review Committee made it clear that they do . . .

Since the decision in *Re Charge Card Services Ltd*,[12] statutes have been passed in several offshore banking jurisdictions to reverse its effect. A typical example is section 15A of the Hong Kong Law Amendment and Reform (Consolidation) Ordinance (Cap 23) which I have already mentioned. It reads:

For the avoidance of doubt, it is hereby declared that a person ('the first person') is able to create, and always has been able to create, in favour of another person ('the second person') a legal or equitable charge or mortgage over all or any of the first person's interest in a chose in action enforceable by the first person against the second person, and any charge or mortgage so created shall operate neither to merge the interest thereby created with, nor to extinguish or release, that chose in action.

There is similar legislation in Singapore . . . Bermuda . . . and the Cayman Islands. The striking feature about all these provisions is that none of them amend or repeal any rule of common law which would be inconsistent with the existence of a charge over a debt owed by the chargee. They simply say that such a charge can be granted. If the trick can be done as easily as this, it is hard to see where the conceptual impossibility is to be found.

In a case in which there is no threat to the consistency of the law or objection of public policy, I think that the courts should be very slow to declare a practice of the commercial community to be conceptually impossible . . .[13]

C. Pressure Relieved—Loose Ends

The *BCCI (No. 8)* decision was welcomed by the FLP (which had specifically **2.08**
requested both the Court of Appeal and the House of Lords to rule on the

---

[12] [1986] 3 All ER 289.

[13] The case is a further example of the English courts' desire to keep in step with market practice (and keep English law competitive) whenever possible. Lord Hoffmann's language can, eg, be compared with that used by Colman J in *Lordsdale Finance v Bank of Zambia* [1996] 3 All ER 156, when, in upholding a default interest provision (under attack as a 'penalty') he compared the situation in New York (where such clauses are upheld): 'It would be highly regrettable if the English courts were to refuse to give effect to such prevalent provisions while the courts of New York are prepared to enforce them. For there to be a disparity between the law applicable in London and New York on this point would be of great disservice to international banking.'

charge-back point) and the market generally.[14] Although many of those who held the other view will probably never be completely persuaded of the logic of it, the 'conceptual impossibility' point is now almost certainly of academic interest only. The requirements of the market have, it would seem, prevailed. There are, however, a few loose ends.

2.09 On a purely technical, but important, level, the Hoffman dicta are not sufficiently authoritative to constitute cast-iron, judge-made law (even though the decision in question was by the highest court, the House of Lords). This is because the remarks were obiter, ie not strictly necessary as part of the reasoning for the court's decision. The remarks are not binding on judges who might have to decide questions on charge-backs in new cases. It is, therefore, possible—in theory—that a court in the future would not follow the Hoffman approach. (It must be accepted, however, that this seems extremely unlikely.)

2.10 Academic opinion remains somewhat less than totally convinced by Lord Hoffman's views. Goode, in particular, has expressed well-known reservations even though he acknowledges that 'the force of business practice cannot be denied'. In his authoritative book *Legal Problems of Credit and Security*[15] he summarizes the position:

> The provision of cash collateral to banks and brokers is commonplace. Accordingly conceptual problems such as the blurring of the distinction between property and obligation, and policy problems such as the fact that the only method of distinguishing a charge-back from a contractual set-off is *by the label given to the transaction by the parties*, must yield to business practice and legislative developments designed to accommodate it.[16]

2.11 Meanwhile neither law-makers nor regulators seem completely content that charge-backs are legally 'established' beyond doubt. As indicated above, the Law Commission has published a series of draft regulations which include a provision that would, if it becomes law, give statutory authority to the charge-back. Presumably, the Law Commission is not completely convinced that the law is already sufficiently clear.

2.12 Meanwhile, the FSA, which needs to be confident that its requirements for cash collateral held by the banks are the most effective form of security available, states that 'the main mechanism by which cash collateral held by a bank can be

---

[14] See FLP paper 'Security over Cash Deposits: a Valediction', April 1998. *BCCI (No 8)* was in fact the third of a series of three immensely important judgments by Lord Hoffmann on set-off issues given in the 1990s. The other two are considered in detail in 3.44–3.57 below.

[15] 3rd edn, 94.

[16] Emphasis added. In the preface to the third edition of his book, *Commercial Law*, Goode has apparently become more reconciled to the force of the 'business logic' and warns that although 'concepts are essential to law, we must never allow them to become our masters'.

enforced is through the legal right of set-off'.[17] The FSA also suggests that 'another way of ensuring that a bank does not have to repay cash collateral is through the use of flawed asset provisions, which have the same risk weighting as cash collateral' although such provisions 'should be accompanied by a charge or set-off arrangement'.[18] If anything, the use of set-off as the favoured means of creating security for financial market transactions only seems to have increased over the years. The FSA requires, of course, that legal opinions are obtained in all relevant jurisdictions as to the efficacy of the arrangements referred to above.[19]

An informal survey conducted by the author (in 2005) suggests that most **2.13** leading law firms in London still use the 'triple cocktail' or some variation of it.[20] We should not forget that many borrowers will tend to prefer avoiding the need to create an express charge (for example, because of negative pledge restrictions) if their lenders can be persuaded that a right of set-off and 'flawed asset' is adequate protection. The position seems to be, therefore, that charge-backs are almost certain to be upheld by the courts but that, in the meantime, the 'triple cocktail' of set-off, flawed asset, and charge is still regarded as the route of least risk for those documenting bilateral security over cash deposits (and some may be content with the first two of the cocktail's ingredients).[21] *Plus ça change, plus c'est la même chose.* If there is any uncertainty here, it is manageable. It is not driving any business offshore.

---

[17] See FSA, *Interim Prudential Sourcebook: Banks*, NE: Section 1, para 4.2.1, 3.

[18] FSA, ibid at NE: Section 1, para 4.2.2, 7   [19] See para 11.16.

[20] An article published by a leading practitioner shortly after the *BCCI (No. 8)* case put the question of whether the triple cocktail should still be used and concluded that: 'Although the document could be simplified, lawyers might be naturally cautious in some cases about discarding the safety nets provided by this form of security. The safety nets are useful, for instance, if the charge were attacked as being merely floating and not a fixed charge because the amount of the deposit had fluctuated as a result of dealings by the charging company.' See Yeowart, 'House of Lords upholds charge-backs over deposits' (January 1998) IFLR. See also Hughes, *Selected Legal Issues for Finance Lawyers*, 98 and the comments of The City of London Law Society Financial Law Sub-Committee on various questions raised by HM Treasury on the implementation of the Collateral Directive, which sets out various advantages of set-off over a charge and states that: 'Market practitioners must be free to choose, on a transaction by transaction basis, which method is most appropriate.' For a slightly different view (and a very useful exposition of the potential advantages of a charge over a mere right of set-off in insolvency) see Calnan, 'Security Over Deposits Again: BCCI (No. 8) in the House of Lords' (1998) 4 JIBFL 125.

[21] It should be noted that there may be some inconsistency in providing for both a charge and a right of set-off; in the case of the insolvency of the 'chargor' the court might have to decide which is to prevail, since, in that situation, the legal position may vary according to which element of the 'cocktail' is thought to apply.

3

SETTLING DIFFERENCES

Insolvency set-off is probably the most direct and piercing indicator of financial law. The bulk of international opinion favours the remedy as an important technique for risk and cost reduction. The apparent doubts in some of the transition economies starting with a more or less clean slate show a continuing global split on the issue. The advantages are considered to be paramount.[1]

A. Early (but Perennial) Concerns about Set-off and Netting

In this chapter, we shall examine some of the other legal uncertainty issues, **3.01** principally in relation to set-off and netting, that were troubling various sectors of the financial markets at around the time of the *Hammersmith and Fulham* and *Charge Card* cases.[2] Although these may be regarded as 'early' legal risk issues when viewed from a historical perspective, it would be wrong to assume that they have now, in some sense, 'gone away'. It is true that English law in these areas is now much clearer than it was[3] but the position is still evolving, especially in relation to transactions that have an overseas element, have an impact on the working of an EU single market in financial services, or are affected by recent legislation (considered below) implementing EU

---

[1] Philip R Wood, *Maps of World Financial Law* (University Edition, Allen & Overy LLP, February 2005) 47

[2] According to the FLP, 'the establishment of the Panel coincided with an upsurge of concern, throughout the global financial markets, on the legal efficacy of arrangements (whether statutory or contractual) which permitted the netting of financial transactions as a way of controlling credit risk'. See FLP First Annual Report to Subscribers, October 1994.

[3] A purist would no doubt contend that the law always was clear, the problem being that it had not manifested itself through case law at the earlier time. However, as will be explained below, the Financial Collateral Arrangements (No 2) Regulations 2003, SI 2003/3226, ('FCA(2)') and the Insolvency (Amendment) Rules 2005, SI 2005/527, have recently removed any lingering doubts that may have been left in certain key areas by case law.

Directives.[4] One of the most interesting aspects of the transaction structures that involved legal uncertainty issues in the earlier years, is that many of the concepts that appeared in the documentation at that time (the late 1980s and early 1990s) have now found their way into the substantive law. For the architects of those transaction structures this must indeed be the sincerest form of flattery.

3.02 We shall look, first, at a number of general, but very important, concerns that lawyers in the market had in relation to the operation of set-off and netting; secondly, at a particular form of transaction that featured many of those (and other) concerns; and, finally, at some of the more significant case law and legislative developments. In reviewing these issues, we should bear in mind the huge importance that 'certainty' in this area of the law has now assumed. As Goode puts it:

> . . . in dealings on an organised market the legal protection of netting and set-off has in recent years been seen as fulfilling a much more fundamental need, namely the reduction of systemic risk, hence the issue of EC Directives and of implementing national legislation designed to ensure that rules of insolvency law do not imperil rights of set-off in market contracts.[5]

3.03 There is very little risk tolerance in relation to the question of whether or not set-off 'works' (or, to be more specific, whether carefully crafted contractual provisions designed to enable set-off, or laws that require set-off, 'work'), whether in the context of insolvency or otherwise. 'Penumbral' areas of uncertainty are not generally permissible here.

B. General Issues

3.04 Philosophers have for many years debated whether law has, and must have, some moral content. Must all law be based on some assessment of justice or right and wrong? Does law have to have some 'internal morality'? Such questions may seem far removed from the day-to-day realities of financial markets in the modern era. The old-school approach of 'my word is my bond', knowing what is done and not done, and the 'light touch' of a powerful but essentially benign regulator, concerned to see 'fair play' (together with a good deal of self-regulation) seem distant memories. And yet the fundamentals of financial law

---

[4] For a description of some of the concerns felt by EU lawyers regarding set-off and netting even after the Collateral Directive, see the Report by the European Financial Market Lawyers Group on 'Protection for Bilateral Insolvency Set-Off and Netting Agreements under EC Law', October 2004; for a review of some more recent English set-off concerns, see Turing, 'Setting Off Down a New Road' (2004) 9 JIBFL 349.

[5] Goode, *Legal Problems of Credit and Security* (3rd edn) 238.

(which is itself a hotchpotch of contract, tort, commercial, banking, regulatory, and corporate law, amongst other things) turn upon questions which are moralistic in nature. Whether or not debts should be repaid is a moral question. There is a broad consensus that someone who properly incurs debts should be obliged to repay them.[6] Most (but not all) societies have no problem, in principle, with an obligation to pay interest on debts. Indeed, in the context of commercially powerful debtors, such as large store chains, there is a concern that creditors such as small suppliers should have a right to interest. Interest rates, however, should not be excessive and certain sectors of society should be protected against unscrupulous 'loan sharks' and the like. Some societies, however, find the payment of any interest morally repugnant.

If the obligation to repay properly incurred debt is one of the founding principles of this branch of the law, a principle of close to equal importance, and which exists in the interest of doing 'substantial justice between the parties',[7] is the principle that you should not have to repay a creditor who is himself in debt to you where that debt has fallen due and remains unpaid, at least to the extent that you are owed money by that creditor. If A owes B £100 but B owes A £120, it will come as a surprise to no one that the law will not generally compel A to pay B if B is in breach of his obligation to pay A. A will be entitled to set off B's debt to him against any claim that B may make against him for the £100 debt, with the result that A does not have to pay B anything but can claim against B for the balance in A's favour of £20. Obviously, if B's debt to A was £70, A would, by virtue of the same logic, be required to pay the balance in B's favour of £30. **3.05**

But how do these set-off principles work in more complex situations? Supposing, for example, A and B are both companies and: **3.06**

(1) A's debt to B falls due for payment a week before B's debt to A; or
(2) B is insolvent and can only pay its creditors 20 pence in the pound; or
(3) B is insolvent but has not borrowed money from A; B has, however, guaranteed a debt of £100 owed to A by X and X's debt falls due for payment after A's debt to B; or
(4) B's debt to A is for US$ 150; or
(5) B does not owe any money to A but owes £100 to A's subsidiary; or
(6) B does not owe any money to A but does owe £100 to C, who in turn has defaulted on a £100 debt to A; or

---

[6] The moral questions become much more complex, of course, as to the sanctions that should apply if it becomes apparent that a debtor does not have the means to repay. In this context, we are much more debtor-friendly (or insolvent-friendly) than we used to be.

[7] See judgment of Parke B in *Forster v Wilson* (1843) 12 M&W 191, 204, quoted by Lord Hoffmann in *Stein v Blake* [1996] 1 AC 243. See also para 3.19.

(7) B's debt of £100 to A is owed to A in A's capacity as trustee of an educational charity, but A's debt to B is owed by A for goods bought by A for A's own business; or

(8) B's claim against A is not for unpaid purchase moneys but for the return of property belonging to B (worth £100) which B alleges A wrongfully removed from B's factory; or

(9) A's debt to B falls due for payment several days before B's debt to A, but although B has complied with all B's obligations to A, and is not, as yet, insolvent, A has cause for concern about B's financial condition, having heard that B has defaulted on other debts to other creditors; or

(10) A and B are incorporated under the laws of different countries; or

(11) A assigns the debt owed to him by B to C (for par value) and then B, when asked for payment by C, sets off the debt owed to B by A against C.

3.07 One can, of course, continue to add layers of complexity. Should the position be affected, for example, by whether or not the debts between A and B were incurred under a single contract as opposed to a range of different transactions, possibly quite different in nature, between the two entities? However, the points of principle are fairly clear. They revolve around variations of the same question: in what circumstances is it legally justifiable to pay less than the full amount of a debt by setting off against that debt an amount owing, or possibly to become owing, by the person to whom the debt is owed? This setting off of one debt against another is sometimes called set-off and sometimes referred to as netting. There is a degree of overlap between the meanings of the two phrases,[8] but 'netting' tends to be used only in the context of procedures which are laid down by contract (usually, but not always, to apply where the contract is being terminated so as to produce a single net balance payable),[9] whereas 'set-off' can also refer to the exercise of a right or the implementation of a procedure that does not depend on contractual terms (for example, where one party simply

---

[8] FCA(2), SI 2003/3226, para 3 defines a 'close out netting provision' as a specific kind of transaction (considered below) that, in effect, results in a net payment being required between the parties (or acceleration of dates for payment so as to produce an 'estimated current value or replacement cost') '*whether through the operation of netting or set-off or otherwise*' (emphasis added). These regulations are considered in more detail at paras 3.58.

[9] A major exception to this is so-called 'netting by novation' which involves an 'umbrella' (or master) agreement between the parties providing for continuous amendment and updating of the net balance between the parties as a matter of course. The technique is described in the FSA *Interim Prudential Sourcebook: Banks*, according to which the netting 'should have the effect of legally discharging performance of the original obligations and substituting the single net amount as the sole remaining obligation between the counterparties for the relevant value date. Thus a single legally binding new contract extinguishes the former contracts.' It is thought that netting by novation restricts the ability of a liquidator to disclaim individual deals (or 'cherry-pick') because there is always only one net amount payable (at least per value date and, in some cases, per currency).

refuses to pay the other the full amount due under one contract because it is owed money under another contract, or where one party has become insolvent and set-off becomes mandatory).[10] As will be explained below, both concepts can be further subdivided, according to the particular circumstances in which the action is taken. Netting, in particular, is the term used where the arrangement involves more than two parties (ie 'multilateral netting').[11]

C. Why the Concerns Became Acute

Although the principles are relatively clear, finding the answers to specific ques-   **3.08**
tions relating to set-off and netting has, over the years, given rise to some difficulty. This was especially the case in the 1980s and early 1990s, when the concerns became acute. There were a number of reasons for this.

First, it has to be understood that the questions have tended to arise in the   **3.09**
context of market operations and transactions that have involved enormous sums of money, raising issues that are central to the manner in which certain markets actually function. The questions, arguably, go now to the legal founda-tions of the international financial system itself. As noted earlier, it is vital for banks to know whether there is a solid legal basis for assessing their exposure to counterparties, in a wide range of markets, on a net basis. This question arises in foreign exchange operations, in securities lending and 'repo' markets,[12] and in many derivative markets, as well as basic commercial lending. If banks could not rely on contractual provisions to net, or set off, payments, the exposures would have to be measured on a gross basis and the markets would simply cease to function in the way they have done to date, if they could function at all. The increase in exposure would be catastrophically enormous, as would be the impact on regulatory capital adequacy requirements. If any one active bank relied on such provisions but they were shown to be legally invalid, the con-sequences could include the financial collapse of that bank and the potential triggering of insolvency of other institutions affected by its inability to honour its commitments. The legal points thus have a direct bearing on the regulators' worst nightmare, systemic risk.

---

[10] A statutory definition of netting (in the context of payment and securities settlement systems) can be found in the Financial Markets and Insolvency (Settlement Finality) Regulations 1999, SI 1999/2979, reg 2(1), ie: 'the conversion into one net claim or obligation of different claims or obligations between participants resulting from the issue and receipt of transfer orders between them, whether on a bilateral or multilateral basis and whether through the interposition of a clearing house, central counterparty or settlement agent or otherwise'. See para 3.72 below.

[11] See para 3.59 et seq.

[12] See further para 3.59 et seq. below, as regards securities (or stock) lending.

3.10   The legal issues associated with netting were considered at length by the Bank for International Settlements in a report of November 1990,[13] which made the observation that:

> By reducing the number and overall value of payments between financial institutions, netting can enhance the efficiency of domestic payment systems and reduce the settlement costs associated with the growing volume of foreign exchange market activity. Netting can also reduce the size of credit and liquidity exposures incurred by market participants and thereby contribute to the containment of systemic risk.[14]

3.11   Some years later, in June 2002, the European Parliament and Council of the European Union expressed similar sentiments in the Recital clauses to the Collateral Directive (which is concerned, amongst other things, with the validity of close-out netting arrangements, and was implemented in the UK by the Financial Collateral Arrangements (No 2) Regulations 2003 ('FCA(2)')), which states (in para 3): 'A Community regime should be created for the provision of securities and cash as collateral under both security and title transfer structures[15] including repurchase agreements (repos). This will contribute to the integration and cost efficiency of the financial market *as well as the stability of the financial system in the Community.*'[16]

3.12   Paragraph 14 of the Recitals to the Collateral Directive also emphasizes the need to facilitate the role of netting and set-off as a means of credit risk management:

> Sound risk management practices commonly used in the financial market should be protected by enabling participants to manage and reduce their credit exposures arising from all kinds of financial transactions on a net basis, where the credit exposure is calculated by combining the estimated current exposures under all outstanding transactions with a counterparty, setting off reciprocal items to produce a single aggregated amount that is compared with the current value of the collateral.

3.13   Reducing the legal risk enables more effective management of credit risk.[17] This in turn enables regulators to allow a more favourable capital adequacy treatment, since legally effective netting has such a dramatic impact on bank

---

[13] Report of the Committee on Interbank Netting Schemes of the Central Banks of the Group of Ten Countries (generally known as the 'Lamfalussy Report').

[14] The Lamfalussy Report recommended 'collective policy responses' to facilitate effective netting schemes and issued six minimum standards that should apply to such schemes, including a requirement that they should have a well-founded legal basis under all relevant jurisdictions.

[15] Explained at para 3.28 below.   [16] Emphasis added.

[17] As will be seen, by the time of the Collateral Directive, English law in this area was regarded as robust, the Treasury's 'Regulatory Impact Assessment' (for FCA(2) which implemented the Collateral Directive in the UK) noting that the 'Laws in the UK are already amongst the most amenable to collateral arrangements in the EU'.

exposures, resulting in reductions of approximately 50 per cent on average. In the UK, the FSA's policy is generally to 'accommodate the use of netting and collateral as long as the agreements have a firm legal basis and the bank has adequate systems and controls'.[18]

Secondly, the transactions under consideration frequently involve parties in more than one jurisdiction. Since the legal questions are not merely straightforward questions of contract interpretation but involve considerations of insolvency law, the law relating to security interests and 'recharacterization' risks,[19] as to which the law and public policy varies greatly from country to country, it has been difficult (until recently) to produce an analysis confined to only one legal system that would satisfy a market that has been getting bigger and more globally based with each passing year, and especially in relation to transactions where set-off and netting provisions are crucially important. Further, the approach of many legal systems to set-off in insolvency was rather different to that which applied in England, producing results that were far less satisfactory for the markets. **3.14**

Thirdly, as at the time of the formation of the Legal Risk Review Committee (LRRC) and the Financial Law Panel (FLP) (when concern in London about legal risk in the financial markets, especially Type 2 risks, was at its height) the law in this area appeared to feature a combination of case law and legislation which fell somewhat short of enabling practitioners to issue categoric statements of advice except in relation to very specific factual situations. There was a dearth of authority on, for example, how the courts would treat foreign exchange contracts in the event of the insolvency of one of the parties. There were particular concerns about the liquidator's right to disclaim unprofitable contracts and whether this would enable a liquidator to cherry-pick and perform only the 'in the money' deals (which would still leave the liquidator with an obligation to pay compensation for the disclaimed deals, but how this would be assessed was not as clear as some would have wished). There were also uncertainties as to how insolvency set-off would operate in relation to contracts with a settlement (ie payment) date which fell after the commencement of liquidation.[20] Rule **3.15**

---

[18] See FSA, *Interim Prudential Sourcebook: Banks*, NE: section 2, at para 2.1 (subpara 4). The FSA's requirements for legal 'robustness' (which need to take into account the cross-border aspects and are thus not concerned only with English law legal risk) are substantial. NE: section 5 para 5.4 sets out extensive requirements in relation to legal opinions, which are considered further in Part IV of this book. See para 11.16.

[19] See Ch 9 below.

[20] One doubt that was sometimes expressed was as to whether the express right of set-off embodied in most close-out netting provisions might constitute a registrable charge because, in providing for set-off of claims that were payable after the commencement of liquidation, it might

4.90 of the Insolvency Rules 1986[21] (especially the use of the word 'due') also posed some difficulties of interpretation, which have only recently been clarified by statutory amendments to the rule, although, as we shall see, case law in the 1990s effectively removed the most serious worries.

3.16 Even now, opinions on some of these issues are couched in carefully guarded terms, with a large number of highly technical qualifications. However, during the intervening years, the market (aided to an extent by recent case law and legislation, considered at 3.44 to 3.57 below) has become more accustomed to the technical issues. It is now accepted that English law, essentially, provides the 'right answers'.

D. The FLP's First Guidance Notice

3.17 But it was not always like that. The concerns about legal uncertainty that were experienced by the markets following the *Hammersmith and Fulham* and *Charge Card* cases were centred on a number of issues, but none was more pressing than the question: do these set-off and netting provisions really work, especially if one party becomes insolvent? This topic was the subject of the FLP's first Guidance Notice, issued in November 1993.[21a]

3.18 The press announcement accompanying the Guidance Notice was robust, quoting Colin Bamford (the FLP's Chief Executive) as follows: 'The purpose of the Guidance Notice is to remind the markets that the legal foundation in England for systems and structures of netting is at least as strong and deep as in any other jurisdiction. In an area of great technical complexity, we believe this clear principle will help achieve a proper focus on the problems of detail.'

3.19 The Guidance Notice took the form of a Statement of Law, recording 'a consensus of the views of leading practitioners in the fields of insolvency and banking law'. Drafted by a leading insolvency barrister, Michael Crystal QC, it read:

> Where a company goes into insolvent liquidation in England and there have been mutual credits, mutual debts or other mutual dealings between the company and another party prior to liquidation, set off applies. An account must be taken of the mutual dealings and the ultimate net balance only is required to be paid to the liquidator or proved for in the liquidation.

---

be going further than setting out the rights that the party exercising set-off would have under general law. Case law developments (not least those following the *Charge Card* case) have since shown this view to be erroneous, but it was a difficult call to make in the mid- to late 1980s.

[21] See App 1, Part 1 below, for the language of Rule 4.90, as in effect until 1 April 2005, when it was amended by The Insolvency (Amendment) Rules 2005 (described in App 1, Part 2 below).

[21a] This is now available on the FMLC's website at <http://www.fmlc.org>.

This rule of English law is now contained in Rule 4.90 of the Insolvency Rules 1986.[22] The object of the rule is to achieve substantial justice between the parties having regard to the whole of their mutual dealings. The rule achieves this result by imposing a requirement for a complete set off in respect of all the mutual dealings between the parties.

All obligations in respect of the mutual dealings are required to be brought into account.

The set off applies whether or not there is any contractual entitlement to the same. The requirement for set off in respect of all mutual dealings is mandatory and cannot be excluded by agreement between the parties.

Where a bank and its corporate customer enter into various transactions with each other prior to the customer's insolvent liquidation and the customer goes into liquidation before the transactions are closed mandatory set off applies. The bank will have a claim (or obligation) on a net basis only to receive from (or pay to) the liquidator the net amount in respect of the transactions taken as a whole.

3.20 The Guidance Notice made it clear that the statement was intended to apply to 'contracts for forward and spot foreign exchange, cross-currency and interest rate swaps, currency and interest rate options (including caps, floors, and collars), forward rate agreements and similar commodity and equity-related derivatives, as well as loans by and deposits with the bank'. It was not intended to apply to other transactions. The Statement (inevitably) was accompanied by a list of qualifications, ie:

> The Statement of Law does not consider the effect of situations where any of the following apply:–
> — the counterparty's insolvency is governed by the law or procedures of a jurisdiction other than England;
> — either the bank or the counterparty was acting outside the scope of its legal powers in entering into any of the transactions, or was otherwise behaving unlawfully or improperly;
> — one or both of the parties was acting as an agent for a third party, and not in its own right;
> — the transactions concerned are affected by the rules of an organised market, or by some other form of multilateral netting arrangement;
> — the bank was aware of the counterparty's insolvency when, or the liquidation of the counterparty had commenced before, one or more of the transactions were concluded;
> — the circumstances giving rise to the transactions do not involve mutuality between the bank and the counterparty.

3.21 This is a long list but, for the purposes of the markets most directly affected, it was an acceptable one. The cross-border exception represented a risk outside the UK's control. It was problematic, but the important thing was for banks to be

---

[22] The text of Rule 4.90 as in effect at the time of this Guidance Notice is set out in App 1, Part 1 below.

aware of the need to take foreign legal advice if set-off and netting were material to their dealings with foreign counterparties. Unauthorized, *ultra vires*, or illegal dealing by a counterparty was another difficult but manageable risk, as was the risk of deals being affected by insolvency existing at the time they were entered into. The reference to organized markets and multilateral arrangements would have been understood in the context of recently enacted legislation containing special provisions for dealings and 'clearing house' arrangements on recognized exchanges;[23] and it was known and accepted that the general law on set-off on insolvency was applicable to two-party (ie bilateral) situations (for example, between a bank and its customer or a bank and another bank), not multiparty (or multilateral) situations.[24] The references to agency and mutuality were concerned with the technical requirement (for set-off to apply) that each party's claim should be held 'in the same right'. This means that, for example, a trustee, claiming in that capacity (ie on behalf of someone else, the trust's beneficiaries) cannot set off that claim against a debt owed by the trustee in its personal capacity (ie for which the person who happens to be the trustee is responsible but in respect of which no claim lies against the trust assets). It also means that a personal claim (typically for the payment of money, the most common kind of claim in the financial markets) cannot be set off against a property claim (for example, for the return of property wrongfully withheld). Obviously, the set-off has to operate as between the same two entities. The insolvency set-off rules do not, for example, permit a parent company to set off against a claim owed to its subsidiary. Mutuality is a complex and difficult requirement but, again, represented a manageable risk for bilateral market arrangements. As regards multilateral netting arrangements (typically found in clearing houses and investment exchanges), the mutuality requirement and the general insolvency rule requiring creditors of the same class to be treated equally (or *pari passu*) gave rise to significant (but very clear) problems, which had been addressed by legislation (in the Companies Act 1989, Part VII). Multilateral netting is considered in more detail below.[25]

3.22 The Statement went out of its way to refer to the oft-repeated moral objective being served by the law, ie 'to achieve substantial justice between the parties'. There is, at least to an English lawyer's eyes, something repugnant about the notion that a creditor might be required to pay 100 pence in the pound to a liquidator for a debt owed to an insolvent company but only receive, say, 20 pence in the pound (if that) for debts owed to that same creditor by that company.

3.23 The Statement was endorsed by twenty-three well-known City law firms, whose names were listed in an appendix. It was followed, in September of the following

---

[23] See para 3.70.   [24] See para 3.67 below.   [25] See para 3.59 et seq. below.

year, by a similar statement (also in the form of a guidance note) by the Banking Law Sub-Committee of the City of London Law Society. This note was concerned only with foreign exchange transactions, but it covered substantially the same area of law, ie set-off. The note described the transactions to which it applied in the following way:

> It is common practice for foreign exchange transactions in London to be the subject matter of a master agreement between the two parties to the transactions containing terms applicable to all of the transactions. The master agreement will usually contain provisions which provide for the close-out of all outstanding transactions if certain events have occurred in relation to a party. The trigger events will commonly include insolvency, non-payment and cross-default. The master agreement will normally provide that, on the close-out, the notional gains and losses of each party are computed by reference to the then prevailing market rates for the value dates and currencies concerned, and the notional gains and losses are then netted out so that only a net balance is payable one way or the other.

3.24 The note then went on to state that such provisions 'in a properly drafted master agreement' were effective under English law. Similar (but not identical) qualifications were made to those set out in the FLP Guidance Note.

E. Problems with Stock Lending Documentation—a Case Study

3.25 In February 1991 Ian Plenderleith[26] gave a 'keynote address' to a conference on 'exploiting new securities lending opportunities'. In the speech he referred to an issue 'that came at us unexpectedly'. This was 'the doubts that arose recently over the legal status of collateral given under stock lending agreements'. He was able to report that a legal problem had been identified, which was of considerable significance, but that, happily, it had been speedily resolved. Legal risk and uncertainty had raised its head, but it had been swiftly dispatched. There was, however, a lesson to be learned: 'The episode illustrates very well the point . . . that securities lending, if it is to thrive, needs to take place in a properly regulated framework on the basis, inter alia, of sound legal agreements.'

3.26 The episode also provides an excellent example of how legal risks, if quickly and precisely identified, can often be managed and perhaps even eradicated. Further, the issues and problems involved in the stock lending transaction structure and the solutions found (which at the time seemed somewhat esoteric and specific to the facts) have echoed down the years and, as we shall see, references

---

[26] At the time, Associate Director and Government Broker, Bank of England, and Chairman of the Stock Borrowing and Lending Committee.

can now be found to them in recently introduced legislation with a much broader ambit than stock lending.[27]

3.27 However, before we go further, a brief explanation of what securities lending is, and why it is done, is necessary. According to the website of the International Securities Lending Association:

> Securities lending began as an informal practice among brokers who had insufficient share certificates to settle their sold bargains, commonly because their selling clients had mislaid their certificates or just not provided them to the broker by the settlement date of the transaction. Once the broker had received the certificates, they would be passed on to the lending broker. This business arrangement was subject to no formal arrangement and there was no exchange of collateral.

> Securities lending is now an important and significant business that describes the market practice whereby securities are temporarily transferred by one party (the lender) to another (the borrower). The borrower is obliged to return the securities to the lender, either on demand, or at the end of any agreed term. For the period of the loan the lender is secured by acceptable assets delivered by the borrower to the lender as collateral.

> Under English law, absolute title to the securities 'lent' passes to the 'borrower', who is obliged to return 'equivalent securities'. Similarly the lender receives absolute title to the assets received as collateral from the borrower, and is obliged to return, 'equivalent collateral'.

3.28 The arrangements regarding collateral, as described above (and considered further below), are an example of what is defined in the Financial Collateral Arrangements (No 2) Regulations 2003 as a 'title transfer financial collateral arrangement'. This term, according to FCA(2), means:

> . . . an agreement or arrangement, including a repurchase agreement, evidenced in writing, where—
> (a) the purpose of the agreement or arrangement is to secure or otherwise cover the relevant financial obligations owed to the collateral-taker;
> (b) the collateral-provider transfers legal and beneficial ownership in financial collateral to a collateral-taker on terms that when the relevant financial obligations are discharged the collateral-taker must transfer legal and beneficial ownership of equivalent financial collateral to the collateral-provider; and
> (c) the collateral-provider and the collateral-taker are both non-natural persons.[28]

3.29 The definition of 'equivalent financial collateral' in FCA(2) is worthy of note here since it embodies a concept that is fundamental to the legal analysis of securities lending and was extremely important to the solution devised for the legal problems identified in 1990. It reads as follows:

---

[27] The term 'stock lending' has now been largely replaced by 'securities lending'. The latter term will be used in the rest of this chapter.

[28] FCA(2), para 3.

'equivalent financial collateral' means—

(a) in relation to cash, a payment of the same amount and in the same currency;

(b) in relation to financial instruments, financial instruments of the same issuer or debtor, forming part of the same issue or class and of the same nominal amount, currency and description or, where the financial collateral arrangement provides for the transfer of other assets following the occurrence of any event relating to or affecting any financial instruments provided as financial collateral, those other assets;

and includes the original financial collateral provided under the arrangement; . . .'

The same concept (developed somewhat to deal with a number of specific **3.30** contingencies) can now be found in the definition of 'Equivalent' (as applied to 'Securities' or 'Collateral') contained in ISLA's standard form 'Global Master Securities Lending Agreement'.[29] The concept was developed for the first time in 1990 to deal with the issues described below:

(1) In 1990, stock lending and borrowing in the UK domestic markets was carried out through intermediaries known as money brokers. The role of a money broker was to assist with the financing of market making by lending stock and money. Money brokers, in performing this role, *acted as principal*.[30]

(2) If a market-maker asked to borrow securities, the money broker would meet the request by borrowing (as principal) from an institution, such as an insurance company, bank, pension fund, or building society. (Gilt-edged market makers and discount houses were also available as lenders of gilt-edged stock.) It would then 'on-lend' to the market maker (again, acting as principal).

(3) The market-maker would usually deposit cash with the money broker as collateral until the 'borrowed' securities could be 'returned'.[31]

(4) This cash would then generally be lent back to the same market-maker who would typically secure the loan with a deposit of securities. These securities would then be 'on-pledged' by the money broker as collateral to the relevant investment institution until the return of the borrowed securities.

(5) The arrangement described in (4) above did not (in 1990) involve anything like a 'title transfer financial collateral arrangement'. The collateral was

---

[29] This can be found on the ISLA website at http://www.isla.co.uk, together with a guidance note and legal opinion.

[30] The lending of securities allowed market-makers to operate with more confidence in complying with their obligation to offer the market a continuous two-way price for securities. They could quote prices in larger quantities of stock than they held on their books in the knowledge that, if necessary, they could borrow stock to cover any sales and borrow money to finance any purchases. In this way, securities lending provides vital liquidity to the system. If securities lending was thought to involve unacceptable legal risk, the securities market would be in danger of seizing up.

[31] The obligation was of course to deliver 'equivalent' securities.

taken by the money broker as conventional security, with the money broker only acquiring a security interest in the collateral assets.

(6) The market-maker would have the right to substitute the security provided as collateral with securities of equivalent value.

3.31 The following questions arose:

(a) Did any of the security transactions involve registrable charges (for example, floating charges or charges over book debts)?

(b) Was the purported 'on-pledge' by the money broker (in favour of the investment institution, the original 'lender') valid, given that the asset pledged was in fact an asset belonging to the market-maker, pledged in the first place by the market-maker to the money broker to secure the obligations of the market-maker to the money broker?

3.32 The questions were sufficiently important, and the problem sufficiently urgent, for the Bank of England to set up a special Working Party, which included lawyers from two major City law firms (who consulted one of the leading barristers in the field), to consider, and find solutions to, the potential problems.[32]

3.33 The first of the two questions referred to above did not, it was decided, give rise to difficulties. None of the arrangements constituted registrable charges. Those that related to cash collateral were either (1) not charges at all, because the arrangements were 'bilateral' and therefore simply rights of set-off as described by the (in this context, extremely helpful) judgment of Millett J in the *Charge Card* case, or (2) not charges over book debts, because the cash deposit, in properly kept books of account, would be entered as 'cash at bank' rather than a book debt.[33] The arrangements for the substitution of collateral had a superficial resemblance to certain aspects of a floating charge but, after certain adjustments to the drafting, it was felt that the risk of this analysis being favoured by a court was small.

3.34 In any case, as far as securities lending was concerned, these issues became academic because, in order to solve the problems cause by the second question, the legal structure of the transaction was radically altered.

3.35 The second question did give rise to difficulties. One cannot generally create security over an asset that belongs to someone else.[34] That seemed to be what the

---

[32] The LRRC and FLP did not, of course, exist at this time.

[33] See *Re Brightlife Ltd* [1987] Ch 200 and *Northern Bank Ltd v Ross* [1990] BCC 883. The cases are not strictly authority for the interpretation of CA 1985, s 395, being concerned with the construction of similar language in debentures, but they (together with obiter dicta of Lord Hoffmann in *BCCI (No 8)*) are thought to provide reliable guidance to judicial thinking on the point. See also Calnan, 'Security Over Deposits Again: *BCCI (No. 8)* in the House of Lords' (1998) 4 JIBFL 125.

[34] It might be possible to create a sub-mortgage or sub-charge over the (limited) interest

money brokers were purporting to do when they provided collateral (by way of the 'on-pledge' referred to above). As a result, the ultimate 'lenders' of the securities were understandably concerned that the collateral they received from the money brokers might be invalid. The Bank of England assembled a group of market and legal experts to devise a solution as quickly as possible. After a certain amount of burning of midnight oil, it was decided that, to solve the problem, the securities that were intended to be provided as collateral—both between market-maker and money broker and between money broker and 'lender'—should in fact be transferred outright, with full legal ownership passing. The recipient of this 'security' would be obliged to return securities of the same issue (or 'equivalent securities') on the unwind date. The commercial purpose of the arrangement would still be the provision of collateral but the legal analysis of the transaction would be that the recipient of the collateral would in fact become its absolute owner. The provider of the collateral would lose any equity of redemption that he would otherwise have had and only be left with a right of set-off vis-à-vis his counterparty. In other words, if, on the date the transaction was to be unwound, the recipient of the collateral failed to 'return' it (or, to be more precise, securities of the same nature as those originally provided as collateral), the provider of the collateral would have to rely on such rights as it might have to withhold performance of the primary obligation for which the collateral was actually provided in the first place. It was absolutely essential, therefore, to incorporate into the documentation a carefully crafted right of set-off. The clause used for this purpose was deliberately drafted to follow closely the wording of rule 4.90 of the Insolvency Rules 1986. The current version of that clause[35] reads as follows:

> . . . if an Event of Default occurs in relation to either Party, the Parties' delivery and payment obligations (and any other obligations they may have under this agreement) shall be accelerated so as to require performance thereof at the time such Event of Default occurs (the date of which shall be the 'Termination Date' for the purposes of this clause) so that performance of such delivery and payment obligations shall be effected only in accordance with the following provisions:
>
> (i) the Relevant Value of the securities which would have been required to be delivered but for such termination (or payment to be made, as the case may be) by each Party shall be established in accordance with paragraph 10.3; and

---

conferred by the original mortgage or charge (which would be subject to the original debtor's equity of redemption) but that would not have been commercially acceptable to the ultimate 'lender'. It would not have been possible, in 1990, to maintain that the money broker had a 'right to use' the collateral, including the right to dispose of, or charge it for its own purposes.

[35] See the ISLA standard form Global Master Securities Lending Agreement, cl 10.2.

> (ii) on the basis of the Relevant Values so established, an account shall be taken (as at the Termination Date) of what is due from each Party to the other and (on the basis that each Party's claim against the other in respect of the delivery of Equivalent Securities or Equivalent Collateral or any cash payment equals the Relevant Value thereof) the sums due from one Party shall be set-off against sums due from the other and only the balance of the account shall be payable (by the Party having the claim valued at the lower amount pursuant to the foregoing) and such balance shall be payable on the Termination Date . . .

3.36 As indicated by the above language, there are other provisions dealing with valuation of securities to be delivered. What is striking about this text, given the difficult legal issues raised by it in 1990, is its simplicity. It is not particularly 'legalistic'. A reasonably sophisticated non-lawyer would understand it on first reading. A 'commercial' language paraphrase might read: 'If either of us has good grounds for bringing this agreement to an end early, and does so, we will bring forward to an earlier date the time for delivering what we owe each other, value what we owe each other as at that earlier date, and the one who owes the more will pay the net balance to the other.'

3.37 Now, such an arrangement falls within the definition of 'close-out netting provision' in FCA(2), which reads as follows:

> 'close-out netting provision' means a term of a financial collateral arrangement, or of an arrangement of which a financial collateral arrangement forms part, or any legislative provision under which on the occurrence of an enforcement event, whether through the operation of netting or set-off or otherwise—
> (a) the obligations of the parties are accelerated to become immediately due and expressed as an obligation to pay an amount representing the original obligation's estimated current value or replacement cost, or are terminated and replaced by an obligation to pay such an amount; or
> (b) an account is taken of what is due from each party to the other in respect of such obligations and a net sum equal to the balance of the account is payable by the party from whom the larger amount is due to the other party . . .

3.38 As a result of falling within this definition, the provision in clause 10.2 of the ISLA document (and other similar provisions) gains important, statutory protection (provided by FCA(2)) which was not available in 1990. For example, paragraph 12 of FCA(2) makes the simple, but vitally reassuring, statement that a 'close-out netting provision shall . . . take effect in accordance with its terms notwithstanding that the collateral-provider or collateral-taker under the arrangement is subject to winding-up proceedings or reorganisation measures'. There are a number of important exceptions to this general principle[36] which apply if, for example, a bank (in relation to its insolvent customer) was aware or should have been aware that the customer's winding-up proceedings had already

---

[36] See FCA(2), para 10(2).

started (ie a court had made a winding-up order) at the time it entered into the arrangement that included the close-out netting provision. These exceptions need to be studied carefully by anyone seeking to rely on this kind of arrangement, but they are fair (in striking a balance amongst the interests of different creditors of an insolvent) and not such as to pose a problem for normal market activities.

FCA(2) represents the law as it is now. How were these issues dealt with in **3.39** 1990? It was felt that the 'outright transfer' method of creating 'security' was effective for its purpose, and not, for example, subject to 'recharacterization' risk.[37] The transactions were outright transfers of assets. It was true that they were entered into for the purpose of creating security in the commercial (as opposed to legal) sense, but this in itself did not justify them being recharacterized by the courts as, say, the creation of some kind of charge, not least because the transferee could dispose of the securities and was not obliged to hold any alternative securities or assets (in which the transferor might, it could be argued, have an equity of redemption) and, of course, the transferor had no rights whatsoever to the return of the same securities (ie a right to 'redeem') as were transferred at any point. The transferor's rights, when the transaction was 'unwound', were to the delivery of equivalent securities, a crucial distinction.[38]

The more difficult questions arose in relation to set-off. Clearly, the new struc- **3.40** ture would not be satisfactory, and not acceptable commercially, if the set-off provision[39] was ineffective. It was known that any such provision, by its nature,

---

[37] See *Re George Inglefield* [1933] Ch 1 and, generally, Ch 9 below.

[38] Goode (op. cit. 220, footnote 57) takes the view that, notwithstanding the language used in documentation regarding equivalent securities, 'contrary to the general understanding, what is transferred on the reverse leg of the transaction is not simply the *equivalent* of the securities but the identical securities, since the holding of securities is no more than co-ownership of a single asset, the issued share or loan capital relating to the issue in question. Accordingly the immunity of title transfer from attack as a security interest rests solely on the fact that it is intended as an outright transfer of ownership, not on any argument that the seller does not have a right to repurchase the same asset as that which it transferred.' The author would respectfully differ from this view, believing that distinctions can be made between a shareholding in a company and an undivided share in, say, a tank of petroleum and that a court would hold that where a company has, say, 1,000 shareholders, each of those shareholders has an asset (its shareholding) which can be bought and sold, charged, given away, etc separately, without regard to what any other shareholder might do with its own shareholding, and that, consequently, each shareholding is a distinct asset from each other shareholding. Further, if a shareholder has, say, 100 shares and creates a charge over 50 of them, it can dispose of the other 50 free of the charge because they are not the *same* shares as the charged shares (even though they are identical to the charged shares). For a more erudite and reasoned rationale for this view, see Morton, 'Commentary on "The Dematerialisation of Money Market Instruments" ' in Worthington (ed), *Commercial Law and Practice* 291. The point, however, is now largely academic in view of FCA(2).

[39] There was no material difference between the set-off provision devised in 1990 and that contained in the extract of the ISLA standard document quoted above.

would be of limited application insofar as the statutory rules[40] (rather than the contractual provision) would prevail if one of the parties became insolvent. Nevertheless, the statutory rules were considered satisfactory, subject to two points:

(1) credits advanced after a petition for winding-up had been presented would not be eligible for set-off (and, for this purpose, credits advanced would include any transaction under which a party put itself in the position where it relied on the other party performing its side of the bargain—for example, the provision of 'security' or the 'lending' of stock); and

(2) statutory set-off took place as of the date of winding-up and therefore it was at least arguable that the relevant claims to be set off had to be valued as at that date rather than at the (earlier) date that contractual set-off might have taken place.[41]

The market was prepared to live with these risks.

3.41   A view had to be taken on the meaning of the word 'due', as used in Rule 4.90.[42] Subsequent case law, and some very recent legislation,[43] has clarified that meaning but in 1990 there were concerns that 'due' might mean that the date for payment should have arrived; it would not, for example, be normal practice for a banker to say that a sum due for repayment on Friday was 'due' on the preceding Monday (even though it was of course correct to say the money was 'owing', and constituted a debt, on that day). It was felt that the correct construction of 'due' in the context of rule 4.90 was that it was a reference to an obligation that would result in a debt; ie a broad construction, going some way beyond 'due and payable' was permissible. The following extract from Millett J's judgment in the *Charge Card* case was influential:

> In the first place the general rule does not require that at the moment when the winding up commences there should be two enforceable debts, a debt provable in the liquidation and a debt enforceable by the liquidator against the creditor claiming to prove. It is enough that at the commencement of the winding up mutual dealings exist which involve rights and obligations, whether absolute or contingent, of such a nature that afterwards in the events that happen they mature or develop into pecuniary demands capable of set off. If the end contemplated by

---

[40]   ie the Insolvency Rules 1986, rule 4.90.

[41]   See comments of Lord Hoffmann in *Stein v Blake* [1996] 1 AC 243, 252 (as to 'the general principle of insolvency law . . . which governs . . . conversion of foreign currency'), set out at para 3.54, and see further para 3.58 as to the current law, as modified by FCA(2).

[42]   The rule provides that 'sums due' between the relevant parties are to be set off. See App 1 and see further below.

[43]   See the judgment of Lord Hoffmann in *Stein v Blake* [1996] 1 AC 243, 252 (considered further para 3.52 below and the Insolvency (Amendment) Rules 2005 (considered at para 3.58 below).

the transaction is a claim sounding in money so that, in the phrase employed in the cases, it is commensurable with the cross demand, no more is required than that at the commencement of the winding up liabilities shall have been contracted by the company and the other party respectively from which cross money claims accrue during the course of the winding up.

Although the above statement of law was based on section 31 of the Bankruptcy **3.42** Act 1914, and the corresponding language in rule 4.90 was different, the prevailing view was that no change in law had been intended by the change in drafting.

No one had any doubt that the set-off provision would be effective in accord- **3.43** ance with its terms, as a matter of contract, in situations not involving insolvency. The form of security may now be generally referred to as 'title transfer collateral' but its effectiveness depends entirely on the law relating to set-off, especially set-off where one party is insolvent.

F. Case Law and Legislative Developments

As can be seen from the first part of this chapter (and Chapters 1 and 2), the **3.44** early 1990s were difficult times for those concerned about legal risk and legal uncertainty, even though, in practice, lawyers were generally able to find workable solutions to such problems as were presented to them. The law regarding set-off was satisfactory, but not exactly free from niggling doubts. Many of these doubts were, fortunately, dispelled during the course of the decade as market practice developed and, in particular, as the more important issues came up for consideration in the courts. Not only did the case law help to clarify the more difficult issues, it also demonstrated, for anyone who might have had doubts, that the judiciary understood very clearly where the areas of uncertainty lay and that it was desirable to remove that uncertainty if at all possible.

We should begin under this heading with two cases on set-off, both heard in **3.45** the 1990s and both featuring judgments by Lord Hoffmann which one commentator has described as 'masterly analyses'.[44]

The first of these cases was *MS Fashions Ltd v Bank of Credit and Commerce* **3.46** *International SA (No 2)* (also referred to as *BCCI* (No 2)).[45] The facts can be briefly stated. Two brothers had executed a mortgage deed (in 1984) to secure advances by the bank, BCCI, to two companies. The main purpose of the

---

[44] See Goode, *Legal Problems of Credit and Security* (3rd edn) 283.
[45] [1993] Ch 425, affirmed [1993] Ch 439. In this case, Lord Hoffmann was still Hoffmann LJ, sitting at first instance.

document was to create security over property owned by the brothers, but it also contained a covenant by which the brothers (defined, with the two companies, as 'the principal debtor') undertook to pay on demand in writing all moneys owed by the 'principal debtor' ie by each of the brothers themselves and the companies. About eighteen months after executing the mortgage deed, one of the brothers (a Mr Sarwar) provided additional security by placing a deposit with BCCI and signing a letter of charge by which he charged that deposit to secure the liabilities of the companies. He agreed that BCCI could apply the deposit at any time to satisfy the companies' indebtedness, without notice to him, and that 'the liabilities hereunder shall be as that of principal debtor'. He also signed two unlimited guarantees of the companies' liabilities, which were expressed to be additional to any other security that BCCI might have.

3.47 It was noted that the references to the brothers being 'principal debtor' in the mortgage was 'odd' because there was no express liability taken on by the brothers in the mortgage. However, Hoffmann LJ felt it was 'a tenable view that such charges over deposits can be analysed as the creation of a liability on the part of the chargor for the company's debt, not exceeding the amount of the deposit, which can be set off against BCCI's liability to repay the deposit'. He so construed the language in the mortgage, making an interesting passing reference to the (by this time well-known) controversy generated by the *Charge Card* case[46] (and foreshadowing his own judgment in the later case of *BCCI (No 8)* in indicating that set-off might not be 'the only way in which they can take effect'.

3.48 Approximately seven years later, BCCI was compulsorily wound up. At that time Mr Sarwar had about £300,000 in the deposit account with BCCI and his companies owed BCCI about £572,000. Mr Sarwar claimed to set off what he was liable for in respect of the company loans against his deposit, which set-off would also, he argued, extinguish the companies' liabilities to BCCI, to the extent of that deposit. If Mr Sarwar failed, he would lose all of his deposit and still be liable to BCCI's liquidators in respect of the companies' loans. But, in order to win, he had to overcome a difficult problem: BCCI's liquidators had not at any time demanded any money from him. If he had not been asked to pay under the mortgage, what was there for him to set-off against the deposit? If the liability of Mr Sarwar remained only contingent at the time of the court hearing, it would not be possible to effect a set-off. It was not permissible, in insolvency set-off (as the rules stood at the time of this case),[47] to set-off a claim by a creditor of the insolvent company against a liability of that creditor that is

---

[46] See Ch 2 above.

[47] The policy that militated against an insolvent company being able to set off on account of a contingent claim owned by it (as opposed to against it) has now been reversed by The Insolvency (Amendment) Rules 2005. See App 1, Part 2 below.

only contingent (for example, on a demand being made). Hoffmann LJ, in finding for Mr Sarwar, overcame this problem by deciding that the 'principal debtor' language in the various documents referred to above had 'the effect of creating primary liability for the purposes of the rule that the debt is not contingent on demand'. As a result, he was able to find that 'one therefore has on the one hand a liability of BCCI to the individual director against a several liability of the director to pay the same debt as that for which the company is liable. Such liabilities may be set off against each other.'

It should be emphasized that the problems that used to exist (prior to the coming into effect of The Insolvency (Amendment) Rules 2005 in April 2005) relating to the contingent nature of a creditor's liability to the insolvent company were not, and are not, a concern where the contingency relates to a creditor's *claim*. Such contingent claims can be valued (if necessary, ie if the relevant event has not occurred at the time of liquidation and distribution of assets) and then set-off can take place, even though the contingency may not occur until some time later. This is consistent with the dicta of Dixon J in *Hiley v People's Prudential Assurance Co Ltd*[48] quoted by Dillon LJ in the Court of Appeal judgment affirming Hoffmann LJ's judgment at first instance: **3.49**

> ... In the first place, the general rule does not require that at the moment when the winding up commences there shall be two enforceable debts, a debt provable in the liquidation and a debt enforceable by the liquidator against the creditor claiming to prove. It is enough that at the commencement of the winding up mutual dealings[49] exist which involve rights and obligations whether absolute or contingent of such a nature that afterwards in the events that happen they mature or develop into pecuniary demands capable of set off. If the end contemplated by the transaction is a claim sounding in money so that, in the phrase employed in the cases, it is commensurable with the cross-demand, no more is required than that at the commencement of the winding up liabilities shall have been contracted by the company and the other party respectively from which cross money claims accrue during the course of the winding up.

It may be felt that the finding of a personal liability on the part of Mr Sarwar, by reason of the 'principal debtor' language, was an example of somewhat imaginative judicial reasoning, employed, no doubt, in the interest of what was perceived to be a just result. This aspect of the case should not blind us to the fact that it is possible for assets (including money) to be charged or otherwise used as security on the basis that their owner undertakes no personal liability (even of a **3.50**

---

[48] (1938) 60 CLR 468, 498

[49] In the later case of *Secretary of State for Trade and Industry v Frid* [2004] UKHL 24, the House of Lords has held (Lord Hoffmann giving the principal judgment) that 'dealings' should be interpreted 'in an extended sense which includes the commission of a tort or the imposition of a statutory obligation'. As a result, debts which are eligible for set-off in insolvency may have arisen 'by contract, statute or tort, voluntarily or by compulsion'.

limited recourse nature) for the obligation secured. (Such arrangements are sometimes termed 'naked collateral'.) In the case of Mr Sarwar's deposit, the 'odd' language used in the documentation obviously led to a different conclusion.[50]

3.51 The *MS Fashions* case (*BCCI (No 2)*) is, however, cited most frequently because of the very clear (and very welcome) statement of principles relating to insolvency set-off provided in Hoffmann LJ's judgment. In referring to rule 4.90,[51] he says:

> Certain principles as to the application of these provisions have been established by the cases. First, the rule is mandatory (the mandatory principle). If there have been mutual dealings before the winding-up order which have given rise to cross claims, neither party can prove or sue for his full claim. An account must be taken and he must prove or sue (as the case may be) for the balance. Secondly, the account is taken as at the date of the winding-up order (the retroactivity principle). This is only one manifestation of a wider principle of insolvency law, namely that the liquidation and distribution of the assets of the insolvent company are treated as notionally taking place simultaneously on the date of the winding-up order (see Oliver J. in *Re Dynamics Corp of America* [1976] 2 All ER 669 at 673, [1976] 1 WLR 757 at 762). Thirdly, in taking the account the court has regard to events which have occurred since the date of the winding-up (the hindsight principle). The hindsight principle is pervasive in the valuation of claims and the taking of accounts in bankruptcy and winding-up. A good example of the principle being applied outside the context of set-off is *Re Northern Counties of England Fire Insurance Co, Macfarlane's Claim* (1880) 17 Ch D 337 in which the value of a claim under a fire insurance policy was determined by reference to the loss suffered in a fire which occurred a month after the insurance company had been wound up.

3.52 The existence of the mandatory principle was well known. However, elucidation of the retroactivity and hindsight principles (and the impact of the hindsight principle on contingent claims and their valuation) was especially helpful. For those concerned by the issues described in the earlier part of this chapter, this statement had a greatly reassuring effect. But more was to come. In the case of *Stein v Blake*,[52] Lord Hoffmann took the opportunity to clarify other obscure areas relating to insolvency set-off. As was arguably the case with *MS Fashions*, the specific facts of the case (which was concerned with the bankruptcy of an individual rather than the insolvency of a company) required a decision on a rather narrow point, but they nevertheless provided the occasion for an

---

[50] In the later case of *BCCI (No 8)* [1998] AC 214, which involved central facts very similar to those in *MS Fashions* but without there being any language in the documents suggesting personal liability on the part of those who had made security deposits, the anomalous nature of the latter case (described as involving 'a very unusual security document') was acknowledged by the House of Lords (with Lord Hoffmann once again delivering the principal judgment).
[51] See App 1 below.   [52] [1996] 1 AC 243.

exposition of the law that would have been welcomed by market participants. Lord Hoffmann's summary of the facts cannot be bettered for its succinctness:

> If A and B have mutual claims against each other and A becomes bankrupt, does A's claim against B continue to exist so that A's trustee can assign it to a third party? Or is the effect of section 323 of the Insolvency Act 1986 to extinguish the claims of A and B and to substitute a claim for the net balance owing after setting off the one against the other? And if the latter is the case, can the trustee assign the net balance (if any) before it has been ascertained by the taking of an account between himself and B? If yes, is that what the trustee in this case has done? These are the issues in this appeal.

Section 323 of the Insolvency Act 1986 (or at least the relevant part of it) is the same for all relevant purposes as Rule 4.90, except that it applies to individuals, not companies (and, as a result, there are some technical differences to take account of this which do not concern us here). The statements of Lord Hoffmann in this case, referred to below, are of equal application to companies, notwithstanding that the case concerned an individual's bankruptcy. **3.53**

In the course of his judgement, Lord Hoffmann embarked on a general review of the law relating to bankruptcy set-off. Set out below are some extracts which are of important general application: **3.54**

- **Set-off as quasi security:** 'Bankruptcy set-off . . . affects the substantive rights of the parties by enabling the bankrupt's creditor to use his indebtedness to the bankrupt as a form of security. Instead of having to prove with other creditors for the whole of his debt in the bankruptcy, he can set off pound for pound what he owes the bankrupt and prove for or pay only the balance.'

- **The meaning of 'due':** (1) 'Bankruptcy set-off . . . requires an account to be taken of liabilities which, at the time of bankruptcy, may be due but not yet payable or may be unascertained in amount or subject to contingency. Nevertheless, the law says that the account shall be deemed to have been taken and the sums due from one party set off against the other as at the date of the bankruptcy. This is in accordance with the general principle of bankruptcy law, which governs payment of interest, conversion of foreign currencies etc., that the debts of the bankrupt are treated as having been ascertained and his assets simultaneously distributed amongst his creditors on the bankruptcy date . . . It is clear, therefore, that when section 323(2) speaks of what is "due" from each party,[53] it does not mean that the sums in question must have been due and payable, whether at the bankruptcy date or even the date

---

[53] The relevant language is in the same terms as rule 4.90(2); see App 1 below. See also para 3.41.

when the calculation falls to be made. The claims may have been contingent at the bankruptcy date and the creditor's claim may remain contingent at the time of the calculation, but they are nevertheless included in the account.' (2) '. . . I think that "due" merely means treated as having been owing at the bankruptcy date with the benefit of hindsight and, if necessary, estimation prescribed by the bankruptcy law.'[54]

- **How contingent claims (of either a creditor or the bankrupt/insolvent company) are dealt with:** 'How does the law deal with the conundrum of having to set off, as of the bankruptcy date, "sums due" which may not yet be due or which may become owing upon contingencies which have not yet occurred? It employs two techniques. The first is to take into account everything which has actually happened between the bankruptcy date and the moment when it becomes necessary to ascertain what, on that date, was the state of account between the creditor and the bankrupt. If by that time the contingency has occurred and the claim has been quantified, then that is the amount which is treated as having been due at the bankruptcy date . . . But the winding-up of the estate of a bankrupt or an insolvent company[55] cannot always wait until all possible contingencies have happened and all the actual or potential liabilities which existed at the bankruptcy date have been quantified. Therefore the law adopts a second technique, which is to make an estimation of the value of the claim . . . This enables the trustee to quantify a creditor's contingent or unascertained claim, for the purpose of set-off or proof, in a way which will enable the trustee safely to distribute the estate, even if subsequent events show that the claim was worth more. There is no similar machinery for quantifying contingent or unascertained claims against the creditor, because it would be unfair upon him to have his liability to pay advanced merely because the trustee wants to wind up the bankrupt's estate.'

3.55 The above statements confirmed that the view of the law that underpinned close-out netting provisions of the kind considered earlier in this chapter was correct. To the extent that the principles of insolvency set-off were confirmed or established in cases such as *MS Fashions* and *Stein v Blake*, those principles, combined with rule 4.90 and other legislation, formed a model that (with a certain amount of fine tuning, as introduced by FCA(2) which is considered further below) was ideally suited to a market that was becoming more and more reliant on set-off and netting as a means of reducing and controlling risk on a

---

[54] The meaning of 'due' has recently been clarified by The Insolvency (Amendment) Rules 2005, which, in effect, give statutory confirmation of Lord Hoffmann's interpretation; see App 1, Part 2 below.

[55] The reference to a company in a judgment that was concerned with the bankruptcy of an individual only confirms that Lord Hoffmann was seeking to provide a description of the law that would be of general application.

massive scale. The Insolvency (Amendment) Rules 2005,[56] as regards the issues described above, represented the 'icing on the cake', giving statutory authority to what the courts had already decided. It is perhaps just as well that the financial markets, thanks largely to the courts and robust opinions from eminent barristers, did not have to wait until 2005 for the clarification that eventually came to the rules originally promulgated in 1986.

We should not, however, leave the case of *Stein v Blake* without recording that, as **3.56** to the specific point requiring decision, the court held that, with reference to the summary of facts set out by Lord Hoffmann quoted above, the trustee in bank-ruptcy could assign the net balance owing after bankruptcy set-off, even at a time before it was known what that balance would be. (The trustee would not have been able to assign the gross claim, ignoring the set-off, because 'the original chose in action ceases to exist and is replaced by a claim to a net balance' on the bankruptcy date.) It mattered not that no account had been taken at the time of the assignment because bankruptcy set-off is 'self-executing' (in addition to being mandatory) and 'does not require the trustee or anyone else to execute it'. The net balance was thus 'like any other chose in action' and capable of assignment.

The case of *BCCI (No 8)*[57] completes a trilogy of important cases on set-off **3.57** featuring judgments from Lord Hoffmann. This case has been considered above (at para 2.07) because of its significance in, it would seem, laying to rest the spectre of 'conceptual impossibility' in the context of charge-backs.

This string of cases on set-off gave the markets the reassurance they wanted, if **3.58** indeed they needed any more after the various efforts of the FLP to calm such concerns as may have arisen in relation to insolvency set-off. It is sometimes observed that although the common law system delivers great flexibility, its ability to deliver anything at all depends on the right issues coming before the right judges at the right time. It would seem that the insolvency of BCCI did have at least a few beneficial side-effects as regards the development of English law on set-off. That development was, some years after the cases just considered, taken to a further stage by the legislation implementing the Collateral Directive in the UK, FCA(2).[58] The regulations contained in FCA(2) address a number of different issues, including, for example, conflict of laws questions[59] and the removal of various formal and registration requirements that might otherwise have applied to financial collateral arrangements. They also address such rechar-acterization risks as may have remained following the case law developments in the previous decade. In this chapter, we are chiefly concerned with the impact of

---

[56] See App 1, Part 2 below.   [57] [1998] AC 214.
[58] And, even more recently, by The Insolvency (Amendment) Rules 2005; see App 1, Part 2 below.
[59] See further Ch 7 below.

FCA(2) on set-off and netting, especially close-out netting (which, as mentioned above,[60] is the subject of a special definition in the regulations). As one commentator has noted, 'many of the issues that the Collateral Directive is intended to remedy were not problematic under English law'[61] (although they were certainly problematic under the laws of other EU countries) but the following reforms have been helpful, as regards close-out netting:

(1) It is expressly stated that close-out netting provisions take effect in accordance with their terms, notwithstanding the insolvency of either of the parties.[62]

(2) The contractually agreed mechanism for converting foreign currency claims will now apply (rather than the rate applying on the insolvency date) as long as it does not involve the use of an 'unreasonable exchange rate'.[63]

(3) Various parts of insolvency law that might otherwise have cast doubt on the effectiveness of close-out netting provisions and related security in certain situations are expressly disapplied.[64]

(4) 'Rights of use' are expressly recognized as valid, so that a collateral taker can, in effect, use and dispose of collateral (if the documentation so provides) if it is replaced with 'equivalent' collateral.[65]

(5) Although not required by the Collateral Directive, arrangements which involve certain kinds of floating charge receive the same advantages as those involving fixed charges; the floating charge has to be one where the assets subject to it are in the possession or under the control of the chargee (which of course is not usually the case with a run-of-the-mill floating charge, but more likely to be the case with financial collateral).[66]

G. Multilateral Netting—the *British Eagle* case and its Aftermath

3.59 The cases and legislation referred to so far in this chapter on set-off and netting are concerned with bilateral situations, ie those that concern only two parties

---

[60] See para 3.37.

[61] See Freshfields Bruckhaus Deringer publication, 'Structured Finance News', Summer 2004.

[62] See FCA(2), Art 12; a number of exceptions (which are not problematic) to this principle are set out in Art 12(2); note the extended benefit conferred by Art 13 where, eg a financial collateral arrangement is 'innocently' entered into on the same day as winding-up commences.

[63] See FCA(2), Art 14.   [64] See FCA(2), Arts 8 and 10.   [65] See FCA(2), Art 16.

[66] See definition of 'security interest'; the effect of the provision is to protect arrangements where, because of the chargor having the right to substitute assets held as collateral, there is a risk of the arrangement being construed as a floating charge. (It is expressly provided that such substitution rights do not prevent the collateral being regarded as controlled or possessed by the chargee.)

(the mutuality principle applicable to insolvency set-off requires, in effect, that only two parties are involved).[67] However, multilateral netting arrangements are also extremely important to the smooth functioning of the financial markets, particularly in the context of investment exchanges and payment and settlement systems involving clearing houses.

A classically simple and clear description of a clearing house was provided by **3.60** Lord Cross in the House of Lords' judgment in the leading case on how such arrangements are generally treated in English insolvency law, *British Eagle International Airlines Ltd v Compagnie Nationale Air France*:[68]

> . . . if the members of a group of traders are entering day in day out into numbers of transactions with one another it may be much to their mutual advantage to agree that the liabilities arising out of the individual transactions shall not be settled directly between the members concerned but that a 'clearing house' shall be set up to which every member will give notice of each transaction to which it is a party and which will at regular intervals strike a balance between them all showing what, as a result of all the transactions into which it has entered during the relevant period, is the net amount which each member is in credit or in debit as the case may be. Those in debit will then pay to the clearing house the amounts of their debits, the total of which will of course be the same as the total of the amounts owing to the members in credit, and the clearing house will in turn pay over to such members the sums due to them.

A description of the origins of a clearing system for payments amongst banks **3.61** can be found in the award of Bingham J (as he then was), sitting as arbitrator in the reported case of *Barclays Bank plc and ors v Bank of England*:[69]

> The origins of the clearing house as it exists today can be traced back to a device adopted by bank employees in the eighteenth century, largely (as it would seem) for their own convenience. During the early years of the eighteenth century the banks employed walk clerks whose task it was to call at other banks in the City and the West End of London to present cheques for payment and obtain cash in exchange. As the use of cheques increased, so this task became increasingly laborious. As a result, a practice grew whereby, instead of visiting other banks on foot, the clerks would meet at a central point, exchange cheques and settle the difference between the total exchanged. To begin with, the meeting place was unofficial and unrecognised but the advantages of this central exchange were obvious and in due course a room was hired and, in 1833, a building erected on the present site . . . The clearing house is only one part, although a central part, of the complex and sophisticated clearing system which now operates in this country.

---

[67] See para 3.21.
[68] [1975] 2 All ER 390; it should be stressed that there are important exceptions to the position at common law, established by statute, which are considered at 3.70 et seq.
[69] [1985] 1 All ER 385.

3.62 It may assist understanding of clearing and multilateral netting if we bear in mind a very simple example. Let us suppose that, following various transactions involving A, B and C, the state of accounts amongst them is that:

> A owes B £100;
> B owes C £50; and
> C owes A £100.

Let us also suppose that all these debts fall due for payment at the same time on the same day. It would be possible for the debts to be settled by three payments (by each of A, B and C). However, if one analyses each party's net position (looking at the state of accounts on a multilateral basis, ie taking into account the position of all three parties), it is clear that:

> A has a nil balance (because its debits equal its credits);
> B has a credit balance of £50; and
> C has a debit balance of £50.

If the parties so agree, the debts amongst them can therefore be settled by one payment only (instead of three) i.e. a payment by C to B of £50. This is, essentially, the logic that underlies the operation of clearing houses. Clearing (sometimes called 'clearance') is of crucial importance to banking and the financial markets. Clearing systems are used to settle all manner of 'trades' in the markets, including transactions in securities, payments of money and the settlement of derivatives transactions.

Some definition of terms used in this context can be found in the First Giovannini Clearing and Settlement Report.[70]

> '. . . the clearing and settlement procedure can be described in terms of four main activities . . .:
> • Confirmation of the terms of the trade as agreed between the buyer and seller;
> • Clearance, by which the respective obligations of the buyer and seller are established;
> • Delivery, requiring the transfer of the securities from the seller to the buyer; and
> • Payment, requiring the transfer of funds from the buyer to the seller.
> Delivery of securities and payment of funds may occur simultaneously but only when both delivery and payment have been finalised is settlement of the securities transaction achieved.'

3.63 The Report also contains a very helpful summary of typical clearance procedures, together with a description of the significant advantages of multilateral netting:

> Once the terms of a securities transaction have been confirmed, the respective obligations of the buyer and seller are established and agreed. This process is

---

[70] The first of two reports delivered by the EU 'Giovannini Group' (named after its chairman, Alberto Giovannini) on 'Cross-Border Clearing and Settlement Arrangements in the European Union', delivered in November 2001.

known as clearance and determines exactly what the counterparties to the trade expect to receive. Clearance is a service normally provided by a clearinghouse, a central securities depositary (CSD) or international central securities depositary (ICSD). The latter two also hold securities and allow them to be processed by book entry. Clearance can be carried out on a gross or net basis. When clearance is carried out on a gross basis, the respective obligations of the buyer and seller are calculated individually on a trade-by-trade basis. When clearance is carried out on a net basis, the mutual obligations of the buyer and seller are offset yielding a single obligation between the two counterparties. Accordingly, clearance on a net basis reduces substantially the number of securities/payment transfers that require to be made between the buyer and seller and limits the credit risk exposure of both counterparties. Clearance can also be continuous (typically when settlement of a transaction is on a gross basis)[71] or discrete (typically when settlement is on a net basis).

Securities markets may avail of a central counter party (CCP), which is an entity that interposes itself legally between the buyers and sellers of securities by a process of 'novation'. In consequence, the buyers and sellers of securities interact directly with the CCP and remain anonymous to each other. Some CCPs also offer a netting facility, whereby the CCP offsets all obligations i.e. amounts owed by and to participants in the market and reduces all outstanding residuals to a single debit/credit between itself and each member (rather than a multiplicity of bilateral exposures between members). This further facilitates the management of securities and payments transfers and reduces the credit exposure, margin requirements and liquidity needs of buyers and sellers.[72]

So why did the *British Eagle* case (decided in 1975) cause, or potentially cause, **3.64** concern for those who relied on multilateral netting arrangements? The case came about because of the insolvency of an airline company that was party to a clearing house arrangement operated by the International Air Transport Association (IATA). The clearing house arrangements (as is generally the case) constituted a contract between each of the members *inter se* as well as between each member and IATA (which was incorporated in Canada). The airline industry generates a great many inter-airline obligations for which a clearing house system seems particularly suited. As Lord Cross observed:

---

[71] So-called 'Real Time Gross Settlement' is the payment system now used by clearing banks in the UK. As described in the Bank of England's notice: 'In April 1996, the UK Clearing Banks switched to a new electronic system for settling same day sterling payments. Payments are processed through the Clearing House Automated Payment System (CHAPS) individually and continuously during the day in real time. Previously, payments were processed as a single net transaction at the end of the day *and exposed the settlement banks to massive losses if one of the banks were to fail.*' (Emphasis added.)

[72] The Second Giovannini Clearing and Settlement Report also contains a definition of 'clearing/clearance' in its glossary of terms. This is: 'the process of transmitting, reconciling and, in some cases, confirming payment orders or security transfer instructions prior to settlement, possibly including the netting of instructions and the establishment of final positions for settlement. Sometimes the terms are used (imprecisely) to include settlement.'

A clearing house system is peculiarly appropriate to the operations of international airlines since each of them is every day carrying passengers and cargo on behalf of other airlines which will have received payment from the passenger or consignor of the full amount payable for the whole distance covered though only part of it is going to be flown in the aircraft of the airline issuing the ticket, the remainder being flown in the aircraft of another airline, to which the issuing airline will be liable to make an appropriate payment. Instead of a vast number of cross remittances in a variety of different currencies one has, under the clearing house system, a single payment to or by the clearing house in either dollars or sterling which, to use the words of the IATA clearing house Manual of Procedure, 'concurrently collects and settles a member's world-wide debts'.

3.65   Of the gross inter-airline obligations, 91 per cent were dealt with by the offsetting of debits and credits with only 9 per cent requiring actual payments to or by the clearing house. Of crucial importance was the court's analysis that although the arrangements required the payment of obligations to be made via the medium of IATA, they did not amount to a continuous extinction of the inter-member obligations and replacement thereof with debts owing to and by IATA as a principal. The arrangements did not (except upon completion of a clearance, as described below) involve 'netting by novation' (as is now commonly the case with clearing houses). What they did involve was the taking of an account, on a monthly basis, of the various debits and credits of members, with the account for month 1 being closed on the thirtieth day of month 2 (after appropriate provision of information to the clearing house) and the members being notified of their position (debit or credit) by telegram within five working days after that. (Members in debit had to pay within seven days ('Call Day') of such notification.) One of the members (British Eagle) had gone into winding-up on 8 November 1968 and its liquidator was contending that payments due to it in respect of the preceding September and October should be paid gross, and not subject to the multilateral netting arrangement constituted by the IATA rules. With regard to the 'September clearance', the court found that the 'Clearance in respect of business done in September was "completed" or "effected" on 4th November, before the winding-up resolution was passed'—4 November was the date of the telegram notice referred to above with respect to the September business and the court determined that this event (not the later Call Day) was the event that constituted closure of the clearance for that month. Once clearance was closed, the original debits and credits 'were all satisfied and replaced by an obligation on British Eagle to pay the clearing house £44,771' (ie the net balance owing by it). The September clearance thus escaped the liquidator, since it was a transaction that was closed and completed before liquidation commenced.

3.66   The same could not, however, be said of the October clearance. This had only been completed after the commencement of the winding-up. Here, the liquidator's argument rested on the principle of insolvency law, then enshrined in section 302 of the Companies Act 1948, that 'the property of a company shall, on its winding up, be applied in satisfaction of its liabilities *pari passu*, and, subject to such application, shall, unless the articles otherwise provide, be distributed among the members according to their rights and interests in the company'. The House of Lords agreed with the liquidator that this provision was mandatory and that, insofar as the IATA clearing house arrangements amounted to an attempt by the IATA members to 'contract out' (by means of a 'mini liquidation') of what should happen on insolvency with regard to *pari passu* distribution to unsecured creditors, the arrangements were void. As a result, the October clearance was not upheld and the liquidator was entitled to make recoveries of sums due as a result of October business without regard to the IATA clearance arrangements. To hold otherwise would have had the effect of giving those members the benefit of a quasi-security over the assets of British Eagle represented by some of its claims against IATA members. It would be as though, taking the simple example set out in para 3.62 above, if A went into liquidation with no assets sufficient to pay unsecured creditors, B could recoup half of the debt owed to it by A by offsetting £50 of the debt owed by C to A (C being a creditor of B for £50). There was, of course, no mutuality of debtor and creditor to justify insolvency set-off and no charge had been registered over British Eagle's 'book debts' to take what would have been in effect a security interest outside the scope of the general winding-up. As Lord Cross remarked:

> ... the parties to the 'clearing house' arrangements did not intend to give one another charges on some of each other's future book debts. The documents were not drawn so as to create charges but simply so as to set up by simple contract a method of settling each other's mutual indebtedness at monthly intervals. Moreover, if the documents had purported to create such charges, the charges ... would have been unenforceable against the liquidator for want of registration ...

3.67 The *British Eagle* case therefore serves as a reminder that multilateral netting arrangements can be vulnerable on insolvency. The case, however, has not given rise to unmanageable risk. There are three reasons for this.

3.68 First, it is apparent from the logic of the judgment of Lord Cross that the *pari passu* problem simply does not arise if insolvency set-off is available. If, therefore, the mutual debts of the clearing house members are owed, instead of to each other, to the clearing house as a principal, the clearing house (which would not be a mere medium of payment, as in *British Eagle* prior to clearance completion) should be able to implement the netting, even where a member goes into liquidation, without the risk of the *pari passu* principle being infringed. It is possible to structure the rules of a clearing house so as to achieve this effect.

3.69 Secondly, novation of members' mutual debts to the clearing house as principal can be achieved on a continuous basis (with documentation adopting Lord

Cross's reference to debits and credits being 'satisfied and replaced' by debits and credits to and from the clearing house) so that the risk of liquidation intervening before 'completion' of a clearance has been effected is minimized.

3.70 The third, and most important reason, is that there have been a number of statutory adjustments to the basic insolvency law principle as described in the *British Eagle* case. The first of these came with the Companies Act 1989. This legislation was the first of a number of legislative measures in recent years which have accorded special treatment to certain kinds of financial market transactions, effectively shielding them from the most severe legal risks posed by general insolvency law. The Act achieved its objectives by protecting[73] what are defined as 'market contracts' of 'recognised investment exchanges and clearing houses'.[74] Market contracts are defined to include contracts subject to the rules of a recognized clearing house[75] which are 'subject to the rules of the clearing house entered into by the clearing house for the purposes of or in connection with the provision of clearing services for a recognised investment exchange'. Of great significance were the new requirements for recognition added by Sch 21 to the 1989 Act. These have now been replaced by regulations made under section 286 of the Financial Services and Markets Act 2000.[76] The requirements include the following:

- The clearing house must have default rules which, in the event of a member of the clearing house being or appearing to be unable to meet his obligations in respect of one or more market contracts, enable action to be taken to close out his position in relation to all unsettled market contracts to which he is a party.

- The rules must provide: (1) for all rights and liabilities of the defaulter under or in respect of market contracts to be discharged and for there to be paid by

---

[73] The protection takes the form of providing (in CA 1989, s 159) that market contracts and default rules of recognized clearing houses and investment exchanges 'shall not be regarded as to any extent invalid at law on the ground of inconsistency with the law relating to the distribution of the assets of a person on bankruptcy, winding up or sequestration, or in the administration of an insolvent estate'.

[74] In 1989 the recognition in question was pursuant to FSA 1986, but it is now pursuant to FSMA 2000.

[75] Comparable provisions apply to recognized investment exchanges (market contracts including, in that context, contracts entered into by a member of the exchange which are subject to the rules of the exchange. Unless otherwise stated, what is said in the rest of this chapter about clearing houses can be taken to apply generally to investment exchanges. Clearing houses currently recognized by the FSA are CRESTCO Ltd and LCH Clearnet Ltd. Recognized investment exchanges include London Stock Exchange plc, The London Metal Exchange Ltd, and The International Petroleum Exchange of London Ltd.

[76] These are The Financial Services and Markets Act 2000 (Recognition Requirements for Investment Exchanges and Clearing Houses) Regulations 2001, SI 2001/995. The requirements quoted can be found in Part IV of the Schedule to these regulations.

or to the defaulter such sum of money (if any) as may be determined in accordance with the rules; (2) for the sums so payable by or to the defaulter in respect of different contracts to be aggregated or set-off so as to produce a net sum; (3) for that sum (a) if payable by the defaulter to the clearing house, to be set off against any property provided by or on behalf of the defaulter as cover for margin (or the proceeds of realisation of such property) so as to produce a further net sum, and (b) if payable by the clearing house to the defaulter, to be aggregated with any property provided by or on behalf of the defaulter as cover for margin (or the proceeds of realization of such property).

The policy of the law in the UK, from 1989 onwards, has been clear. Multi-   **3.71**
lateral netting in the financial markets, provided it is within the 'safe harbour' of recognized systems and exchanges, should be allowed to take effect notwithstanding insolvency law on *pari passu* distribution. In the EU, similar sentiments, in favour of both bilateral and multilateral netting in such circumstances, came to the fore during the 1990s and resulted in a number of directives such as the Collateral Directive[77] and the Settlement Finality Directive. The Settlement Finality Directive, which led to further changes to English law in this area in 1999, refers, amongst other things, in its recitals to:

(1) 'the important systemic risk inherent in payment systems which operate on the basis of several legal types of payment netting, in particular multilateral netting';
(2) the 'paramount importance' of 'the reduction of legal risks associated with participation in real time gross settlement systems';
(3) 'the utmost importance' of reducing 'risk associated with participation in securities settlement systems, in particular where there is a close connection between such systems and payment systems'; and
(4) the desirability of laws of member states aiming 'to minimise the disruption to a system caused by insolvency proceedings against a participant in that system'.

The objectives of this directive, concerned primarily with payment and secur-   **3.72**
ities settlement systems, were implemented in English law by The Financial Markets and Insolvency (Settlement Finality) Regulations 1999.[78] In similar manner to the application of Part VII of the Companies Act 1989 to 'market contracts', the regulations give precedence to 'the default arrangements of a designated system' and 'transfer orders' over the general insolvency regime (so that *pari passu* and *British Eagle* concerns are not relevant). A 'transfer order' is defined as:

---

[77] Considered at 3.58 above.   [78] SI 1999/2979.

91

    (a)   an instruction by a participant to place at the disposal of a recipient an amount of money by means of a book entry on the accounts of a credit institution, a central bank or a settlement agent, or an instruction which results in the assumption or discharge of a payment obligation as defined by the rules of a designated system . . .; or

    (b)   an instruction by a participant to transfer the title to, or interest in, securities by means of a book entry on a register, or otherwise . . .

3.73 A payment or securities settlement system may be 'designated' (by either the FSA or the Bank of England, depending on its functions) under the regulations[79] if it satisfies the requirements set out in the Schedule to the regulations, and these include the requirements that the system must be 'a system through which transfer orders are effected' and that the system's rules 'must have default arrangements which are appropriate for that system in all the circumstances'. The term 'Default arrangements' is given an extended definition. The arrangements are 'put in place to limit systemic and other types of risk' which might arise on a participant's default and otherwise are to contain default rules comparable to those applicable to recognized clearing houses and investment exchanges[80] in relation to netting, the close-out of open positions, and the application or transfer of collateral security. Crucially, the rules of the system must also specify the point at which a transfer order takes effect as having been entered into the system, specify the point after which a transfer order may not be revoked by a participant or any other party, and prohibit the revocation by a participant or any other party of a transfer order from the point so specified.[81] The rules must thus specify what amounts to 'finality' and, in relation to this, the rules will prevail over provisions of insolvency law that might otherwise result in revocation of a payment.[82]

---

[79] The designating authority, in deciding whether or not to make a designation order, is expressly required, by para 4(2) of the regulations, to 'have regard to systemic risks'.

[80] See above. To the extent there is overlap between the market contract default regime in the Companies Act 1989 and the regulations (ie if a market contract is also a payment order) the regulations' default regime prevails (see para 21 of the regulations).

[81] See para 5(1) of the Schedule to the regulations.

[82] See para 17 of the regulations. Other aspects of payment and securities settlement systems are considered in Ch 7 below.

PART II

CHARACTERISTICS

4

DEFINITION

A general definition of legal risk would facilitate proper risk assessment and risk management, as well as ensure a consistent approach between EU credit institutions. It would also be worthwhile examining the extent to which one should take into account the fact that legal risks are inherently unpredictable and do not generally conform to a pattern. In addition, the management of legal risk would have to be consistent with the management of operational risk as a whole.[1]

A. Background and Context

The expression 'legal risk' is not a term of art. It may become one as the details **4.01** of the new regulatory regimes being ushered in by Basel II become clearer. However, at the present time it is simply a phrase that has slipped into common usage in the media and the financial markets. It can evidently mean different things according to the context—there is no clearly right or wrong usage. But although there may be no pressing need for a definition drawn as tightly as one might see in a legal document, some consensus on what we mean by legal risk when we speak of it in the context of financial markets is desirable.

To put the defining exercise in context, before we embark on the detailed issues **4.02** involved in formal definitions, let us take stock of the main points that have arisen in the first part of this book. These can be summarized as follows:

(1) Over the last twenty years the financial markets have experienced great changes. With the relaxation of exchange controls, the advent of international arrangements like the EU's 'single market', the huge growth in the trading of derivative products, and fundamental technological and cultural changes in the manner in which business is carried on, the risks involved in

---

[1] From opinion of the European Central Bank of 17 February 2005 on Capital Requirements Directive (CON/2005/4) para 55.

the day-to-day operations of banks and other financial institutions have become far more complex than those that used to arise in traditional bank lending.

(2) Regulators now seek more control and influence over operational risks taken on by banks and regard operational risks as including legal risks. There is, however, no universally accepted definition of legal risk.

(3) Legal risk and its travelling companion, legal uncertainty, cannot be completely eradicated from any civilized legal system. However, we have seen that bodies like the Financial Markets Law Committee (FMLC) and the Financial Law Panel (FLP) can play a vital role in 'sounding the alarm' when appropriate and articulating the case for such changes as may be desirable to eliminate, or at least reduce, certain kinds of avoidable legal uncertainty.

(4) English commercial judges are now perhaps more sensitized to the issues involved in court decisions that affect financial market practice than ever before (even though they have always had a very keen awareness of the need to respect sound market practice and custom). It also appears that the relationship between the 'judges' job' of providing effective and respected resolution of commercial disputes (albeit as a last resort), the 'legislators' job' of keeping commercial law up-to-date, and the political objective of keeping the UK an attractive centre for financial business is closer than ever.

(5) The EU has, however, become an important new source of new laws and regulations that affect the financial markets in the UK. The European Commission, which is the body chiefly responsible for EU legislative initiatives, does not carry any brief to safeguard the UK's pre-eminence as a financial market centre. It is fair to say that, at best, it is indifferent to the continuance of such pre-eminence. Nevertheless, certain EU initiatives, such as the Collateral Directive, can easily be implemented into English law with beneficial effect as regards removing legal uncertainty.

(6) On a broader international front, the world's financial regulators now have a greater awareness of the importance of legal risk and its significance in relation to, for example, how netting arrangements should be viewed in the context of capital adequacy requirements.

(7) Finally, regulators such as the Financial Services Authority (FSA), and in the US, the Securities and Exchange Commission (SEC), are clearly determined to pursue, and be seen to pursue, wrongdoers in the financial markets and exact appropriate retribution. In the criminal law context, the Serious Fraud Office is equally vigilant in its desire to punish financial crime. This phenomenon takes place against the background of an increasingly litigious climate for business and a worrying spread of the so-called 'compensation culture' (which some feel goes hand-in-hand with a risk-averse, or responsibility-averse culture).

Michael Taylor, in an article published in 1998,[2] made a more general, but **4.03** crucially important, point:

> It is undoubtedly true that banking has experienced a profound cultural change in the last two decades. This has been associated with a change from a situation in which the supply of credit was limited to one in which . . . it has been in plentiful supply. As a result, the role of bankers has changed from being rationers of credit to its marketers. But with this change in credit culture has gone a neglect of the basic principle that banks are, in the last resort, the stewards of other people's money.

Since 1998 the 'cultural change' has gathered pace. Over the past thirty years, **4.04** we have lived through a time of extraordinary social and political change. This has had a profound impact on how we live our lives and, as part of this, how risks in general, and financial and business risks in particular, are perceived; legal risk is no exception.

B. Changing Perceptions of the Meaning of 'Legal Risk'

The perception of what 'legal risk' means (at least in the context in which the **4.05** phrase is most commonly used) has shifted during the period we have examined. At the time of the formation of the Legal Risk Review Committee (LRRC), in the early 1990s, legal risk was generally thought of by practitioners in terms of Type 2 risks. Lawyers and market participants feared that perhaps the law had not kept pace with the changes seen in the markets. Commentators talked of 'legal black holes'. If such holes existed, we needed to find them quickly and fix them—or at least erect suitable warning signs. However, as we now look back more than a decade later and observe that very few strictly 'legal' disasters have actually occurred in the UK's financial markets (although there have been plenty of other problems in the UK and elsewhere caused by non-legal operational risk) we can see that legal risk is still a cause for concern but that the focus of attention is now more on Type 1 risks. When commentators and participants talk of legal risk nowadays they are usually referring to the risk of court actions or regulatory sanctions. This is, for example, evidenced by the very brief explanatory wording about legal risk to be found in Basel II.[3] Influential bodies like the Centre for the Study of Financial Innovation, when they talk of legal risk, focus only on litigation risk.[4]

The change is not a reflection of complacency about Type 2 risks; legal **4.06** uncertainty is still the principal focus of bodies like the Financial Markets Law

---

[2] M Taylor, 'Risk, Uncertainty and Other People's Money' (1998) 11 JIBFL 499.
[3] See para Intro 1.24 n. 37 above.
[4] See 'Banana Skins 2005—the CSFI's annual survey of the risks facing banks'.

Committee (FMLC) and UNIDROIT.[5] It is more a reflection of two market phenomena. First, the near panic that was induced by the *Hammersmith and Fulham* case and related developments has receded. There are, of course, still the risks that one would expect to find in any highly innovative market but there are no significant 'legal black holes', at least not in English law as it relates to these markets. Secondly, the litigious atmosphere has intensified. Rightly or wrongly, it seems that dissatisfied consumers, regulators, insolvency practitioners, etc are more prepared than ever to 'have a go' in the courts or other tribunals. Not only have claimants become more zealous, the range of potential causes of action (and jurisdictions with courts prepared to hear the claims) against internationally active institutions and their officers and employees seems to have been broadened, partly at least as a result of the relative ease with which legal actions can apparently be brought in a country like the US without the need for any particularly strong connection between any of the parties (or the act complained of).[6] In addition, recent legislative and political trends seem to have made it easier for a claimant to challenge the legitimacy of primary legislation itself (for example, on the grounds of perceived infringements of 'human rights') with the result that a determined litigant, with sufficient resources, can continue through an extended hierarchy of tribunals for some considerable time before he finally has to take 'no' for an answer.

4.07   The risk of litigation has also been increased by the apparent growth in financial fraud involving banks. Financial crime, at times, seems to be almost as innovative as the financial markets and it has often been noted that the increasing use of 'electronic banking' methods appears to make fraud easier to perpetrate. Further, the fall-out from major corporate scandals almost always seems to include claims against the collapsed company's banks from unpaid creditors (or the liquidator on their behalf), alleging that the banks' behaviour contributed to the fraud, even though the chief wrongdoers were clearly members of the company's management. As has been noted above,[7] the claims against banks involved in transactions with Enron, for example, run to several billion dollars.

---

[5] The organization 'Risk Psychology.net', somewhat against the trend, still focuses on Type 2 risks, its definition being: 'Legal risk is the risk of loss from a contract that cannot legally be enforced.' This definition (as is apparent from the organization's website) is heavily influenced by the *Hammersmith and Fulham* case and a similar case in the US, *County of Orange v Merrill Lynch & Co, Inc, et al* (1996). It is suggested, on the website, that legal risk includes 'transactional risk', which in turn includes 'documentation risk'.

[6] The recent extradition treaty between the UK and the US also suggests that it has become alarmingly easy for the US authorities to require the extradition of UK citizens (eg bankers involved in alleged corporate frauds) for alleged crimes committed, essentially, in the UK, which the UK authorities themselves do not, apparently, wish to prosecute. See Goodhart, 'Extradition of Bankers to the USA' (2005) 03 JIBFL 96.

[7] See para Intro 1.22 n. 32.

These market phenomena need to be seen against the backdrop of what many **4.08**
now perceive to be the 'risk society'.[8] We have become preoccupied with risk,
and especially the risk of being asked to take the blame for something (a very
prominent concern of the modern politician and certain kinds of organization
leader) or, worse, being sued for damages—(a fear that we have seen creeping
into many forms of occupation (teaching, medicine, law, accountancy, etc)
which traditionally used to feel much more able to absorb the risks involved in
their day-to-day responsibilities. As a result, we have also become preoccupied
with risk management (and Basel II reflects this to an extent).[9]

As Power has cogently put it:[10]   **4.09**

> A functional explanation for the phenomenon [of the growing preoccupation with
> risk management] suggests that the emergence of a systematic, generic and broad
> approach to risk management is a *rational* response to the fact that the environ-
> ment of individuals and organisations, indeed the world, has become genuinely
> 'more risky'. So, the argument runs, financial markets have become more volatile,
> organisational activities have become more dangerous with ever greater negative
> externalities, new large-scale threats exist from epidemics, from terrorism, from
> climate change. Individual states are ever weaker to control their destinies in a
> system of global interconnectedness, while technology advances to create both
> new opportunities and threats (GM foods, nanotechnology). The image is of a
> 'runaway world' in need of new forms of risk governance. In such a world, the
> reinvention of risk management and its repositioning as a critical model of good
> organisational control seems a natural response. It is reinforced and justified by
> each new dramatic headline event, from Barings to Enron and Parmalat, from

---

[8] See, eg, Ulrich Beck, *Risk Society* (page 12/13): 'The argument is that, while in classical
industrial society the "logic" of wealth production dominates the "logic" of risk production, in the
risk society this relationship is reversed . . . The productive forces have lost their innocence in the
reflexivity of modernisation processes. The gain in power from techno-economic "progress" is
being increasingly overshadowed by the production of risks. In an early stage, these can be
legitimated as "latent side effects". As they become globalised, and subject to public criticism and
scientific investigation, they become, so to speak, out of the closet and achieve a central importance in social and political debates.' In a more recent work, Barbara Hudson, *Justice in the Risk
Society*, the author comments: ' "Risk society" analyses of contemporary life suggest that risk has
become a central, generalised preoccupation, to the extent that it is configuring contemporary
institutions and contemporary consciousness', and that 'we now think of the negatives—the
risks—associated with modernity, rather than the benefits'.

[9] The regulators' approach to their role, understandably, focuses on risk, and how well the
regulated manage it. In a speech given on 8 February 2005, Dr Thomas Huertas (Director of the
FSA's Wholesale Firms Division), commented that 'we approach supervision in a risk-based way.
We concentrate our resources on the areas that are likely to pose the most significant risks to our
statutory objectives under FSMA. Over the coming year, we will focus a good deal of attention on
the implementation of Basel 2 and the Capital Requirements Directive (CRD). The CRD will
mark a huge step forward in developing a modern capital framework that will improve the risk
sensitivity of capital standards across the EU.' The FSA publishes a Risk Outlook at the beginning
of each calendar year.

[10] M Power, 'The Risk Management of Everything', a paper produced for Demos (2004),
http://www.demos.co.uk.

Challenger to Columbia, from BSE to mobile phones, and from 11 September 2001 to 11 March 2004 (the date of the Madrid train bombings).

4.10 If perceptions about the meaning and significance of risk, risk management, and legal risk can change (and there is no reason to suppose that current perceptions should be any more permanent than those which were more dominant fifteen years ago), is the pursuit of a definition of legal risk likely to have lasting value? The answer must surely be 'yes'. If we record how we understand the concept now, we can better understand how and why that understanding might change in the future. Definition is not an empty exercise. We cannot expect to tackle the serious, practical question of how to manage a specific kind of risk if we cannot say what we mean when we refer to it. In this part of the book we shall therefore consider how best to define legal risk in the context of the financial markets. We shall also look at the closely related question of legal risk sources, ie the social phenomena that generally cause legal risk to arise. An understanding of these sources is crucial if we are to understand the causation chains that generally give rise to 'legal risk problems'. When these causation chains are understood, both the definition of legal risk and the most appropriate means of managing it can be better understood.

C. Do We Need a Definition?

4.11 Notwithstanding what has been said above, there is a school of thought that holds that a definition of legal risk is not necessary. Rather like those who see no need to define what an elephant is 'because you know one when you see one', some would argue that there is sufficient (unwritten) consensus on the point to render the fine-tuning involved in a precise, written definition a waste of time. Others seek to rely on definitions (such as 'it's what lawyers advise on') that beg so many questions that they serve little purpose.[11] This seems to stem from a reluctance to 'get bogged down in detail'—combined perhaps with a dislike of the 'legalese' that detailed (ie precise) definitions can sometimes involve.[12] Running away from making our meaning clear is understandable but it is not,

---

[11] It is, of course, quite different for an in-house lawyer to say (as many do, somewhat ruefully) 'If I'm responsible for it, it's legal risk' when that statement is part of the justification for requiring a precise description of the area of responsibility. In any event, it is helpful, as a practical test of any definition to consider whether the scope of matters covered by it would generally be thought to fall within an in-house lawyer's area of responsibility.

[12] There is also a fear in some quarters that a definition that establishes legal risk as a distinct kind of risk might lead to 'double-counting' by regulators, ie that a bank could be asked to set aside capital twice for the same substantive risk because it happens to fall within another definition as well. (It has to be said that this seems unlikely; see, however, the example considered in Ch 5 below.)

in the final analysis, acceptable. Although many institutions have successfully managed legal risk in the past without the formality of a definition, the increasing scrutiny applied to banks' internal procedures (typically in the wake of a major financial scandal) by the media, regulatory authorities and, on occasions, litigants seeking someone to take the blame for a 'black hole' in a company's finances means that we now have to face up to the need to write down what may have simply been understood as common sense by earlier generations. Getting the details right is important. Defining legal risk is not a simple matter, and is not an exercise free of controversy, so it is worth analysing why the task is worth the effort.

Allocation of responsibility and effective risk management

First, we should recall that legal risk is regarded by the regulators (or at least by Basel II) as a category of operational risk.[13] Following the disappearance of exchange controls and the arrival of the deregulated, globalized era in financial markets, operational risk has assumed an enormous importance. We have seen how a single 'rogue trader'[14] (an example of operational risk) can fatally undermine a bank's capital with the stroke of a pen (or, more likely perhaps, the push of a button, the pressing of a computer key, or a telephone call). Derivative transactions involve risks on future events and market movements such as the price of oil or other commodities, equity and debt investments, interest rates and currency values that are very difficult to evaluate and even more difficult to regulate effectively. The operational risks involved here (whether or not they involve fraud) could, if triggered, have systemic effects on the financial system as a whole. The potential domino effect caused by the collapse of a major institution could be catastrophic. And that situation, it would seem, is much more likely to arise as a result of operational risk (say, a series of very badly misjudged positions taken by a bank's trader on commodities markets or the Tokyo Stock Exchange) than 'traditional' credit risk (where an important customer becomes insolvent and cannot pay its debts to the bank). **4.12**

So responsibility for operational risk management within a bank or other institution is immensely important, and the lines, and demarcation, of responsibility have to be very clear. Although the ultimate responsibility for risk management must lie with senior management, it seems sensible that the legal function in any institution should be significantly involved in the management of legal risk.[15] If responsibility is to be allocated to the lawyers effectively, it is important that all **4.13**

---

[13] See para Intro 1.24 n. 37 above. See, however, the views of Whittaker (General Counsel of the FSA) referred to below.
[14] See para 4.42 below.   [15] See Ch 10 below.

concerned have a common understanding of what legal risk actually is. A vague definition (or, worse, no definition at all) increases the risk of misunderstanding. It is, for example, in the interest of the lawyers particularly to correct the common misconception that legal risk is essentially the risk of being sued. Not every event that results in legal proceedings is necessarily attributable to legal risk (even though the management of those proceedings is likely to be the responsibility of lawyers). And the institution as a whole has to understand where and why the line is drawn. A definition is needed to facilitate this.

Impact on policy

4.14   It would, however, be wrong to see the definition as relevant only to the allocation of responsibility. Defining what we mean by legal risk also helps us to understand how the various component parts of the risk can best be managed. Further, the management of risk has an impact on a range of business policies undertaken by institutions. If we take, for example, a bank's policy on the selection of legal advisers,[16] we can see at once that this is likely to have some relevance to legal risk management. Suppose that a bank has a number of different law firms (sometimes called a 'panel') as its regular legal advisers. It might justify the panel composition with something like the following:

> We chose law firm A because we have a high regard for their knowledge of the credit derivatives market and their documentation skills in connection with that, as well as in other areas where we do business.

> We chose law firm B because they have a first-class litigation department and since a large bank like ours is always going to have a certain amount of court work (some of which can be very high-profile) we wanted the best people on our side.

> We chose law firm C because they have an excellent office in Moscow and we do an increasing amount of business there.

4.15   In making these policy decisions, the bank has, even if only subconsciously, thought about various kinds of risk (which most would see as legal risk) that it thinks law firms can help with. (It might, of course, have taken into account other factors as well. If the senior partner of the Moscow office of law firm C knows key figures in the local business community, the bank might find his advice and assistance on such matters very valuable, even though the advice does not relate to legal risk.) If, however, the bank was asked whether, in making its selection, it thought about its lawyers' expertise in preventing fraud by senior staff, its response would probably be something like:

> We want lawyers who would be good at helping us handle the consequences of fraud if it happens, but we have other, better qualified personnel and advisers to

---

[16] This is considered in more detail in Ch 10 below.

help us combat the risk of fraud occurring. For example, we have extremely rigorous vetting procedures for all new hires in all positions of any responsibility. Fraud is taken very seriously here but we do not see it as a legal risk as such.

The bank's selection processes, especially its selection criteria, are virtually **4.16** certain to involve assessment of different aspects of legal risk, and its management, whether or not it analyses its decisions by reference to such concepts. The policy is influenced by how the bank perceives legal risk. This role of risk assessment could also be illustrated by other examples not directly involving lawyers. For example, a decision as to whether or not to enter a new market may well be influenced by the legal risks associated with that market. If, say, a bank wishes to open a new office in Ruritania and trade in derivatives there, its procedures would be defective if it looked only at the litigious climate in the country and not at the local laws that were very uncertain (or hostile) as to the enforceability of various kinds of derivative contracts. If legal risk is relevant to a policy decision, it is important that all the relevant aspects of legal risk are considered. An incomplete or very vague definition is more likely to lead to errors.

Responsibility for corporate misbehaviour

Secondly, it should be recognized that the attribution of loss to legal risk tends, **4.17** for some, to soften the blow of accepting not just responsibility but some degree of fault or blame. Legal risk has the air of 'technical reasons' about it. In certain contexts, blaming loss on legal risks even comes close to implying that the non-lawyers in the institution deserve our sympathy. After all, how could they be expected to cope with the infernal complexities that the legal and regulatory system presents? 'My lawyer told me I could do this' or 'the legal department raised no objection' are sentiments that we often hear voiced when things go wrong. Blaming lawyers for misfortunes or worse has a long (and, of course, sometimes justifiable) track record. Blaming the law itself is a more modern habit (especially if it is a 'foreign' law). These habits may be hard to shake but, as a matter of corporate governance, they are not generally healthy. There is no reason why bad laws should not be criticized as much as bad lawyers. But recklessness, gross negligence, and other forms of corporate misbehaviour should not generally be confused with legal risk. Vagueness in definition (and especially in the context of related causation chains) makes it easier to fall to this temptation. The specific difficulties of framing a definition that covers appropriate Type 1 risks but excludes the more egregious forms of corporate misbehaviour are considered in more detail below.[17]

---

[17] See para 4.41.

Advantages of a 'norm'

4.18   Thirdly, although it is obviously right to allow institutions a degree of latitude as to how they approach risk management, it must surely be advantageous to be able to compare different management techniques by reference to a risk category about which a substantial degree of consensus as to meaning has been achieved. One needs to be able to compare like with like. It is also desirable that an institution that departs from 'the norm' knows what the norm actually is, so that it can justify its different stance.

4.19   We have seen how, in other contexts, the series of norms representing market practice is a major influence on the law as it applies to financial transactions. If a bank finds itself defending a lawsuit in connection with transactions involving, say, a fraudulent customer or rogue trader, it is likely to be of at least some assistance if it can show that its internal 'know your customer' and other procedures took into account legal risk, as that phrase is generally understood by other comparable market participants.

Need for flexibility

4.20   The meaning of legal risk may vary according to the context. An institution concerned, for example, with financial stability might have a different perspective (focusing more on Type 2 risks) than a 'supervising' regulator which is concerned more with consumer protection (and Type 1 risks). As an example, we could look at the approach of the FMLC. That body is evidently concerned primarily with legal uncertainty. It therefore tends to look at legal risk in the context of legislative or case law developments that might introduce an unacceptable level of uncertainty into market activities. It also looks at market developments that, in a sense, 'get ahead of' the law, where the legal basis for the new kind of transaction might not be clear. It would also be concerned if certain kinds of market transaction might result in institutions attracting significant exposure to lawsuits, but that would tend to be seen from the perspective of market stability rather than consumer protection. A market participant needs to be alert to all these legal risks. A reasonably detailed definition is more likely to raise the alarm when necessary than a very general one.

4.21   Finally, as the International Bar Association (IBA) definition set out at para 4.40 below shows, there are advantages in accepting that it may not be appropriate to strive for one perfect, all-encompassing definition as long as there is sufficient consensus around the core of the meaning. Not only do different institutions have different perspectives, depending on their business or role, we have seen that it is possible that the public perception of legal risk may change, over time, reflecting, amongst other things, changes in market behaviour. For example, our media now tend to concentrate much more on Type 1 risks (rather than Type 2 risks) than was the case in the early 1990s; this is a reflection, partly, of their close interest in the evolving role of the FSA as regulator and also, to some extent, in consumer rights.

Flexibility is not, however, to be confused with vagueness. Variations on a **4.22** central theme may be justifiable but the process of justification should itself be thorough. A proper definition of legal risk is to be welcomed, not for doctrinal reasons, but because it is useful. A 'high-level', very generally framed, definition may have some superficial appeal, but will not be of much help to those charged with risk management. To paraphrase certain definitions of this kind, it does not really advance things very much to state that 'legal risk is the risk that, in relation to one's legal position, things do not turn out as expected'. Such a definition may not be technically incorrect. But it is not a great deal of use.

D. The FSA's Definition

There is, as yet, no all-purpose, official definition of legal risk. However, the **4.23** FSA has published a definition for insurers as follows:[18]

> For insurers, legal risk is the risk that the law is proved to operate in a way adverse to the interests or objectives of the insurer where the insurer:
> a) did not consider its effect;
> b) believed its effect to be different; or
> c) operated with uncertainty as to its effect.

In principle, it would seem that a definition as broad as this should apply to **4.24** banks and other financial institutions as well, but the FSA's position on this is not yet clear. The definition raises a number of interesting questions:

(1) What is the purpose of the reference to 'proved'? Why not, for example, simply say 'the law operates'? What, in any event, constitutes proof? Would an adverse court decision qualify? What if it is subject to appeal? The reference also suggests that when there is a change in the legal assessment of an insurer's position that renders previously confident, positive advice to change to advice that doubts have arisen as to whether the legal position is satisfactory, no legal risk has materialized until the later advice is confident (and proven to be right) that there really is a legal problem that had not been appreciated before. This seems unnecessarily restrictive.
(2) Reckless behaviour (for example, refusing to take legal advice when a prudent businessman would do so) and, possibly, even deliberate criminal

---

[18] Previously contained in Guidance Note P3 of the FSA Interim Prudential Sourcebook for Insurers (this is currently deleted).

activity could be said to give rise to legal risk on the basis of this definition (either because of a failure to consider effect or because of a reckless mistake as to effect). It is questionable whether that is an appropriate application of the concept of legal risk, notwithstanding that the behaviour obviously has legal consequences.[19]

(3) The language relies heavily on an elastic interpretation of what is meant by the 'law operating'. If a party overlooks an important term in a long, complex contract that is against his interests, is that an instance of 'law operating'? If a party is aware of a term that appears to be in its favour but does not realize that it is unenforceable, presumably the fact of its unenforceability is a case of 'law operating'. But simply overlooking a term that is adverse to the party's interests is not such a case, at least not in the ordinary sense of the words. It is the contract that 'operates' in an unexpected way, not the law. And yet most would think that an error of this kind was an example of legal risk.

(4) The definition does not cover an adverse change in law. A new law may be introduced in a jurisdiction where a party carries on business that is clearly adverse to its interests. The party is aware of it and correctly assesses its implications. The definition is not satisfied. This may be because the FSA regards change in law as a political risk rather than a legal risk. It is true that there is a grey area here. However, there is a body of opinion that would regard change in law as legal risk and it would perhaps be desirable to clarify what is intended.

4.25 As with all definitions, the degree of precision is likely to be improved over time in the light of practical experience.[20] The FSA's definition can be compared with other definitions considered below.

---

[19] See para 4.41 below.

[20] It should be noted, however, that the FSA does not appear to favour too precise a definition. In his paper presented to an IBA Conference on 22 May 2003 (which is published on the FSA's website), Andrew Whittaker (the FSA's General Counsel) gave a list of various kinds of risk, including internal and external fraud, incomplete legal documentation, improper trading and money laundering and 'sales of unauthorised products' and expressed the view that 'these can all be described equally well as forms of legal risk, and as forms of operational risk. It is not necessarily helpful to try to draw a distinction between one or the other in deciding how they should be addressed . . . It should be emphasised that the mere fact that there are legal aspects to operational risk does not mean that there are not also legal aspects to other forms of risk, including market risk, credit risk, and indeed strategic and reputational risk. The fact that the Basle Capital Accord refers to legal risk in the context of operational risk should not be taken to mean that all forms of legal risk must be treated as operational risk—the legal aspects of operational risk should be dealt with alongside operational risk, while the legal aspects of other forms of risk can be dealt with alongside those other forms of risk.' In Hadjiemmanuil, 'Legal risks and fraud: capital charges, control and insurance' in Alexander (ed), *Operational Risk: regulation, analysis and management* the author also notes the 'abrupt manner' in which Basel II brings the concept into discussion but then leaves it 'undeveloped', and that 'Significantly, the Committee takes it for granted that legal risk is part of the broader notion of operational risk. This is neither self-evident nor universally accepted.'

E. A Bank of England Definition—the Cause-based Approach

In its paper entitled 'Oversight of Payment Systems' of November 2000, the **4.26**
Bank of England defined legal risk in the context of risk in payment systems as,
'the risk that unexpected interpretation of the law or legal uncertainty will
leave the payment system or members with unforeseen financial exposures and
possible losses'.

This definition is obviously intended for a narrower purpose than the FSA **4.27**
definition and has to be read in that light. Nevertheless, there are a number of
interesting points of comparison:

(1) The definition is cause-based. Its structure is: 'something untoward happens
    and this causes exposure and possible loss'. In this context the 'something' is
    'unexpected interpretation of the law' (by a court or perhaps by a regulatory
    authority) or (and this is much more general) 'legal uncertainty'. The com-
    parable part of the FSA definition is simply concerned with the way 'law is
    proved to operate'.
(2) The definition does not turn upon the acts or omissions of the person
    affected. There is no equivalent of paragraphs a), b), and c) of the FSA
    definition (see para 4.23 above) for the 'payment system or members'.
    However, it is a requirement that the exposure and (as a result) the losses are
    'unforeseen'.
(3) It would seem impossible for reckless 'corporate misbehaviour'[21] to fall
    inside the Bank of England definition.

There are advantages in the cause-based approach (as opposed to an effects- **4.28**
based approach). As described in more detail in Chapter 5 below, the key criteria
of legal risk are generally described by ordinary businessmen by reference to the
'legal' nature of the event that might (if the risk materializes) cause loss. It is
important, as we shall see, that the link between such event and the possible loss
is, in some sense, causal (even if the event is only a contributory cause). If, at
the time the event occurred, it was clear that the loss was going to be suffered
any way, it would be wrong to regard the loss as attributable to legal risk even
though (a) a legal risk arose and (b) a loss followed.

We may contrast this approach with effects-based approaches to the definition. **4.29**
This is the approach that is followed where an event is characterized as
involving legal risk because it leads on to, or has the effect of, 'legal consequences' (for example, fines or penalties). The effects-based approach has

---

[21] See para 4.44.

superficial attractions but is flawed. It is an easy trap to fall into because when we use expressions like 'health risk', 'financial risk', or 'injury risk', we are evidently qualifying the risk by reference to the nature of the potential effect or consequence. But when we talk of legal risk in the specialized context of its being a sub-category of operational risk we must have in mind a narrower concept than 'risks that can have legal consequences'.[22] What we have in mind is that there is something in the nature of the events and surrounding circumstances that imbues the risk with a 'legal' quality. Thus, if a bank does not take appropriate steps to keep its legal documentation up to date with the law or fails to ensure that its staff are trained with regard to changing regulatory requirements, it is (a) taking operational risks and (b) exposing itself to risks that, by their nature, have a 'legal' quality about them because (in these examples) the bank is causing 'legal risk events' to occur by not being sufficiently diligent in the safeguarding of its rights under documentation or by increasing the risk of falling foul of legal requirements. This legal quality may relate to the bank's contractual rights, its compliance with laws and regulations, the effectiveness of security taken by it, or other comparable concerns. It is true that all these situations may ultimately result in the bank being involved in legal proceedings (although that is not certain) but the essential 'legal' nature of the risk is identifiable at the earlier point, at the time of the event that causes the risk to arise.

F. The FLP's Approach

4.30 In a draft paper circulated by the FLP to various interested parties (shortly after the formation of its steering group on legal risk in July 2001)[23] the FLP set out a description of various sets of circumstances that 'might be thought to constitute legal risk'. This was, it must be emphasized, very much a preliminary paper for

---

[22] Otherwise, all operational risks would be legal risks. This may be consistent with the view expressed by Whittaker, referred in n 20 above, that in this context one should be concerned with 'legal aspects of operational risk' rather than legal risk as a category of risk in its own right. However, the better view, which is supported by the prevailing usage of the expression, is that there is something peculiarly 'legal' about the events giving rise to the risk that justify it being described as legal risk. This view clearly explains the approach taken by the FLP and the IBA, referred to below (and seems to be more consistent with Basel II). Further, as Hadjemmanuil (n 20 above) points out: 'All financial events affecting a bank can be expressed as legal events' and 'all banking risks could be redescribed as legal risks.' Hadjemmanuil focuses on three main categories of examples of, in effect, causes ie: '(a) legally flawed actions of the bank or its employees and agents; (b) uncertainties regarding the requirements and effects of the law itself; or (c) the relative inefficiency of a country's legal system'. See also the categorization used in Ch 5 below.

[23] See para Intro 1.16. This is now available on the FMLC's website at <http://www.fmlc.org>.

the purpose of stimulating comment and discussion, but it is nevertheless a very clear indication of what many market participants would have thought 'legal risk' meant at that time. It is unlikely (having regard to the various subsequent responses to the work of the IBA working party on legal risk)[24] that the general perception has changed much since. The relevant part of the paper read as follows:

> Legal risk situations affecting a commercial institution ('the company') might be grouped under three headings . . .

Organisational Legal Risk

This is the risk connected with the maintenance of the company's assets and property and with the internal affairs of the company. Examples:

1. The risk that the company might fail adequately to protect its intellectual property assets or that the ownership and/or value of these assets might be successfully challenged by third parties.

2. The risk of liability to shareholders or that shareholders might be able to compel action contrary to the wishes of the management of the company.

3. The risk that management action may fail to take proper account of employment law or of the rights of employees or trade unions.

4. The possibility that the company may fail to see the consequences of an act or omission because of:
   i) failure to take appropriate legal advice;
   ii) shortage or inadequacy of in-house legal advice; or
   iii) defects in internal procedures for identifying when legal advice is needed

Legal Methodology Risk

This is the risk that the methods adopted and steps taken to protect the company's assets against claims by others or to protect against liability to pay damages or compensation to others are inadequate. Examples:

1. In a commercial transaction, the company does not take warranties from its counterparty, but relies instead on its due diligence procedures. The due diligence procedures fail to reveal a defect, leaving the company with no legal recourse.

2. The use of standard or 'generic' legal opinions on the content of legal rules in overseas jurisdictions may fail to reveal an issue relevant to a particular transaction because of the general nature of the opinion given.[25]

3. The risk that the only available method of taking protection can never be completely effective. For example, opinions given about the ownership of and capacity of 'tax haven' companies with bearer shares can never, in practice, avoid the possibility of fraud.

---

[24] See below.
[25] The use of formal legal opinions is explored further in Ch 11 below.

Conduct-of-Business Legal Risk

This is the risk that, in the course of the conduct of the company's commercial operations, it will incur obligations or liabilities that were not foreseen, or are greater than were foreseen or that its rights and claims prove to be fewer, or of a lower value, than had been expected. Examples:

1. The possibility that contractual rights will be void or unenforceable because of:
    i) illegality;
    ii) a technical defect (e.g. lack of restriction or registration);
    iii) lack of capacity (of either party).

2. The possibility that a contractual or statutory provision may be interpreted differently by a court than by the company either:
    i) because of misunderstanding by the company; or
    ii) because of misunderstanding by the court.

    This risk is particularly acute where the contractual documentation is complex and the court is not specialist (e.g. if a technical point of insurance or shipping law comes before a bankruptcy court in a country that is not a major commercial jurisdiction).

3. The possibility that a court will take a view on a technical point that is different from the view on which the company has relied, with adverse consequences e.g. a court may categorise a contract as a gambling contract (and, accordingly, unenforceable under local law) contrary to the view taken by the company.[26]

4. The possibility that legal proceedings will have an adverse consequence greater than expected (or a favourable consequence lower than expected) e.g. the company takes an over-optimistic view of the outcome of litigation or regulatory proceedings.

5. The operations of the company produce unforeseen liabilities to third parties e.g. the company becomes liable to compensate third parties or account as a constructive trustee because of the default or fraud by another party to a transaction with the company.

6. The possibility that the company's operations might infringe the legal rights of third parties e.g. breach of copyright or patent infringement.

7. The risk that the company's claim, although sound in law, will not be capable of satisfaction in practice e.g. a counterparty may refuse to honour its obligations and precipitate litigation as a delaying tactic. The company's claim, although sound in law, will not be satisfied because of the insolvency of the debtor.

8. The risk that a claim by the company, although it appears likely to succeed, may fail because of unforeseen events occurring during the litigation process (e.g. the loss of a crucial witness).

9. The risk that the company's rights, although they appear secure in law, may need to be enforced in an overseas jurisdiction with which the company is unfamiliar. Its right to claim may, therefore, be subject to difficulties of procedure of which it is unaware.

---

[26] See Ch 9 below.

Although these examples do not themselves constitute a definition of legal risk, **4.31**
they are immensely helpful in illustrating what many would regard as the core of
the concept. The tripartite classification of 'Organisational', 'Methodology',
and 'Conduct-of-Business' is also likely to be at least one useful way of looking
at legal risk issues from the perspective of risk management.[27] It will be apparent
that Type 1 and Type 2 risks could fall into any of the three classes, although
Type 1 risks are more likely to arise under 'Organisational', whereas Type 2 risks
seem more likely in the context of the other two classes.

G. A Definition Proposed by UNIDROIT

In its explanatory notes to the draft Convention discussed in more detail in **4.32**
Chapter 7 below, UNIDROIT (in the context of risk associated with multi-
tiered securities holding systems) notes that: 'Legal risk commonly refers to a
situation where the applicable law does not provide for a predictable and sound
solution.' It goes on to observe:

> For example, legal risk might arise in scenarios where the relevant factual issue is
> not addressed by the law. Even where there were rules in place, these could be
> contradictory or give rise to different interpretations. In such a 'gap' or 'lack of
> clarity' situation, parties may enter a transaction without knowing about the
> specific risk they face, which they might then realise later. Or, parties may know
> the risk beforehand but then have to invest time and money filling the gap or
> overcoming the lack of certainty by way of contractual agreements. Legal risk
> might also refer to situations where the answer provided by the applicable law does
> not fit the market reality, or where the law unnecessarily complicates or burdens a
> transaction. Often, legal requirements that are rooted in traditional legal concepts
> and created to promote legal certainty lose their original purpose when applied to
> modern securities holding and transfer structures. The consequence of imposing
> requirements that complicate a transaction can be time-consuming and costly.
> Furthermore, a complicated procedure makes each process of perfection of a
> transaction specifically vulnerable to mistakes. On the other hand, in other cases,
> the law provides for legal concepts that make the use of specific kinds of transac-
> tion that are used in or requested by the practice impossible and thereby creates a
> barrier.

It sometimes appears that the law has become out of date, or that the practices **4.33**
of the market have raced on ahead of the law, apparently regardless of whether
or not the law will give effect to the new way of doing things. (If the risk of
'getting too far ahead of the law' has been appreciated and 'priced in' this is not
always obvious.) It also, regrettably, often seems to be the case that legislators are
slow to make the changes that are needed to bring the law up to date. The risks

---

[27] See Part IV of this book.

of delay do not always catch the eye—another facet of low probability/high impact scenarios that are usually represented by Type 2 legal risk.

H. Two Definitions Used by Banks' Lawyers

4.34 Most bank in-house lawyers use a working definition of legal risk. Some are much more precise than others. Some pre-date Basel II, others have evidently been greatly influenced by it. The following definition of legal risk was suggested, in the course of discussions with the author, by a senior lawyer working for a major bank in London:

> As far as the financial institution is concerned, legal risk is the risk of having legal action taken, or a legal sanction enforced, against that institution, or the institution being unable to enforce a legal right, arising directly or indirectly out of the legal relationship between the institution and a contractual counterparty, a third party, or a governmental or non-governmental authority.

4.35 This definition is admirably brief, precise, and comprehensive. It reflects the distinction between Type 1 and Type 2 risks and, although it is not explicitly phrased in terms of cause of loss, that is clearly the implication. However, the events described (legal action, legal sanction, inability to enforce legal right, etc) are essentially effects of some other (unspecified) event and, as a result, the definition could be interpreted as meaning that any event that gives rise to a legal action against the bank is an event involving legal risk. In that respect, the definition, if taken literally, may be too wide, if it is used to define the lawyer's area of responsibility.

4.36 Another definition which emerged in discussions with bank in-house lawyers is as follows: 'legal risk is failure to understand (and/or act in accordance with) the legal environment (including any legislation, law, contracts and duties) relevant to the bank's rights, obligations or assets or to the achievement of the bank's strategic and business objectives'.

4.37 This language is really 'one step back' from defining legal risk. It describes events (failure to understand the legal position or to comply with legal requirements, etc) that can give rise to legal risk without stating what that risk actually consists of. In this regard, the first of the two definitions considered here (which spells out consequences, such as sanctions) is preferable. However, if it is permissible to read into the second definition a phrase to the effect that it is concerned with 'the risk of loss arising from' these events, this problem is easily solved. The definition also has the advantage that it is clearly cause-based rather than effects based. It makes no distinction between deliberate non-compliance and negligent non-compliance. This difficult aspect of all attempts to define legal risk is considered further below.

What these examples show (and others could be quoted)[28] is that bank lawyers **4.38**
are concerned to have the concept of legal risk defined, but that, to date, there is
not only a lack of 'custom and usage' about the definition, there is in fact
considerable disparity in the various approaches taken.

I. The International Bar Association's Definition

As mentioned above,[29] the FLP initiated a steering group to look at legal risk in **4.39**
July 2001.[30] The FLP, however, was disbanded before the steering group could
make much progress. At the suggestion of various individuals who had been
involved, the work of the FLP steering group was taken up by a specially formed
working group of the International Bar Association (IBA).[31] This group undertook a number of activities, including the production of a paper (by Joanna
Benjamin) on the sources of legal risk (which is referred to in more detail in the
next chapter) and the organization of a symposium on legal risk issues in
October 2003.[32] At the time of the symposium, the definition set out below was
circulated to participants and formed part of the discussions.

The definition produced by the IBA working party reads as follows: **4.40**

*(NB: This definition needs to be read with the accompanying notes, which affect how it
should be interpreted).*

Legal risk is the risk of loss to an institution which is primarily caused by:–
(a) a defective transaction; or
(b) a claim (including a defence to a claim or a counterclaim) being made or some
     other event occurring which results in a liability for the institution or other
     loss (for example, as a result of the termination of a contract); or
(c) failing to take appropriate measures to protect assets (for example, intellectual
     property) owned by the institution; or
(d) change in law.

---

[28] The First Giovannini Clearing and Settlement Report defines legal risk as 'the possibility of
an unexpected application of a law/regulation or because a contract cannot be enforced' (*sic*) and
comments that 'Cross-border settlement involves multiple legal jurisdictions, such that this risk is
increased'. Other examples of definitions used by bank, and other, in-house lawyers can be found
in (July/September 2005) 1(1) *Law Department Quarterly*.

[29] See para Intro 1.16.

[30] The members of the FLP's steering group were Lord Eatwell, Francis Neate, Ernest Patrikis,
Antonio Sainz de Vicuna, Paul Tucker, and the author. The group was chaired by the FLP's Chief
Executive, Colin Bamford.

[31] The members of the IBA working party were Joanna Benjamin, Michael Crystal QC, Derek
Arnott, Sebastian Hofert, Klaus Loeber and, as co-chairs, Hugh Pigott and the author. The
working party was formed under the auspices of Sub-committee E8 (International Financial Law
Reform) of the IBA's Banking Law Committee (Committee E).

[32] The proceedings of this symposium (co-chaired by Hugh Pigott and the author have been
published as a special supplement to Butterworths JIBFL, April 2004.

The reference to a defective transaction in (a) above includes:–

    (i) entering into a transaction which does not allocate rights and obligations and associated risks in the manner intended;

   (ii) entering into a transaction which is or may be determined to be void or unenforceable in whole or with respect to a material part (for whatever reason);

  (iii) entering into a transaction on the basis of representations or investigations which are shown to be misleading or false or which fail to disclose material facts or circumstances;

  (iv) misunderstanding the effect of one or more transactions (for example, believing that a right of set-off exists when it does not or that certain rights will be available on the insolvency of a party when they will not);

   (v) entering into a contract which does not, or may not, have an effective or fair dispute resolution procedure (or procedures for enforcement of judgements/arbitral decisions) applicable to it;

  (vi) entering into a contract inadvertently;

 (vii) security arrangements that are, or may be, defective (for whatever reason).

All references above to a transaction shall include a trust, any kind of transfer or creation of interests in assets of any kind, any kind of insurance, any kind of debt or equity instrument and any kind of negotiable instrument.

All references to entering into a transaction include taking an assignment of a contract or entering into a transaction in reliance upon a contract which is itself a defective transaction.

NOTES:

1.   The consultation paper of 1 July 2003 issued by the EU Commission Services contains a 'Working Document' setting out proposed risk-based capital requirements for financial institutions. Article 106 of that document states:–
   'Operational risk is the risk of loss resulting from inadequate or failed internal processes, people and systems or from external events, including legal risk.'
   It is arguable therefore that a legal risk which has been deliberately and prudently taken would not fall within the concept of legal risk described in Article 106 (since it would not result from inadequate or failed internal processes, people or systems) unless it can in some sense be attributed to an 'external event'.

2.   The document referred to in note 1 above does not offer any definition of 'legal risk'.

3.   The attached definition should not be regarded as prescriptive. Each institution may wish to adapt the definition for its own particular purposes and, especially, to reflect any allocation of responsibility within that institution (for example, to the legal department) which may not be consistent with the definition as it stands. Any specific views of regulators, as they become known, will also, obviously, need to be taken into account.

4.   With regard to paragraph (b) of the definition, institutions may wish to make a distinction between claims which reflect a risk that has been anticipated (but nevertheless deliberately taken) and claims which come as a genuine 'surprise'. It is not thought necessary to make any distinction between contractual, tortious or other claims in this context (but see 5 below).

However, the prevailing view (and, it is submitted, best practice) is that risks which arise from wilful or reckless behaviour (including fraud) – although they are operational risks – should not properly be regarded as legal risks.

5. It is suggested that the risk of loss caused by contractual commitments to pay money (e.g. indemnities or guarantees) entered into voluntarily should not be regarded as legal risk. The risk of loss caused by a breach of contract is a more difficult question. It is suggested that each institution is likely to have its own procedures for ensuring that clear contractual commitments (e.g. to pay a sum due on a due date) are properly complied with, and may take the view that failure to follow those procedures is primarily a non-legal operational risk. However, it is arguable that extremely complex contractual arrangements might give rise to a more technical risk of breach simply on the grounds that the requirements of the contract have not been fully appreciated. Institutions may, in appropriate cases, regard such situations as an example of legal risk.

6. Situations may arise in the context of paragraphs (a), (b) or (d) which have strong political overtones and may more properly be regarded as examples of political risk or at least a combination of legal risk and political risk. Whether or not any such situation is to be treated as legal risk will largely reflect the allocation of responsibility within any given institution and may also reflect how that institution perceives political risk in any particular country. It is suggested, for example, that outright confiscation of assets by a governmental authority is, generally, pure political risk and not legal risk. On the other hand, some institutions might regard political interference with the judicial process as a form of legal risk. (See also paragraph (v) of the definition.) How responsibility is allocated will no doubt reflect the institution's own judgement as to which departments or officers are best placed to provide advice on such risk situations.

7. 'Change in law' has been added as paragraph (d) in order to cover situations where such a change (whether as a result of statute or case law) does not also lead on to a loss under paragraph (a) or (b). It should be noted that, in certain contexts, a change in law may be more properly regarded as a political risk event rather than true legal risk (see 6 above).

Key features of the IBA definition are as follows: **4.41**

(1) Sub-paragraphs (a) and (b) deal with Type 2 risks and Type 1 risks respectively. The two kinds of risk sit alongside each other somewhat uneasily, having nothing in common of substance except the fact that the market has evidently decided to apply the epithet 'legal' to both of them.

(2) Subparagraphs (c) and (d) address two other situations that members of the IBA working party felt were commonly regarded as examples of legal risk. A failure to register a security interest in the appropriate official registry would be an example falling within (c). Although there would be situations where (a) and (d) overlap, it was felt that a change in law might, of itself, affect an institution's legal or financial position adversely without necessarily

involving a defective transaction. Change in law therefore appears as a separate head of legal risk in the definition.

(3) Subparagraphs (i) to (vii) give a number of illustrations of what subparagraph (a) is intended to cover. On the purely technical level, these subparagraphs may not be necessary for the definition (although they do result in the concept of 'defective transaction' being given a very comprehensive, if not extended, meaning). However, it was felt that it would be useful to market participants (and assist with risk management) to provide these examples, some of which are more obvious than others.

(4) The 'grey areas' which are felt to be unavoidable in the definitional exercise are, in a sense, acknowledged by the notes, which significantly qualify the literal text of the definition.

(5) The difficult borderline between legal risk and political risk is referred to in Note 6. The general purpose of the notes is to explain where some of the more difficult borderline issues lie and to assist institutions in forming their own view as to the appropriate parameters of legal risk for the purpose of risk management. Political risk will often have a number of the characteristics of legal risk (for example, a confiscatory law may render certain contractual rights invalid under the law of the jurisdiction in question) and, in some countries, the judiciary may in any case be somewhat 'politicized'. A country that poses excessive legal risk, in effect, invites those who do business there to take a political decision. It was felt that there should be a degree of flexibility in decisions as to which situations fell on which side of the legal/political line.

(6) An even more difficult borderline is addressed in Note 4. As indicated earlier in this chapter, it seems appropriate (and this was the view of the working party) to draw a line that separates wilful or reckless behaviour from 'innocent' mistakes or misjudgements. Those who deliberately fly in the face of well-known legal requirements create serious operational risks, but it seemed to the working party to be a misuse of language to characterize the consequences as legal risk. However, there is certainly a case for distinguishing between bad institutional behaviour and the behaviour of a rogue individual or group of individuals which is unanticipated. It is at least strongly arguable that the 'surprise' element (as mentioned in Note 4 to the IBA definition) is important for the purpose of drawing the line between legal risk and other risks. It is also important as regards the insurability of the risk. This is considered further below.[33]

---

[33] See para 4.43 et seq.

(7) The definition does not make any specific reference to reputational loss. Obviously, a legal risk event (especially if it involves a Type 1 risk) could give rise to reputational loss, and this could be a very serious matter not only for an individual institution, but also for market confidence generally. The management of reputational risk is now enormously important for many institutions, particularly following well-publicized bank involvement in corporate scandals such as Enron, Worldcom, and Parmalat. However, it was felt by those who framed the definition that, in the context of the private sector, reputational loss was ultimately important only as an interim step (albeit a very important one) on the way to financial loss, which of course is covered in the 'effects' part of the definition.[34] Banks, as corporations, cannot really complain about hurt feelings, caused by damage to reputation, as a head of damage independently of financial loss. It should be noted, however, that very different considerations apply to regulators, politicians, and others in the public sector, who are likely to be only too conscious of reputational risk, quite independently of any financial consequences.[35] Further, even in the private sector, it would perhaps be unwise to overlook the potential damage to reputations of individuals working in financial institutions which become involved in financial scandals or other operational mishaps which are triggered by Type 1 risks. Tony Williams, formerly managing partner of Andersen Legal, put the point in the form of a question that every senior in-house lawyer should consider: 'Are you aware of the legal *and* reputational risks for your company? As general counsel you should know the legal risks that confront your business. However, a "legal" transaction may have significant reputational consequences for your company.'[36] In his article 'Bankers in the business of managing risk', published in 1998, Tiner stressed the virtually priceless nature of a bank's reputation:

> Financial service organisations worldwide have one asset, which is not on their balance sheet and indeed is perhaps not even capable of being valued, but which is their very life blood—their reputation. With a product which is intangible, fungible and instantly transferable, confidence is paramount. An

---

[34] It should be noted, however, as Power has pointed out in his paper, 'The Risk Management of Everything', that a relatively minor legal infringement, such as having a company pay directors' parking fines, can, if given adverse treatment in the media, have a disproportionate reputational effect, which then leads on to much greater financial consequences than might have been envisaged. The management of reputational risk in its own right (however it may be linked to legal risk) has become enormously important.

[35] Certain aspects of reputational risk management are, of course, not entirely dissimilar to the dark art of 'spin'.

[36] Article in *Global Counsel*, May 2003.

institution whose reputation is sound can generally compete on fair terms in the market place. An institution whose reputation has deteriorated over time or taken a severe shock risks losing the confidence of its customers, employees and shareholders, and will find the market place has upwardly repriced its borrowing costs.[37]

Many banks appear to look at legal and reputational risk management together, when designing risk management functions and some feel that reputational risk management is best handled primarily by lawyers. As was demonstrated by Citibank's recent controversial eurozone government bond trades, which led to the bank apologizing for the 'inappropriate, unrealistic and . . . juvenile' behaviour of some of its staff and investigations by several European regulators, it would seem that the borderline might not always be clear.[38]

(8) The definition selects certain kinds of causes of loss as the central component of its answer to the question: what is legal risk? How is that selection justified? The causes of loss all have the 'legal quality' referred to above, but the answer to this question is pragmatic rather than conceptual. The selection is based on how the term 'legal risk' is most commonly used rather than on 'pure' logic. The 'grey areas' in the definition follow from this, reflecting the divergence of practice in the market. There seems to be little merit in taking a hard-and-fast view on whether, say, a certain kind of political risk is or is not a legal risk. As long as those responsible for risk management are aware that a risk exists and that it may fall on either side of the line, it is best for their judgment to prevail, given that the regulatory treatment will most likely be the same however the risk is categorized. Notwithstanding the grey areas, a loss which is properly attributable to legal risk will feature one or more of the events described in the definition in the causation chain leading to the loss.[39]

J. The 'Rogue Trader'

4.42 The analysis of the nature of the risk posed by the employee who 'goes off the rails', or the 'rogue trader' raises a number of interesting issues. As noted above, it seems inappropriate, as a matter of general principle, to classify an institution's wilful or reckless behaviour (or its consequences) as giving rise to legal risk (although it clearly involves a form of operational risk) notwithstanding the

---

[37] (1998) 8 JIBFL 323. [38] See *Financial Times*, 2 February 2005.
[39] See further Ch 5 below.

obvious 'legal' connotations. However, although a bank cannot escape responsibility for its rogue traders, there is, in certain cases, an element of fortuity (from the perspective of the bank) about activities carried on by a dishonest employee, out to line his own pockets, which could almost be compared to theft from the employer. The risk posed by such activities is potentially much more serious than conventional theft, since it may have either a direct financial consequence sufficient to bring down the bank or a reputational consequence that leads to the same result. It would be understandable if this combined potential effect of rogue behaviour, at least in certain situations, was felt by some institutions to come so close to legal risk as to merit the same or a very similar response as regards its management.

Categorization of this kind of risk may be assisted by considering how it is now **4.43** regarded by the insurance market. In October 2003 the Lloyd's Market Association announced the publication of a new Wordwide Financial Institutions Professional Liability policy (NMA 3000) which it described as 'Lloyd's future mainstream financial institutions' professional liability policy'. The accompanying press announcement included a number of comments that were clearly relevant to rogue traders (or, to quote the language of the policy in relation to the relevant head of risk covered, 'loss caused by a Dishonest or Fraudulent Act or Omission by an Employee'). It was, for example, said that the policy provided cover for 'realistically insurable professional risks. It is infused with the principle of fortuity, which is fundamental to the concept of insurance, and provides cover for those risks which are unplanned, unintended and unanticipated.' The policy is 'intended to supplement good management practice, good communication and a controlled environment, and provide coverage for those risks which, despite "best efforts" to avoid them, nevertheless result. In line with this, the Policy does not cover claims which result from an insured's management's intentional wrong doing, calculated business decisions or conscious risk-taking.'

In relation to Type 1 risks, many would maintain that a similar exclusion **4.44** should apply.[40] To describe intentional wrongdoing by a bank's management as

---

[40] The position is different for Type 2 risks. A bank which has bought a large number of trade receivables from a customer might, for example, take a calculated risk in not serving notice of an assignment on debtors (perhaps because it would be costly or impractical to do so). This involves a deliberately taken legal risk (because serving notice confers a number of important protections, eg removing the right of the debtor to get a good discharge if it pays the bank's customer instead of the bank). This 'behaviour' by the bank is not 'corporate misbehaviour'. It involves no criminal offence, tort or breach of regulation. On the contrary it is a very common way of proceeding. The risk taken would be regarded in the market as a legitimately taken legal risk (even though it might not strictly fall within the Basel II 'definition'—see note 1 to the IBA definition). The deliberate commission of an offence or tort (giving rise to Type 1 risk) would not be regarded in this way.

'taking a legal risk' seems unacceptably economical with the truth. One would not say that a burglar takes a legal risk when he decides to break and enter. It would be rather like describing a footballer who deliberately maims an opponent to stop a goal being scored as committing 'a professional foul'. The implicit suspension of moral judgment in the language used is completely inappropriate.

4.45 The wording of the Lloyd's Market Association policy expands on the distinction between institutional bad behaviour and the behaviour of an individual 'rogue' in a number of areas. One of these is in relation to mis-selling. The risk of loss arising from mis-selling is excluded from cover but there is an 'exclusion from the exclusion' as the language set out below shows.

> Underwriters shall not be liable for payment of Loss[41] incurred in connection with any Claim ... based on arising out of, relating to or involving, directly or indirectly, the actual or alleged non-suitability or misdescription of, or act, error, omission or misrepresentation concerning the nature or purpose of, any investment product (including securities, commodities, currencies, and options and futures transactions and all other forms of derivatives) designed, issued or marketed by or on behalf of the Assured, whether such investment product was sold by or on behalf of the Assured or by or on behalf of some other person or entity *except where such Claim as based on, arises out of, relates to, or involves the failure by an individual full-time or part-time Employee of the Assured, while acting in the ordinary course of his or her employment by the Assured, to observe, follow and/or implement the applicable rules, guidelines and policies of the Assured and such Claim is otherwise covered under this Policy*[42]

4.46 One obvious conclusion to be drawn from this language is that, to benefit from cover, a bank (which would be the 'Assured') should have in place 'rules, guidelines and/or policies' that relate to the activities described.[43] The approach of institutions to the content of such rules, guidelines, and policies is considered in more detail in Part IV of this book. The general point to be noted here is that it should be possible to lay down rules and policies that record clearly how an institution expects its employees to behave in relation to activities that may expose the institution to claims and it is in the institution's own interest that it does so. It seems reasonable to suggest that an individual who breaks those rules or policies exposes the institution to legal risk (and possibly other risks) but where the fault really lies with the

---

[41] The reader should appreciate that some of the expressions quoted have their own defined meanings in the policy. To understand the full meaning of any passage quoted, there is no substitute for reading the policy as a whole.

[42] Emphasis added.

[43] There is explicit language elsewhere in the policy that states that there will not be cover if such rules, etc do not exist.

institution's own management[44] the legal risk label is likely to be misleading and inappropriate.

---

[44] The LMA Policy also excludes cover where a claim results from 'any Corporate or Business Policy of the Assured' the latter expression being defined as:

... any activity which has been expressly or impliedly approved, condoned, ratified or endorsed by any two or more members of the Assured's management and which results in a financial disadvantage to any two or more of the Assured's former or existing customers to whom the Assured owes or owed a legal duty or obligation; and either

(a) the Assured ... received revenue or some other financial benefit to which they are not entitled . . .; or

(b) the Financial Services Authority or any equivalent ... regulatory body ... or court or tribunal ... orders ... the Assured ... to pay a fine or penalty or punitive or exemplary or aggravated or multiplied damages . . .

It will be appreciated that the existence of rules and policies, etc will not let management (and therefore the institution) off the hook (and thus allow cover) if they knew of the misbehaviour and expressly or impliedly condoned it.

5

SOURCES

One final problem with credit default swaps was that, as with any insurance policy, payment hinged on the language describing what was covered—the definition of a default. A loan agreement was a lengthy document that typically specified numerous standard events of default . . . In contrast, credit swap agreements were slim documents that allowed the parties to use any definition of 'default' . . . In their effort to develop highly customized credit default swaps, banks had created unforeseen difficulties. Having done hundreds of billions of dollars of credit default swaps based on simple documentation, the banks finally understood why the underlying loan agreements had been so lengthy.

The consequence was that parties to credit default swaps bore *legal risk* associated with whether obligations had been triggered. A party that believed it was hedged might be whipsawed if the language in one credit default swap required payment while the language in an offsetting swap did not.[1]

A. Sources of Legal Risk

We may have developed a reasonably common understanding of what legal risk **5.01** is, but why does it arise at all? In a paper presented in November 2003 to a UNIDROIT seminar on 'Legal Risk and Market Efficiency',[2] Morton, reflecting on, essentially, Type 2 risks, points out that:

A law may be uncertain, widely misunderstood or not clearly defined, or a law may be very clear and well understood but simply not up to the task. It may be defective; it may be incomplete; it may leave gaps which simply do not permit people to do the transactions they would like to do, or it may be burdensome; it may impose irrelevant antiquated or simply over engineered procedural requirements which make it expensive and cumbersome to operate.

---

[1] Partnoy, 'Infectious Greed', p. 382.   [2] See further Ch 7 below.

5.02 Defects in the law such as those described above present a readily identifiable source of legal risk. However, there are others. For example, as indicated in the quotation at the start of this chapter, legal risk may arise simply as a result of poor documentation. In the 2003 paper produced for the IBA working party, referred to at para 4.39 above, Benjamin identified four categories of social phenomena that represent sources of legal risk.[3] These are:

(1) the behaviour of financial institutions themselves;
(2) the nature of the financial markets;
(3) problems within the law; and
(4) the interaction of law and finance.

5.03 Understanding the sources of legal risk is at least as important as understanding the component parts of a detailed definition. Only in this way can we understand why legal risks arise in the first place. Developing such an understanding is crucial if we are to design systems and procedures intended to manage the risks. The sources of legal risk identified by Benjamin are considered in turn below.

B. The Behaviour of Financial Institutions

5.04 Benjamin subdivides this heading into four further subcategories, ie limited legal awareness; implementation failure; exploiting the letter of the law; and outsourcing.

Limited legal awareness

5.05 Ignorance of the law, as we all know, is 'no excuse', but it does provide a rich source of legal risk. It is, of course, a comparatively rare phenomenon in the case of major, well-managed financial institutions, who are in a position to access the best legal advice available. However, even with the very sophisticated, errors do inevitably occur from time to time in a market which is constantly in search of 'new products', which usually require a great deal of legal ingenuity to devise (and, sometimes, to sell). It may seem a harsh judgment on those involved but the *Hammersmith and Fulham* case certainly appears to fall into this category (the less likely alternative being that a known risk was deliberately taken).

---

[3] See Joanna Benjamin, 'Sources of Legal Risk for Financial Institutions', set out in App 1 to the Report of the IBA Symposium on Legal Risk (October 2003) published as a special supplement to Butterworths JIBFL, April 2004. As Benjamin acknowledges, the categories are not exhaustive and there is a certain amount of overlap. This chapter (with very minor changes) adopts Benjamin's categorization throughout, although the author, of course, accepts sole responsibility for the text. References in this chapter to Benjamin's work are all references to the above paper.

The issues of law involved were complex but, as we have seen, not particularly novel.

In a common law system, 'ignorance' of the law can be a misleading expression. **5.06** English judges do in fact 'make law' and can be unpredictable, but if we do not anticipate a 'new' ruling on a point we are, according to accepted doctrine, 'ignorant' of the law, not merely bad at predicting which way a court will decide. There are times when this lack of knowledge (caused by uncertainty in the law) can persist across a market for many years (as has been the case with the law on fixed charges over book debts)[4] but, under this heading, we are principally concerned with a lack of knowledge that is peculiar to a given institution. It should also be mentioned that the heading includes not only limited awareness of a given part of the substantive law but also lack of understanding of the legal implications of a particular course of action (including failure to understand the nature of legal commitments being entered into as a result of a misunderstanding of documentation).

The availability of legal advice from in-house and external lawyers makes, or **5.07** should make, the likelihood of complete legal ignorance relatively small. Problems are most likely to occur where (a) advice is not sought when it should be; (b) the lawyer is not properly briefed as to the facts; or (c) advice is not understood. All of these situations can arise in even the best-managed institutions. They are more likely to arise (especially situations (b) and (c)) when, as is often the case, the advice is needed as a matter of great urgency or when, for other reasons (including under-staffing), the legal department (where the advice is being provided in-house) is under great pressure to deliver advice to a time-table that does not permit due consideration or a comprehensive explanation to the client of the issues raised. External lawyers can find themselves subject to the same pressures, especially as the competitive environment in which legal services are provided continues to intensify. It should be emphasised that the difficulties do not generally arise because the lawyer does not know the law (although he may have precious little time for any research) but because he has either not fully understood what is required (whether that is his fault or his client's) or because the client has not fully appreciated the advice given (especially any notes of caution or assumptions that a careful lawyer might have mentioned in conveying the advice).

The difficulties referred to above can increase exponentially where advice is **5.08** needed in relation to more than one jurisdiction. First, the international dimension will almost certainly require the use of several lawyers. Their advice, which will relate to several different legal systems and may be received in several

---

[4] See Ch 9 below.

languages (or, if in English, may, albeit with the best of intentions, be mistranslated or lack precision) will require very careful coordination, assessment, and explanation to the client. The initial advice may well generate follow-up questions. Pressure of time will aggravate what is already a difficult exercise. Confusion over the exact responsibilities of lawyers involved (for example, as between in-house lawyer and external lawyer or as between the 'transaction' lawyer and 'local counsel')[5] will also be a risk.[6] Advances in technology allow documents to be produced, amended, and distributed at remarkable speed—an all-day negotiation meeting followed by an overnight 'turnaround' of an updated version of the document under discussion is by no means unusual. However, the human brain (even of the most gifted and determined) can still only function effectively, absorbing and assessing new information, seeking clarification of new data and authorization for decisions, if given adequate time. This is not always allowed, and the inevitable risks follow.

Implementation failure

5.09 Even where legal advice has been properly given and understood, it may not always be followed. Lawyers are naturally cautious. They are duty-bound to advise clients of potential risks and at times a very cautious lawyer can give the impression of being 'negative'. But it is the client's privilege to ignore the advice if he chooses, or to be selective in its application. As we have already observed, the modern financial markets place a premium on innovation and the ability to deliver what the customer wants at a keen price and with minimum delay. A bank that steps out of line with general market practice as regards the acceptability of a risk will lose business. So, to take an example used earlier, if an important customer wants to raise money (by, say, a securitization or bulk discounting of trade receivables) using a transaction structure that involves the risk that follows from not serving notice on trade debtors, the bank will not welcome losing the business (to a rival who may not be so 'fussy') by insisting on serving the notice. A similar dilemma may confront a bank wishing to take security for a loan in an overseas jurisdiction where the documentary taxes payable in connection with the perfection of that security are excessive. The borrower will put commercial pressure on the bank to 'make do' with, say, a

---

[5] The terminology commonly used in the market distinguishes between (a) the lawyer (or law firm) charged with producing the principal documentation (which would be governed by the law of the jurisdiction on which this lawyer is qualified to advise) and generally coordinating other advisers, and (b) the lawyer who is asked to advise on legal issues in a particular (different) jurisdiction whose laws are relevant to the transaction. It will be apparent that this analysis is not concerned only with wholesale financial market transactions or capital market 'products' but also with negotiated finance transactions of all kinds.

[6] See further Ch 11 below.

negative pledge[7] rather than insist on security over assets. This may be far less satisfactory from the bank's perspective, especially if the provider of the negative pledge is not itself very creditworthy (and therefore not likely to be worth suing even if it breaks that pledge). However, commercial pressure may well cause the bank to ignore the legal advice it has received.

The above examples involve banks taking informed, commercial decisions to ignore legal advice. This happens every day and is a feature of any dynamic, competitive market. Taking risks, including at least some kinds of legal risk, is what we expect commercial enterprises to do. The resultant risks should, ideally, be priced into the transaction by the bank. **5.10**

Less frequent is failure to follow advice in circumstances where the interests of the institution are not being served. This is likely to involve some form of breach of duty, even criminality. It may be rare but it can happen. As discussed elsewhere,[8] there will be doubts in some cases as to whether it is even proper to regard the resultant risks as legal risks. **5.11**

Exploiting the letter of the law

English law generally looks to the form of transactions rather than their substance and in construing the meaning of provisions in transaction documents will adopt an objective method of interpretation (based on what the parties might reasonably have been thought to mean) rather than a subjective method (based on the court deciding what the parties true intention actually was). There are a number of important exceptions (especially in tax law) to this rather general statement and, perhaps as a result of the growing influence of EU law, those exceptions seem to be increasing. However, at the present time, it is the 'objective' approach that prevails.[9] This has greatly assisted the development of innovatory **5.12**

---

[7] A negative pledge is an undertaking not to create security; it confers no security interest in its own right

[8] See para 4.41.

[9] A certain amount of controversy has been generated by dicta of Lord Hoffmann in the case of *Investors Compensation Scheme Ltd v West Bromwich Building Society* [1998] 1 WLR 896 where he re-stated the principles that the courts should apply to the interpretation of contracts. The specific concerns relate to the extent to which the court should be able to overturn apparently unambiguous language by considering issues which suggest an alternative meaning, as evidenced by the 'background'—which Lord Hoffmann described as including 'absolutely anything which would have affected the way in which the language of the document would have been understood by a reasonable man', as long as this 'background' was 'reasonably available to the parties'. It was acknowledged that the 'background' could not include evidence of pre-contractual negotiations and the parties' declarations of subjective intent, which can only be put before the court in actions for rectification. Various subsequent cases have feature references to this aspect of the judgment which suggest that it has not been wholly welcomed. For a detailed analysis of issues raised, see McKendrick, 'The Interpretation of Contracts: Lord Hoffmann's Re-Statement' in S Worthington (ed), *Commercial Law and Practice*.

transaction structures in the financial markets. Not all of the innovations are particularly complex or ingenious. For example, the use of reservation of title clauses can permit the (commercially effective) creation of 'security' for an obligation without the transaction involving a security interest that would be categorized as such as a matter of law. This can have certain advantages.[10] A restriction on providing guarantees might be avoided by entering into a put option under which the guarantor agrees to buy a debt at par value if the borrower defaults. Other examples include the use of financial leases to achieve the same effect as secured lending and the title transfer collateral arrangements considered above.[11]

5.13 What these examples have in common is a reliance on the unwritten, but fundamental, rule in English law that, in general, you are entitled to enter into whatever transactions you may wish, as long as you do not fall foul of the law, and even though a given kind of transaction may have the same effect as another kind of transaction (and may have been entered into for the clear purpose of avoiding some adverse consequence that would be attracted by the other kind of transaction), the law will respect the method and form of transacting business that you have chosen and not seek to 'recharacterize' it as something else. One result of this is that there are many different ways of raising money under transactions subject to English law and, notwithstanding that they may all achieve the same commercial effect as lending and borrowing, some, if not all, of these different ways are likely to be available 'on the menu' to those devising a financing exercise, and the choice should be relatively free of legal risk.

5.14 The creativity[12] involved in this 'exploitation' can be put to positive use, not merely used for avoiding restrictions. For example, some years ago the secondary market in bank loans was revolutionized by the development of a contractual structure that enabled participations in syndicated loans to be transferred in a manner that resulted not only in an assignment of the selling bank's rights but also the transfer (by a special form of novation) of its obligations. This meant that the selling bank could genuinely 'exit' the loan transaction completely, without needing to rely, say, on indemnities from the buying bank, and its balance sheet and capital requirements would reflect this. The development of securitization in the 1980s and the general trend in favour of 'disintermediation', with resultant cost savings, have also relied heavily on legal ingenuity of the kind under consideration.

---

[10] eg it would not be necessary to register the 'security' under CA 1985, s 395. It might also escape certain kinds of negative pledge restrictions that would apply to conventional security interests.

[11] See Ch 3 above.

[12] Academics sometimes call this kind of transaction structuring 'creative compliance'.

So, if this 'objective' approach of English law is such good news, why are we **5.15**
concerned that taking advantage of it may be a source of legal risk? The concerns are, for the most part, general in nature rather than specific. As the tax
cases on substance over form have shown, the courts may not be sympathetic if
they think that a good thing is being abused. For example, over-aggressive
transaction structures that seek to achieve the benefits of security, in effect, but
which are clearly unfair to the general body of an insolvent's creditors (because
no security interest has been publicly registered) may still perhaps be subject to
'recharacterization' risk by a court in the future if it is felt that they infringe
fundamental principles of insolvency law.[13] Recent Law Commission proposals
have shown[14] that there is already a body of opinion that too many 'quasi-
security interests' (including reservation of title clauses, as referred to above) are
escaping the requirement for registration. This is just one example of an area
where some kind of reaction to the relatively unrestricted freedom of contract
enjoyed by the financial markets might be brewing up. The reaction might
take the form of legislation, case law, or (perhaps more likely) intervention by
regulators, but it would be foolish to discount the risk of it becoming more
pronounced. One man's creativity is another man's sharp practice. 'Creative
accounting' is already a pejorative term. If taking advantage of the letter of the
law is used in highly sensitive areas such as 'balance sheet dressing' or to deceive
regulators or shareholders, the institutions involved will expose themselves to
legal and reputational risks and the ability to continue to use techniques such as
those discussed here may be eroded.

Outsourcing

As Joanna Benjamin observes: **5.16**

> Outsourcing has been an important trend among financial institutions in recent
> years. It involves generally the delegation of (usually) non-core business functions,
> which are generally involved in providing services to clients, in circumstances
> where these functions were previously provided in house. These functions may be
> 'back office' operational functions, or ancillary business lines.

The Bank for International Settlements (BIS) described the issues that concern **5.17**
regulators in a paper published in February 2005:[15]

> Outsourcing has the potential to transfer risk, management and compliance to
> third parties who may not be regulated, and who may operate offshore. In these
> situations, how can financial service businesses remain confident that they remain
> in charge of their own business and in control of their business risks? How do they
> know they are complying with their regulatory responsibilities? How can these
> businesses demonstrate that they are doing so when regulators ask?

---

[13] See further Ch 9 below.   [14] See para 9.08 n. 9.
[15] 'Outsourcing in Financial Services'.

5.18 Outsourcing is a phenomenon that is not confined to the financial markets. It usually brings cost savings and should, in theory, result in a better, more specialized service. But a bank that subcontracts out a service, typically a 'back-office' function, by outsourcing is still liable to its customer if the service is not delivered properly and the customer suffers loss as a result. Indemnities from the subcontractor (who may, as the BIS noted, be located offshore) are likely to be of limited value. Further, 'back office' functions, and their effective management and supervision, although lacking glamour, are vitally important not only to the proper administration of a bank but also to risk control and management.[16] Failure to check, for example, that a confirmation has been obtained may mean that a vitally important contract on which the bank is relying is not actually entered into. This is legal risk at its most basic, and may also spill over to reputational risk. The outsourced supplier may not have the assets or insurance cover necessary for such risks.

5.19 Some specific concerns in this area in relation to credit derivatives were highlighted in a letter, dated February 2005, from the FSA to institutions active in the market for those instruments:

> . . . we believe that more can be done to reduce operational and settlement risks. The difficulties of back-office functions keeping pace with the rapidly developing front office trading activity were highlighted during the Joint Forum's investigation[17] and the FSA's soundings of firms confirmed this.

> Specifically we are concerned about the level of unsigned confirmations with some transactions remaining unconfirmed for months. Although we recognise that work undertaken in 2004 is helping to reduce the backlog, levels of unsigned

---

[16] Failure to control and oversee back-office functions properly is sometimes alleged to be one of the principal operational defects that led to the downfall of Barings Bank. According to a paper published by the International Financial Risk Institute (see: risk institute.ch/137580.htm): 'The back-office records, confirms and settles trades transacted by the front office, reconciles them with details sent by the bank's counterparties and assesses the accuracy of prices used for its internal valuations. It also accepts/releases securities and payments for trades. Some back-offices also provide the regulatory reports and management accounting. In a nutshell, the back-office provides the necessary checks to prevent unauthorised trading and minimise the potential for fraud and embezzlement. Since Leeson was in charge of the back-office, he had the final say on payments, ingoing and outgoing confirmations and contracts, reconciliation statements, accounting entries and position reports. He was perfectly placed to relay false information back to London.' For a fuller account of what went wrong at Barings, see Pigott, 'Lessons from Barings' (1995) 4 JIBFL 159. See also App 3 Part 2 below, Principle 6; in commenting on this principle, the BCBS states: 'Segregation of duties is a basic internal control measure designed to reduce the risk of fraud in operational processes and systems and ensure that transactions and company assets are properly authorised, recorded and safeguarded. Segregation of duties is critical to ensuring the accuracy and integrity of data and is used to prevent the perpetration of fraud by an individual. If duties are adequately separated, fraud can only be committed through collusion.'

[17] This is a reference to a cross-sectoral group combining the Basel Committee, the International Organization of Securities Commissions (IOSCO), and the International Association of Insurance Supervisors (IAIS), which conducted a 'wide-ranging investigation' into credit derivatives.

confirmations and master agreements remain relatively high and raise serious issues for market efficiency and market confidence.

We ask you to consider your firm's operational processes and risk management frameworks—and the resourcing of these in relation to credit derivatives—to assess their robustness in this rapidly evolving market. Confirmations and other documentation should be issued and affirmed promptly after the transaction has been agreed.

This letter was, in part, an echo of an earlier warning given by the then **5.20** Chairman of the FSA, Sir Howard Davies, in a speech to the Human Resources Group Conference in June 2001:

Over the past year, on behalf of the old self-regulators, we have disciplined a wide range of institutions, many of them household names, for back-office administrative failures such as poor reconciliations, miscalculation or misapplication of dividends. The one common feature in these cases seems to us to be that firms were not giving enough priority to these important back-office functions.

More anecdotal evidence of the problem can be found in a *Financial Times* **5.21** article of 24 February 2005 (by Batchelor and Larsen) commenting on the Parmalat scandal:

A sudden shift in market sentiment or problems at an individual company—a so-called 'reference entity' on which credit default swaps have been written—could leave traders exposed to large losses. For example, credit derivatives written on Parmalat formed part of dozens of collateralised debt obligations—portfolios of underlying bonds, loans and CDs—when the Italian dairy group went bust in late 2003.

'It was a nightmare to find out where exposure was at Parmalat', says Mr. Nakachi.[18] 'Banks were going through their filing cabinets. There were "confirms" outstanding. That and the default made a double whammy.'

A few days after the publication of this article (and the FSA's warning letter **5.22** referred to above) the *Financial Times* reported[19] that 'some banks have cut back their trading of credit derivatives to clear up their backlogs of unconfirmed trades'. It was noted that 'unlike more established and standardised interest rate and equity derivatives, credit derivative trades have to be backed up with lengthy documentation outlining the terms of the deal'. This complexity and lack of standardization obviously heightens the potential legal risk.

The FSA has, more generally, indicated that it has concerns over the risks that **5.23** outsourcing can involve for regulated institutions. A recent 'sting' operation, involving a tabloid newspaper paying an Indian IT worker a few thousand

---

[18] A senior analyst at Calypso Technology, which, according to the article quoted, provides back-up systems for trading credit derivatives.
[19] See article by Batchelor, 'Moves to speed up derivatives trading', 3 March 2005.

pounds to obtain private information relating to bank customers, has highlighted some of the security issues involved. Policies and guidelines in this area are evolving and will be of considerable importance to any general framework of risk management.[20]

C. The Nature of the Financial Markets

Financial innovation

5.24 You cannot usually innovate in business without taking some risks, and the financial markets thrive on innovation. Further, law is one of the principal tools of innovation. There is nothing new in this. One of the early landmarks in the development of 'financial law' in England was the recognition by English courts, in the 1870s, of the floating charge as a legitimate form of security interest.[21] That innovation (which, together with the recognition of assignments of 'future property',[22] is still one of the hallmarks of our financial law, distinguishing it from many other legal systems) facilitated the financing of industrial activity on a grand scale and still vitally underpins transaction structures used for the development of large-scale capital projects, such as North Sea oil and gas projects and the Channel tunnel. (These transaction structures have been 'borrowed' heavily for virtually all Private Finance Initiative and Public Private Partnership projects carried out by successive UK governments since the early 1990s.) The floating charge remains controversial to this day[23] and is frequently the subject of re-examination both in the courts and in the legislature,[24] as well as in academic critical comment.

5.25 Many of the more recent innovations have been mentioned already. The development of the eurobond market itself, syndicated loans, multicurrency options, revolving underwriting facilities, certificates of deposit, swaps, transferable loan certificates, title transfer collateral arrangements, 'double dip' financial leases,[25] 'direct agreements',[26] perpetual bonds . . . all of these financial market

---

[20] A description of the current (as at November 2004) FSA requirements can be found in Taylor, 'Financial Services Outsourcing and the FSA's Guidelines' (2004) 10 JIBFL 405. For a description of 'sound practices for managing outsourced e-banking systems and services' (which includes suggestions regarding the 'adequacy' of outsourcing contracts) see the BCBS paper of July 2003 entitled 'Risk Management Principles for Electronic Banking', App II.

[21] See Ch 9 below.   [22] See Ch 9 below.

[23] See para 9.20.   [24] See para 9.28 et seq.

[25] So called because they took advantage of favourable tax treatment (such as the use of capital allowances to 'shelter' income against tax liability) in more than one jurisdiction.

[26] These were first devised (it is thought) in the Eurotunnel limited recourse project financing. By establishing a direct contractual relationship between the lending banks and the host governments dealing (amongst other things) with what should happen in relation to the concession agreement if the security is enforced, such agreements provide a vital enhancement to the rights

phenomena (and many others) have justified the epithet 'innovative' in their time. The desire to innovate, fuelled to some extent by huge advances in information technology as well as by sheer competitive pressure, continues unabated. The most striking example of innovation in recent years has been the growth and expansion of transaction structures known as derivatives. The idea behind derivatives (which involves trading in risks in things as diverse as interest rates, borrower defaults, and adverse weather conditions) took off slowly at first, with banks providing 'bespoke' currency and/or interest rate swaps to corporate customers. It is now the idea that provides the basis for what has become the most prominent feature of the international financial market place.[27]

Many of the early legal risk concerns associated with derivatives centred on set-off and close-out netting provisions, as considered in Chapter 3. In certain contexts, they still persist. 'No other legal issue has resulted in as much concern, attention, lobbying and general angst among derivatives dealers over the last 15 years.'[28] New forms of derivative will continue to be devised and each new development will raise new legal questions in its own right, some of them highly technical and some of them relating to more basic documentation and procedural issues. Recently, there has, for example been an increased level of concern about credit derivatives. These instruments were helpfully described, in a recent Joint Forum paper,[29] as falling into two major product categories:

5.26

---

and remedies available under traditional security instruments. Direct agreements are now used in virtually all PFI/PPP and other project financings in the UK and elsewhere.

[27] The *Financial Times* reported the size of the interest rate swap market in 2004 as US$184,000 bn. See Batchelor, 'Credit Derivatives market set for weekly fixing', *Financial Times*, 20 March 2005.

According to Pretzick and Silverman, 'What Goes Around', *Financial Times*, 31 January 2002, the Bond Market Association estimated that the market in the US alone for asset backed securities (see futher below) grew from US$15bn in 1995 to US$1,048bn in 2001. In the same period, the market in collateralized debt obligations (see further below) grew from US$1bn globally to US$ 300–400bn. It was estimated that the global market for credit derivatives reached US$1,581bn in 2001, a ninefold increase from 1997.

In March 2005 the *Financial Times* estimated that the market in credit default swaps would reach more than US$8,000bn (gross outstanding value) by 2006.

When the 'hedge fund', Long Term Capital Management collapsed in 1998, requiring a US$3.6bn bail-out by the US Federal Reserve, its bankers had an estimated exposure of US$125bn. See Wighton, 'Risk Management: Keeping Pace with Effective Results', *Financial Times*, 27 January 2005.

A study released in March 2005 by the investment bank, CSFB, claimed that investment banks worldwide had earned US$25bn from hedge funds, about an eighth of their total income (see *Financial Times*, 10 March 2005).

[28] Henderson, 'Master Agreements, Bridges and Delays in Enforcement, Part 1' (2004) 10 JIBFL 394.

[29] 'Credit Risk Transfer,' March 2005; see also Brown, 'Legal, Documentation and Regulatory Issues of Credit Derivatives' (1997) 3 JIBFL 119.

(1) credit default swaps, which bear credit risk that is similar though not necessarily identical to that associated with a bond, and

(2) collateralised debt obligations (CDOs), where the credit risk of a portfolio of underlying exposures is 'tranched' into different segments, each with unique risk and return characteristics.

5.27 Credit derivatives, in many ways, serve a very valuable market and social purpose by facilitating risk spreading and diversification, but their complexity does result in hazards. John Tiner (Chief Executive of the FSA) recently noted:[30]

> As firms take on more risk through complex and relatively illiquid instruments, risk management may become more difficult and operational and legal risks are likely to increase. For example, in the wholesale markets, the use of credit derivatives has provided another means for credit risks to be spread, but, their rapid growth has also put pressure on firms' back office and documentation procedures.[31] And as collateralisation and netting agreements become more widespread it is essential that legal documentation is clear, enforceable and up-to-date.

5.28 In addition, the trading and marketing of derivatives appears to have become a source of Type 1 risk. We have seen recently a number of lawsuits by banks against other banks, complaining of mis-selling.[32] We will probably see more (notwithstanding that the market has become more sophisticated since the time of the transactions that gave rise to some of this litigation). In its March 2005 paper on 'Credit Risk Transfer' (referred to above) the Joint Forum commented on legal risk in the derivatives markets as follows:

> In regard to legal risk more generally, market participants are cognizant that legal issues have previously arisen in the broader financial derivatives market in several areas. These include the risk that counterparties did not have the appropriate legal authority to enter into the transactions and the risk that a counterparty or customer may seek to avoid payment based, for instance, on the market participant's failure to make adequate disclosures, or to assess the appropriateness of the transaction and its risks for the counterparty or customer. Market participants understand the need to reduce such risks as much as possible, and thus far the credit derivatives market seems to have been largely successful at absorbing the lessons of past experience in this regard. Nevertheless, the very nature of these risks will require continued vigilance by participants and regulators.

5.29 Another innovation, considered in more detail in Chapter 7 below, is the use of intermediaries, such as 'depositaries' or 'custodians', in connection with the holding of securities. Traditionally, an investor in the equity or debt securities of a company would have a direct, contractual relationship with that company. If the company failed to pay interest or dividends due on the securities, the investor would have a direct claim against the company and, if the

---

[30] Speech given at AIG Conference, 20 January 2005.   [31] See para 5.18.
[32] See para 5.59 et seq.

company went into liquidation, the investor would have an appropriate, direct entitlement to a distribution, depending on the nature of the security (and, of course, the ratio of assets to liabilities). When investments are not held in this 'traditional' manner, but are represented by, say, a book-entry in an account maintained by an intermediate nominee of some description,[33] the investor's immediate contractual relationship is not with the company that has issued the security but with the intermediary. What then is the position of the investor if the company defaults or if the intermediary defaults? Does the investor have protected rights to claims represented by the underlying security if the inter-mediary goes into liquidation or is the investor just an unsecured creditor of the intermediary? How does the investor create a security interest over his investment if he wants to use it as collateral? What law applies to any dealings or claims? Holding securities through book-entry systems has become very widespread and owes its popularity to the increased efficiencies available in a 'paperless' system for recording holdings, transfers, collateral, etc. However, there are concerns that the practice of the market, not for the first time, may have got somewhat ahead of the law. As with close-out netting in the early 1990s, it would be highly desirable for there to be some clarification that the respective rights of investors and others will, as a matter of law, be as the market believes they are.[34] Until that time there is, inevitably, a degree of legal risk accompanying the innovation.

5.30 Not all innovation results in risk. Some of the innovatory techniques mentioned above actually reduced or removed risk. However, the pressure to deliver solutions, develop market opportunities, and be at the forefront, or 'cutting edge', is very strong in the financial market sector and deeply embedded in the culture of most international banks.[35] The challenge is to be sure that the legal risks (if any) that are involved in a new development, and especially in its marketing, are identified quickly and then, if necessary, either to adapt the innovation

---

[33] See Ch 7 below, for a fuller description of investment structures involving custodians, sub-custodians, etc.

[34] See Ch 7 below.

[35] The 'Banana Skins 2005' Survey (CSFI) comments on the 'pressure to take risk': 'The pressure to outperform their peers ranks high among the risks facing banks. Many of our respondents saw banks fishing downmarket, slackening credit standards, engaging in imprudent innovation or diversification, even skimping on risk management to boost earnings . . . [one] respondent saw banks going in for innovation "in desperation to recover market share, leading to highly esoteric products, little understood by management, risk committees etc".' This competitive pressure is also currently causing lenders to be less exacting in the financial covenants they require from borrowers, according to the *Financial Times* of 14 March 2005: 'The ratio of average debt/earnings before interest, tax, depreciation and amortisation that investors are prepared to live with, for example, is 5.8 times, according to Standard and Poors—which is higher than in 1999.' Why are lenders prepared to do this? 'One reason is excess supply of credit. Easing up on covenants may seem preferable to simply competing on price. Another reason is that there has yet to be a big default. But as interest rates rise, the true cost of looser covenants may start to show.'

(and its marketing) so as to keep the risks within reasonable bounds or, in more difficult cases, to lobby for legislative or regulatory change to permit the innovation to proceed with less risk, if the potential benefits are sufficiently compelling.

New market sectors and convergence

5.31 Banks are now providers of many more varieties of financial services than they were twenty-five years ago. Deregulation of financial markets has facilitated the growth of the 'universal bank', offering not merely deposit-taking, foreign currency and loans (in retail and wholesale markets), but also insurance (sometimes termed 'bancassurance'), stockbroking, investment advice, fund management, and a range of other products. We also see convergence taking the form of retailers, and even newspapers, marketing financial products and services.[36] Recently, a mobile phone company announced that it was contemplating an alliance of some kind with a bank or financial institution 'to help offer financial services such as payment settlements through mobile handsets'.[37]

5.32 One result of this deregulation is that banks and other financial institutions are keen to take advantage of 'cross-selling' opportunities—consider how many tempting offers are laid before you next time you visit your local high street branch—and, apparently, willing to acquire new businesses in virtually all kinds of financial sector, with no preconceived limits as to the countries where the target businesses may be located. A recent visit to the author's local 'high street' bank yielded marketing materials for customers covering credit cards, travel agency, insurance (including car breakdown cover), various kinds of investment, and stockbroking and a wide range of more traditional banking products.[38]

5.33 Some of these expansions have been very successful, some less so. They will no doubt continue, especially if the retail banking market in the EU is allowed to develop more freely than has been the case to date. However, such ambitions (like the product innovations considered above) do involve risks, including legal risks. The difficulties that many institutions have experienced with mis-selling claims stem, for the most part, from operations in (for the institution) new

---

[36] For a thorough analysis of the convergence phenomenon, see Cheyne, 'The Convergence of Financial Services in the UK' (1995) 1 JIBFL 5.

[37] See *Financial Times*, 13 April 2005 (article about NTT DoCoMo).

[38] As Cranston points out in *Principles of Banking Law* (2nd edn) 214: 'there is a . . . category of presumed undue influence where, for instance, the person proves a relationship as a result of which he or she has generally reposed trust and confidence in the other party or in which the other party has acquired an ascendancy. There is no reason that this other party cannot be a bank. The circumstances in which this can occur are multiplied as the modern multifunctional bank holds itself out to customers as financial adviser, planner and confidant.'

areas. The role of derivatives in diversifying risk is crucial here, in that certain kinds of derivatives have the legal and economic effect of transferring risk from those institutions which would have traditionally borne it to institutions in a different sector. Thus, the growth in the market of collateralized debt obligations (CDOs) and asset backed securities (ABSs) has resulted in enormous amounts of credit risk, traditionally borne by banks, in areas such as corporate loans, mortgages, and credit card loans, being 'repackaged' and sold, in the form of derivative instruments, to investors such as insurance companies and investment funds. The regulators have, from time to time, voiced concern as to whether these investors, to put it crudely, really know what they are doing in buying these risks. Sir Howard Davies, when he was Chairman of the FSA, feared that insurance companies might be buying excessive credit risks from banks and warned that they 'may not be pricing these risks appropriately, perhaps because they lack the sophisticated technology to price them which investment banks possess'. As Pretznick and Silverman observed in 2002:[39]

> The FSA's concern that insurance companies may not have fully known what they were doing in buying such instruments is plausible. Even sophisticated financial conglomerates have admitted that they had trouble understanding the complex instruments marketed by Wall Street. Last summer, American Express disclosed that it had lost money on CDO investments it did not fully understand. Amex had wrongly calculated that the diversity of the underlying credits would offer protection. 'It is now apparent that our analysis of the portfolio did not fully comprehend the risk underlying these structured investments during a period of high risk', said Kenneth Chenault, Amex's chairman.

5.34 It might be thought that the legal risk involved in a 'big boys' market', where complex instruments are traded amongst banks, insurance companies, and investment funds, should be slight, in that such institutions should be able to look after themselves. However, recent experience of mis-selling claims being made between banks suggests otherwise.[40]

5.35 The desire to offer a wider range of services also increases the risk of accusations of conflict of interest. This is, for example, virtually inevitable for any institution which not only trades in marketable securities as a principal but also advises others on such trades and investments, arranges new issues of such securities and advises on important transactions which provide it with price-sensitive

---

[39] Pretzick and Silverman, 'What Goes Around', *Financial Times*, 31 January 2002 and JIBFL, March 2002

[40] See para Intro 1.07 n. 7. See also remarks of Michael Gibson, head of trading risk analysis at the US Federal Reserve, as reported in the *Financial Times*, 12 April 2005: 'What we are hearing from market participants is that there is a minority of CDO investors, perhaps 10 per cent, who do not really understand what they are getting into.'

information relating to marketable securities. Recent history has provided a number of examples of banks getting into difficulties where the temptation to take advantage of information gained in one role for the purpose of making money in another (regardless of the interests of clients) has proved too strong to resist.

Cross-border business

5.36 Joanna Benjamin observes that cross-border business is 'arguably . . . the major source of legal risk in the financial sector'. Many of the new markets targeted by banks are outside their 'home' jurisdiction and some are located in parts of the world where the potential size of the market may not be matched by a particularly well-developed legal infrastructure.[41] The continuing expansion of the EU, the emergence of new market economies following the collapse of Soviet communism, and the gradual opening up of China to foreign investment are just some of the better-known new opportunities for financial market activity that have been experienced in recent years. But such new markets present a range of legal hazards for the unwary. The following may feature in some or all of the countries presenting such opportunities:

(1) there may be no clear legal mechanism for obtaining security over a borrower's cash flows (which might be the borrower's most valuable asset);

(2) it may be prohibitively expensive (because of notarial fees, stamp duties, or similar taxes) to perfect a security interest over other assets, such as land and buildings;

(3) there may be no means of recording a security interest in a public registry and no certainty that it will prevail against a third-party rival creditor or upon the borrower's liquidation;

(4) it may be unlawful to have important documentation governed by anything other than local law—a problem that may be compounded by the fact that the judiciary is known, or suspected, to be corrupt and that international arbitration would not be respected by the local courts;

---

[41] This expression, which has now slipped into common usage, is intended to mean a range of things. The wish list for an acceptable legal infrastructure for cross-border financial business would generally include: (1) an impartial, reasonably efficient judiciary and court system, immune to political interference; (2) a commercial legal system that has a well-developed law of contract and tort and insolvency and company law, as well as laws that enable lenders to take (and enforce) effective security and conclude reasonably conventional financing documentation with nationals in the jurisdiction (whether or not governed by the local law) that they can reasonably expect will be valid and enforceable; (3) a system of regulation for banking and financial services that is not unreasonably discriminatory; (4) a reasonably transparent legislative process (preferably involving at least the basic democratic elements); and (5) respect for the rule of law throughout government institutions. Obviously, the ambitions and hopes represented by such a wish list may not always be fully realized.

(5) the concept of the trust (and the difference between legal and beneficial ownership) may not be recognized;

(6) there may be a risk of penal withholding taxes or regulatory restrictions being applied to payments (including payments of interest) by the borrower to the bank or the borrower's access to the foreign currency needed to make such payments;

(7) the bank's security may be at risk if a new government opposes a project being funded by the bank; this risk may also be compounded if there are no clear laws entitling the bank or its customer to compensation in the event of nationalization or confiscation;

(8) a project being funded by the bank may require regular renewal of key permits and licences and there may be no clear right of appeal against a refusal of renewal, which may occur for relatively arbitrary reasons;

(9) it may not be clear whether the bank's transacting business in a country will result in it being liable to pay taxes there or require some form of regulatory consent and/or ongoing consent to regulatory requirements (even though the bank has no branch or office there); and

(10) it may not be clear whether certain of the products that the bank wishes to market fall foul of local laws on, for example:

(a) the payment of interest,

(b) gaming, or

(c) the marketing of securities,

there may also be doubts as to the extent of the bank's potential liability (criminal and civil) in connection with such marketing.

This is an extensive list, but it is no more than a summary of a handful of the **5.37** legal risk issues that tend to surface in connection with cross-border financial activity. In the context of heavily negotiated, one-off transactions, the normal process of obtaining detailed legal advice from experts in all relevant jurisdictions would generally enable the relevant risks to be identified and evaluated. It is well known that some of these risks exist in certain jurisdictions and, because they act as a deterrent to investment (or, at best, permit investment to proceed but at a higher cost), efforts are being made at international levels to bring about legal reforms.[42] More serious problems will tend to arise when the risks affect day-to-day financial activities and trading, when the participants are less likely to have the time or budget to seek detailed advice. The dangers are arguably greater now that financial institutions have become so accustomed to trading in a 'global market place'. A constant reminder is needed that, however global the market may be, law remains, for virtually all relevant purposes, a creature of national jurisdictions, and therefore can vary, sometimes quite alarmingly,

---

[42] See para Intro 1.39.

from country to country. This is the case even in the EU, after many years of 'harmonization' initiatives. We are still a very long way from having comprehensive EU-wide laws on basic contractual concepts, security instruments, methods of assignment, trusts, and so on. Reforms such as the Collateral Directive have been extremely valuable but very limited in scope, and even when a helpful attempt at harmonization emerges there is no guarantee that implementation into national laws will be followed throughout the EU on a uniform basis. Outside the EU, one finds major differences of approach around the world. Some jurisdictions, for example, tend to be more 'creditor-friendly' than others in the context of insolvency laws.[43] This can have an important impact in areas such as the validity of close-out netting provisions on liquidation. Some jurisdictions are clearly hostile to forms of security like the English floating charge, taking the view that it places too much power in the hands of the secured creditor. There are a number of major conceptual differences between common law systems and civil law systems. They are rarely differences that can be avoided by skilful drafting.

5.38   For those who wish to reduce legal risk, the challenge represented by the fact that the global market does not operate within a single, global legal system is probably the greatest of all. It will take the longest time for there to be anything approaching a successful response. In the meantime, cross-border financial business continues to grow. The market is, for the most part, managing the risks.

D. Problems Within the Law

Bad law

5.39   It happens. We do, from time to time, find that our legislators impose laws and regulations on us that simply do not function properly. This is not a question of political preferences. It is a question of laws that just do not work. Fortunately, in a democratic society, we are generally able to bring sufficient pressure to bear to get bad laws changed, especially where the adverse impact is being felt in an area as sensitive to the economy as the financial markets. Some of the more recent examples of bad laws (for example, provisions of the Proceeds of Crime Act 2002 which apparently would require a bank to notify the appropriate authorities if it received funds from a French fox hunter or a Spanish matador) are considered in more detail in Chapter 8 below.

---

[43] See paras 7.17 and 7.18.

Policy concerns

It is a policy decision to require regulation of those who provide financial **5.40**
services in the first place. The policy relates to a perceived need to protect
consumers, punish 'cheats', and promote orderly financial markets, with minimum risk of systemic instability. Banks and other institutions accept that there
is a legitimate public interest here, even though, understandably, there will be
concerns on their part about over-regulation.[44] An inevitable consequence of
this is that Type 1 risk is likely to be increased. The presence of such risk in
one form or another, for example the possibility of fines by a regulator or civil
claims by customers, is a necessary deterrent for the wrongdoer and also, perhaps, a useful discipline for those who might otherwise be inclined to be over-
exuberant. However, as discussed in more detail below,[45] regulators are not
merely the producers and enforcers of regulations; they are also a prolific source
of 'soft law', which may take the form of codes of conduct, guidance, statements
of policy, descriptions of market standards, warnings about what is 'inappropriate', etc. This is not the place to comment on the merits or otherwise of any
particular policy, but it seems inevitable that such activity, combined with the
regulators' assumed brief, to protect customers of financial institutions, will
tend to produce a body of soft law that places more duties upon banks than
might otherwise have been the case.

There is also a sub-variant of this policy, which produces legal risks for banks **5.41**
(and others) that can be extremely difficult to manage. Over the past few years,
governments in many countries, including the UK, have introduced legislation
which is intended to assist the law enforcement authorities in their attempts to
combat serious crime such as drug peddling and terrorism. Laws concerned with
money-laundering and related issues have proliferated. Banks and banking practices have inevitably been affected by these laws because it has been necessary,
for example, to disapply what might otherwise have been duties of confidentiality to enable the authorities to have access to information possessed by banks
regarding the financial aspects, and fruits, of such criminal activity. Banks'
conflicts of duties with regard to confidentiality alone have resulted in a good
deal of litigation. However, some of the laws go much further than merely
requiring banks' cooperation with police enquiries. The most serious risk problems arise for banks in the context of laws that place obligations on banks to
disclose information not merely in response to enquiries, but on the banks' own
initiative if they suspect, or should reasonably suspect, something untoward.

---

[44] This was, eg the 'easy first' in the CSFI's 2005 Banana Skins Survey of risks facing banks.
One 'senior banker' was quoted in that survey: 'The Financial Services Authority is interfering
more and more, costing the banking industry millions in order to comply with many meaningless
regulations. Interference, regulation and compliance are out of control.'
[45] See para 5.56 et seq.

The policy appears to be to make the banks active assistants in the crime detection process. The legislation is unsatisfactory in a number of respects, which are considered further in Chapter 8 below.

5.42 Less obvious, but more traditional policy issues can be found embedded in much of the case law that comprises 'financial law'. Joanna Benjamin lists the following examples:

> insolvency displacement rules (unhelpful to collateral takers; designed to protect general creditors);
>
> rules protecting the equity of redemption (unhelpful to collateral takers; designed to protect collateral givers);
>
> equitable defences to payment under guarantees (unhelpful to guaranteed parties; designed to protect guarantors);
>
> the rule in *Barclays v. O'Brien*[46] (unhelpful to mortgagees; designed to protect spouses of mortgagors).

5.43 Thus, although the English courts will lean in favour of respecting the customs and usage of the financial market place, they also tend to lean in favour of 'the little guy' against 'the big guy', and there have, not surprisingly, been a number of decisions (especially where individuals are involved) where the banks have been perceived as 'the big guy'. The same approach can be detected in the attitude of regulators. As Huertas has pointed out,[47] 'we [the FSA] focus on helping retail customers achieve a fair deal. Such retail customers need our help. Wholesale firms by and large do not.' As a result, one finds that retail customers are constantly being reminded of their rights, almost to the point of being encouraged to make claims.[48] Such legal risks now seem to 'come with the territory'. But they come at a cost.

5.44 The regulatory regime appears to be getting much tougher in the US as well. There have been complaints of a 'regulatory blizzard', but the results so far do seem to be the unearthing of a disturbing number of questionable practices in the markets and the increased zeal of the regulators seems to have popular support. In a recent article,[49] Roel Campos, a commissioner at the US Securities and Exchange Commission (SEC)—writing in a personal capacity—commented, in defence of the (somewhat controversial) policy of fining corporate entities for frauds committed by their officers or employees:

> If the SEC charged only individuals, causes of fraud would be left unaddressed. For example, a company may have a culture where cheating is tolerated or where

---

[46] *Barclays Bank plc v O'Brien* [1994] 1 AC 180; see also *Royal Bank of Scotland v Etridge (No 2)* [1998] 4 All ER 705.

[47] Speech by Thomas Huertas (Director, Wholesale Firms Division, FSA), 8 February 2005.

[48] See further para 5.59.   [49] See the *Financial Times*, 12 April 2005.

internal controls are ineffective. The corporate penalty is in part to punish and shame the company and its officers for those failures and to require remedial action. Corporate penalties also provide deterrence. As a former business executive, I can assure you that no officer or director wants corporate penalties imposed under his or her watch. Penalties against individuals alone produce far smaller recoveries for victims . . . Recognising the enormous losses suffered by investors from corporate fraud, Congress in 2002 showed extraordinary wisdom in authoris-ing the SEC to use penalties to help restore investor losses. Corporate penalties now add significantly to overall recoveries (which include private and criminal actions) for defrauded investors, without imposing legal costs. Last year, the SEC recovered more than $3bn that will be distributed to investors to offset some of their losses.[50]

Surveys show that investors have not forgotten the devastating losses from Enron and that they strongly support all types of penalties. Agencies worldwide increas-ingly use corporate penalties. For example, last autumn Callum McCarthy, Britain's chief regulator, announced the largest monetary fine ever imposed by his agency against Royal Dutch/Shell.[51]

Campos acknowledged that regulation is not welcomed by business but stressed that when he was in business, 'My real enemy was a competitor who might be cheating and thus obtaining more and cheaper capital to use against my business'. **5.45**

Inaccessible law

It can sometimes be difficult to advise with certainty how a given legal rule should apply in a specific situation. This is inevitable for any legal system that has to relate to economic activity of any degree of complexity. A law that purports to lay down rules of behaviour for every conceivable situation (as opposed to clear principles which have to be sensibly applied to the facts) will be **5.46**

---

[50] Stephen Cutler, the recently retired head of enforcement at the SEC, is on record (*Financial Times*, 16 March 2005) as being enthusiastic about the deterrent effect of the 2002 Sarbanes-Oxley legislation in the US: 'We are trying to achieve a greater degree of deterrence. We want to ensure that the executive does not view the prospect of a sanction as just another cost of doing business.' The SEC, however, is clearly concerned about the adverse publicity that Sarbanes-Oxley s 404 has attracted and has issued guidance (16 May 2005) as to the application of the requirement for management to assess whether or not a company's internal controls provide reasonable (as opposed to absolute) assurance regarding the accuracy of its accounting.

[51] The fine, imposed by the FSA pursuant to FSMA 2000, for market abuse and breaching the listing rules, was £17m. The wrongdoing related to false or misleading statements about petroleum reserves. At around the same time, the SEC imposed a fine for parallel US offences of about £65m (US$120m). Announcing its fine, the FSA commented: 'The FSA views timely and accurate disclosure to shareholders and markets as fundamental to maintaining the integrity of the UK's financial markets. The size of the penalty reflects Shell's misconduct and the impact it had on markets and shareholders.' The implications of the case for risk management are considered at para 10.33 below.

inflexible, impractical, and probably unjust. So a degree of uncertainty has to be tolerated.

5.47   The common law system has both the advantage of built-in flexibility that enables law to evolve in a way that recognizes changing social conditions and the disadvantage of, at times, being frustratingly unclear as to how a given rule might apply in a situation which has not actually come before the courts. We have seen[52] how this troubled the markets (in some countries more than others) for some time in relation to set-off insolvency. The *British Eagle* case[53] has also, on occasions, given rise to worries (largely ill-founded) as to whether the *pari passu* principle as therein described could be seen to be inconsistent with subordination agreements and arrangements[54] which are very common in the market. Concerns about whether certain kinds of arrangements give rise to registrable charges (and what exactly is a charge over book debts) will, it would seem, always be with us. One could give many other examples of such doubts and fears that tend to arise from time to time. Within limits, the market can accommodate such uncertainty. It now has the mechanisms to make its feelings known if the limits are being exceeded.

Unpredictable judicial reasoning

5.48   Again, part of the price to be paid for the flexibility inherent in the common law system is the fact that one can never be absolutely certain how a piece of litigation will be resolved by the courts. As Hughes, in his paper presented at the IBA legal risk symposium observed, 'judicial unpredictability is a logical outcome of a precedent based system—decisions have to be taken and justice has to be done and if (sometimes) that means breaking with precedent, then so be it . . . We will approve of judicial unpredictability where it delivers the results we want; we will disapprove of it where we do not like the result.'

5.49   Despite the reaction of the markets to the cases referred to in Chapters 1 and 2 above, English courts are not regarded as a serious source of legal risk, whether because of unpredictability or otherwise. There have always been, and always will be, court decisions that may come as an unpleasant surprise to banks, but risk under this heading is reasonably manageable.

---

[52] See Ch 3 above.   [53] [1975] 2 All ER 390. See, further, para 3.59 et seq.
[54] Under a subordination agreement, a creditor (or group of creditors)—often known as 'junior creditors'—agree (usually at the time money is advanced) that some or all of their rights against a given debtor will rank behind the rights of one or more other creditors—often known as 'senior creditors'. This may be upon the debtor's insolvency and/or possibly in other circumstances. It is not, therefore, an instance of a class of creditors trying to 'steal a march' on the others (the 'mischief' that the *pari passu* principle, as applied in *British Eagle* is counteracting) but rather the reverse.

E. Interaction of Law and Finance

Hard and soft law

'Soft law' is the expression commonly used to describe codes of conduct, rules, **5.50** guidance, statements of approved practice, etc that emanate from various agencies, associations, and other institutions and have sufficient authority in the market to influence participants' and their advisers' responses to legal and other questions, and, possibly, to influence the courts but do not in themselves constitute 'law' (ie do not have the force or status of law, such as case law, regulation, or statute—the latter being known in this context as 'hard law'). The term is also applied to market practice habits that typically originate from accepted interpretations of law or views on best practice which derive from professional bodies and 'committees of the wise' or otherwise become part of the 'folklore' that influences how financial lawyers perceive certain well-known legal issues.[55]

One example of soft law is Basel II itself. Although the substance of Basel II **5.51** will be implemented by legislation in many countries around the world, and it is of course an extremely authoritative document, it has no legal effect itself. Another example is the very sensible practice of trade associations like ISLA and ISDA of producing and publishing not only standard form documentation but also legal opinions from well-known law firms which comment on the validity and enforceability of that documentation. Such opinions acquire a status in the market. Everyone knows that they are not 'law' but there is a very high degree of confidence that the opinions will have been thoroughly researched and can reasonably be relied on as to the statements of law that they contain.

A further example is the publication of papers by bodies like the Financial Law **5.52** Panel (FLP) (and, now, the Financial Markets Law Committee (FMLC)) and The Law Society and City of London Law Society (and their various technical committees), commenting on, for example, proposed new legislation or case law developments. These papers contain a great deal of material which, in effect, is a commentary on the existing law. Because of the composition of the various bodies concerned, who are able to call upon leading practitioners in London and elsewhere, from many different sources, these commentaries carry considerable weight. Indeed, if this were not the case, the FLP's practice of issuing 'guidance notices' would not have been worthwhile, since they would not have

---

[55] See also examples given by Cranston, in *Principles of Banking Law* (2nd edn) 50.

had any influence. Whether or not they are acting through the medium of bodies like these, the market practice of, and consensus of opinion built up by, finance lawyers practising in the City and elsewhere also plays a part in developing behaviour that responds to perceived legal risks. As Whittaker has observed, 'as practitioners, we influence the way in which law develops by formulating standard terms of business, helping develop common understandings of the legal position in areas of uncertainty, and contributing our bit to the development of custom and practice. Our authority comes from our skill and influence, and the respect which others may accord to it.'[56]

5.53 Soft law can be extremely useful. It fills gaps left by the unavoidable uncertainties that are produced from time to time by the common law system and constantly changing market practice (which produces a parallel constantly changing list of legal questions requiring answers). It also helps to address the impracticality of expecting every market participant to get its own detailed legal advice, and compare it with advice obtained by other participants, on every issue that may come up for consideration (including amendments to market documents that are already extremely complex). It is also part and parcel of the lobbying process and 'bridge to the judiciary'[57] that is now recognized as necessary if we are to keep financial law up to date and responsive to legitimate market expectations. It is doubtful that many of the advances made in financial law, in the UK, the EU, and elsewhere, could have been made as successfully as they have been in recent years if soft law developments had not led the way.

5.54 There are, however, risks involved in over-reliance on soft law sources (especially when combined with a reluctance to check things out for oneself). Markets, by their nature, tend to act from time to time on 'herd instinct'. Rumours of both legal problems and legal solutions will spread quickly. If it is whispered in one part of the City in the morning that, say, a new case has given rise to a significant legal issue, only the exceptionally ill-informed will not have heard about it (and started to worry about it) by the end of the day. So if it is argued by even a relatively small group of eminent lawyers that, for example, case law makes it difficult to create certain kinds of security under English law, there is every likelihood that the argument will develop into an established, even institutionalized, view in a relatively short period of time. Whether or not the argument is correct (which, of course, may be the case) the fact that most market participants believe it presents legal risk issues that will have to be dealt with. The most obvious risk (which is more likely to arise from a 'solution' rumour than a 'problem' rumour) is that market participants become lulled into believing that

---

[56] See Whittaker, 'Commentary' on 'Property, Private Government and the Myth of Deregulation' in S Worthington (ed), *Commercial Law and Commercial Practice* 115.
[57] The FMLC's own description of a key part of its role.

statements from soft law sources have become so authoritative that they do indeed represent the law and, as a result, take risks that are not justified and turn out to be misjudged in the light of subsequent case law. Over-reliance might also lead to the pressure for real (hard law) clarification and/or reform being eased up when, in fact, it should be increased.

A slightly different risk arises from the understandable desire to save on legal **5.55** costs by over-reliance on a standard, published opinion in circumstances that are not, on close analysis, addressed in that opinion. Formal legal opinions are highly technical documents. Typically, they contain a number of relatively short paragraphs expressing a view (the essence of the opinion) on the validity and enforceability of certain contractual provisions but those paragraphs are accompanied by longer, and more complex, paragraphs stating both assumptions (including assumptions of fact) made by the opinion-giver and qualifications to the opinion itself (for example, 'we express no opinion on the validity of provision (x)'). If an assumption of fact (for example, 'we have assumed the correctness of the opinion dated 3 March, 2005 of Messrs Blank and Blank, as to matters of Ruritanian law') turns out to be incorrect, that can undermine the entire opinion, rendering it, in effect, worthless. Such hazards may not always be apparent to a busy layman, who does not look beyond a trade association's statement that a given standard document has been considered by a well-known law firm, who have issued an opinion on it. Unfortunately, there are always going to be situations where you have to talk to your own lawyer if you are to keep legal risk under control.

Finally, there are evidently Type 1 risk implications resulting from the soft **5.56** law impact and potential influence on case law of the relatively recent proliferation of codes of conduct and similar documents. As is apparent from any visit to, say, the FSA's website, regulators maintain a constant output of information, guidance, advice, and warnings, in addition to the issuance of rules and regulations themselves. The FSA is also required by statute to issue documents such as the Code of Market Conduct.[58] Such promulgations (whether by the

---

[58] This is required by FSMA 2000, s 119. It must contain 'such provisions as the Authority considers will give appropriate guidance to those determining whether or not behaviour amounts to market abuse' (which is subject to penalties imposed by the FSA under FSMA 2000, s 123. Because the definition of market abuse in FSMA 2000 is somewhat vague (see s 118) the Code contains, amongst other things, provisions for 'safe harbours' which, where they apply, protect firms from being accused of market abuse (see s 122(1)). If a firm transgresses the Code, this may have evidential force against it in connection with any allegation of market abuse, since s 122(2) states that the Code 'may be relied on so far as it indicates whether or not . . . behaviour should be taken to amount to market abuse'. See further, Ch 8 below.

The relationship between the Code of Market Conduct and the City Code on Takeovers and Mergers is covered by FSMA 2000, s 120. The provisions for consultation as to the contents of the Code of Market Conduct are set out in s 121.

FSA or otherwise) can, and generally do, have the effect of (at least) soft law.[59] This may simply be because regulators' advice is not lightly ignored[60] or there may be other reasons why, say, a code of conduct, although theoretically requiring only 'voluntary' compliance, in fact has rather sharp teeth. This, for example, is the case with the Combined Code of Corporate Governance, in relation to which listed companies are required (by paragraph 12.43A of the Listing Rules) to 'comply or explain' in their annual report and accounts; and, of course, as indicated above, the FSA's Code of Market Conduct has its own statutory 'teeth' in relation to the possible imposition of penalties for market abuse.[61]

5.57 Statements about 'sound practice', 'market standards', 'appropriate' behaviour, etc, which, in most cases, go some way beyond encouragement merely to

---

[59] The FSA's Handbook distinguishes: (a) rules (designated by the icon **R**, made under various sections of FSMA 2000 which, for the most part, create binding obligations on firms and may be subject to enforcement action or actions for damages (these include the 'core' principles (or 'Principles for Business') referred at 10.07); (b) 'evidential' and similar provisions (icon: **E**), which, although rules, are not binding in their own right but relate to some other rule (they include descriptions of situations which create 'rebuttable presumptions' of compliance or contravention, they also include various paragraphs of The Code of Practice for Approved Persons and the Code of Market Conduct); (c) 'guidance' (icon: **G**) given under s.157 FSMA 2000, s 157, which is not binding and is not intended to have 'evidential' effect, although the FSA does state that 'if a person acts in accordance with general guidance in the circumstances contemplated by that guidance, then the FSA will proceed as if that person has complied with the aspects of the rule or other requirement to which the guidance relates'; (d) directions and requirements (icon: **D**) given pursuant to powers under FSMA 2000 (these are binding on the persons to whom they are addressed (e) 'legislative material' (eg Acts of Parliament, EU directives or statutory instruments) (icon; **UK** or **EU**, depending on origin); (f) Statements of Principle for approved persons (icon: **P**) made under FSMA 2000, s 64 and (g) 'descriptions of behaviour that, in the opinion of the FSA do not amount to market abuse' (icon: **C**)—see FSMA 2000, s 119(2)(b).

[60] The implications of various soft law initiatives for banks in the pre-FSA era were considered by Trust and Harris in 'Trends in Legal Risk' (1997) 7 JIBFL 291: 'The British Bankers' Association's . . . key principles for dealing with customers in financial difficulties were developed in response to industry-wide rejection of the DTI's consultative document on imposing a creditors' voluntary arrangement or a minimum 28-day moratorium on the appointment of receivers of an insolvent company's assets. The key principles set industry standards for banks in the way in which they deal with small- and medium-sized companies in financial difficulties. For example, the principles say that a bank will add its support to a rescue proposition which it believes will succeed. Unlike the other codes (such as The Bank of England's London Code of Conduct) the key principles may be tailored by individual banks which may allow for competitive advantage. Breach of the principles may affect awards made by the Banking Ombudsman. There is a risk that although the key principles are not legally binding, a court would interpret them as such if a customer sued a bank for not supporting them when they were in financial difficulties.'

[61] See n 58 above. The FSA also has power to issue 'statements of principle' under FSMA 2000, s 64 (and, if it does, it must also issue a related code of practice); s 64(8) helpfully provides that 'failure to comply with a statement of principle under this section does not of itself give rise to any right of action by persons affected or affect the validity of any transaction'.

comply with the law[62] do not just influence current behaviour; they can have a long-term effect on 'hard' law as well. Over time, such statements may well, through case law development based on evidence of market practice, become part of the legal fabric that applies to the financial markets. This could be the case, for example, in relation to the evolving law applicable to the acceptable management of 'Chinese walls' (and related conflict of interest questions) as well as the disclosure duties of those selling financial products of various kinds, even in the 'professionals market'.[63] There may be no harm in that (and perhaps it is what is intended), but the possibility of law developing in this way should be borne in mind if the exhortations to do what is 'appropriate' or expressions of concern about treating customers 'fairly', etc lack sufficient precision. It also needs to be borne in mind that soft law of this kind is more susceptible to ongoing political interference and influence in its interpretation and application. What is fair or appropriate (and other similarly vague concepts may also apply) may vary with the eye of the beholder, especially if the beholder is not subject to the rigours that apply to judicial proceedings and a decision-making process that is required to observe the constraints of precedent.

Further, not all such exhortations originate from regulators. Many companies **5.58** (including banks), mindful of the need to demonstrate sound 'governance' practices, environmental awareness,[64] politically acceptable employment policies, etc now have their own codes of conduct for officers and employees covering a wide range of issues, and these, in turn, tend to be grist to the mill for potential litigants, ranging from aggrieved employees to dissatisfied investors.[65] It is not

---

[62] eg see the letter dated 17 September 2004 from Hector Sants (Managing Director, Wholesale and Institutional Markets, FSA) to various investment banks regarding conflicts of interest. He says: 'I am writing to remind you of your responsibility to implement appropriate processes and procedures for the effective management of conflicts of interest and risks arising from financing transactions . . .' The letter states that it is only describing existing requirements (or 'standards') rather than announcing new ones and then goes on to set out 'practices of management which we expect to see in a well managed firm'.

[63] See also the examples considered at 8.17–8.23 below of how compliance with a code of conduct may be taken into account by the FSA in determining whether or not market abuse has occurred.

[64] An increasing number of banks are now formalizing their 'environmental awareness' policy statements by agreeing to comply with the 'Equator Principles'.

[65] The interaction between law and notions of correct 'corporate governance' has given rise to a number of concerns (including the responsibility of in-house counsel, considered in Ch 11). The views of the US Chamber of Commerce are particularly strident:

The unintended expansion of corporate governance rules and excessive compliance demands will cost the nation's 17,000 public companies billions of dollars this year [2005]. Entire industries have been consumed by multiple, sweeping demands from competing regulators for their data, emails and correspondence. These excesses have discouraged bold business decision making, have sent both domestic and foreign companies fleeing from public markets, and have hurt efforts to attract strong board members and executives to public companies.

always apparent that the formulation of documents of this kind is subject to the rigour that might be appropriate, given their potential effect on individuals' and market participants' rights and liabilities. Nor are such documents always given the publicity and accessibility that they merit (although, as indicated above, the FSA is subject to the publicity and other requirements of FSMA 2000 with regard to codes issued by it).

Interaction of 'soft law' with consumerism

5.59 As has been noted above,[66] the FSA, like most regulators, has a specific concern for the interest of consumers and 'small investors' and much of the content of codes of conduct (issued by the FSA and others) reflects this. There is a balance to be struck here in relation, on the one hand, to the 'consumer-friendly' policy that underlies much soft law and, on the other hand, to the risk of creating (or perpetuating) a climate where people believe that for every ill there must be a remedy, and the remedy takes the form of a claim for compensation. It has been mentioned elsewhere[67] that there are signs that the 'compensation culture' has been allowed to grow unchecked for too long and that this is beginning to have damaging social consequences. And yet, in the field of financial services, we seem to have become so concerned about 'consumer rights' that we come perilously close to encouraging the disappointed to 'have a go' (as Lord Falconer might have put it). For example, the author recently received correspondence from an insurance company relating to an endowment policy that he owned. The policy had been a slightly disappointing investment, reflecting a period of stock market turbulence. The insurer's letter referred to an enclosed 'FSA factsheet' and advised: 'Do read this carefully and think about what action you should take.' The 'factsheet' (an FSA publication) included the following text:

> This information sheet sets out what you can complain about and how you go about making a complaint.
>
> **Do I have grounds for making a complaint?**
> You may have grounds for making a complaint if your adviser did not:
> - tell you how your money would be invested and explain the risks involved;
> - explain that an endowment policy is a long-term commitment that often gives a poor return if you cash it in early;
> - check you were comfortable with the risks of your money being linked to investment performance, including the stockmarket;
> - check there was a reasonable expectation you would be able to keep up payments until the end of the term; and

---

Outside groups with special interest agendas—such as trial lawyers, labor unions, public pension funds . . . and rating agencies . . .—are exploiting concerns about corporate governance to win concessions and advance their interests.

[66] See para 5.43.   [67] See para Intro 1.48.

- explain any fees and charges and how they would affect the return on your savings. If you bought your policy between 29 April 1988 and 1 January 1995, you should have been given 'product particulars' including charges and surrender values for the first five years. If you bought your policy on or after 1 January 1995, you should have been given a Key Features document with details of fees and charges and their effect on your savings over the longer term.

Some of the above advice ('you may have grounds for making a complaint if **5.60** ...') verges on the suggestive, not least because so many complaints of the kind described would turn on 'your word against mine' disputes, which an out-of-pocket investor may well be tempted to launch (and which are difficult to defend). There was also information provided on how to make a complaint, guidance on specific scenarios that might or might not justify a complaint, and a reference to the FSA's Consumer website.[68]

Recently, Abbey National was fined £800,000 by the FSA for failing to handle **5.61** customer complaints properly (and also providing 'misleading information' to the FSA).[69] The 'factsheet' referred to above is mentioned in the FSA's final notice to Abbey National. It was first released in October 2000 as part of measures taken to ensure 'redress for those customers who had lost out as a result of mis-selling'. The FSA took the view that the complaints handling procedures of regulated firms were a better mechanism for redress than a 'blanket industry-wide review'. According to the final notice:

> In the period from 1 January until the end of September 2002 Abbey received approximately 5,900 mortgage endowment complaints. From October 2002, Abbey experienced a sudden increase in the volume of its mortgage endowment complaints, receiving a further 9,653 complaints during Q4 2002 alone. The dramatic rise in the number of mortgage endowment complaints received by Abbey from October 2002 was due to a general increase in awareness on the part of consumers that their endowment policy might not generate enough money to pay off their mortgage loan at maturity. This increased awareness resulted from 'reprojection' letters that were issued to all mortgage endowment policy holders from 2002 onwards. The purpose of the reprojection letters was to provide all mortgage endowment policy holders with clear and timely information about any shortfall they might be facing on their endowment and the options for addressing that shortfall. The reprojection letters were also accompanied by the FSA factsheet 'Endowment Mortgage Complaints' . . . Complaint volumes continued at a similar level from the period Q4 2002 onwards . . . In the four year period from 1 January 2001 to 31 December 2004, Abbey received approximately 65,000 mortgage endowment complaints . . .

---

[68] http://www.fsa.gov.uk/consumer.
[69] See 'Final Notice' to Abbey National from the FSA, dated 25 May 2005. Previous fines for similar offences had been levied by the FSA on Friends Provident (£675,000 in December 2003) and Allied Dunbar (£725,000 in March 2004).

5.62   Whatever one might feel about the particularities of the Abbey National case (and the text of Abbey's decision letter to customers, rejecting complaints, as cited in the final notice, does not make for very comfortable reading) there can be no doubt of the effectiveness of documents like the 'factsheet' in stimulating complaints. There may well have been substance to most of them and, in this regard, perhaps the consumer has been well served by the FSA's efforts. The impact on legal risk, however, is unmistakable.

5.63   It is also striking that the 'offences' that justified the fine were breaches of two of the very broadly worded Business Principles of the FSA,[70] namely:

1)   A bank must conduct its business with due skill, care and diligence (Principle 2); and
2)   A bank must pay due regard to the interests of its customers and treat them fairly (Principle 6).

5.64   Principle 2 was held to be infringed by both the mishandling of the complaints and also Abbey's communications with the FSA on the subject. Principle 6 was held to be infringed (also) by the mishandling of the complaints. The FSA, amongst other things, found that 'on occasions Abbey placed its own interests above those of its customers and it communicated with customers in such a manner that may have discouraged customers from exercising their rights and referring their complaints to the [Financial Ombudsman Service]'.[71] Even though Abbey may have been at fault in this case (and it has agreed to pay 'full redress to customers whose complaints should have been at fault') the risk implications of the existence of what is, in effect, a 'law' (whether one judges it to be soft or hard) that may be paraphrased as 'conduct your business properly' (Principle 2) are considerable. As noted elsewhere[72] the FSA is conscious that its Principles are not framed as rigid 'rules' (although they are, technically, rules for the purposes of the regulatory regime) and therefore not something that can be avoided easily on the basis of the technical drafting. This may be laudable insofar as it makes it much more difficult for the wrongdoer to escape punishment on technical grounds. The problem (and it is a problem with all laws of this nature) is that it makes it difficult for the citizen (in the form of the regulated entity) to know where he stands and, in particular, where the border-line is to be drawn between (a) not being very good at his job (for which he suffers by virtue of poor returns in his business), and (b) being so bad at his job that he is causing others material harm (for which he should also be punished by law). There is also a serious difficulty in that the law tends to put too much

---

[70] See para 10.02.
[71] Some of the implications of the Abbey decision for risk management are considered in para 10.32.
[72] See paras 10.02 and 10.03.

power into the hands of the executive. One is, and should always be, instinctively mistrustful of broadly drawn penal laws[73] that appear to 'catch' activity that most would not regard as meriting criminal (or quasi-criminal) punishment but which are justified by the executive on the grounds that they would 'be reasonable' about how they apply them. Even the regulated are entitled to the protection implicit in the rule of law. The citizen's guilt should not turn upon the exercise of executive discretion.

Shortly after receiving the factsheet referred to above, the author also received a **5.65** document accompanying his bank statement, informing him about the Banking Code[74] and his high street bank's 'key commitments' to its customers. These commitments included: 'We will deal quickly and sympathetically with things that go wrong and consider all cases of financial difficulty sympathetically and positively', as well as assurances about confidentiality, clear information about services, honest advertising, and so on. There was also a separate section on 'How to make a complaint'. This was slightly less forthcoming than the FSA document, informing the reader: 'If you ask us, we will tell you how to make a complaint and how quickly we will deal with it.' At best, this is rather cold comfort. One wonders whether statements of this kind, which are no doubt made with the best of intentions, really serve any useful purpose.

There are, of course, very good reasons for making sure that consumers are **5.66** aware of their rights. To the extent a question is being raised here about such materials, it is a question of degree. Is there a danger that we might, for example, be prompting those who *knowingly* bought a financial product or service that involved a degree of risk to avoid the consequences of that willingly accepted risk by making claims that rely on an ever-expanding definition of mis-selling or duty of disclosure? ('You told me there were risks involved in this kind of investment, but you did not *explain* those risks sufficiently fully or clearly, at least not in terms that a layman would find easy to understand; you did not treat me fairly, and you can't prove that you did.')

There are signs that the combination of consumer protection policy and our **5.67** litigious culture may be tilting the balance too far off centre. This concern is evidently felt by the Financial Services Practitioner Panel, which, in its Annual Report for 2004/5, commented on the FSA's 'Treat Customers Fairly' initiative (TCF) that: 'The Panel feels strongly that it is not possible to consider TCF in

---

[73] See further Ch 8 below.
[74] The latest version of 'The Banking Code' was issued in March 2005, under the auspices of the British Bankers Association, The Building Societies Association, and APACS (the Association for Payment Clearing Services). It is 'monitored' by the Banking Code Standards Board, 'whose directors include a majority of independent members as well as representatives of financial institutions'.

isolation from the principle of caveat emptor (buyer beware). The responsibilities that consumers themselves must take for their investment decisions—an obligation that remains enshrined in the FSMA legislation—should not be overlooked by the FSA.'[75]

5.68 There seems to be a built-in assumption that investors, over time, only become more, not less, naive and that they are entitled to legal protection against the consequences of that naivety. Many of us have become accustomed to being informed that the value of investments can go down as well as up; we also receive warnings that 'where an investment is denominated in a foreign currency, changes in rates of exchange may have an adverse effect on the value of the investment in sterling terms'. The regulators' requirements can extend to compelling the regulated not merely to make 'warning' or 'informational' statements but also to make statements that clearly could have contractual effect and this often seems to follow, directly or indirectly, from the issuance of codes of conduct.[76] This is soft law with a cutting edge. There is a cost associated with 'cotton wool balling' the consumer. The cost arises not only because firms who sense they are at risk will price that risk, and the cost of managing it, into their products and services but also because of the influence that is spread into other areas and the general contribution to the compensation culture. One concern is that the trend towards encouraging the making of claims in situations where the fault of the person complained against is far from self-evident is encouraging 'deep-pocket' litigation—or at least complaints to the Financial Ombudsman Service.[77] In some cases, no consumers may be involved. Liquidators of failed financial companies, for example, seem to be particularly imaginative. This may be good news for lawyers but how far do we want to go?

---

[75] The Panel has a statutory basis under FSMA 2000, s 9; it comprises 'senior figures from a cross-section of the financial services industry, to provide a high-level body available for consultation on policy by the FSA and which is able to communicate to the FSA views and concerns of the regulated industries'. Its views on the FSA's consumerism were expressed in more trenchant terms in its preceding Annual Report: 'Too much emphasis on over-regulation, reviews of disclosure and selling practices, and Government-imposed product designs pose a serious threat to the competitiveness of UK firms. It is worth considering at what point the regulator, in seeking to protect consumers, actually starts to damage competition and innovation, so disadvantaging the very people whose interests it is seeking to safeguard.'

[76] Ellinger, Lomnika, and Hooley, *Modern Banking Law* (3rd edn) 61, point out that the provisions of the Banking Code, eg 'will no doubt be treated as implied terms in the banking contract'.

[77] According to the FOS' Annual Review and Report and Financial Statements for 2004/5, complaints to it in that year increased by 12% over the preceding year, and complaints about mortgage endowment policies represented 63% of all complaints. About 12% of all mortgage endowment complaints were referred to the FOS by 'claims management' (no win, no fee) companies.

Globalization

Many of the source categories considered involve, or emanate from, the **5.69** phenomenon known as globalization. Under this heading we are concerned with what might loosely be termed the import and export of legal concepts and transaction structures. Much of the innovation in financial law has originated in common law jurisdictions, because that is where the main financial markets are located. If we again take the example of limited recourse project finance techniques, developed to a significant extent in UK North Sea financings but then extended to infrastructure financings such as Eurotunnel and the UK's PFI and PPP programme, we can see that a fundamental element in the security structure required by project lenders is the floating charge,[78] pursuant to which the banks can obtain valid and effective security over all the project assets. In this context, project assets include physical assets such as land, buildings, and machinery, as well as intangible assets such as rights under contracts and revenues from the exploitation of the project. Since the financing is limited recourse (with the banks being expected to look to the success of the project for repayment, thus taking 'project risk') it is vital to the banks that they have 'first call' on project assets, through enforcing security, if problems arise and they need to take legal action to recover the project loans. It is also vital, since the borrower's most valuable asset will usually be the income produced by the project rather than physical assets, that the banks can have effective security over future cash flows. All of this can be done relatively easily in common law jurisdictions. In civil law jurisdictions the position is different. It is not at all easy for banks to obtain security of this kind.

Much has been written about the difficulties that arise in civil law jurisdictions **5.70** with regard to security instruments, especially for those seeking something akin to a floating charge or a charge over 'future property'. It is an area so far untouched by EU legal harmonization. There have, however, been a number of important law reform initiatives launched by bodies such as the European Bank for Reconstruction and Development (EBRD), UNCITRAL, and the Organization for Economic Cooperation and Development (OECD). All of these initiatives are designed to enable countries who wish to attract investment for infrastructure improvement, and other purposes, and who wish to facilitate transactions for trade financing, to reform their laws relating to security interests so that they allow lending banks to take security of the kind described above. These initiatives involve a degree of 'import/export' of legal concepts. They are not easy to devise or implement and, sometimes, they conflict with deeply felt convictions and values regarding business and commercial reality. They cannot

---

[78] See para 9.19 for discussion of the floating charge as an example of innovation.

just be 'bolted on'. They have to function alongside related laws on insolvency, property, and contract. But the reform process has gathered a head of steam and is likely to continue.

5.71 Other examples of cross-pollination can be found in more specific areas, such as the validity of close-out netting provisions, and various insolvency law initiatives. As we have seen,[79] the law relating to set-off is of extraordinary importance to the financial markets. Set-off has many of the characteristics of traditional security instruments, such as mortgages and charges but, unlike such instruments, is 'international' in that it is not a creature of any particular national legal system; it is a contractual device recognized by most modern legal systems. It is, arguably, the ideal security device for a global market. However, it has to be treated with caution, and this is where the serious legal risk arises, because however easy it may be under various laws to enter into a contractual set-off arrangement, the way those various laws treat the rights of a party relying on set-off in the event of the other party's insolvency varies enormously from country to country. There are serious limits to how much financial law has been globalized, especially in comparison to the markets that rely upon it.

5.72 The international law reform initiatives that have been taken in relation to netting, insolvency, etc are designed to reduce risk. However, the fact that the initiatives are needed, and are being taken at such high levels, demonstrates that, for the time being at least, there are significant legal risks involved in the markets' assuming a globalization of legal concepts that, in reality, is only just beginning and, consequently, not having adequate regard to the variety inherent in the many legal cultures that underpin the global financial market.

---

[79] See Ch 3 above.

6

CAUSATION

... what or who has caused a certain event to occur is essentially a practical question of fact which can best be answered by ordinary common sense rather than by metaphysical theory.[1]

The first point to emphasise is that common sense answers to questions of causation will differ according to the purpose for which the question is being asked. Questions of causation often arise for the purpose of attributing responsibility to someone, for example, so as to blame him for something or make him guilty of an offence or liable in damages. In such cases, the answer will depend upon the rule by which responsibility is being attributed. Take, for example, the case of the man who forgets to take the radio out of his car and during the night someone breaks the quarterlight, enters the car and steals it. What caused the damage? If the thief is on trial, so that the question is whether he is criminally responsible, then obviously the answer is that he caused the damage. It is no answer for him to say that it was caused by the owner carelessly leaving the radio inside. On the other hand, the owner's wife, irritated at the third such occurrence in a year, might well say that it was his fault. In the context of an inquiry into the owner's blameworthiness under a non-legal, common sense duty to take reasonable care of one's own possessions, one would say that his carelessness caused the loss of the radio.[2]

A. Risks and Causation Chains

What is the relationship between the sources of legal risk identified by Joanna **6.01** Benjamin,[3] as considered in Chapter 5 above, and the causes of loss attributable to legal risk identified in the IBA definition? Whereas the sources describe the

---

[1] *Per* Lord Salmon in *Alphacell Ltd v Woodward* [1972] AC 824, 847.

[2] *Per* Lord Hoffmann in *Environment Agency (formerly National Rivers Authority) v Empress Car Co (Abertillery) Ltd* [1999] 2 AC 22.

[3] Benjamin, 'Sources of Legal Risk for Financial Institutions' in the Report of the IBA symposium on Legal Risk (October 2003) App 1, published as a special supplement to the JIBFL of April 2004.

social circumstances that cause legal risk to arise, the definition is concerned with how an institution, when faced with a legal risk-originated problem (or a potential such problem), should answer the question: how did this happen (or how can we prevent this happening)? Consideration of the sources helps us to understand why legal risks arise in the broader social context but it is the definition that provides the pointer to the more immediate causes of risk and loss in any specific context. If a loss arises that appears to be attributable to legal risk, questions will be raised as to whether the risk was properly managed by those responsible and what lessons can be learned for the future. Such questions are essentially questions of causation, and they are important to an institution's assessment of whether its legal risk management system[4] is working properly.

6.02 In considering causation, it is helpful to distinguish the various different kinds of event that may be involved in causing risk, and then loss, to arise. The following components will generally be present in a legal risk causation chain:

- **Legal risk events:** These are the events or circumstances that cause the risk to arise. Examples include failure to take legal advice when necessary, employing poorly qualified advisers, understaffing the legal department, misunderstanding advice, failing to follow internal compliance rules, and so on.[5]

- **Definitional causes of loss:** These are the causes of potential loss that are 'built into' the legal risk definition. Examples include adverse claims in the courts and defective documentation. (It is easy to confuse the definitional cause of loss with the legal risk event. They are not the same thing. Any number of events or circumstances might cause the *risk* of loss to arise. The cause of actual loss, if it is to be attributed to legal risk, has to fit within the narrower range of causes contained in the definition.)

- **Loss trigger events:** These are the events that are the most proximate cause of loss. They include the insolvency of a customer, adverse government action (such as the confiscation of assets) and the commencement of litigation against the institution.

- **Intermediate events:** These events precede loss trigger events in the causation chain, but do not fit into any other category. An example would be a decision to extend a credit line to a customer which subsequently defaults and cannot honour its obligations. They may be extremely numerous.

---

[4] Legal risk management in general is considered in Chs 10 and 11 below.
[5] Many other examples are provided in the FLP paper, referred to in Ch 5 above.

The categories are not mutually exclusive. One event may qualify for more than **6.03** one category. A simple causation chain involving all the above is set out below as an example:

(1) Bank A launches a new financial product in Ruritania.
(2) Bank A obtains only incomplete legal advice about the laws and regulations applicable to the marketing of the new product in Ruritania.
(3) Bank A sells the product to Customer B, a telecommunications company incorporated, and resident, in Ruritania. This results in the bank having a credit exposure to Customer B (a Ruritanian incorporated company) of £10 million.
(4) Because Bank A has failed to make the appropriate filings in Ruritania, its claims against Customer B rank behind all other creditors of Customer B in the event of Customer B's insolvency.
(5) Customer B becomes insolvent. After its other creditors have been paid there are no other assets available to pay any part of Bank A's claim.

We can see that, applying the classification of events suggested above, the loss **6.04** trigger event is the insolvency of Customer B (see (5) above), the principal legal risk event is the failure to obtain full advice (see (2) above), the subordination of the bank's claims is the definitional cause of loss and the other events described are intermediate events. (The failure to make the appropriate filings is also a legal risk event, although it is of secondary importance as regards causation. If Bank A had actually been advised to make the filings but had overlooked that advice, that failure to follow advice would qualify as the principal legal risk event.)

It is a feature of Type 2 legal risks (such as that described in the above example) **6.05** that the legal risk event or events might lie undetected for some time. Comparison might be made with a failure to take out insurance against one's house being damaged by fire. The risk event (ie the event that causes the risk of financial loss to arise) is the failure to insure. Many years may pass before the seriousness of the risk becomes apparent. The loss is triggered if a fire actually occurs. On the other hand, legal risk events giving rise to Type 1 legal risks tend to be easier to spot and are usually much closer, both in absolute time and the sequence of events, to the loss trigger event. This is because acts or omissions that entitle a third party to bring a legal claim usually trigger some form of complaint at an early stage and the nexus between the complaint and the act complained of is usually reasonably close. With Type 1 legal risks, the loss trigger event may well be the same as the definitional cause of loss. This is likely to depend on how any specific claim is actually handled. There are, however, occasions when the more imaginative claimant, identifying a bank as a 'deep pocket', might seek to establish liability on the basis of causal connections which are far from obvious, and will usually come as a surprise to the bank. In such cases, the nexus between the legal risk event and the loss trigger event may not be so close.

6.06 Legal risk events are thus not necessarily the most proximate cause of loss (or, using the terminology suggested above, the 'loss trigger event'). They may be no more than causes *sine qua non* (sometimes known as 'but for' causes, because the loss would not have been suffered but for the event). There should, however, be a reasonably strong causal connection between the legal risk event, the definitional cause of loss, and the actual loss, if the loss is to be attributed to legal risk and so recorded. The events in the causation chain should be more than mere conditions of the loss occurring. Therefore, taking the example set out above:

(1) it would be wrong to attribute Bank A's loss to legal risk if Customer B had no assets to satisfy *any* of its creditors; and

(2) it would be wrong to attribute Bank A's loss to its decision to launch the new product in Ruritania; it could have done this with much less risk if it had taken proper advice. However, if it is known that the laws of Ruritania are very unclear as regards the rights of foreign banks in the insolvency of a Ruritanian company, it is not difficult to envisage a situation where that decision alone might constitute a legal risk event (perhaps together with other events that could be properly so described).

6.07 A more difficult question arises as to whether Bank A's loss should be attributed to credit risk in the telecommunications sector (or the Ruritanian telecommunications sector). Consider also, how one might attribute the loss if Customer B was owned by the Ruritanian state. It could be argued that it was due to 'country risk' or 'sovereign risk' in Ruritania, ie forms of credit or market risk. Whilst one might have misgivings about, in effect, ignoring the legal risk event by attributing the loss in such a way, it does not seem unreasonable, in cases where there are several candidates for 'principal cause', to allow institutions to choose what they think is most appropriate. After all, they should be in the best position to analyse and evaluate the true cause, and that process will, of course, have an impact on their future behaviour (no more risks on Ruritanian telecommunications, or a more rigorous approach to Ruritanian legal advice?) as well as on how they record the cause of the problem. The important thing is that the loss is not 'double-counted' for regulatory and capital adequacy purposes merely because its cause is arguably a combination of more than one kind of risk. As our analysis has shown, the causes of loss that comprise definitional causes of loss for legal risk will very often be followed by other causes of loss, including intermediate events and the loss trigger event itself. However, a later cause is not necessarily the primary cause.

One can summarize the relationship between risk and causation as follows: **6.08**

(1) Causes are not the same as risks. Causes of loss arise for consideration because the loss has actually occurred, or is virtually certain to occur. A risk, on the other hand, arises when there may be a loss in the future, but it is not certain that there will be. This may seem an obvious distinction to make, but it is easily forgotten.

(2) A loss may have more than one cause. This will, in fact, frequently be the case. A typical example is the case of the defective security and the subsequent insolvency. Both the insolvency and the absence of security combine to cause the loss. But, in the typical case, if the security would have given adequate cover, the primary cause of loss is the defective security rather than the insolvency.

(3) The presence of a legal risk event in the causation chain leading to loss is not, by itself, sufficient to warrant the conclusion that the loss is attributable to legal risk. There may be other events that should properly be regarded as the primary cause, or at least as significant contributing factors.

(4) The loss trigger event is, by definition, close in terms of sequence of events to the actual occurrence of the loss, but it may not be the primary cause of the loss.

(5) The fact that an institution has a history of very few losses attributable to, say, legal risk events does not necessarily justify the conclusion that it is managing legal risk well (although it is certainly a positive indicator). A poor goalkeeper in a football team may be protected by an outstanding 'back four'. (The converse is, of course, also true.)

B. Case Law and Common Sense

Causation questions are of course notoriously difficult in law, especially in the   **6.09** context of criminal and tort liability.[6] Some of the more complex fact scenarios considered in the cases on negligence illustrate why a 'but-for' test tends to be too simplistic and too easy to satisfy, particularly where the facts suggest multiple causes. The cases also show that our courts are still grappling with novel and complex causation questions. For an institution that is trying to establish the 'real cause' of a particular loss, the various approaches taken by the judges might be instructive (although not, of course, binding on an institution that wishes to take a different view of causation).

In the recent case of *Chester v Afshar*[7] the House of Lords acknowledged that it is   **6.10** 'generally accepted that the "but for" test does not provide a comprehensive or

---

[6] See Hart and Honore, *Causation and the Law* (2nd edn) especially ch V.
[7] [2004] UKHL 41.

exclusive test in the law of tort'.[8] The case is interesting because of the approach taken to causation in an extreme situation where there was clearly a desire to find a remedy for an individual who had (a) not received adequate warning from her surgeon about the risks involved in a back operation, and (b) suffered a serious injury as a result of the operation, which left her partly paralysed. On conventional legal causation logic, the plaintiff's claim was in some difficulties because, although it was accepted that the warning should have been given, it was far from clear that, if she had received the warning, the plaintiff would have refused absolutely to have the operation (although she might have postponed it). As Lord Hope put it:

> . . . how can causation be established when, as in this case, the patient would not have refused absolutely there and then and for ever to undergo the operation if told of the risks but would have postponed her decision until later? The problem is rendered more acute in this case by the fact that the failure to warn cannot be said in any way to have increased the risk of injury. The risk was inherent in the operation itself . . . It can be said that Miss Chester would not have suffered her injury 'but for' Mr. Afshar's failure to warn her of the risks, as she would have declined to be operated on by him on 21 November 1994. But it is difficult to say that his failure was the effective cause of the injury.

6.11 The majority of their lordships, acknowledging 'a narrow and modest departure from traditional causation principles',[9] decided in the plaintiff's favour, achieving a result which they felt was 'in accord with one of the most basic aspirations of the law, namely to right wrongs'.[10] The House was clearly influenced by the very similar Australian case, *Chappel v Hart*,[11] and by a perceived need to respect the patient's 'autonomy and dignity', which, due to the absence of informed consent consequent upon the absence of the warning, were regarded as having been flouted. The law imposed a duty on the surgeon to warn patients about risks involved in operations, and: 'The principal reason for imposing this duty is to promote the patient's decision making autonomy. The law should deem the doctor to have assumed the risk of injury as though, in failing to mention it, he had warranted that it would not materialise. Or one could say that the doctor is estopped from pointing to the existence and unavoidable nature of the risk.'[12]

6.12 The case represented something of a leap from established precedent. It was not long before an attempt was made to test the application of the 'new' approach to causation in the context of the provision of financial advice and a 'failure' to advise on the possibility of making an investment in a less risky manner (buying an annuity) than the one actually chosen. The Court of Appeal case of *Beary v*

---

[8] See dissenting judgment of Lord Bingham, para 8 and also judgment of Lord Hope, para 73.
[9] *Per* Lord Steyn, para 24.   [10] *Per* Lord Steyn, para 25.
[11] (1998) 195 CLR 232.   [12] *Per* Lord Hope, para 77.

Pall Mall Investments[13] concerned advice given to an individual regarding the investment of the proceeds of his self-administered pension fund. It was common ground that the adviser was negligent in not advising the plaintiff that an annuity was an alternative possibility to the investments that were actually chosen (which performed badly). However, the question had arisen in the lower court as to whether, if this possibility had been raised, the plaintiff would in fact have proceeded differently. The judge was not persuaded that he would have done and that conclusion was not challenged in the appeal. In short, it was accepted that there had been negligence but it was not accepted that this caused the losses complained of. The plaintiff's counsel sought to persuade the Court of Appeal that the reasoning in *Chester v Afshar* should apply. It was acknowledged that *Chester* was a case which turned very much on its particular facts and the House of Lords' assessment of policy considerations. But why not treat investment advice as though it was subject to similar policy considerations as those applicable to medical advice? Paraphrasing the argument, Dyson LJ pondered that question: 'Pension advice is as important to an individual's financial health as medical advice is to his or her physical health.'

The argument was roundly rejected by Dyson LJ: **6.13**

> In *Chester v Afshar*, the majority made it very clear that the departure from established principles of causation in that case was exceptional, and was justified by the particular policy considerations that are in play where there is a breach of the doctor's duty to advise a patient of the disadvantages and dangers of proposed treatment so as to enable the patient to give informed consent. The analogy that [plaintiff's counsel] seeks to draw between a breach of the doctor's duty of care and breach of the duty of care owed by financial advisers (whether in relation to pensions or otherwise) is unconvincing. The subject-matter of the two duties is very different. The policy considerations applicable to the duty to give proper financial advice and the duty to give proper medical advice are quite different. The suggestion that the established principles of causation should be rejected in *all* cases of negligent financial advice is breathtakingly ambitious, contrary to authority and, in my view, wrong.

Had the case gone the other way, the repercussions for advisory businesses in the   **6.14**
financial services sector would have been very significant. This was a potential 'surprise case law' legal risk trigger that, fortunately, failed to materialize.

The cases illustrate causal chains that may have parallels from time to time when   **6.15**
legal risk management is under scrutiny. For example, the possibility of incorrect legal advice being received (or correct legal advice being ignored) is a fact of life for all financial institutions. If this happens, legal risks are likely to follow. But suppose the result of the bad advice is that a charge that should have been

---

[13] [2005] EWCA Civ 415.

registered over a borrower's assets is not registered. If the borrower defaults, and the assets would, if realized, have paid off the loan, then any failure to recover as an unsecured creditor (and the related loss) may be fairly attributed to legal risk. But if the assets in question were, in the event, worth only 10 per cent of the loan, the failure to recover has other causes, perhaps reflecting a poor judgement of the borrower's business generally.

6.16 Accidents will happen, but we find it difficult to resist the temptation to rush to pin the blame on someone or something. Accidents in the operating theatre can lead to loss of life or severe physical disability. Accidents in the provision of financial services can lead to a loss of money. Who is to blame? The answer to the question, as the cases referred to above demonstrate, may be complex and require time for thorough investigation and analysis. What would we now say, with the benefit of more than a decade for reflection, was the real cause of the *Hammermith and Fulham* debacle?[14] Was it bad law, a faulty interpretation of the law by the courts, or failure to obtain the best legal advice?

6.17 If one further comparison with case law fact scenarios may be permitted, motor accidents involving negligence by more than one party also offer interesting parallels. Consider, for example, the case of the motorist whose car broke down on a foggy night on a dual carriageway.[15] The car came to rest in the nearside lane. It should have been moved out of the way but it was not. A lorry, travelling at 60 mph (which was far too fast in the foggy conditions) crashed into it, causing enormous damage and seriously injuring a passenger in the back seat. The lorry then continued, out of control, onto the other side of the central reservation where it turned onto its side and blocked the road. Four vehicles hit it, resulting in one death and one serious injury. Who should be held responsible for what consequences? The 'but-for' test would cause most, if not all, the blame to be placed on the head of the driver of the car that broke down. But for the obstruction in the nearside lane, the accident would not have happened. However, the lorry driver was driving negligently and should not escape blame. The Court of Appeal held the car driver and the lorry driver jointly responsible for the injury to the passenger in the broken down car but the lorry driver solely responsible for the collisions on the other side of the dual carriageway. The court placed considerable reliance on what it termed 'common sense standards'. Although resorting to common sense in a technical legal context can, on occasion, be evidence of either a desire to avoid precedent or

---

[14] See Ch 1 above.
[15] See *Wright v Lodge* [1993] 4 All ER 299. For an example of difficult causation issues in the context of reliance on fraudulent misrepresentation, see *Barton v County NatWest Ltd* [1999] All ER 782.

an acceptance that the precedents do not help, those seeking the true cause of loss (by reference to whatever categories of risk may be relevant) in the context of operational problems of banks and other financial institutions could do worse than remember that if the answer to the question 'Who or what is to blame?' does not appear to accord with common sense, it is probably the wrong answer.

Part III

EXAMPLES

7

PROPERTY INTERESTS IN INDIRECTLY HELD INVESTMENT SECURITIES

Ownership, dominium, propriete, Eigentum and similar words stand not merely for the greatest interest in things in particular systems but for a type of interest with common features transcending particular systems. It must surely be important to know what these common features are? . . .

Ownership comprises the right to possess, the right to use, the right to manage, the right to the income of the thing, the right to the capital, the right to security, the right or incidents of transmissibility and absence of term, the prohibition of harmful use, liability to execution, and the incident of residuarity: this makes eleven leading incidents. Obviously there are alternative ways of classifying the incidents; moreover, it is fashionable to speak of ownership as if it were just a bundle of rights, in which case at least two items in the list would have to be omitted.[1]

Drafters of other international instruments have found it unexpectedly difficult to use ostensibly common legal concepts such as 'property' or 'possession' in a manner which would be interpreted in the same sense in all legal systems.[2]

A. Market Practice Compared with Law

We have seen, in Chapter 3 above, how English law, through a combination of **7.01** case law and legislation (and a certain amount of 'soft law' and practitioner ingenuity), exorcised various legal risk demons associated with set-off, netting, and payment systems that arose during the final two decades of the twentieth century. Following the various cases involving BCCI referred to in Chapter 3, the Companies Act 1989, and numerous regulations implementing EU directives

---

[1] From essay on 'Ownership' by AM Honore in *Oxford Essays in Jurisprudence*, 1961.
[2] From the Explanatory Notes to UNIDROIT's 'Preliminary Draft Convention on Harmonised Substantive Rules Regarding Securities Held with an Intermediary', December 2004 (see n 3 below).

on settlement finality and financial collateral (as well as recent regulations updating the Insolvency Rules 1986) the position under English law on the more difficult set-off and netting questions is now reasonably clear. We cannot, however, afford to be complacent. Legal risk issues are still providing food for thought and a degree of concern, and, as ever with low probability/high impact events, may slip under our guard if we allow them to be perceived as of interest to academics only.

7.02 As noted in Chapter 4, the markets' preoccupation now is with Type 1 risks rather than Type 2 risks. This reflects the litigious and highly regulated age in which we live. Examples of current Type 1 risks will be considered further in Chapters 8 and 9 below. In this chapter, however, we shall examine a Type 2 risk that has not yet been fully addressed by law reform, although its existence has been recognized both by the Financial Markets Law Committee (FMLC) in the UK and by the Giovannini Group in the EU. It has also been the focus of a great deal of work by UNIDROIT.[3] The issues involved have been described by the FMLC as giving rise to a 'high level of legal risk'.[4] They arise because, once again, the financial markets appear to have run some way ahead of the law, in this case, in relation to the manner in which ownership structures for securities and related transactions are set up. Apart from the concerns expressed by the FMLC, the discrepancies between law and practice have been described by UNIDROIT as producing a situation where 'the legal risk in the area of securities holding and disposition is particularly high'.[5]

7.03 The risks arise because, although there have been some recent reforms (discussed below), the substantive law regarding the holding and disposal of corporate securities is still, to a significant extent, based on 'paper' securities rather than electronically recorded holdings. In the era when the principal legal rules regarding ownership, methods of transfer, priority questions, and the general relationship between investor and issuer with respect to marketable securities were devised, the standard method used for the issue, and holding, of securities involved a relatively straightforward contractual relationship between the company issuing the securities and the investor. The issuer would raise money by, say, the issue of debentures or shares and the investor would subscribe, paying the relevant price to the company, and become acknowledged (save in the case of bearer securities) in the company's records (some form of register) as the

---

[3] The International Institute for the Unification of Private Law.

[4] See FMLC paper 'Property Interests in Securities' (an analysis of the need for legislation, etc), July 2004, 4.

[5] See UNIDROIT's comments on its study (LXXVIII) for 'Harmonised Substantive Rules Regarding Securities Held with an Intermediary', April 2005.

debenture holder, or member, as the case may be. The terms of the arrangement would incorporate, as appropriate, the company's constitutional documents, such as its articles of association, or the provisions of the instrument establishing the debentures (again, as the case may be). These documents would, amongst other things, set out the rules for transfers of the investment, the payment of dividends (or interest) and return of capital on winding up or, as the case may be, in accordance with the repayment terms of the debenture. In short, all the principal rules regulating the relationship between the investor and the issuing company were a matter of direct agreement between them. The investor would also acquire a certificate, bond, or other comparable document from the issuer, evidencing his investment (and this latter document, generally coupled with a form of transfer for registered (ie non-bearer) securities would be delivered in connection with any transfer of the investment. It would be a comprehensive, self-contained, two-party arrangement. No third party would be materially involved and the rights of the investor would not be directly affected by the economic fortunes of any third party.

Although the above description generally still holds good for private com- **7.04** panies, it is now largely out of date as regards companies whose securities are publicly traded. Most publicly traded securities are now held through intermediaries of various kinds. Shares, for example, are now commonly held by 'custodians' (usually owned by major banks or broker-dealers) on behalf of 'end investors'. Internationally traded debt securities are commonly held by 'central securities depositaries', frequently a chain of such entities, performing a similar role. Securities in the hands of an end investor are now rarely evidenced by any paper, such as a bond or certificate. The investor instead relies on the entry of its name in an account maintained by the intermediary. This aids the use of electronic trading systems, which are cheaper and quicker than systems that require the processing of 'hard copy' documentation. The commercial disadvantages of the old system, in the context of an electronic securities trading, globalized market, have been succinctly summarized by Goode:

> . . . tangible securities, though readily transferable, enjoy four major disadvantages. First, they entail the issue and physical movement of larger quantities of paper, which in recent times grew to such dimensions that it threatened to swamp clearing and settlement systems. Secondly, the certificates and notes are expensive to produce, since they require security printing which incorporates numerous technical features designed to prevent forgery. Thirdly, they are risky, since title passes by manual delivery, so that if the certificates or notes are stolen the thief can pass an overriding title to a bona fide purchaser for value (holder in due course). Fourthly, their *situs*, and therefore the law governing their transfer, is susceptible to constant change and where they are distributed over a number of jurisdictions a lender wishing to take security over the portfolio as a whole will have to comply with a

diversity of national laws, each with its own distinctive perfection requirements and policy rules.[6]

7.05 The concept of book-entry holdings is recognized in, amongst other things, the definition of 'book-entry securities collateral' in the Financial Collateral Arrangements (No 2) Regulations 2003 (FCA (2)), which refers to 'financial collateral subject to a financial collateral arrangement which consists of financial instruments, title to which is evidenced by entries in a register or account maintained by or on behalf of an intermediary'.

7.06 An 'intermediary' is defined as:

> . . . a person that maintains registers or accounts to which financial instruments may be credited or debited, for others or both for others and for its own account but does not include—
>
> (a) a person who acts as a registrar or transfer agent for the issuer of financial instruments; or
>
> (b) a person who maintains registers or accounts in the capacity of operator of a system for the holding and transfer of financial instruments on records of the issuer or other records which constitute the primary record of entitlement to financial instruments as against the issuer.

7.07 In the modern world, securities have thus in many cases, become 'dematerialized', in that the investor no longer has a piece of paper issued by the company in which he has invested to demonstrate his entitlement. He no longer has any direct contractual relationship with that company at all, as a matter of law. Commercially, however, he still regards himself as an investor in the company. So what, exactly, has he got in terms of a proprietary interest in securities? Analysis of the contractual structures now used in the markets shows that the traditional bilateral relationship between issuer and investor has been replaced, in the markets for publicly traded securities (and especially the international markets), by a more complex 'chain-link' structure whereby an issuer might issue a 'global' security in 'immobilized' form to, say, a central, local 'depositary', A. A then holds the rights and interests represented by that security for other depositaries (who might be located in different geographical regions and, therefore, legal jurisdictions)[7] B, C, and D, and the latter might in turn hold their 'sub-interests' for further intermediaries (such as bank custodians or broker-dealers) E, F, G, H, etc (also located in different jurisdictions) who hold

---

[6] See Goode, 'The Nature and Transfer of Rights in Dematerialised and Immobilised Securities' (1996) 4 JIBFL 167. See also Bernasconi, Potok, and Morton, 'General introduction: legal nature of interests in indirectly held securities and resulting conflict of laws analysis' in *Cross Border Collateral: Legal risk and the Conflict of Laws*) ch 1.

[7] In Europe, it is common practice for a common depositary to hold securities issued to it by the issuer for the account of the two leading international central securities depositaries (ICSDs), Euroclear Bank and Clearstream International.

their 'sub-sub-interests' for the end investors, their clients. The various interests up and down the chain are recorded by electronic book-entries. Where an intermediary holds interests for more than one person, as will commonly be the case, the interests are not recorded separately, but pooled. The various links in the chain are commonly referred to by commentators as 'tiers', so that, for example, the intermediary with the direct link with the issuer represents the uppermost tier and the end investors are the lowest tier.

If all the participants involved in such an arrangement were located in common **7.08** law jurisdictions it might be possible to analyse the relevant relationships by reference to trust law (so that a lower-tier custodian would, for example, be treated as holding on trust for its clients all relevant interests that are recorded in its name by any 'higher' intermediary). This would largely accomplish the fundamental objective of ensuring that the end investor is protected in the event of insolvency of an intermediary and would not have to compete with other creditors of the insolvent for access to the interests represented by the book-entries in that investors name.[8] However, as is almost always the case with internationally structured arrangements, common law is unlikely to be of universal application (and it is not without its own areas of uncertainty in this context), many of the relevant jurisdictions do not recognize trusts as a valid legal concept, and, in any case, there is a degree of uncertainty (as regards conflicts of law principles) as to precisely what law should govern some of the relevant relationships.[9]

The issues involved, although at first sight somewhat arcane, go to the heart of **7.09** financial stability. It was estimated at the end of 2004 that the securities held worldwide in 'indirect holding systems' such as that described had a value of roughly €50 trillion and that transaction turnover in collateral transactions in OECD government and corporate securities of more than US$32 trillion (the estimated world GDP) was generated every fifteen trading days.[10] The recent

---

[8] The FMLC paper of July 2004 (n 4 above) comments (at 9) that: 'English trust law and rules of equity do, it is true, go a long way to protecting the interests of the various parties concerned. Thus there is little doubt that, in the absence of agreement to the contrary, investors holding securities with an intermediary relating to interests in securities held in a pool will be considered to have co-proprietary rights in the pool as beneficiaries under a trust so as to be safeguarded against the intermediary's general creditors in the event of its insolvency.' There are, however, still some worrying areas of uncertainty (detailed in the FMLC paper) and, given the reform developments taking place elsewhere (see 7.17–7.36 below) the FMLC is of the view that: 'Given the need to keep the UK competitive in world markets, the commercial disadvantages of delay in improving the position under English law cannot be sufficiently emphasised.'

[9] See 7.12–7.16 below.

[10] See Explanatory footnotes to UNIDROIT's 'Preliminary Draft Convention on Harmonised Substantive Rules Regarding Securities held with an Intermediary', December 2004, para 2.2.4.

FMLC paper on the subject,[11] noting that systemic risk 'looms' over the interests of individual participants, records that dealings in securities in CREST[12] alone average £765,000,000,000 per day.

7.10 The financial system cannot afford a failure by any of the various intermediaries involved, at whatever tier, threatening the rights of investors in securities held by them in such systems. The market, and it is a huge market, is proceeding on the assumption that the investor at the lowest tier has rights of ownership in the securities that are represented by an electronic book entry with the 'nearest' intermediary (say, a broker-dealer) in the chain (and not a mere unsecured contractual claim against that intermediary) even though the issuer of those securities (and the person recorded as investor in that issuer's records) may be several tiers removed, be subject to a different legal system, and have no contractual relationship with the lowest tier investor. It is vitally important that this assumption is correct, but the answer turns upon issues of property and insolvency laws, in the countries where the relevant parties are located, which, in certain important respects, are less than clear. Furthermore, achieving legal reform on an international basis in areas of insolvency and property law (which vary significantly from country to country) is a formidable challenge. Nevertheless, more legal certainty is needed. As the UNIDROIT Position Paper puts it:

> An account holder needs to be confident—
> a) that entries in its accounts with its intermediary represent interests that are good against the intermediary and third parties, even in the case of insolvency of the intermediary;
> b) that such entries cannot be revoked or reversed once certain clearly identifiable and reasonably simple conditions have been satisfied;
> c) that it can give instructions to its intermediary in a reasonably simple and convenient form.[13]

7.11 The Giovannini Group, looking at the issues from the perspective of how improved legal certainty and inter-jurisdiction harmonization and/or compatibility would assist the development of an EU single financial market, summarizes the legal argument as follows:

> 1. The EU needs all countries to treat securities in the same way (what they are, how you own them, how you trade them). At the moment they are treated differently. In particular, in some countries account entries establish ownership; in others they do not.

---

[11] See n 1 above.

[12] CRESTco (which is now part of the Euroclear group) is the Central Securities Depositary for the UK and Ireland and the operator of the Crest system.

[13] See UNIDROIT Position Paper, 'Harmonised Substantive Rules Regarding Indirectly Held Securities', August 2003.

2. Without this common framework, cross-border usage of securities, both in trading and in settlement, cannot consolidate.

3. In a modern market, securities are held through intermediaries: they are recorded in electronic accounts. There needs to be a legal framework across the EU under which, whenever securities have been entered into a book-entry system, it is the accounts that establish ownership of those securities. There would then be a legal identity between ownership and the record of ownership.

4. The recent conflicts of laws measures (EC Directive on Financial Collateral Arrangements and Hague Convention on the law applicable to certain rights relating to securities held with an intermediary) are a huge step towards this, but they do not go all the way.[14]

B. The Hague Convention

The Giovannini Group's references to conflicts of law measures in point 4 of **7.12** the above list are to the establishment of the so-called PRIMA (place of relevant intermediary approach) concept as the rule for establishing, as a matter of conflicts of law, which law should govern the relationship between an investor and an intermediary. The Hague Convention (which is a multilateral treaty) on 'The law applicable to certain rights in respect of securities held with an intermediary' was agreed on 13 December 2002.[15] A uniform legal formula is laid down by Articles 4 and 5 of the Convention as to the law that should apply to:

(a) the legal nature and effects against the intermediary and third parties of the rights resulting from a credit of securities to a securities account;

(b) the legal nature and effect against the intermediary and against third parties of a disposition of securities held with an intermediary;

(c) the requirements, if any, for perfection of a disposition of securities held with an intermediary;

(d) whether a person's interest in securities held with an intermediary extinguishes or has priority over another person's interest;

(e) the duties, if any, of an intermediary to a person other than the account holder who asserts, in competition with the account holder or another person, an interest in securities held with that intermediary;

(f) the requirements, if any, for the realization of an interest in securities held with an intermediary; and

---

[14] See Second Giovannini Clearing and Settlement Report, 16.
[15] An Explanatory Report on the Convention, written by Goode, Kanda, and Kreuzer, can now be found at the Hague Conference on Private International Law website: http://www.hcch.net.

(g) whether a disposition of securities held with an intermediary extends to entitlements to dividends, income, or other distributions, or to sale, or other proceeds.[16]

7.13 The Convention does not deal with purely personal or contractual rights, subject to the overriding principle that it determines the law applicable to the above issues 'in relation to a disposition of or interest in securities held with an intermediary even where the rights resulting from the credit of those securities to a securities account are determined . . . to be contractual in nature'.[17]

7.14 According to Article 4 of the Convention, the applicable law for the above issue should be the law chosen by the parties in the account agreement, as long as the relevant intermediary has an office in the state in question (ie whose law is chosen) that, in effect, carries on the business of an intermediary. If this provision does not produce a result (for example, because no law was expressly chosen by the parties to govern the accounts agreement) various fall-back provisions come into play, with the 'backstop' being that the applicable law should be that of the state in which the intermediary had its principal place of business at the time the account was opened.[18]

7.15 The same, PRIMA, approach is taken in the Collateral Directive as regards the law applicable to:

(a) the legal nature and proprietary effects of book-entry securities collateral;
(b) the requirements for perfecting a financial collateral arrangement relating to book-entry securities collateral and the provision of book-entry securities collateral under such an arrangement, and more generally the completion of the steps necessary to render an arrangement and provision effective against third parties;
(c) whether a person's title to or interest in such book-entry securities collateral is overridden by or subordinated to a competing title or interest, or a good faith acquisition has occurred;
(d) the steps required for the realization of book-entry securities collateral following the occurrence of an enforcement event.[19]

7.16 The EU Commission has proposed that the EU Community sign the Hague Convention, following which consequential amendments will be put forward for the amendment of the Settlement Finality Directive and the Collateral Directive. On the assumption this is done, the clarification of the conflicts of law rule is, and will be, enormously helpful in dispelling some of the legal uncertainty in this area but, as indicated above, it is not the complete answer.

---

[16] Hague Convention, Art 2(1).   [17] ibid, Art 2(2).
[18] ibid, Art 5(2).
[19] See the Collateral Directive, Art 9. As regards English law, this is reflected in FCA(2), para 10.

We may, as a result, know which law to apply, but will that law actually deliver the answers that the market has assumed will be forthcoming? This residue of uncertainty is the focus of the Legal Certainty Group, put in place by the Giovannini Group, and UNIDROIT.

C. Legal Reforms Around the World

Before we examine the reforms proposed by UNIDROIT and others, we should **7.17** note that there has been a significant amount of legal reform in this area at national level already. For example, Belgium and Luxembourg, the home jurisdictions of Euroclear and Clearstream respectively, have both passed similar laws (in 2004 and 2001 respectively)[20] which, according to the description provided by the FMLC, define the investor's interest as a co-proprietary right, or co-ownership right in a pool of securities held by the intermediary for its clients. The right is related to the book-entry rather than the securities (whether or not dematerialized) and does not extend 'up the tiers'. (However, upper tier attachment by creditors of other intermediaries at higher levels, is forbidden.) The rights of the investor have characteristics on the insolvency of the intermediary (described as a right of 'revindication') that strongly resemble the rights of a beneficiary under a trust: the investor's claims to the asset represented by the book-entry should prevail over claims of other creditors.

In the US, there have also been reforms in this area, notably a major revision, **7.18** in 1994, of Article 8 of the Uniform Commercial Code so as to produce a new *sui generis* right for the investor *vis-à-vis* his immediate ('next tier up') intermediary, which has been described as a combination of contract and property rights, producing similar, but not identical, results to the Belgian and Luxembourg reforms.[21] Comparable reforms have been made in recent years

---

[20] The Belgian law is Royal Decree No 62 on the deposit of fungible financial instruments and the settlement of transactions involving such instruments, as coordinated by the Royal Decree of 27 January 2004. The Luxembourg law is the Law of 1 August 2001 on the circulation of securities and other fungible instruments.

[21] In February 2005 the FMLC has produced a report which analyses the 1994 revisions to the Uniform Code, Art 8, from the perspective 'of a foreign legal system aiming to design a law which works alongside the US system without friction, matches the realities of the modern wholesale financial markets and changes only those parts of existing English law that really need it'. The FMLC (or, to be precise, its Working Group) comments that the US approach 'modifies traditional concepts of property based on rules of tracing in traditional trust law and substitutes the concept of security entitlement as a package of interests in common and personal rights derived from and exercisable exclusively against the holder's own intermediary through credits to a securities account, while at the same time facilitating settlement finality through clear priority rules in favour of the bona fide purchaser for value who assumes control'. The influence of Art 8, and of the UNIDROIT proposals considered at 7.19 ff below, on the FMLC's own proposals is very apparent.

in France and Japan. So far no such changes have been introduced into English law.[22]

D. UNIDROIT Proposals

7.19 The reforms are helpful as far as they go, but they are of course limited in application to the jurisdictions concerned and result in a patchwork effect for a securities holding system which, by its nature, is now an international phenomenon. The net result is that each of the major jurisdictions has different laws (although, in some cases, the differences may be slight) and there is a lack of certainty as to how compatible the laws are with each other. If, for example, a top-tier intermediary in Country A gets into financial difficulties and has all its assets (including securities held in its name) subject to attachment or similar proceedings, what are the consequences for its customers (lower tier intermediaries) located in countries B, C, and D and the customers of those customers? It is not practical to expect market participants to investigate and understand the interaction of all the relevant countries' laws in order to be sure that a 'problem', such as attachment at any tier in any holding system, will not adversely affect the rights of those at lower tiers. The issues need to be addressed at an international, as well as national, level. That is what the UNIDROIT (preliminary) draft Convention on Harmonised Substantive Rules Regarding Intermediated Securities (latest version at the time of writing: June 2005) sets out to do.

7.20 The draft Convention is published with very helpful Explanatory Notes. They merit detailed examination and consideration. To give some impression of the scope of the exercise and the issues involved, some examples of provisions from the draft Convention are considered below, but the serious inquirer should, of course, also read the original document. The principal features of the draft Convention are as follows:

The rights of an investor

7.21 Pursuant to Article 4.1:

The credit of securities to a securities account confers on the account holder:

(a) subject to paragraph 2, the right to receive and exercise the rights attached to the securities, including in particular dividends, other distributions and voting rights;

(b) the right, by instructions to the relevant intermediary, to cause the securities

---

[22] But see further 7.37 ff below as to the changes recommended by the FMLC.

to be debited to the securities account Article 5[23] and credited to a securities account of another account holder (whether with the relevant intermediary or another intermediary) or to be delivered into the possession or control of a collateral taker under Article 64;

(c) the right, by instructions to the relevant intermediary, to cause the securities to be debited to the securities account under Article 5 and credited to a securities account of the account holder with a different intermediary;

(d) the right, by instructions to the relevant intermediary, to withdraw the securities so as to be held by the account holder otherwise than through a securities account, to the extent permitted under the law under which the securities are constituted, the terms of the securities and the account agreement;

(e) subject to [the] Convention, such other rights as may be conferred by the domestic non-Convention law.

Article 4.2 provides that: **7.22**

Where securities are credited to a securities account of an account holder who is acting in the capacity of intermediary with respect to those securities, that account holder has the rights specified in paragraph 1(a) only if that account holder, or another intermediary through which, directly or indirectly, it holds the relevant securities, is entitled to those rights against the issuer under the terms of the relevant securities and the law under which the relevant securities are constituted.

There are a number of specially defined terms that are of particular interest. For   **7.23**
example, 'intermediated securities' (previously referred to in an earlier version as 'securities held with an intermediary') means 'the rights of an account holder resulting from a credit of securities to a securities account'.[24] In effect, this means that the 'property' element in the ordinary meaning of the word 'securities' (as in, 'I own £100 worth of securities') is replaced by a list of 'rights' (ie those described above) which, at first sight, appear to be contractual only. However, as we shall see, these rights do in fact include rights which, for all practical purposes are as good as those that generally flow from being the owner of 'property'. 'Securities' are defined to mean 'any shares, bonds or other transferable financial instruments or financial assets (other than cash) or any interest therein'. 'Intermediary' is defined to mean 'a person that in the course of a business or other regular activity maintains securities accounts for others or both for others and for its own account and is acting in that capacity'. This covers banks, brokers, central securities depositories, and other such entities as might be likely to be found at the various tiers in an indirect holding system.

The rights of the investor are expressly stated to be 'effective against the relevant   **7.24**
intermediary and third parties' but, generally, may only be enforced against the

---

[23] See further 7.30–7.32 below.
[24] The same language is used in the corresponding definition in the Hague Convention referred to above.

relevant intermediary and only in limited cases against the issuer.[25] The 'relevant intermediary', an expression used throughout the draft Convention, is 'with respect to an account holder, the intermediary that maintains the securities account for the account holder'.

7.25 The rights of the investor are 'effective against the insolvency administrator and creditors in any insolvency proceeding in respect of the relevant intermediary'.[26] Also, pursuant to Article 17, the securities held by an intermediary or credited to its account with another intermediary 'shall be allocated to the rights of the account holders of that intermediary to the extent necessary to ensure that the aggregate number or amount of securities [of each relevant description] so allocated is equal to the aggregate number or amount of such securities credited to securities accounts maintained by the intermediary'. This Article also provides that the securities so allocated 'shall not form part of the property of the intermediary available for distribution among . . . its creditors' if the intermediary becomes insolvent. In other words, the position is broadly that which would have arisen if a trust had been created.

7.26 The language used in this article reflects UNIDROIT's approach of avoiding the use of legal expressions like 'trust'—which belong to a particular kind of legal system (ie the common law system, in this case) but may be alien to others—if it can achieve the required effect with the so-called 'functional approach' of describing all the attributes and effects of (in this case) a trust (or some form of proprietary interest) without using the term itself. It is not possible for the draft Convention to remain silent on the question of what happens on the insolvency of an intermediary, since this is the most important area of uncertainty that needs attention. Equally, the 'functional' definition of what 'intermediated securities' actually means, since it avoids notions of property and beneficial interests (or title), begs all the most important questions, ie what rights *does* the investor (or 'next person down' from the insolvent intermediary) have in such a situation? The answer provided by Article 17.2 is expressed as a negative. The 'securities allocated' (which would include securities credited to an account in the name of the insolvent intermediary) do 'not form part of the property of the intermediary available for distribution'. This is, of course, an enormously important principle. But it does not tell us the whole story, since we are not told by Article 17.2 what does happen to the securities (or the rights that relate to them). Instead, Article 17.3 points us in the direction of 'domestic non-Convention law'. The point is somewhat obscurely expressed in that it is stated that the 'allocation' (an undefined term) required by Article 17.1 'may be effected by the domestic non-Convention law and, subject to the domestic

---

[25] Art 4.3.   [26] Art 12.

non-Convention law, arrangements made by the relevant intermediary'. The draft Convention has deliberately allowed flexibility for different legal systems to 'use different techniques for ensuring that securities held for account holders are protected from the insolvency of the intermediary', the principle being that 'it is for the applicable law to determine the precise technique by which the appropriation (or allocation) is effected and the procedure by which the account holders' rights are enforced'.[27]

The draft Convention also protects investors from the perils of 'upper-tier attachment', Article 9 providing that: 'No attachment of or in respect of intermediated securities of an account holder shall be granted or made against the issuer of those securities or against any intermediary other than the relevant intermediary.' An aggrieved creditor of an investor can thus pursue the investor's 'relevant intermediary' for attachment of the securities held by the investor with it, but cannot go 'higher' in the tiers of the system. 'Attachment' is defined to mean 'any judicial, administrative or other act or process for enforcing or satisfying a judgement, award or other judicial, arbitral, administrative or other decision against or in respect of the account holder or for freezing, restricting or impounding property of the account holder in order to ensure its availability to enforce or satisfy any such judgement, award or decision'. **7.27**

What if, despite the intermediary's duties to keep the accounts 'in balance' there is a shortfall, for example on the intermediary's insolvency, so that there are not enough 'securities' (of any relevant class) held by the intermediary to go round? Article 18 provides that where the intermediary is an operator of a clearing or settlement system, the rules of the system (if they cover such a situation) shall apply, or, failing that, the shortfall shall be allocated to the unfortunate investors who hold the relevant class of securities on a pro rata basis. This is a risk that would not be present where securities are held directly from the issuer, but it is hard to see how else the problem could be fairly addressed. **7.28**

Finally, a provision that almost certainly improves investors' rights where they hold through intermediaries can be found in Article 20, which provides that rights of set-off should not be precluded *vis-à-vis* an issuer by virtue of the lack of any direct contractual relationship between it and an investor several tiers 'below'. **7.29**

---

[27] See Explanatory Notes to the draft Convention, 33. The notes also make the comment that: 'Under a legal system which treats securities held with an intermediary as owned by the underlying account holders, the legal structure will of itself ensure that such securities are not available for realisation for the benefit of the general unsecured creditors of the intermediary.' In relation to the functional approach generally, the Explanatory Notes (in para 3.2.1) explain the attractions of avoiding being too 'intrusive' with respect to individual countries' laws: 'The means by which the required result is to be achieved in a concrete legal system are not decisive and remain within the national legislator's discretion, provided they are compatible with other rules of the preliminary draft Convention.'

Acquisitions, disposals, and creating security interests

7.30   How does one buy and sell securities held in indirect holding systems? The ease of process of such transactions is supposedly the *raison d'être* of the systems themselves, so what does it involve? The answers provided by Article 5 of the draft Convention show the simplicity and elegance of the system (and the legally crucial role played by the intermediary) when difficult questions of insolvency are not involved.

7.31   Securities held with an intermediary are acquired by an account holder by the credit of those securities to a securities account of that account holder and they are disposed of by the debiting of the account.[28] 'No further step is necessary, or may be required by domestic non-Convention law, to render the acquisition or disposition of intermediated securities effective against third parties.'[29] It does not matter, for example, that the intermediary may not have entered into a matching transaction at a higher level. This provision, as well as the definition of 'intermediated securities' itself, the ban on upper tier attachment, and the shortfall rules referred to above, reflect what the FMLC calls the 'no-look-through-principle'. This is the general principle that an investor's claim should only lie against 'its own' (ie the 'relevant') intermediary. It negates any concept based on showing some kind of chain of title between an issuer and the end investor. At any level or 'tier' the interests held by an intermediary which match (or should match) the interests of its own customers may have been derived from a number of sources and may have been the subject of a netting of transactions at various points, with the result that it is very unlikely that any particular holding of an investor can be accurately traced through a series of transactions at higher tiers. Even if it could, the time and effort involved in the necessary investigation would be prohibitively expensive. It is noteworthy that these provisions are at the more 'intrusive' end of the scale for the draft Convention; not much discretion is left to national legislatures as to what is needed to effect an acquisition or disposal.

7.32   Debits and credits may be made on a net basis. This also reflects the principles referred to above. As the Explanatory Notes say:

> An intermediary should be entitled to effect a net settlement. That is, to the extent that there are matching debits or credits to accounts maintained by the intermediary for its account holders, there need not be precisely matching entries in the intermediary's accounts maintained with the upper tier, but such entries should simply reflect the net overall change in the aggregate balances of its account holders taken together.

---

[28] See Arts 5.1 and 5.3.   [29] Art 5.2.

Security interests (or 'collateral') over indirectly held securities are also the sub- **7.33**
ject of a simple book-entry regime. Article 6.1 provides that they may be created
by the account holder:

(a) entering into an agreement with the collateral taker providing (in whatever
terms) for the grant of such security interest; and

(b) delivering the intermediated securities into the possession or control of the
collateral taker in accordance with paragraph 2 [which sets out more detailed
requirements for delivery into possession or control].

Other provisions

Other items of note in the draft Convention include lengthy provisions on the **7.34**
duties of intermediaries, focusing chiefly on the obligation to keep accounts in
balance and a special provision protecting the position of what English lawyers
would call the 'bona fide purchaser for value without notice' (termed the 'innocent acquirer' in Article 11). There is also a provision, in Article 19, stating that:

Any rule of law of a Contracting State, and any provision of the terms of issue of
securities constituted under the law of a Contracting State, which would prevent
the holding of securities with an intermediary or the effective exercise by an
account holder of rights in respect of intermediated securities shall be modified to
the extent required to make possible the holding of securities and the effective
exercise of such rights.

Examples are given of restrictive laws that could be affected by the above provi- **7.35**
sion. These include laws that do not give the end investor adequate access to
copies of notices, accounts, circulars, etc issued by a company to investors, and
restrictions on voting, either through a proxy or representative.

The UNIDROIT draft Convention represents the most advanced work, at **7.36**
international level, that has been done in relation to the analysis of potential
legal problems caused by indirect holding systems, and the best solutions to
those problems. It was the first item to which the Giovannini Legal Certainty
Group gave detailed attention (as evidenced by its published minutes and the
memorandum of 7 February 2005 produced for the group by Morton, Dupont,
and Maffei). It has obviously influenced the thinking of the FMLC on the
subject and will no doubt continue to influence any detailed proposals for
English law reform in this important area. To date, the most detailed such
proposals are those of the FMLC itself.

E. The FMLC Proposals

A number of references to the FMLC papers on Proprietary Interests in **7.37**
Investment Securities have already been made in this chapter. If reform of

English law does proceed, it seems likely that it will be modelled to a significant extent on the FMLC's ideas. The FMLC has not proposed draft legislation as such, but has put forward a series of Principles for an Investment Securities Statute (together with a detailed commentary). The principles are based on three 'central concepts' ie:

1) The root of title to securities held with an intermediary is the credit to a securities account;
2) Unless otherwise agreed, investors in a particular issue of securities held by an intermediary in a common pool have co-proprietary interests in the pool;
3) Except as otherwise provided by a contract or provision in a deed poll or trust deed, an account holder's rights are solely against its own intermediary, with no look-through to an upper-tier intermediary or the issuer and, in consequence, no upper-tier attachment.

7.38 The most significant principles put forward by the FMLC for the new statute may be summarized as follows:

(1) Contracting out of (all or part of) the new regime by the intermediary and its customer is to be permitted, although this can of course only affect their bilateral relationship and will not change the position of third parties affected by the provisions.

(2) The rights of an investor *vis-à-vis* its intermediary comprise both personal rights against the intermediary and 'property rights in relation to the securities'. (In this latter respect, the overt reference to property rights does, of course, contrast strongly with the language used by UNIDROIT, although the net effect of the proposals may not be very different.)

(3) The property rights in a pool of securities held with an intermediary are 'proportionate' to the extent of the entitlement of the investor.

(4) The intermediary must appropriately record entitlements in its books.

(5) The intermediary must avoid shortfalls.

(6) The intermediary must pass on to the investor dividends, interest, and other income derived from the securities and follow the investor's instructions on voting.

(7) Investors (and persons claiming through them) can only exercise rights against 'their' intermediary (no 'look-through'). 'However, this is subject to any direct rights of action against the issuer or other intermediary provided under the terms of issue of the securities or of a deed poll or contract or arising under general law against persons not acting in good faith.'

(8) Intermediaries should follow their customers' instructions.

(9) Securities held by an intermediary who becomes insolvent are not to be available to its general creditors.

(10) Shortfalls are to be borne proportionately by the class of investors affected.

(11) Although dealings in securities (transfers, creation of security interests, etc) may be carried out informally as between the parties to the dealings, in order to bind third parties a 'transfer of control' will be necessary. This can be done, for example, by having securities credited to the account of the transferee or chargee or by having the intermediary acknowledge that it will comply with the transferee's or chargee's instructions, without the need for any consent from the transferor or chargor.

(12) A good faith purchaser without notice of fraud, etc is protected (against claims from the original owner) where there has been fraud or other wrongful disposition by the intermediary.

(13) The fact that securities are held indirectly will not preclude set-off as between an issuer and an investor.

The Law Commission's Ninth Programme of Law Reform, published in March **7.39** 2005, includes reform of the law in the areas covered by the FMLC as 'Project 9'. The Law Commission acknowledges that: 'It is necessary for the law to catch up with current trading practice. This work will need to consider the wider EU context and it is possible, and indeed to be hoped, that the UK may lead the way for forming EU law on this issue.'

It is important that this area of uncertainty is not seen as a suitable case for **7.40** 'letting sleeping dogs lie'. It would be dangerous to assume that the potential problems that have been identified with tiered holding systems simply will not come up in practice, however improbable the insolvency of a major intermediary may seem, or that, if they do, the courts (of each jurisdiction affected) will have sufficient laws, precedent, and judicial inventiveness at their disposal to come up with a market-friendly solution. The groundswell of opinion behind the need for reform, at international, EU, and the domestic level, appears to be strong and should be sufficient to ensure that the necessary changes are made.

8

VAGUE LAWS

... the courts will ordinarily construe general words in a statute, although literally capable of having some startling or unreasonable consequence, such as overriding fundamental human rights, as not having been intended to do so.[1]

Parliamentary sovereignty means that Parliament can, if it chooses, legislate contrary to fundamental principles of human rights. The Human Rights Act 1998 will not detract from this power. The constraints upon its exercise by Parliament are ultimately political, not legal. But the principle of legality means that Parliament must squarely confront what it is doing and accept the political cost. Fundamental rights cannot be overridden by general or ambiguous words. This is because there is too great a risk that the full implications of their unqualified meaning may have been missed in the democratic process.[2]

A. Over-ambitious Legislation

The current President of the US is apparently of the view that it is possible to **8.01** pass laws that 'guarantee honesty' in the financial markets and the boardrooms of companies.[3] In the UK we have not perhaps gone that far in our ambitions, but we do tend to pass laws with ambitious titles, that suggest they can, for example, 'prevent' fraud or terrorism.[4] Why not, if this works, simply pass a law 'preventing' murder, maiming, or theft? The truth of the matter is, of course, that no amount of legislation will ever eradicate bad behaviour simply by making it an offence. Over time, legislation may have an influence on moral

---

[1] From the judgment of Lord Hoffmann in *R (Morgan Grenfell & Co Ltd) v Special Commissioner for Income Tax* [2002] UKHL 21.

[2] From the judgment of Lord Hoffmann in *R v Secretary of State for the Home Department, ex p Simms* [2000] 2 AC 115.

[3] See speech by President George W Bush of 2 June 2005, announcing the nomination of Christopher Cox as the new Chairman of the SEC.

[4] See Prevention of Fraud (Investments) Act 1958 and Prevention of Terrorism Act 2005.

perceptions in society (for example, the laws against certain kinds of racialist activity, introduced in the UK in the 1960s) and that, in turn, may affect the way a substantial number of people behave. But you cannot stop someone from behaving badly simply by passing a law against what he is doing. (In all likelihood, he is probably breaking an existing law already). Ultimately, the enforcement of acceptable behavioural standards is a matter for the executive and the judiciary, not the legislature. And society will generally demand that the executive's powers are properly controlled and exercised in accordance with law and that the judiciary imposes, and observes, certain basic norms that recognize the right to a fair trial. Keeping this 'balance', to ensure that those accused of crimes are treated fairly, can at times seem inconvenient to the executive, and it may well have the result that not as many wrongdoers are punished as is desirable, but we lose this balance at our peril.

8.02   The danger with over-ambitious legislation is that it tends to be oppressive. One could, for example, probably achieve a reduction in some crime figures by imposing a curfew on the entire population from dusk until dawn. One could extend the executive's powers of detention without trial. The social price, however, would be too high. Nevertheless, the political imperative to combat serious crimes such as drug trafficking and terrorism is very strong (and since the terrorist incidents in the US on 11 September 2001 has become even stronger than before). This has had the result that, in recent years, law-makers have resorted to more extreme forms of legislation in an effort to catch serious criminals. The new legislation tends to require those who may know, or suspect, that something untoward is going on, especially in relation to the financial proceeds of crime, to take responsibility for bringing it to the attention of the executive. Thus the 'primary' offences of, say, insider dealing or drug-trafficking are now joined by new laws requiring those who know about transactions involving the proceeds of the primary offence (or suspect it, or have enough information that they should reasonably suspect it) to inform the relevant authorities, on pain of committing a criminal offence themselves if they fail to do so. Such laws have a particular impact on banks and the providers of financial services because in their ordinary line of business they are likely to come into possession of information about financial transactions and money transfers generally that may point to 'something suspicious'.[5] They also lead to a series of practical difficulties, for example:

---

[5] It is for this reason, of course, that banks were singled out for special attention as long ago as the 1991 EU directive on money laundering, which provides, in Art 6, that:

'Member States shall ensure that credit and financial institutions and their directors and employees co-operate fully with the authorities responsible for money laundering:
- by informing those authorities, on their own initiative, of any fact which might be an indication of money laundering,
- by furnishing those authorities, at their request, with all necessary information, in accordance with the procedures established by the applicable legislation.'

(1) Which crimes should be the subject of such reporting requirements?

(2) Should it matter if the 'crime' is not in fact a crime in the country where the event takes place, even though it would be a crime if committed in the UK?

(3) What if the event or crime took place a long time before the relevant information came to the attention of the potential informer?

(4) Is it practical to expect potential informers to have enough knowledge of the law in all relevant countries to be capable of anything other than identifying the most obvious signs of activity that is widely accepted in most societies as criminal?

(5) Is it fair to impose a test that is more severe than actual knowledge or actual suspicion of a crime (for example, requiring reporting because an individual 'should reasonably have been suspicious')?

(6) How can the authorities cope with banks and others who, erring on the side of caution, report transactions to an excessive degree?

(7) If employees of banks are to be put under greater duties than others, what should the duties of the 'ordinary citizen' be?

(8) Should lawyers, who come into possession of information in circumstances that are arguably unique to them because of their role in society, be put under the same obligations to inform as everyone else?

B. The Proceeds of Crime Act 2002

The legislation in the UK which has illustrated these difficulties most fully is the Proceeds of Crime Act 2002 (POCA 2002), particularly Part 7 of the Act (which is concerned with 'Money Laundering' and is in implementation of two EU directives on the subject).[6] This law has been criticized by the Financial Markets Law Committee (FMLC) as giving rise to legal uncertainty, especially with regard to 'in what circumstances conduct outside England and Wales is criminal within the meaning of POCA'.[7] This uncertainty, in turn, leaves banks and many other businesses in 'the regulated sector'[8] unclear as to 'who has to be reported to the UK authorities as a suspected money-launderer and which

8.03

---

[6] These are Council Directive of 10 June 1991 (91/308/EEC) and Council Directive of 4 December 2001 (2001/97/EEC), also known as the first and second Money Laundering Directives.

[7] See FMLC Papers of October 2004 and January 2005.

[8] Defined initially in Sch 9 to the POCA 2002, but now defined in the Proceeds of Crime Act 2002 (Businesses in the Regulated Sector and Supervisory Authorities) Order 2003 (SI/3074) to include banks and most kinds of financial service providers as well as businesses in the property sector (and casinos). Lawyers fall within the definition if they participate 'in a financial or real property transaction (whether by assisting in the planning or execution of any such transaction or otherwise by acting for, or on behalf of, a client in any such transaction)' (see para 1(1)(l) of the Order) and might also be caught by the definition if they give advice in connection with tax matters, trusts, or companies. Accountants are also likely to be caught by the definition.

transactions need consent'. The 2002 Act has been controversial from the outset and has already given rise to litigation, going as far as the Court of Appeal,[9] on difficult issues of interpretation arising under section 328, which applies to everyone, not just the regulated sector, and reads as follows:

(1) A person commits an offence if he enters into or becomes concerned in an arrangement which he knows or suspects facilitates (by whatever means) the acquisition, retention, use or control of criminal property by or on behalf of another person.

(2) But a person does not commit such an offence if—

(a) he makes an authorised disclosure under section 338 and (if the disclosure is made before he does the act mentioned in subsection (1)) he has the appropriate consent;

(b) he intended to make the disclosure but had a reasonable excuse for not doing so;

(c) the act he does is done in carrying out a function he has relating to the enforcement of any provision of this Act or of any other enactment relating to criminal conduct or benefit from criminal conduct.

8.04 There are other, more onerous provisions creating new offences that are specific to the regulated sector alone, considered further below. As regards, section 328, the Court of Appeal's decision in *Bowman v Fels* concerned what the court itself described as:

> . . . an issue of public law of very great importance which is causing very great difficulties in solicitors' offices and barristers' chambers and in the orderly conduct of litigation through the country. . . . Since the Act came into force lawyers have become concerned that this section may mean that they themselves are exposed to the threat of criminal sanctions if they do not make 'an authorised disclosure' of any information which leads them to know or suspect their client—or some other person, often the opposing party in family proceedings—is involved in the acquisition, retention, use or control of property derived from criminal conduct, *however minor*. They then feel obliged to wait for 'the appropriate consent' before they take any further steps for their client.[10]

8.05 Although the issue raised in *Bowman v Fels* (considered in more detail below) is, at first sight, of more importance to lawyers than to banks,[11] the case illustrates the difficulties that vague, 'catch-all' drafting can cause. In any event, the issues raised by the case have implications that extend beyond the legal profession. The

---

[9] See *Bowman v Fels* [2005] EWCA Civ 226.

[10] Emphasis added. The section is not limited by reference to 'serious crime'.

[11] But for an example of how POCA 2002, s 328 can affects banks and their customers, see *Squirrell v National Westminster Bank plc* [2005] 2 All ER 784, where it was noted by Laddie J that the provision 'is . . . of particular concern to banks'. Squirrell, the bank's customer, had had its account frozen by the bank and no explanation had been provided. The judge noted that 'Natwest says it wishes to comply with Squirrell's instructions in relation to the account but that it was forced to block it because of . . . s.328(1) [of POCA]. Furthermore, because of the anti-tip off provisions of that legislation, it was also prevented from explaining to Squirrell the reasons for so acting.' It emerged that the bank must have had some suspicions falling within the scope of the

ambit of the words 'enters into or becomes concerned in an arrangement which he knows or suspects facilitates (by whatever means)' is wide enough to trouble those involved in many kinds of financing transaction, especially when the broad definition of 'criminal property' (considered further below) is taken into account. The importance of the case beyond the specific concerns of solicitors and barristers may be summarized as follows:

- It provides an illustration of how a court might approach the construction of language in a statute like POCA 2002, which includes references to not only 'entering into an arrangement' but also 'the vaguer concept of "becom[ing] concerned in an arrangement" '.

- It demonstrates the extremely broad ambit of the definition of 'money laundering': the case concerned a dispute over ownership of a house that had been the subject of certain works which one of the parties had wrongfully put through the books of his company as business expenses. This had the effect, under the Act, of potentially causing the house to be 'criminal property' and causing those advising on a dispute about it in the courts (or any settlement of such a dispute) to be guilty of money laundering if they did not make the required disclosures to the authorities. (The relevant definitions are considered further below.)

- The judgment makes a number of observations about how the UK legislation goes significantly further than necessary for the implementation of the EU directives. For example, the legislation 'defines money laundering to include property known *or suspected* to constitute or represent a benefit from criminal activity' and, also, it applies to 'any type of criminal conduct' (not just serious crime). The FMLC, in its paper of October 2004, was particularly critical of the latter point and the absence of a *de minimis* threshold:

> In the domestic context, this means that a person is under the same onerous duties both to report and, more importantly, to suspend transactions pend-ing consent from the authorities, in circumstances where the criminal con-duct does not raise the same public interest issues as serious crime involving matters like fraud, corruption, drugs, pornography, such as:

---

section (with regard to a possible VAT offence) and Laddie J accepted that its course of action was 'unimpeachable'; the bank had made the authorized disclosure and had not received the necessary consent to enable the account to be unblocked; the law gave it virtually no choice. However, the judge also had 'some sympathy for parties in Squirrell's position. It has not been proved or even alleged that it or any of its associates has committed any offence. It, like me, has been shown no evidence raising even a prima facie case that it or any of its associates has done anything wrong. For all I know, it may be entirely innocent of any wrongdoing . . . if Squirrell is entirely innocent it may suffer severe damage for which it will not be compensated. Further, the blocking of its account is said to have deprived it of the resources with which to pay lawyers to fight on its behalf. Whether or not that is so in this case, it could well be so in other, similar cases. Whatever one might feel were Squirrell guilty of wrongdoing, if, as it says, it is innocent of any wrongdoing, this can be viewed as a grave injustice.'

a breach of intellectual property laws;

regulatory or technical breaches (e.g. some offences under the Financial Services and Markets Act 2000 and Part X of the Companies Act 1985);

events in the past which are so stale as to be of no practical interest or use to law enforcement agencies (e.g. unlawful confiscations during the Second World War).

8.06 The potential practical difficulties created by section 328 for the regulated as well as the unregulated sector are also illustrated in an example set out in the FMLC 2004 Paper:

> . . . in the context of a corporate transaction where something comes to the attention of a professional adviser which prompts him to make a report, the professional adviser in question may not take any steps in relation to the transaction for fear of committing the offence under section 328 of POCA 2002. Nor may he explain the situation to his client for fear either of tipping off [12] or prejudicing an investigation: if the professional adviser is a lawyer, English law principles of client confidentiality and legal professional privilege are modified in this context . . . It is disproportionate to deny the client access to his advisers at the very point at which he needs them: it might not even be the client, but a counterparty, who is implicated in a crime.

8.07 Although the court in *Bowman v Fels* achieved the 'right result' (and held that section 328 did not apply), in order to do this it had to rely extensively on analysis of the two EU directives that gave rise to the legislation combined with an application of 'fundamental principles' (of human rights or otherwise 'not lightly to be interfered with', ie the right to have 'access to legal advice on a private and confidential basis') in order to conclude that (in reaching its decision on the central issue): 'Parliament cannot have intended that proceedings or steps taken by lawyers in order to determine or secure legal rights and remedies for their clients should involve them in "becoming concerned in an arrangement which . . . facilitates the acquisition, retention, use or control of criminal property".' Some 'linguistic' arguments were also used ('to describe a judgement or order as an "arrangement" is a most unnatural use of language') but, whilst one may applaud the result, one cannot help feeling some disquiet both at the uncertainty involved in having to appeal to an argument based on human rights (a point which also troubled the FMLC)[13] and also at the vast range of ordinary professional and financial activity that does not qualify for the '*Bowman v Fels* exemption' (because it does not involve legal proceedings).

The case also supports the trenchant criticism of POCA 2002 made by Chamberlain:

---

[12] An offence in its own right under POCA 2002, s 333; the definition is complex but, broadly, covers making disclosures of information that would be likely to prejudice an investigation.

[13] See FMLC October 2004 Paper, para 14.

... poor legislation produces poor compliance which shows itself in a number of ways. The first is that the person subject to the requirement simply misunderstands its scope and application, and inadvertently fails to comply. The second arises where, driven to distraction by the range of possibilities of construction, the person affected simply decides to operate on the basis of what he thinks would be a sensible law. The third kind of compliance, which is equally problematic for the authorities, is compliance with a literal interpretation. As noted by the FMLC, in the case of POCA the effect of such an approach is that the authorities will receive a mass of information which is of no use in countering the real crime that damages society and which should be the proper subject of anti money-laundering legislation.[14]

As indicated above, the facts of the case concerned a dispute over the ownership **8.08** of a house where the parties had lived for ten years. In the course of routine fact-finding inquiries by one of the solicitors involved it became apparent that one of the parties had been involved in some suspicious-looking bookkeeping, having 'included the cost of the work he had carried out at the property within his business accounts and his VAT returns, even though these works were unconnected with his business'. His solicitors believed that section 328 of the 2002 Act might apply and therefore made the disclosure to the authorities which is, in effect, required by section 328(2)(a). This led to delays and, ultimately, a question—to be considered by the Court of Appeal—as to whether or not the section really did apply to this situation. The point turned on whether or not section 328 'applies to the ordinary conduct of legal proceedings or any aspect of such conduct—including, in particular, any step taken to pursue proceedings and the obtaining of a judgement'. A related question was whether or not the section could apply to 'any consensual steps taken or settlement reached during legal proceedings'.

The Court of Appeal determined that section 328 did not apply. Even though **8.09** the literal wording of the section evidently gave rise to some difficulties, the Court was clearly influenced by the fact that the sections of POCA 2002 that apply to the regulated sector do in fact provide a defence for 'a professional legal adviser' if the relevant information 'came to him in privileged circumstances'.[15] This is in line with Article 6 of the 1991 EU Directive, as amended by the 2001 Directive, which provides, in paragraph 3, that the general requirements need not apply to 'notaries, independent legal professionals, auditors ... with regard to information they receive from or obtain on one of their clients, in the course of defending or representing that client in, or concerning judicial proceedings, including advice on instituting or avoiding proceedings'. The court felt that the

---

[14] See Chamberlain, 'The Proceeds of Crime Act 2002—FMLC Highlights Key Legal Uncertainties' (2004) 10 JIBFL 435.
[15] See s 330(6)(b) and (10).

fact that 'the absence from s.328 of any equivalent protection to that contained in respect of the regulated sector in s.330(10) is a strong argument for a restricted understanding of the concept of "being concerned in an arrangement" '.

8.10 The court also made an important statement about settlements out of court:

> The consensual resolution of issues is an integral part of the conduct of ordinary civil litigation. If, as we consider, article 7 was intended to leave unaffected the ordinary conduct of litigation, then it seems implausible to suggest that it was intended to apply to legal professionals negotiating or implementing a consensual resolution of issues in a litigious context . . . Similar considerations apply with regard to s.328 of the 2002 Act . . . It would be a strange policy which treated the ordinary conduct of litigation as outside the scope of s.328, but only to the extent that the parties refrained from agreeing on any step involved in its conduct and/or from agreeing to resolve any of the issues arising by settlement rather than by litigation to judgement.

8.11 It was noted that this resulted in a distinction between deals done to resolve litigation and other types of transactions, but this seemed to be an inevitable consequence of the structure of the first and second Money Laundering Directives.

8.12 *Bowman v Fels* is a welcome decision. The *Law Society's Gazette*, reporting the case, expressed the relief felt by the legal profession (or at least those with contentious practices):

> The ruling in *Bowman v Fels* [2005] EWCA Civ 226 puts an end to a wide interpretation of the rules that has caused considerable difficulties for lawyers and delays in litigation.
>
> Thousands of family cases in particular had been affected, with solicitors believing they were obliged to report suspicions of minor tax evasion to the National Criminal Intelligence Service (NCIS) and then be unable to work on the case until they received NCIS consent . . . Robin Booth chairman of the Law Society's money laundering taskforce said, '. . . What this judgement does is to protect the whole process of litigation. It does not just depend on professional privilege, but on the principle that people should have access to justice and the courts without having their action disrupted by executive action.'[16]

8.13 But although the process of litigation may now be protected from POCA 2002, most routine banking and financial business is not. As mentioned above, these businesses are in the 'regulated sector' for the purposes of the 2002 Act, and therefore they are not only subject to section 328 but also to section 330, the first part of which provides:

> (1) A person commits an offence if each of the following three conditions is satisfied.

---

[16] LS Gaz 10 March 2005, 1.

(2) The first condition is that he—
    (a) knows or suspects, or
    (b) has reasonable grounds for knowing or suspecting,
    (c) that another person is engaged in money laundering.

(3) The second condition is that the information or other matter—
    (a) on which his knowledge or suspicion is based, or
    (b) which gives reasonable grounds for such knowledge or suspicion,
    (c) came to him in the course of a business in the regulated sector.

(4) The third condition is that he does not make the required disclosure as soon as is practicable after the information or other matter comes to him.

8.14 The required disclosure was originally to the National Criminal Intelligence Service (NCIS), but will in future be to the Serious and Organised Crime Agency. Defences are provided by section 330(6) if the person has 'a reasonable excuse for not disclosing', if he is a professional legal adviser and the information came to him in privileged circumstances (as discussed above), or if he does not actually know about or suspect the money laundering and has not received appropriate training by his employer (as specified by order of the government).

8.15 This section is potentially tougher than section 328 because the offence does not depend on actual knowledge or suspicion (which is what is required for the section 328 offence). However, the real problem with the section is the definition of money laundering itself, which, as *Bowman v Fels* shows, catches activity that many would not have thought would generally be covered by a law whose ostensible purpose was to combat serious crime. The definition is worth close analysis. Money laundering is any offence under sections 327, 328, or 329 of POCA 2002. All of these sections are concerned with some kind of misbehaviour (for example, concealing, converting, or using) with respect to 'criminal property'. By virtue of section 340(3), property is criminal property if:

    (a) it constitutes a person's benefit from criminal conduct or it represents such a benefit (in whole or part and whether directly or indirectly), and
    (b) the alleged offender knows or suspects that it constitutes or represents such a benefit.

8.16 There are numerous provisions which expand on the basic concept. For example, it is stated to be immaterial who carried out the criminal conduct, who benefited from it, and whether or not the conduct occurred before or after the passing of the Act. In section 414(1), property is defined to be: . . . all property wherever situated and includes—

    (a) money;
    (b) all forms of property, real or personal, heritable or moveable;
    (c) things in action and other intangible or incorporeal property.

8.17 The definition of criminal property, however, must be read with the definition of 'criminal conduct' (and it is here that criticisms from the FMLC and others have been most fierce). In section 413(1), this is defined to mean:

> . . . conduct which
> (a) constitutes an offence in any part of the United Kingdom, or
> (b) would constitute an offence in any part of the United Kingdom if it occurred there.

8.18 If these words are taken literally, money laundering could arise as a result of dealing with the proceeds of an activity carried out overseas, which did not constitute a crime in the country where it was carried out, and which did not result in any offence being committed in the UK (although it would have done if the activity had been carried out in the UK). In other words, money laundering may occur in circumstances where no other crime of any kind (let alone a serious crime) has actually been committed. Further, the activity that triggers the money laundering may have occurred a long time ago and may have been relatively minor.

8.19 The FMLC Paper of October 2004 reflects on whether, to take an extreme example, driving (in France) on what would be the 'wrong side' of the road in England (but is the right side in France) could trigger the legislation. It concludes, with certain misgivings, that it would not. More difficult, however, are activities that are permitted elsewhere (such as bullfighting in Spain) but are illegal in the UK. As the FMLC point out, 'the Spanish matador who buys a house in England is, under POCA 2002, laundering the proceeds of criminal conduct'. It follows that those in the regulated sector who might come to know of the matador's house buying must notify the authorities if they are not to be at risk of committing an offence themselves. This result is, of course, patently absurd. Real practical difficulties have resulted for banks and other regulated entities. For example, to quote once more from the FMLC Paper of October 2004 para 11:

> The ambiguities of the legislation make it particularly difficult for large financial institutions to develop clear and consistent guidelines for their myriad customer-facing staff. The fact that the Home Office has declined to issue material guidance on the legislation's interpretation, despite calls from many corners of the regulated sector, only worsens the sense of unease. Some global institutions have considered avoiding the pressures which difficulties in interpreting POCA have placed on certain areas of their business, by simply transferring whole teams of staff into a different jurisdiction. Even if this has not occurred in any particular case, the fact that it has been considered makes this an influential factor in determining where to locate a business, and could be detrimental to the UK economy . . .
>
> The consequences of making a report are extremely difficult to reconcile with the ongoing duties that a financial institution such as a bank normally owes to its customers. When a client seeks to recover what they consider to be their money from an account, only to be told that it is not currently available to them (because a

report has been filed without their knowing), conflict is inevitable; there have been cases of customers making threats of physical violence to bank staff. When consent is subsequently given to the transaction, it is very difficult to explain to a client why their account is functioning normally, without revealing why it did not do so previously (as this could be tipping off).[17] It has even been known for customers to claim damages from the bank for the loss of a business opportunity during the period of the account's suspension pending NCIS response.

The government responded to the FMLC's criticisms (particularly the 'Matador point') with the amendments to POCA 2002 contained in the Serious Organised Crime and Police Act 2005 (SOCPA 2005),[18] which do not change the definition of criminal conduct but, instead, create a new defence to the various potential money laundering charges for a person who is able to show that he knew or believed on reasonable grounds that the relevant criminal conduct took place outside the UK, as long as the conduct is not unlawful in the country where it did take place and as long as it is not of a description to be prescribed by order (as to which details are not currently available). It is helpful that a defence is now available to cover acts which are not criminal where they took place. However, it would have been more helpful if the offence itself had been redefined. The onus on the (potential) defendant, when deciding whether or not to make a disclosure, may be considerable, since the new provision requires him to establish that the act in question is lawful where it takes place; it is not sufficient that he believed this, or had reasonable grounds to believe this, to be the case. As the FMLC comments in the January 2005 Paper: **8.20**

> The only course would be to conduct due diligence as to actual compliance with local law, which would be disproportionate in an 'all crimes scenario', and in many cases could be impossible ... The defence places an obligation on the person concerned to inquire into and definitively establish the criminal law of a foreign jurisdiction. He would have to do so, whether or not the conduct raises public interest issues such as those involved in serious crime, or whether it involves other historic, strict liability or other offences which might not be considered to be of interest to the UK authorities.

The criticism is amplified by Margaret Chamberlain: **8.21**

> In many cases it will not be worth the expense and effort involved in ascertaining that the defence would be available and firms will be left with the choice as to whether or not to make a report to NCIS and obtain NCIS' consent to their particular involvement in a transaction. The prospect that this defence will reduce

---

[17] See *Bowman v Fels* [2005] EWCA Civ 226.
[18] See SOCPA 2005, s 102, which contains amendments to POCA 2002, ss 327, 328, 329, 330, and 331. The legislation also introduces the concept of a *de minimis* 'threshold amount' (initially set at £250), which excuses deposit-taking institutions for what would otherwise be money laundering offences involving criminal activity relating to very small amounts.

the number of reports to NCIS, or assist in resolving the uncertainties, is therefore illusory.[19]

8.22 The potential consequences of firms erring on the side of caution in making 'disclosures' and swamping the authorities with an enormous number of unnecessary reports is a real practical difficulty that will have to be managed as the new law 'beds down'. 'Suspicious Activity Reports' (SARS) numbered some 90,000 in 2003–4.[20] Recent statements from the law enforcement agencies suggest that they are very mindful of the need to work constructively with the regulated sector to make the law work sensibly and, one would hope, develop practices that inspire confidence that the legal risk that arises on the literal wording of POCA 2002 can, in fact, be managed in practice.

C. Market Abuse

8.23 The requirement to report suspicious transactions relating to money laundering under POCA 2002 is echoed in rules of the FSA relating to insider dealing and other forms of 'market abuse', as defined in section 118 of FSMA 2000. Paragraph SUP 15.10 of the Supervision Manual, which applies to activities carried on from UK offices of regulated firms, provides that:

> [15.10.2] R   A firm which arranges or executes a transaction with or for a client in a qualifying investment admitted to trading on a prescribed market and which has reasonable grounds to suspect that the transaction might constitute market abuse must notify the FSA without delay.

> [15.10.3] R   A firm, that is an investment firm or a credit institution, must decide on a case-by-case basis whether there are reasonable grounds for suspecting that a transaction involves market abuse, taking into account the elements constituting market abuse.

> [15.10.4] G(1)   Notification of suspicious transactions to the FSA requires sufficient indications (which may not be apparent until after the transaction has taken place) that the transaction might constitute market abuse. In particular a firm will need to be able to explain the basis for its suspicion when notifying the FSA.

---

[19] See Chamberlain, 'The Proceeds of Crime Act 2002: Progress, but in Which Direction?' (2005) 04 JIBFL 127. For further criticism of the new provision, see 'Solicitors in "double bind" over crime Act', LS Gaz, 30 June 2005.

[20] This number is referred to in a report issued in 2004 by the Inspector of Constabulary, and quoted in Delahunty, 'Three is one is too many' LS Gaz, 16 June 2005. Higher numbers were quoted at a Financial Times conference, reported on 8 June 2005. As one delegate (the head of financial crime prevention at Lloyds TSB) remarked: 'There is little point in turning on the tap and providing a torrent of information if there isn't a big enough bucket to deal with it.' According to LS Gaz, 14 July 2005, solicitors in England and Wales made 12,740 disclosures to the authorities under POCA 2002 in 2004. The corresponding number under comparable laws in Germany was 15 (and similarly low numbers were recorded in other EU jurisdictions).

Certain transactions by themselves may seem completely devoid of anything suspicious, but might deliver such indications of market abuse, when seen in perspective with other transactions, certain behaviour or other information (though firms are not expected to breach effective information barriers put in place to prevent and avoid conflicts of interest so as actively to seek to detect suspicious transactions).[21]

The following information must be provided with any notification: **8.24**

(1) a description of the transaction, including the type of order (such as limit order, market order, or other characteristic of the order);

(2) the reasons for the suspicion;

(3) the means of identification of the relevant parties to the transaction;

(4) the capacity in which the firm operates (for example, for own account or for client); and

(5) any other information that might be significant.[22]

There is also a provision prohibiting 'tipping off'.[23]

It will be noted that these provisions, like those that apply to regulated entities   **8.25** under POCA 2002, apply an objective test. A firm will not be excused failing to report on the grounds that it genuinely suspected nothing if there are 'reasonable grounds' for suspicion. Having regard to the fact that such a test, in the event of any dispute, will of necessity be applied by a regulator which has the benefit of hindsight, it might prove to be somewhat exacting. Should one's suspicions always be aroused, for example, by orders that emanate from certain kinds of client, from certain parts of the world, or in relation to certain kinds of investment? The FSA does provide some insights as to its own thinking with some 'Indications of Possible Suspicious Transactions', which are considered below. First, however, we should look more closely at what the expression 'market abuse' actually means. If POCA 2002 may be criticized for requiring reporting based on ill-defined criminal conduct, the definition of market abuse surely gives rise to similar concerns, both in relation to the risk of being found in contravention of the reporting requirement and also the substantive 'offence'[24] itself (although, in this context, as explained below, there is a considerable amount of official guidance available as to interpretation).

---

[21] See Ch 5, n 61 above for the significance of the prefixes 'R' (rule) and 'G' (guidance).

[22] See SFA Supervision Manual, SUP 15.10.6R.   [23] ibid, SUP 15.10.9.

[24] Market abuse itself is not a criminal offence but insider dealing is a criminal offence under the Criminal Justice Act 1993, s 52. Because it can attract fines from the FSA, market abuse is often referred to as an offence. It should be noted that the FSA can also impose fines if it is satisfied that a person (A) 'by taking or refraining from taking any action has required or encouraged another person or persons to engage in behaviour which, if engaged in by A, would amount to market abuse' (see FSMA 2000, s 123(1)(b)).

8.26 Section 118 of FSMA 2000 (recently amended as part of the implementation of the EU Market Abuse directive)[25] sets out seven types of behaviour that (wherever qualifying investments on a prescribed market are concerned)[26] can amount to market abuse. It is not appropriate in a work of this kind to analyse the descriptions of relevant behaviour in detail, but they may be summarized as:

(1) insider dealing;

(2) wrongful disclosure of inside information;

(3) other behaviour (not covered by (1) or (2) above) which:

  (a) is 'based on' information not generally available in the market (and which would influence dealings if it was), and

  (b) would be 'likely to be regarded by a regular user of the market as a failure on the part of the person concerned to observe the standard of behaviour reasonably expected of a person in his position in relation to the market';

(4) effecting deals, 'otherwise than for legitimate reasons and in conformity with accepted market practices on the relevant market', which:

  (a) give or are likely to give the wrong impression as to supply or demand (or price) in relation to investments, or

  (b) secure the price of investments 'at an abnormal or artificial level';

(5) effecting deals using 'fictitious devices or any other form of deception or contrivance';

(6) putting out or spreading information, 'by any means', which gives or is likely to give the wrong impression about an investment, where the person concerned knows or should know that the information was false or misleading;

(7) behaviour (not covered by any of (4), (5), or (6) above) which:

  (a) is likely to give a regular user of the market the wrong impression as to the supply, demand, price, or value of an investment, or

  (b) would be likely to be regarded by a regular user of the market 'as behaviour that would distort, or would be likely to distort, the market in such an investment',

and 'the behaviour is likely to be regarded by a regular user of the market as a failure on the part of the person concerned to observe the standard of behaviour reasonably expected of a person in his position in relation to the market'.

8.27 It will be immediately apparent that a number of the concepts that appear in the above descriptions of behaviour (behaviour 'based on' information,

---

[25] Directive 2003/6/EC of the European Parliament and of the Council of 28 January 2003. See Sch 2 to the Financial Services and Markets Act 2000 (Market Abuse) Regulations 2005 (SI 2005/381).

[26] All the most commonly traded forms of security are covered, as are the leading exchanges.

'standard of behaviour reasonably expected', 'legitimate reasons', 'deception or contrivance', etc) are somewhat vague, even nebulous. However, breach of the provisions regarding market abuse can attract unlimited fines, imposed by the FSA,[27] and, as indicated above, failure to report market abuse, if it is (or should reasonably be) suspected, can also be punished by fines. The vagueness of the provisions was heavily criticized when the provisions were being debated in Parliament, and this resulted in the government accepting that the FSA could, in effect, provide some guidance and 'safe harbours' in the Code of Market Conduct. This is reflected in section 119 of FSMA 2000, which requires the production of the Code and states that it may, among other things, specify:

(a) descriptions of behaviour that, in the opinion of the [FSA], amount to market abuse;

(b) descriptions of behaviour that, in the opinion of the [FSA], do not amount to market abuse;

(c) factors that, in the opinion of the [FSA], are to be taken into account in determining whether or not behaviour amounts to market abuse.

Although the requirement to produce a code is helpful, it does, of course, result **8.28** in enormous power being placed in the hands of the FSA. No doubt the regulator would wish to exercise such power reasonably and fairly, but there is nevertheless cause for concern that an entity which is, in effect, an arm of the executive should have powers to make, enforce, and judge compliance with laws which include the power to impose unlimited fines.[28]

The Code of Market Conduct contains the following provisions (among many **8.29** others) regarding some of the vaguer concepts referred to above. These are set out here by way of example as to how clarification can be provided; they should not be regarded as exhaustive or comprehensive or a substitute for reading the Code in full. They do, however, contain material that may be appropriately converted to internal guidance or principles of behaviour for the purpose of legal risk management.[29]

The '*on the basis of*' concept is dealt with as follows: **8.30**

---

[27] See FSMA 2000, s 123.

[28] See Blair et al, 'Banking and Financial Services Regulation' (3rd edn) para 9.52: 'the novelty of the new regime, as regards both its structure, its conceptual framework and the language in which its requirements are couched, has given rise to a significant amount of apprehension among market participants'.

[29] See Chs 10 and 11 below.

E   In the opinion of the FSA, the following factors are to be taken into account in determining whether or not a person's behaviour is 'on the basis of' inside information, and are each indications that it is not:

(1)   if the decision to deal or attempt to deal was made before the person possessed the relevant inside information; or

(2)   if the person concerned is dealing to satisfy a legal or regulatory obligation which came into being before he possessed the relevant inside information; or

(3)   if a person is an organisation, if none of the individuals in possession of the inside information:

(a)   had any involvement in the decision to deal; or

(b)   behaved in such a way as to influence, directly or indirectly, the decision to engage in the dealing; or

(c)   had any contact with those who were involved in the decision to engage in the dealing whereby the information could have been transmitted.

8.31   The Code goes on to state (and the points made here are of course of crucial importance for legal risk management)[30] that:

E   In the opinion of the FSA, if the inside information is the reason for, or a material influence on, the decision to deal or attempt to deal, that indicates that the person's behaviour is 'on the basis of' the inside information . . .

E   In the opinion of the FSA, if the inside information is held behind an effective Chinese wall, or similarly effective arrangements, from the individuals who are involved in or who influence the decision to deal, that indicates that the decision to deal by an organisation is not 'on the basis of' inside information.'

8.32   With regard to '*standards of behaviour*', the Code states that:

E   In the opinion of the FSA, the following factors are to be taken into account in determining whether or not behaviour that creates a false or misleading impression as to, or distorts the market for, a qualifying investment, has also failed to meet the standard expected by a regular user:

(1)   if the transaction is pursuant to a prior legal or regulatory obligation owed to a third party;

(2)   if the transaction is executed in a way which takes into account the need for the market as a whole to operate fairly and efficiently;

(3)   the characteristics of the market in question, including the users and applicable rules and codes of conduct (including, if relevant, any statutory or regulatory obligation to disclose a holding or position, such as under section 198 of the Companies Act 1985);

(4)   the position of the person in question and the standards reasonably expected of him in light of his experience, skill and knowledge;

---

[30] See Chs 10 and 11 below. It will be appreciated that the various statements referred to here that are prefixed by the letter 'E' are, in the FSA's parlance, 'evidential provisions' (not 'safe harbours', for which the prefix would be 'C'—for 'conclusive') and, as such, serve as influential 'pointers' to interpretation, but are not conclusive; see 5.56 n. 59.

(5) if the transaction complied with the rules of the relevant prescribed markets about how transactions are to be executed in a proper way (for example, rules on reporting and executing cross-transactions);

(6) if the organisation has created a false or misleading impression, whether the individuals responsible could only know they were likely to create a false or misleading impression if they had access to other information that was being held behind a Chinese wall or similarly effective arrangements.

The influence of 'soft law'[31] (such as the rules of prescribed markets and applicable codes of conduct) will be apparent here. It is, perhaps, inherent in the concept of 'the standard expected of a regular user', in that it is difficult to see how such a standard could be demonstrated to exist (or what it consists of) except by reference to soft law sources. Whether or not the architects and draftsmen of such material would appreciate its 'hard law effect' (in providing evidence of whether or not market abuse has occurred) is another matter. As with insider dealing, the existence of an effective Chinese wall may, in certain circumstances, be of great significance. **8.33**

With reference to '*legitimate reasons*', the Code states that: **8.34**

E In the opinion of the FSA, the following factors are to be taken into account in determining whether or not a person's behaviour is in pursuit of legitimate business, and are indications that it is:

(1) the extent to which the relevant trading by the person is carried out in order to hedge a risk, and in particular the extent to which it neutralises and responds to a risk arising out of the person's legitimate business; or

(2) whether, in the case of a transaction on the basis of inside information about a client's transaction which has been executed, the reason for it being inside information is that information about the transaction is not, or is not yet, required to be published under any relevant regulatory or exchange obligations; or

(3) whether, if the relevant trading by that person is connected with a transaction entered into or to be entered into with a client (including a potential client), the trading either has no impact on the price or there has been adequate disclosure to that client that trading will take place and he has not objected to it; or

(4) the extent to which the person's behaviour was reasonable by the proper standards of conduct of the market concerned, taking into account any relevant regulatory or legal obligations and whether the transaction is executed in a way which takes into account the need for the market as a whole to operate fairly and efficiently.

E In the opinion of the FSA, if the person acted in contravention of a relevant legal, regulatory or exchange obligation, that is a factor to be taken into account in determining whether or not a person's behaviour is in pursuit of legitimate business, and is an indication that it is not.

---

[31] See para 5.50 et seq. above.

Paragraph (3) above obviously points to the desirability of an in-house rule requiring client consent (or at least non-objection, following proper disclosure) to trading in the relevant circumstances.

8.35 Concerning '*deception or contrivance*', the Code states that:

> E   The following behaviours are, in the opinion of the FSA, market abuse (manipulating) devices:
>
> . . .
>
> (3)   pump and dump—that is, taking a long position in a qualifying investment and then disseminating misleading positive information about the qualifying investment with a view to increasing its price;
> (4)   trash and cash—that is, taking a short position in a qualifying investment and then disseminating misleading negative information about the qualifying investment, with a view to driving down its price.

The colourful expressions aptly describe behaviour which seems to exemplify market abuse in two of its simpler forms.

8.36 In an effort to assist those who may have to decide whether or not a transaction is suspicious enough to justify reporting, the FSA has also given guidance[32] by way of 'examples of indications' of suspicious dealings 'as a starting point for consideration' of whether suspicion is merited, including the following (in relation to insider dealing):

> Possible Signals of Insider Dealing
> 1   . . .
> 2   A client opens an account and immediately gives an order to conduct a significant transaction or, in the case of a wholesale client, an unexpectedly large or unusual order, in a particular security—especially if the client is insistent that the order is carried out very urgently or must be concluded before a particular time specified by the client.
> 3   A transaction is significantly out of line with the client's previous investment behaviour (e.g. type of security; amount invested; size of order; time security held).
> 4   A client specifically requests immediate execution of an order regardless of the price at which the order would be executed (assuming more than a mere placing of 'at market' order by the client).
> 5   There is unusual trading in the shares of a company before the announcement of price sensitive information relating to the company.
> 6   An employee's own account transaction is timed just before clients' transactions and related orders in the same financial instrument.

8.37 As with the statements in the Code of Market Conduct regarding what constitutes market abuse, these 'signals' are potentially very helpful and would no doubt be reflected at the appropriate point in firms' own in-house guidance

---

[32] In the 'Full Handbook', SUP/15/Annex 5.

literature. Nevertheless, a double level of uncertainty remains for those who have to decide about whether or not to make a report:

(1) Was what apparently happened within the definition of market abuse, having regard to the Code of Market Conduct?
(2) How clear is it that the suspicion is justified?

The FSA has made it clear that it will not welcome excessively cautious, 'defen- **8.38** sive' reporting. This might itself be seen as a sign of inadequate internal controls (which may be grounds for a fine under a different head). So it is important that the correct balance is struck. The FSA has acknowledged that the same set of circumstances may give rise to an obligation to make a report under POCA 2002 as under the market abuse provisions, but there are no proposals as yet for combined reporting.

On 1 July 2005 (the day that the new market abuse regime came into force) the **8.39** *Financial Times* reported (under the heading 'FSA fears banks may swamp it with their filings'):

> . . . the Financial Services Authority . . . is concerned that it will be overwhelmed by banks reporting routine transactions as suspicious in order to protect themselves against future fines. That was the experience of the National Criminal Intelligence Service, which has been deluged with 'suspicious activity reports' in recent years as a result of new money laundering legislation governing financial institutions. To prevent it being swamped, the FSA last week wrote to companies to warn that it would come down hard on firms that report suspicious transactions for 'defensive' reasons.

D. Other Recent Legislation

The Pensions Act 2004

Shortfalls in pension funds are a modern social and political problem. Some **8.40** blame taxation policy for the problem, some blame poor management, and some say it's just because we are living longer. Whatever the cause, the problem is serious and has led to legislation in the Pensions Act 2004 which is designed to enable the 'Pensions Regulator' (a new body, established by the Act) to call upon various entities who might have some connection with specific shortfall problems in specific funds to put their hands in their pockets to help out. These entities could include banks who have lent to the company with the pension problem. There are two ways in which the Pensions Regulator might take action that requires a payment (which would have to be made to the specific fund in difficulties rather than the general Pension Protection Fund set up by the Act, which is funded by levy). It could issue a 'contribution notice' under section

38(2) or it could issue a 'financial support direction' under section 43(2). A contribution notice may be issued if the regulator believes the recipient is at fault, in that there has been 'an act or a deliberate failure to act' which in essence relates to an attempt to avoid pension liabilities. The payment required by the notice must be of a sum that in the opinion of the regulator it is 'reasonable' to require the recipient to pay. The sum may be either the whole or a specified part of the shortfall in relation to the relevant pension scheme. A financial support direction may be issued in circumstances where the recipient is not at fault, and (as with contribution notices) the recipient may include anyone 'connected' with the employer. All that is required for this form of notice (instead of fault) is that the regulator 'is of the opinion that it is reasonable to impose the requirements of the direction on the person'.[33] 'Financial support' is broadly defined in section 45 and includes the provision of 'additional financial resources'. Failure to comply can result in a contribution notice being issued.

8.41 Because this legislation is so vague, particularly in its various references to what the regulator thinks is reasonable, there are provisions in the Pensions Act for the application for, and issuance of, 'clearance statements' whereby a person who fears that he might become subject to either form of notice can obtain formal clearance from the regulator (which is binding on it) that, in effect, the notice will not be issued.

8.42 The legislation may apply to banks who fund companies with pension fund shortfalls because the definition of 'connected' persons includes persons who control more than a third of the voting power of the shareholders of a company, and banks which have charges over a sufficiently large percentage of a company's shares might fall into this category. Trustees for bondholders might also find themselves in this position. The point has raised a degree of concern in the financial markets[34] and has been the subject of correspondence (April/July 2005) between Lord Browne-Wilkinson, the Chairman of the FMLC, and the Chair of the Pensions Regulator. The exchanges resulted in informal (non-binding) confirmation from the regulator that the mere fact that a bank or a trustee is a chargee is not going to result in the issuance of either of the notices referred to above. However, if the chargee takes steps to enforce the security, the provisions might come into play. The regulator also said that it expects to clarify its views on these matters in 'guidance' to be published in the near future (although at the time of writing this is still awaited). Guidance from the regulator is intended to supplement its Code of Practice (required under section 90(2) of the Act) but guidance does not have the statutory significance of clearance statements of the Code of Practice itself.

---

[33] See s 43(5)(b).
[34] See Neale, 'Moral Hazards for Lenders—The Pensions Act 2004' (2005).

Section 70(2) of the Pensions Act 2004 also imposes a duty to inform the **8.43** Pensions Regulator in writing if a person to whom it applies (and the category of such persons in widely defined and includes professional advisers) 'has reasonable cause to believe' someone has broken the law in connection with the administration of a pension scheme and that this 'is likely to be of material significance to the Regulator in the exercise of any of its functions'.

This legislation conforms to a broad pattern that we have seen in the context of **8.44** a number of new laws affecting the financial markets. The following features are frequently found:

- The new law is drafted relatively loosely. This makes it more difficult for those who are intended to be caught by it to escape its application. On the other hand, there is an increased risk of unintended, and possibly damaging, side-effects.

- The potential harm caused by the vagueness of the law is partially mitigated by the appointment of a regulator who has power to interpret some of its more difficult provisions.

- However, the regulator is also charged with administering and enforcing the law, issuing codes of conduct, drawing up rules, levying fines (or the equivalent), etc.

- A great deal of reliance is placed on the expectation (or requirement) that the regulator will act reasonably.

- People are expected, and required, to inform on law breakers, usually by reference to an objective test as to what they should 'reasonably' know or suspect rather than what they actually know.

This is a new kind of law making. It has certain advantages, chiefly in relation to **8.45** its flexibility. However, it does result in a plethora of 'soft law' and its inherent vagueness tends to legal uncertainty. It also places enormous power in the hands of unelected bodies for whose actions our elected politicians do not appear to feel much direct responsibility.

The Consumer Credit Bill

The last item to be mentioned under the heading of vagueness is some proposed **8.46** legislation which, at the time of writing, is contained in the Consumer Credit Bill. It would not be appropriate to comment here at length on the Bill because it may, of course, change during its passage through Parliament. However, one provision, in the context of legal risk and uncertainty, is worthy of note even at this preliminary stage. According to clause 19 of the Bill, the courts are to be given powers to make orders which would have the effect, potentially, of completely rewriting agreements between banks and consumer customers (including requiring the repayment of sums paid) if the court determines:

> . . . that the relationship between the creditor and debtor arising out of the agreement (or the agreement taken with any related agreement) is unfair to the debtor because of one or more of the following—
> (a) any of the terms of the agreement or of any related agreement;
> (b) the way in which the creditor has exercised or enforced any of his rights under the agreement or any related agreement;
> (c) any other thing done (or not done) by, or on behalf of, the creditor (either before or after the making of the agreement or any related agreement).

8.47 We have become used to the concept of 'unfair terms' in the context of consumer sales and supply contracts[35] but this is the first time we have seen such a radical extension into consumer credit arrangements and 'relationships'. It remains to be seen how the test of fairness will be developed in this context.

8.48 Clause 19 is potentially severe in its effect on banks, which will lose a considerable amount of contractual certainty as a result of it, and its likely effect as an invitation to litigation can only be increased by virtue of the fact that, in the event of any dispute, it is for the bank to show that the 'relationship' is fair, not for the consumer to show why it is unfair. As with the 'consumerist' approach of the FSA[36] it seems that current policy remains firmly in favour of a compensation culture wherever a 'consumer' is involved. There seems to be a reluctance to allow individuals to have anything approaching full responsibility for their own financial decisions. Legal risks for financial institutions will flow directly from this.

---

[35] See Unfair Terms in Consumer Contracts Regulations 1999, SI 1999/3159.
[36] See 5.59 et seq.

9

RE-CHARACTERIZATION

There is nothing illegal in a party raising finance by a sale of book debts or goods, rather than by a mortgage or charge, if he chooses to do so.[1]

The learned counsel for the respondents spoke of dealings of this sort with an air of righteous indignation as if they were traps for the extravagant and the impecunious . . . I think that is going too far . . . If these agreements are objectionable it is for Parliament to interfere. It is not for the Court to put a forced or strained construction on a written document or to import a meaning which the parties never dreamed of because it may not wholly approve of transactions of the sort.[2]

There may be cases in which banks which have entered into certain kinds of transactions prefer not to raise the question of whether they involve any legal risk. They may hope that if nothing is said, their counterparties will honour their obligations and all will be well, whereas any suggestion of a legal risk attaching to the instruments they hold may affect their credit ratings. There is room for a spectrum of states of mind between genuine belief in validity . . . and a clear acceptance of the risk that they are not.[3]

A. Different Ways of Raising Money

There are many ways for a company to raise money from a bank or other **9.01** financial institution, apart from borrowing. A company may, for example, finance the acquisition of plant and equipment by entering into a financial lease with a bank. The bank would provide the purchase price to be paid to the

---

[1] *Per* Dillon LJ in *Welsh Development Agency v Export Finance Co Ltd* [1992] BCLC 148

[2] *Per* Lord Macnaghten in *Helby v Matthews* [1895] AC 475, 482. Commenting on this passage in 1933 (in *Re George Inglefield* [1933] Ch 1; see below) Eve J remarked: 'Those words were spoken nearly forty years ago, and with the arrival since then of the motor car, and aeroplane, wireless installations and gramophones and the Encyclopaedia Britannica they certainly lose none of their force when applied to the condition of things prevailing today'.

[3] From the judgment of Lord Hoffmann in *Kleinwort Benson Ltd v Lincoln City Council* [1999] 2 AC 349, at 401.

supplier (and become the owner of the asset) and receive lease rental payments from the company (which would possess the asset and have the use of it). The lease payments would take into account any tax benefits (such as capital allowances) that the bank might receive as owner of new plant, and would have a similar economic effect to the payment of interest on, and repayment over time of, capital invested by the bank. Once the bank has 'got its money back'—at the end of the lease—the company would usually have the right to acquire outright ownership of the asset for a nominal consideration. Similar arrangements may be entered into for the acquisition of major capital items such as aircraft or ships.

9.02 Finance is also commonly raised by companies selling their trade debts (or 'receivables') to finance houses, so that the finance house becomes the owner of the expected payment in return for paying a purchase price to the company, which would generally be discounted to the nominal value of the debt in order to reflect the time value of money (or interest) between the date the finance is provided and the date the debt is due for payment. The discount might also reflect the risk taken by the finance house that the debt might not be paid, although in some cases such sales or discounting transactions are made on a 'with recourse' basis, so that the finance house might have full or partial recourse to the company if the debt is not paid. It is well established that a discount, although similar in effect, is not the same as interest:

> When payment is made before the due date at a discount, the amount of the discount is no doubt often calculated by reference to the amount of interest which the payer calculates his money would have earned if he had deferred payment to the due date. But that does not mean that discount is the same as interest. Interest postulates the making of a loan and then it runs from day to day until repayment of the loan, its total depending on the length of the loan. Discount is a deduction from the price fixed once and for all time at the time of payment.[4]

9.03 These forms of financing are common. Less common, but by no means unheard of, are financings for natural resource projects which involve, instead of a borrowing of money, a sale to financiers of the expected production from the project (whether petroleum or other minerals) in return for a capital sum provided by way of 'advance purchase price' at the outset of the construction of the project's facilities. These transactions are sometimes known as 'forward sales' or 'advance purchase' transactions. The British National Oil Corporation raised money through such a transaction in the 1970s. This attracted a degree of controversy because it escaped restrictions that the government had placed upon borrowings by the company; it was not a borrowing, so the restrictions did not apply.

---

[4] *Per* Lord Devlin in *Chow Yoong Hong v Choong Fah Rubber Manufactory Ltd* [1961] 3 All ER 1163, para 217.

The commercial rationale for raising money in one of these 'alternative' ways **9.04** will vary from case to case:

- It may be a desire to escape some form of restriction such as that imposed on the British National Oil Corporation or such as may frequently be imposed by contract in financing documents entered into with other banks or trustees for bondholders. For example, a 'negative pledge' which, perhaps rather carelessly, restricts the granting of security by the company for 'loans' or 'borrowings' only—as opposed to security for the 'raising of money' by any means—would be easily circumvented by most forms of alternative finance structures, including forward sale transactions. Also, 'financial covenants', by which a company's existing lenders may restrict a company's 'gearing', amongst other things, may, in some cases, not apply to the full range of alternative capital raising.

- The commercial rationale may be the opportunity to take advantage of tax allowances that are available to a purchaser of new plant, but which cannot be enjoyed directly by a company because it does not itself have sufficient taxable income (or 'tax shelter') against which to set the allowances. Instead, the company gets the benefit indirectly because the bank that finances the purchase—and has the tax allowance—passes part of the benefit on by way of reduced rental payments under the finance lease.

- The choice of an alternative means of raising money may be influenced by how the transaction is accounted for on the company's balance sheet or whether or not a security interest will require filing or registration.

There may be other reasons. In the 'post-Enron' world, the fact that such **9.05** transactions might involve a degree of complexity (and, in some cases, the use of 'special purpose vehicles') has attracted suspicion.[5] However, although they may often be designed with a view to avoiding some kind of restriction that might apply to a conventional borrowing (or to take advantage of some tax allowances), they do not necessarily involve devious or underhand motives, still less fraud. Off-balance sheet financing has been used by the UK government for many years as a means of raising money for new infrastructure, through the use of PFI and PPP schemes (which are, in effect, forms of project finance). It may have been given a bad name by the excesses of Enron, but off-balance sheet

---

[5] The notorious 'raptor' transactions entered into by Enron prior to its downfall did, of course, involve SPVs and were presented as a form of 'structured financing'. See Eichenwald, 'Conspiracy of Fools' at 'Book Two' and especially, p.143: 'A company could provide 97 per cent of the capital to an off-books partnership, find 3 per cent somewhere else, stir in some legal legerdemain, and—poof!—an "independent" buyer was created. The company could then legally "sell" an asset to the partnership—even if most of the payment originated from its own pockets. The round-trip of cash was complete, the company had converted an asset on its balance sheet into revenue.'

finance should not be equated with wrongdoing. As Ralph Gibson LJ observed in the leading Court of Appeal case of *Welsh Development Agency v Export Finance Co Ltd*:[6]

> I do not think there is any force in the fact that the transactions contemplated were, and were intended to be, 'off balance sheet' . . . Other long-established forms of financing may also be 'off balance sheet', namely factoring and block discounting . . . Those who were concerned with the financial stability of Parrot,[7] over the longer or shorter term, could discover what charges were registered and could ask whether there are any off balance sheet lines of credit. Auditors could insist upon such reference in the accounts to such lines of credit as would, in their judgement, give a true and fair picture. Those who provided credit on security could, if they judged it necessary, insert provisions which would prohibit the use of the sort of arrangement set out in the master agreement.[8] If any mischief arising from off balance sheet financing is judged to be serious it could be prohibited by legislation. Under the law as it now stands, I could see no reason for giving, as it were, bad marks to the master agreement, in that it provides for off balance sheet financing, in the court's approach to the issue of construction.

B. The Risk of Wrong Labels

9.06 When such transactions are arranged, it is important for the parties to have confidence that their choice of 'deal structure' for the money raising will be recognized as such by the courts, if ever challenged. If, for example, a financial lease was deemed by the courts to be a borrowing—because it has the same commercial effect as a borrowing—the expected benefits of the deal structure would be nullified. As we shall see, the English courts rarely indulge in deeming a transaction to be something other than what the parties intended—often termed 'recharacterization' nowadays—but there are policy considerations that may come into play and put the more adventurously structured transactions at risk. It is important that this risk, which is a legal risk, can be understood and evaluated in the more extreme cases and that it is strictly confined to cases where the policy reasons for recharacterization are compelling. Indeed, the use of the term 'recharacterization' (and the reference above to 'deeming') is arguably misleading. It is perhaps more accurate to see the risk as one of incorrect labelling or description of a transaction by the parties. If a court determines that a transaction is, when properly analysed, one of debt on security (and not, as the

---

[6] [1992] BCLC 148.

[7] The company whose insolvency gave rise to the litigation. The facts of this case are considered in more detail at 9.15–9.18 below.

[8] The master agreement provided for a form of off-balance sheet financing to Parrot; see further para 9.15 below.

parties may have described it, one of sale) the court is not, as a matter of law, changing the nature of the transaction, it is making a decision as to what it truly is (and always was). 'Recharacterization risk' would thus be better described as 'incorrect transaction description risk', but the former term is now firmly established and it is not the objective of this book to try to change the markets' preferred linguistic usage.

The risk of recharacterization extends beyond the primary finance-raising trans- **9.07** action to the various forms of security that parties may use for the 'debtor's' obligations. English law does not have a finite, code-defined list of security interests. One of the most commonly used, the floating charge, was, in effect, invented by practitioners (and sanctioned by the courts) relatively recently, towards the end of the nineteenth century. Nevertheless, security interests are subject to a number of important statutory requirements and limitations that affect the degree of publicity that must be given to them by registration, the extent of the debtor's assets that may be covered by them, their priority on the debtor's insolvency, and circumstances in which they may be disregarded completely. Floating charges, in particular, are subject to a number of statutory disadvantages, reflecting a long-standing policy designed to counterbalance the enormous advantages that they would otherwise give to the secured lender on a company's insolvency. Because lenders and borrowers may find advantage in structuring arrangements so that one or more of these statutory provisions does not apply, there have been a number of cases on arrangements involving security interests themselves (or arrangements that have a similar effect to the granting of a conventional form of security), for example, on whether a given kind of arrangement needs to be registered, and, especially recently, on whether a certain kind of charge should properly be regarded as a fixed charge or floating charge.

The range of options available to parties who wish to use a non-conventional **9.08** form of capital raising or security is relatively broad. As the Law Commission noted recently:[9]

> It has been widely recognised for some time that a number of transactions that are not usually treated by the law as creating a security interest do in practice act as a form of security. These functional equivalents are sometimes known as 'quasi-securities' or 'title finance'. Examples include hire-purchase, conditional sales, finance leases, consignments of goods and retention of title clauses. Sales and repurchase ('repos') also represent significant forms of financing in today's modern markets. In each case the financier retains (or in some cases obtains) full title to the assets rather than being granted a charge over the assets, and if the debtor fails to

---

[9] See Consultation Paper, 14 June 2002, 'Registration of Security Interests: Company Charges and Property other than Land', paras 6.2 and 6.7.

pay for the assets (or in other circumstances agreed in the contract) they can be repossessed or (in the case of repos) retained or sold. In addition there are many types of receivables financing including factoring, discounting of receivables and securitisation which seem to perform a 'security function' . . .

Quasi-securities over goods, at least, are most commonly used for 'vendor credit', that is when finance is provided to enable the buyer or hirer to obtain goods. However quasi-securities can also be used as a means of what is in effect secured borrowing on existing assets. A business may own a piece of equipment that it wishes to use as quasi-security. It may agree to sell it to a finance house and then take it back on hire-purchase or under a finance lease ('sale and lease-back'). The functional equivalence to taking a loan secured by a charge over the equipment is evident.

9.09 There are, however, hazards in over-ambitious labelling. If the parties 'get it wrong' and find that their arrangement is recharacterized, the consequences can be very serious. That said, it does at least seem to be the case that many financing structures that are recharacterization-sensitive are adopted in the knowledge that the risk exists, but that it is worth using the 'risky' structure and being prepared to have it tested in the courts if it is challenged. This adventurous approach would seem to be stimulated, at least in part, by the fact that the parties to the transaction do not themselves have any interest in challenging the correctness of the description they have chosen for it. Any challenge is likely to arise in the context of a party's insolvency (which may not happen, at least during the life of the transaction) or perhaps as a result of queries by auditors or regulators. The policy of the law, as reflected in court decisions, thus has to take account of, and achieve a degree of reconciliation between, the following:

- freedom of contract, and associated rights of freedom of private ownership of property, including the right to dispose of it or encumber it, together with the right to structure commercial transactions in such manner as may seem expedient to those involved;

- the policy need to restrict the ability to create security over property in a manner that would be unfair to creditors who do not have the security (for example, because of insufficient publicity or unfairly high ranking on insolvency);

- the law's requirement that transactions be analysed by reference to what they actually consist of rather than by how the parties have chosen to describe them;

- the need to deal with the temptation for parties to use false or incorrect 'labelling' (or 'camouflage') in situations where the only entities that would be adversely affected are third parties; this may be done in good faith in the vast majority of cases (there being at least a tenable argument that the label is the correct one) but in some cases the parties may go a step further and stray into documentation which the courts would consider to be a 'sham'.[10]

C. Essential Differences Between Sale and Security

The starting point (although it is not the earliest case) for analysis of how the courts approach these issues is the 1933 case of *Re George Inglefield*.[11] In that case, a company based in Dorking, Surrey, which carried on a furnishing and drapery business, had gone into liquidation. The company used to let out furniture on hire purchase agreements. It had raised finance from a discount company by assigning to it (by way of purported outright sale) both the furniture which was subject to these agreements and the benefit of the agreements themselves. The discount company paid a purchase price which, in essence, consisted of 75 per cent of the agreements' cash flows 'up front' and the balance in instalments (reflecting the balance of the sums due under the agreements) less a discount or 'finance charge'. The company guaranteed the payments due from the customers (in effect, therefore, a 'with recourse' deal, the financier taking no significant credit risk on the customers). The liquidator of the company challenged the validity of the financing arrangement on the basis that it was really a loan on the security of (unregistered and therefore invalid) charges over book debts. In other words, the transaction (although not a 'sham') was not what it purported to be, and should be 'recharacterized'. **9.10**

It was held (by the Court of Appeal) that the transaction should be upheld as a sale. It was not to be subject to recharacterization. Hire purchase and discount financing were relatively novel at that time but both the Court of Appeal and Eve J at first instance (although he was overturned by the higher court on the recharacterization point) refused to approach the transaction 'with a sinister view'.[12] Lord Hanworth MR defended a businessman's right to raise money in such lawful manner as might be appropriate: **9.11**

> There is nothing improper or wrong in obtaining money in this way any more than there is in going to your banker and obtaining money upon documents. There are, no doubt, provisions . . . which require a charge to be registered, but if you enter into a transaction outside these provisions which require registration as a

---

[10] Under English law, 'sham' transactions are confined to the comparatively limited situations where the documents are intended by the parties 'to give third parties or to the court the appearance of creating between the parties legal rights and obligations different from the actual legal rights and obligations (if any) which the parties intend to create', *per* Diplock LJ in *Snook v London & West Riding Investments Ltd* [1967] 2 QB 786, 802. The test of intention is subjective. Sham transactions are void. See also *Stone v Hitch* [2001] EWCA Civ 63.

[11] [1933] Ch 1.   [12] *Per* Lord Hanworth MR.

condition of validity, you are unaffected by the law. It is not a question of evasion. A transaction is either within or without the law, and malice is not to be attributed to a person who so carried out a transaction that it remains outside the law.

9.12 In the course of his judgment, Romer LJ gave what has come to be regarded as the classic description of the essential differences between a sale on the one hand and a mortgage or charge on the other:

> In a transaction of sale the vendor is not entitled to get back the subject-matter of the sale by returning to the purchaser the money that has passed between them. In the case of a mortgage or charge, the mortgagor is entitled, until he has been foreclosed, to get back the subject-matter of the mortgage or charge by returning to the mortgagee the money that has passed between them . . .
>
> if the mortgagee realizes the subject-matter of the mortgage for a sum more than sufficient to repay him, with interest and the costs, the money that has passed between him and the mortgagor he has to account to the mortgagor for the surplus. If the purchaser sells the subject-matter of the purchase, and realizes a profit, of course he has not got to account to the vendor for the profit . . .
>
> if the mortgagee realizes the mortgaged property for a sum that is insufficient to repay him the money that he has paid to the mortgagor, together with interest and costs, then the mortgagee is entitled to recover from the mortgagor the balance of the money . . .
>
> If the purchaser were to resell the purchased property at a price which was insufficient to recoup him the money that he had paid to the vendor . . . he would not be entitled to recover the balance from the vendor.

9.13 As Dillon LJ remarked in *Welsh Development Agency v Export Finance Co Ltd*, the above distinctions 'do not have the clarity of the distinction between a tenancy and a licence to occupy, viz that it must be a tenancy if the grantee has been given exclusive occupation of the property in question'. They are nevertheless very helpful. Traditional discounting and factoring is, on the basis of this analysis, 'safe' from any recharacterization threat.[13]

9.14 Dillon LJ was of the view that 'there is no one clear touchstone' which incontrovertibly will distinguish a sale from a loan on security. One has to look at the transaction in the round. Lord Herschell's dictum in *McEntire v Crossley Bros Ltd*[14] was thought to point the way:

> . . . I quite concede that the agreement must be regarded as a whole—its substance must be looked at. The parties cannot, by the insertion of mere words, defeat the effect of the transaction as appearing from the whole of the agreement into which

---

[13] At the time of writing, however, it seems possible that the law will soon be changed to provide for the registration of sales of receivables in the same manner as the registration of charges. See draft Statutory Instrument 'The Company Security Regulations 2006', published by the Law Commission, July 2005.

[14] [1895] AC 457, 462–3.

they have entered. If the words in one part of it point in one direction and the words in another part in another direction, you must look at the agreement as a whole and see what its substantial effect is. But there is no such thing, as seems to have been argued here, as looking at the substance, apart from looking at the language which the parties have used. It is only by a study of the whole of the language that the substance can be ascertained.

D. A Very Robust Decision

The *Welsh Development Agency* case[15] must surely represent one of the high water **9.15** marks for the English courts' willingness to take a robust approach to the upholding of the parties' expressed intentions. If any alternative financing structure was ever to run a risk of recharacterization, it was surely the one that featured in this case. However, the court held that the transaction was indeed one of sale and not (as argued) one of loan on (unregistered and therefore invalid) security. The facts were extremely complex, but may be summarized as follows:

- Parrot Corp Ltd. was an exporter of computer floppy disks. It had raised borrowings from financiers (under an agreement dated 31 October 1985) on the strength of a guarantee given to the lenders by the Welsh Development Agency (WDA). This guarantee was the subject of a counter-indemnity given to the WDA by Parrot, which was secured by a debenture over Parrot's assets (which was duly registered).

- Parrot also raised money (under an agreement dated 29 July 1985, as varied in 1988) from Export Finance Co Ltd ('Exfinco'). This did not, on the face of it, involve a borrowing by Parrot. Instead, it was provided in the documentation (which was in Exfinco's standard form) that whenever Parrot had an export sale in prospect, Exfinco made a standing offer to buy all the relevant goods from Parrot (finance thus being provided by way of the purchase moneys) and then Parrot would sell these goods, as Exfinco's agent, to the overseas customer. (Exfinco would be an undisclosed principal.) Exfinco's offer to Parrot was accepted by Parrot sending the relevant invoices to the WDA together with certain other documents.

- The overseas customer would be directed to pay the price into an account in Parrot's name, but the account would be under Exfinco's control: 'Under the terms of the sale to the overseas buyer there was to be retention of title to goods until the price was fully paid, and as a result of the acceptance by . . . Parrot of Exfinco's standing offer the retained title to the goods would be in

---

[15] [1992] BCLC 148.

Exfinco as purchaser from Parrot of the goods to be sold by Parrot to the overseas buyer as agent for Exfinco as undisclosed principal.'[16]

9.16 It was noted in the course of the judgements that a typical bank debenture (such as the one given by Parrot to the WDA) 'might create a fixed charge in equity on future book debts of a company which would prevent the mortgagor-company from disposing of an unencumbered title to the book debts without the debenture-holders consent . . . Alternatively a bank's debenture might include a covenant by the company with the bank not to factor, discount or assign book debts, and a breach of such a covenant might trigger the appointment of a receiver of the company's undertaking.'[17] The arrangement entered into by Parrot and Exfinco neatly avoided any such restrictions since it involved a sale of the goods themselves rather than the debts or receivables.

9.17 The WDA challenged the validity of the Parrot/Exfinco arrangement. If its challenge had been successful, the moneys received and receivable from the overseas customers would have been covered by the WDA's debenture. If not, they would belong to Exfinco. At first instance, Browne-Wilkinson V-C had decided with the WDA's argument that the transaction was in reality a loan on an unregistered security, the decision turning essentially on the very technical point that, at the time of the alleged sale by Parrot to Exfinco, it could not be known whether or not the goods complied with the warranties in the documents (given by Parrot in favour of Exfinco) and therefore it was not clear whether there had been an effective sale to Exfinco or whether Parrot was in fact selling to overseas customers as principal rather than agent. (Exfinco's 'standing offer' only extended to goods which complied with these warranties; on the face of it, this was a good point to take against the contention that 'true sales' were being effected.) The Court of Appeal rejected this argument, finding that it was possible to determine whether or not any warranty was breached after the time of sale: 'The answer can be ascertained by inquiry—if it is ever relevant to do so—and when it has been any possible uncertainty is removed.'[18] The sale/agency 'deal structure' was thus validated.

9.18 The case is a particularly robust decision in view of the fact that the discount in the arrangement was not fixed, but subject to adjustment, and the arrangement also featured a right for Parrot, on termination of the financing, to receive back title in goods for which payment had not yet been received in full from the overseas customers, once it had paid all moneys owed to the WDA. The latter provision certainly looked like a 'right of redemption'—more consistent with a security than a sale. However, the court noted that there was no way that Parrot

---

[16] *Per* Dillon LJ. [17] *Per* Dillon LJ.
[18] *Per* Dillon LJ.

could recover title to goods which had been fully paid for and regarded this 'right of redemption' as consistent with the sale/agency structure.

E. Fixed or Floating?

More difficult recharacterization issues have arisen in recent years in connection **9.19** with the correct categorization of security interests, especially the question of whether an insolvent company's security over book debts or trade receivables, usually given in favour of its bank on standard form documents, is properly regarded as a fixed or floating security. Floating charges are a common law invention which originate from the mid-nineteenth century:

> By the middle of the 19th century industrial and commercial expansion in this country had led to an increasing need by companies for more capital. Subscription for share capital could not meet this need and loan capital had to be raised. But the lenders required security for their loans. Traditional security, in the form of legal or equitable charges on the borrower's fixed assets, whether land or goods, could not meet the need. The greater part of most entrepreneurial companies' assets would consist of raw materials, work in progress, stock-in-trade and trade debts. These were circulating assets, replaced in the normal course of business and constantly changing. Assets of this character were not amenable to being the subject of traditional forms of security. Equity, however, intervened. *Holroyd v Marshall* (1862) 10 HLC 191 was a case in which the debtor had purported to grant a mortgage not only over his existing machinery but also over all machinery which, during the continuance of the security, should be placed in his mill . . . The House of Lords [held] that
>
> '. . . immediately on the new machinery and effects being fixed or placed in the mill, they became subject to the operation of the contract, and passed on equity to the mortgagees' (per Lord Westbury at p.211)
>
> and that
>
> '. . . in equity it is not disputed that the moment the property comes into existence, the agreement operates on it' (per Lord Chelmsford at p.220).
>
> *Holroyd v Marshall* opened the way to the grant by companies of security over any class of circulating assets that the chargor company might possess.[19]

Floating charges have brought many benefits. The reason for the modern **9.20** debate, however, is the same as the reason that banks' documents have for many years sought to create fixed, rather than floating, security over their customers' book debts: floating charges (because, potentially, they are so all-embracing and could operate unfairly *vis-à-vis* creditors who do not have them) are subject to a number of significant disadvantages in the event of the borrower's insolvency,

---

[19] *Per* Lord Scott in *National Westminster Bank v Spectrum Plus Ltd* [2005] UKHL 41.

which do not apply to fixed charges. These disadvantages included, until recently, the fact that, upon insolvency of the customer, a bank's floating charge would rank behind the claims of preferential creditors such as the Inland Revenue—which could be substantial. 'Crown preference' was abolished by the Enterprise Act 2002 but a new disadvantage for floating charge holders has been introduced by legislation in that a prescribed part[20] of the assets of an insolvent company that would otherwise be available to a floating charge holder must now be made available to its creditors generally. There is still a strong incentive, therefore, for a bank to take a fixed charge wherever possible, even though it may be supported by a floating charge over assets that are turned over on a regular basis in the ordinary course of a borrower's business.

9.21 The difficulty with fixed charges over book debts of a trading company is that they represent (when paid) the company's income, and, naturally, the company must have access to that income in the ordinary course. Can it be possible to create a fixed charge over an asset that, upon realization, will generally be required to be freely disposable? Or is it more likely to be the case that the principal characteristics of any security arrangement involving book debts and freely disposable proceeds thereof will resemble much more closely the attributes of a floating charge?

F. Floating Charges Defined

9.22 Before proceeding further, we need to consider the closest thing case law provides to a definition of a floating charge. This is set out in the well-known 'classic and frequently cited definition'[21] of Romer LJ in the leading case of *Re Yorkshire Woolcombers Association*:[22]

> I certainly think that if a charge has the three characteristics that I am about to mention it is a floating charge.
> (1) If it is a charge on a class of assets of a company present and future;
> (2) if that class is one which, in the ordinary course of business of the company, would be changing from time to time;
> (3) if you find that by the charge it is contemplated that, until some further step is taken by or on behalf of those interested in the charge, the company

---

[20] This is equal to 50% of the first £10,000 of assets and 20% thereafter, subject to a maximum of £600,000 of assets. There remains a more limited category of preferential debts, e.g. up to four months' unpaid remuneration of employees. Other disadvantages are considered by Yeowart in 'Spectrum Plus: The Wider Implications' (2005) 08 JIBFL 301.

[21] Per Lord Scott in *National Westminster Bank plc v Spectrum Plus Ltd* [2005] UKHL 41, at para 99.

[22] [1903] 2 Ch 284, 295.

may carry on its business in the ordinary way as far as concerns the particular class of assets I am dealing with.

This certainly looks like a definition. However, Romer LJ also said (and this is a **9.23** remark that has opened the door for a number of fine distinctions as well as speculation as to what might now, following more recent case law, be regarded as a floating charge): 'I certainly do not intend to attempt to give an exact definition of the term "floating charge", nor am I prepared to say that there will not be a floating charge within the meaning of the Act, which does not contain all three characteristics . . .'

It has been pointed out on several occasions that the first two of Romer LJ's **9.24** characteristics are also capable of being present in the context of a fixed charge. It is the last characteristic that tends to be the 'hallmark' of a floater. However, it should be noted that the last characteristic does quite clearly refer back to a class of assets (which, on a proper construction must be 'present and future'). It would be wrong to look at the third characteristic in isolation from the first.[23]

A further definition, contrasting a floating charge with a fixed (or 'specific') **9.25** charge was provided by Lord Macnaghten when the same case went to the House of Lords:[24]

> A specific charge, I think, is one that without more fastens on ascertained and defined property or property capable of being ascertained and defined; a floating charge, on the other hand, is ambulatory in nature, hovering over and so to speak floating with the property which it is intended to affect until some event occurs or some act is done which causes it to settle and fasten on the subject of the charge within its reach and grasp.

G. The Lender's Dilemma

What is to be done, therefore, if you are a lender who wishes to take fixed **9.26** security over a customer's trade debts but commercial reality requires that the customer must have access to the proceeds of those debts (ie the cash in his bank account when the debts are paid) on an unrestricted basis? You have to overcome this dilemma:

(1) The customer may accept that he cannot sell or assign the debts (or charge them) to anyone else. That is not commercially unreasonable and does not

---

[23] This has become an important point, in view of Lord Scott's remark in the *Spectrum* case (at para 107) that 'if a security has Romer L.J.'s third characteristic I am inclined to think that it qualifies as a floating charge, and cannot be a fixed charge'.

[24] Heard under the name *Illingworth v Houldsworth* [1904] AC 355, 358.

hinder the carrying on of business in the ordinary course. It is also consistent with a fixed charge.

(2) However, debts are, in a sense, disposed of when they are collected and turned into cash. Can you impose a genuine restriction on the use of the cash? If you can do this (by, for example, requiring proceeds of debts to be paid into a 'blocked account' from which withdrawals are only permitted if you give permission at the time) you may succeed in creating a fixed charge. But if the customer objects to the account being blocked (which he usually would do, because he needs access to his money on a daily basis for his business) what kind of charge do you have?

(3) You might seek to document your arrangement by drawing a distinction between the asset represented by the uncollected debts and the asset represented by the cash when received. Can you take a fixed charge over the former but allow your customer the flexibility he needs by taking a floating charge only over the latter?

9.27 The structure described in (3) above was, broadly, that of the document under consideration in the case of *Re New Bullas Trading*[25] where the Court of Appeal upheld the distinction between the two assets and allowed that there could be a fixed charge over one and a floating charge over the other.

H. The *Spectrum* Case

9.28 The *New Bullas* decision provoked a good deal of criticism[26] but the opportunity for a thorough review by the House of Lords of the case law in this area (and a chance to overrule *Bullas*) did not arise until the House of Lords' decision in *National Westminster Bank plc v Spectrum Plus Ltd*,[27] which is now the leading case on these issues. Again, the relevant provisions of the debenture given by Spectrum to its bank purported to create a fixed charge on its book debts but

> . . . left Spectrum free to deal with debtors who owed the debts and, in particular, to collect the debts in the normal course of business . . . Paragraph 5 required that the debts be paid into [Spectrum's current account] . . . It enjoyed the overdraft facility of £25,000 . . . Provided that overdraft limit were not exceeded, Spectrum was free to draw on the account for its business purposes . . . This account was in all respects a normal bank current account with an overdraft facility.[28]

9.29 The House of Lords refused to 'perpetuate' what Lord Scott described as 'the *New Bullas* heresy' and held that 'the critical question' was whether or not the

---

[25] [2002] 1 BCLC 485.

[26] See in particular *Agnew v Commissioners of Inland Revenue* [2001] 2 AC 710, where the Privy Council held that *New Bullas* was wrongly decided.

[27] [2005] UKHL 41.   [28] *Per* Lord Scott, para 82.

customer could draw on its account and, since this was the case, determined that the charge over the book debts, although described in the documentation as a fixed charge, was in fact a floating charge. It should be noted that fixed charges on book debts, present and future, are still 'conceptually possible'[29] but a greater degree of control over the proceeds will be required to achieve this than is generally acceptable in a conventional bank/customer relationship.

The decision, which, for various reasons, had been awaited for some consider- **9.30**
able time by the banks and insolvency practitioners, did not come as a great shock and, although not of course welcome to the banks, seems to have been accepted as at least a desirable clarification of the rules of the game. It must be emphasized that the point at issue was concerned with a charge over debts which, by their nature, eventually turn into 'proceeds', ie cash. The case was not concerned with, and is not authority for, the re-characterization of fixed charges over contracts which themselves produce (but do not turn into) debts and proceeds of debts. The case could be regarded as a 're-characterization' case (and a number of commentators have used this term for it) but, in reality, this is an area of law where the writing has been on the wall for some time. No doubt banks and their advisers will be revising standard documentation to try to create another legal mechanism that upgrades their position from that of a mere floating charge holder. It may not turn out to be 'bullet proof' but it may be worth a try. Perhaps, in due course, and as a result, there will be another novel arrangement to be tested in the courts. This is one of the ways in which the common law develops. There should be no cause for alarm, although it does seem that both policy and legal practice in this area are still evolving.

---

[29] *Per* Lord Walker, para 136.

Part IV

MANAGEMENT

10

THE ESSENTIALS OF LEGAL
RISK MANAGEMENT

Risk taking is an essential part of the business and managers have to create an environment where people take necessary risks without being reckless. It is an instinctive thing . . . Management in any business is an art not a science; in investment banking it is voodoo art.[1]

A. The General Approach of Regulators to Risk Management

The Financial Services Authority (FSA) claims that it takes a 'risk-based **10.01** approach' to the regulation of banks and other financial institutions. It is important to the success of such an approach that the regulator, which in this regard is implementing the underlying philosophy of Basel II, is satisfied as to (although it does not assume responsibility for) risk management procedures adopted by regulated institutions. In this area, as in many others, great emphasis is placed, by the FSA as well as other regulators, on principles rather than rigid, narrowly drawn rules.[2] Further, what matters to the FSA is compliance with the substance of its enunciated principles, not merely with their form. 'Creative compliance' and trying to find 'ways round' a clearly stated FSA principle are not options.[3] This fundamental is arguably an unwritten principle in itself and its implications have to be carefully considered by any risk management function. It may be felt by some that this tends to lead to over-regulation and excessively cautious behaviour, but, as the current regime stands, it is a fact of life.

The FSA's eleven core principles for regulated businesses (set out in the first **10.02** part of its Handbook) have important consequences for risk management (and

---

[1] Augar, *The Greed Merchants*, p.123.
[2] Confusingly, however, some of the FSA's principles have the status of 'rules', breach of which may attract fines. See para 5.58 n. 59.
[3] See para 5.63.

especially legal risk management). They were recently outlined by Thomas Huertas (Director, Wholesale Markets Division of the FSA) in a speech given on 8 February 2005 to the first Joint Conference of the Association of Foreign Banks and the Association of Corporate Treasurers. The principles state that a bank must:

(1) conduct its business with integrity;

(2) conduct its business with due skill, care, and diligence;

(3) take reasonable care to organize and control its affairs responsibly and effectively, with adequate risk management systems;

(4) maintain adequate financial resources;

(5) observe proper standards of market conduct;

(6) pay due regard to the interests of its customers and treat them fairly;

(7) pay due regard to the information needs of its clients, and communicate to them in a way which is clear, fair, and not misleading;

(8) manage conflicts of interest, both between itself and its customers and another client;

(9) take reasonable care to ensure the suitability of its advice and discretionary decisions for any customer who is entitled to rely upon its judgment;

(10) arrange adequate protection for clients' assets when it is responsible for them; and

(11) deal with its regulators in an open and cooperative way, and must disclose to the FSA appropriately anything relating to the bank of which the FSA would reasonably expect notice.

10.03 These principles are of general application—'not quite as simple as the Ten Commandments, but close to it', according to Huertas.[4] Since they act as signposts for key risk management issues, they are also of particular relevance to the issues under consideration in this Part of this book. Principles 3, 5, 6, 7, 8, 9, and 10 are especially notable for their strong legal risk overtones. The principles have the status of 'rules'.

10.04 It is also an FSA rule that: 'A firm must take reasonable care to establish and maintain effective systems and controls for compliance with applicable requirements and standards under the regulatory system and for countering the risk that the firm might be used to further financial crime.'[5] This rule has self-evident implications. How can you establish that you have taken the reasonable

---

[4] And thus, evidently, a good example of (at least) 'soft law'; see para 5.50 et seq. above.

[5] FSA rule SYSC 3.2.6R. For FSA approach to risk management more generally, see FSA Handbook, SYSC 3.2. Also PRU 1.4 and PRU 6.1 (which contain material relevant across a wider context than insurance—to which they specifically apply). With regard to money laundering specifically, see further Ch 8 above.

care required and how do you test the effectiveness of your systems and controls? Who is responsible for compliance with this rule and determining that reasonable care has been taken, and how frequently is that compliance tested? Huertas' speech also provides more specific guidance on other areas that touch upon risk management.

Focus on people

The FSA is frequently at pains to make it clear that risk management and compliance is the responsibility of senior management, not the FSA. (It would certainly be surprising if this were not the case; perhaps this is an instance of the FSA indulging in a little risk management on its own behalf?) In his letter of 17 September 2004, to various senior officers in investment banks, Hector Sants[6] of the FSA tells us that the FSA is 'initiating further work' on legal and reputational risk issues associated with financing transactions but, in the meantime, takes the opportunity to 'remind senior management of their accountability for managing the full range of risks that arise from all financing transactions in the businesses for which they are responsible. It is the responsibility of senior management to ensure systems and controls are in place to manage not only the market and credit risks of such transactions but also to ensure that related legal and reputational risks are appropriately considered.' We are also told that the FSA will be 'taking an increased interest in this dimension of management and controls'. **10.05**

The FSA will be keen to evaluate how well individuals with management responsibilities discharge these functions. The regulator will, for example, look closely at the following: **10.06**

- To what extent is control and compliance part of the culture of the bank—or does pressure to 'deliver numbers always' interfere with the duty of 'right behaviour always'?
- Does the bank adequately resource its audit and compliance functions?
- Does the bank have independent non-executive directors on its board, who challenge the management effectively?
- How strong a voice do the control functions have in determining how the business is run, or are they discounted?
- If a breach of the rules occurs, how does the firm handle the situation? Does the firm ignore the breach, or even attempt to hide it?

---

[6] Managing Director, Wholesale and International Markets. The same letter also contains material on standards applicable to managing conflicts of interest. This is considered in Ch 11 below.

- Alternatively, does the firm report the breach, discipline those responsible, and take measures to lessen the probability that such breaches will occur again?

10.07 Anyone designing risk management procedures for a bank which is subject to the FSA's regulation (and perhaps even those who are outside the FSA's regulatory scope) should take heed of the above. The questions need to be put to the appropriate people within the institution and the answers fully documented and substantiated. The values underlying the questions are, arguably, of universal application, whoever may be the regulator. They are, for example, reflected in various parts of the Turnbull Report, which is intended to apply to all companies listed on the London Stock Exchange. According to that report, the board of directors, in considering its policies on 'internal control' is expected to look at the following:

- the nature and extent of risks facing the company;
- the extent and categories of risk which it regards as acceptable for the company to bear;
- the likelihood of the risks concerned materialising;
- the company's ability to reduce the incidence and impact on the business of risks that do materialise; and
- the costs of operating particular controls relative to the benefit thereby obtained in managing the related risks.

10.08 The board should also require regular reports from management, which should 'in relation to the areas covered by them, provide a balanced assessment of the significant risks and the effectiveness of the system of internal control in managing those risks'. Such an approach seems entirely appropriate for financial institutions, whether or not quoted on a stock exchange. The Appendix to the Turnbull Report, which sets out various questions that a company's board of directors should 'consider and discuss with management' when reviewing risk-related issues is set out in full in Appendix 2 below.

Priorities

10.09 Huertas gave an illuminating reference to the current priority areas for the FSA during 2005–6, where the regulator would be undertaking cross-firm reviews. These priority areas included:

- **Conflicts of Interest:**

    Conflicts of interest are endemic to the financial services industry. Clearly, banks do not need to eliminate conflicts. But they do need to manage them, and they must not abuse them. Conflicts are particularly likely to arise where a firm, acting as an agent for its clients, purchases goods or services from another firm. What costs should be for the account of the client, and what costs should be for the account of the agent? Absent rigorous control from the client, the agent may be tempted to push some of its costs onto the client's account . . . we are undertaking a review of how a sample of firms identify and manage the conflicts of interest they face—taking a holistic view of the firm or group, how does senior management know the conflicts it faces are being addressed?

- **Structured transactions:**

  We are also looking at the risks banks face when participating in financing transactions. This was prompted by the high-profile Enron, Worldcom and Parmalat cases. It's clear that firms can face significant risks, particularly risks to their reputation, when they participate in transactions that may be used by their clients to avoid regulatory or reporting requirements, evade tax liabilities or for other improper behaviour. Experience shows that there are reputational risks even where the transactions technically comply with legal, accounting and regulatory frameworks. We will be reviewing with a sample of firms how they evaluate the risks associated with such structured transactions and how they decide which structured transactions to decline.

- **Corporate governance:**

  . . . we place a great deal of emphasis on the importance of corporate governance . . . The critical issue here is really how firms reconcile global functional management with regional control and legal entity responsibilities . . .

- **Stress testing:**

  The FSA is taking forward in its discussions with firms their use of stress testing and scenario analysis within their risk management . . . Within this broad subject, one particular area of interest is how firms identify and assess the most extreme scenarios—those of a scale such that, if they were to occur, they might potentially pose a risk to financial stability.[7]

It is striking that the first two items on the above list raise obvious legal risk **10.10** issues. Whether described as such or not, legal risk is a dominant feature in the regulator's thinking. But the list as a whole sends strong signals to those concerned with risk management, especially legal risk management. Stress testing, for example, is a technique that can be very useful in 'playing out' the consequences for an institution (or for the market as a whole) of classic 'what if' scenarios, such as the 'surprise' court case that has repercussions in the financial markets as a whole or for a particular institution's business. A graphic approach of this kind will often assist with various aspects of risk management, including 'early warnings' and efficient information flows, as well as, in some cases, pointing up exposures to certain events that might not otherwise have been apparent. The concerns over conflicts of interest and structured transactions will of course be amongst the many legal risk issues that a risk management system needs to address.

In statements like those summarized above, the FSA is not saying anything that **10.11** would come as a surprise to those familiar with Basel II. Basel II places much greater emphasis on operational risk, and procedures for its management, than

---

[7] The FSA issued a Discussion Paper, 'Stress Testing', DP05/2, in May 2005.

any previous regulatory regime. The responsibilities of senior management for effective risk management are clear. Legal risk management, as such, is not often addressed specifically (or by name) by regulators, but it is evident from Huertas' remarks that legal risk is a key risk to be dealt with and very much on the regulators' agenda.

B. Risk Management Principles

10.12   It would be a mistake to see the management of legal risk as some special sub-category. Although it may have a number of special features, the management of legal risk should be consistent with the management of operational risk as a whole and anyone with responsibilities in this area or concerned with operational risk management generally will need to be familiar with the paper published by the Basel Committee on Banking Supervision (BCBS) in February 2003, 'Sound Practices for the Management and Supervision of Operational Risk'. Much of what follows is based on the contents of that paper, particularly the principles set out in paragraph 10 (as well as the FSA Principles). The BCBS Principles are set out in Appendix 3, Part 1 below. Other principles promulgated by BCBS in relation to (a) risk management in the context of electronic banking (which touch upon a number of legal risk issues), and (b) the operation of the compliance function[8] in banks (which function should be directly involved in legal risk management, especially as regards Type 1 risks) are set out in Appendix 3, Parts 2 and 3 respectively.

10.13   As is apparent, there are a great many principles that could apply in any given situation. Taken together, they represent a summary of good business practice for risk management with which few could disagree. Some of them perhaps verge on the platitudinous; this is a topic that it is difficult to address without resorting, at least occasionally, to very general statements of principle. There is certainly a degree of overlap. However, these principles cannot be ignored in a world where risk management is expected to be visible, valued, and verifiable.

10.14   Account should also be taken of issues raised by the proposed Interagency Statement on Sound Practice Concerning Complex Structural Finance Activities, published in May 2004 by various US regulatory agencies. Although the Proposed Interagency Statement is essentially concerned with products such as

---

[8] The compliance function is defined by BCBS as: 'An independent function that identifies, assesses, advises on, monitors and reports on the bank's compliance risk, that is, the risk of legal or regulatory sanctions, financial loss, or loss to reputation a bank may suffer as a result of its failure to comply with all applicable laws, regulations, codes of conduct and standards of good practice.' See BCBS Paper, 'The compliance function in banks', October 2003.

financial derivatives, asset backed securities, etc, many of the proposals contained in it are likely to have some influence on legal risk management generally. But before examining the implications of the BCBS Operational Risk Paper and the Proposed Interagency Statement, we should look first at some basic examples of legal risk management techniques.

C. The Scope of the Risk Management Function

> The fact is that bankers are in the business of managing risk. Pure and simple, that is the business of banking.[9]

What do we mean by 'risk management'? We cannot mean the complete eradi-   **10.15** cation of all risk, since we know that is impossible. Nor do we simply mean risk reduction, since there are many situations that warrant risk-taking. Banks, insurance companies, and many others in the financial sector are in the business of taking risk, including extremely complex and technical risk. They must therefore also be in the business of risk management (by whatever name)—it is central to the running of the business, not a specialization. Risk management can be defined by reference to its desired objectives (for example: not too much risk, either overall or by reference to particular types; effective risk pricing; no 'surprise' risks; avoidance of catastrophic risk, etc) or by reference to the process involved (identification, assessment, analysis, etc) and, no doubt, also by reference to other criteria. Tiner proposes a working definition of risk management: 'A behavioural system by which an organisation plans for, evaluates, deals with and monitors risk to achieve its strategic goals and objectives.'[10]

The emphasis is, rightly, on behaviour; so, when it seeks to 'manage' a risk, what   **10.16** does a commercial enterprise actually do? There are a number of courses of action that are commonly followed. These include, at a generic level:

(1) controlling, as far as possible, the situations that generally cause unwanted risk to arise (including making it less likely that such situations will occur);
(2) limiting the scale of loss that a risk is likely to give rise to;
(3) making it less likely that loss trigger events[11] will occur, even though a risk may have arisen;
(4) transferring risk by insurance or by appropriate derivative instruments and the like; and
(5) transferring (or avoiding the acceptance of) risk in the course of negotiating, or structuring transactions to which it becomes a party.

---

[9] Walter Wriston, former Citicorp Chairman.
[10] Tiner, 'Bankers in the Business of Managing Risk' (1998) 8 JIBFL 323.
[11] See Ch 6 above.

10.17 These courses of action are deceptively easy to describe. Putting an institution in the position where these options are realistically open to it and are understood as important by its employees (which is surely the essence of risk management) is more difficult. Indeed, it would be wrong to believe that the required result can always be obtained by the institution acting alone. Very often, it will be necessary to take concerted action with other market participants, for example, either to achieve changes to the law (or proposed new law)[12] or to develop more satisfactory market documentation. Sometimes this can best be accomplished through trade associations, sometimes through bodies like the Financial Markets Law Committee (FMLC). Other aspects of risk management include the analysis of risks that are unavoidable or voluntarily taken and, where appropriate, the pricing of those risks in the context of transactions which cause them to arise. A great deal of legal risk management (whether or not recognised as such by the protagonists) actually takes place in the course of negotiation of specific transactions, as well as in the structuring of more complex transactions.

D. Examples of Risk Scenarios

10.18 It is not possible to provide an exhaustive list of legal risk management techniques. The potential fact scenarios give rise to endless permutations. However, it is possible to describe different kinds of management techniques by way of illustration. Let us compare some examples of risk scenarios that arise from time to time:

A   Market standard documents contain a serious legal defect that no one in the market has hitherto appreciated (see, for example, the stocklending problem that arose in 1990, discussed in paragraphs 3.25 *et seq* above).

B   The situation is as in A, but although some institutions know of the problem, others do not.

---

[12] An interesting example from the US can be found in the testimony of Dennis Oakley, a managing director in a department of Chase Manhattan Bank, in connection with the proposed Commodity Futures Modernization Act (2000), which was intended to 'promote the legal certainty of over-the-counter derivatives transactions'. He says:

> We believe we have a good risk management regime at Chase from credit officers approving extensions of credit to our group who manage the risk once it is on our balance sheet. We have good credit underwriting skills, superior MIS, and portfolio analytics to help us understand our risk. We are aggressive in managing our credit exposure to maximize the return for our shareholders.
>
> Unfortunately I don't have any tools that can help me manage the legal risk associated with the billions of dollars of foreign exchange and derivatives credit risk. Having those contracts declared null and void would be like having all of our counterparties default simultaneously. This event would adversely impact the financial condition of Chase. The only way I know to manage this risk is to come to Washington and ask you to change the laws and remove the legal uncertainty.

C   An institution understands there is a legal risk, because of legal uncertainty (for example, it is not clear (pre-FCA(2)) which exchange rate would apply in the event of insolvency) but decides to take that risk.

D   In the course of negotiations on a complex transaction, a legal risk emerges which no one has foreseen, and about which there is no clear agreement either as to its importance or who should bear it.

E   The law is clear but the institution decides to take a risk for commercial reasons (for example, it decides to take an assignment of receivables, outright or by way of security, without serving notice on the debtors).

F   An institution's 'back office' fails to get 'confirmation' of a transaction.

G   An institution fails to appreciate lack of capacity or corporate power relating to an important counterparty.

All the above situations involve legal risk but, because they are quite different   **10.19**
from each other, they require different risk management responses. For example, we have seen how something like **Situation A** can be dealt with very effectively by concerted market action, involving a wide range of institutions, including the regulator. It would have been possible for an institution to have devised solutions to the problem for itself, acting alone, but what would have been the point? The resultant changes to documentation (which would have been perceived as deviations from the standard) would have needed explanation, which would have led to piecemeal distribution of information about the problem, how to solve it, and a breakdown in the use of standard documents. This in turn would probably have triggered other risks. The market would also fail to get the valuable benefit that came with a firm, widely shared legal opinion (in the broadest sense) on various key issues, including issues which were of fundamental importance to the validity of close-out netting clauses and title transfer collateral techniques. Working together with other market participants will generally be the best risk management response to a situation like Situation A.

Situation B presents different problems. One's first reaction to such a scenario   **10.20**
is likely to be, 'How did this arise? How could a group of institutions be left "in the dark"?' Such questions, in effect, describe the heart of the problem. There are, of course, solutions but, on the assumption that the 'ignorant institutions' remain so, they are all going to be in the nature of damage limitation once the hidden risk has materialized into a known loss or potential loss. Far better to take risk management measures that would make it much less likely for such a situation to arise. These would include the formation of trade associations (if they do not exist) and, of course, joining those that do exist and participating fully in their activities, especially those that involve the dissemination of information that has a bearing on legal risk. Other sources of market information germane to legal risk should also be identified and exploited. These might include the various activities of major law firms active in the financial markets

(who regularly hold free seminars and distribute free newsletters, etc) as well as bodies like the FMLC, the City of London Law Society, and the more commercially minded academic institutions. One might, for lack of a better phrase, regard this as a form of continuing legal education. The purpose of participation is, however, far from academic. The objectives must be targeted to the needs of the institution. Indeed, one of the more difficult aspects of this kind of legal risk management is the management of information overload. This part of the law now attracts so much attention that any new development tends to result in an avalanche of commentary, some of it very useful, some of it less so. In this context, separating the wheat from the chaff is part of legal risk management.

10.21 **Situation C** arises in practice with great frequency. We have seen that, notwithstanding the ongoing, perpetual quest for legal certainty, the market does in fact have a degree of legal risk tolerance. The 'standard' qualifications one finds in formal legal opinions are evidence of this.[13] To take just a few examples, every experienced market participant knows (or should know, if they read such opinions!) that equitable remedies are in the discretion of the court, that clauses that are 'penalties' in the eyes of the law are unenforceable, and that a bank puts itself at risk as regards its ability to claim from a guarantor if it agrees important changes to a loan (for example, regarding repayment dates or rate of interest) without getting the guarantor's consent.[14] Legal risk management in such situations often consists in not allowing the institution's systems and 'risk antennae' to become dulled by repetitiveness. There will be times when the standard qualifications will be acutely important, perhaps because the factual scenario is anything but standard. In any event, if the risk is deliberately taken, it will be important to record the discussions and reasoning that led to the decision, with appropriate note being taken of any non-standard features of the facts or issues, as well as whether or not the taking of the risk was in line with market practice (if known), previous decisions of the institution, or any relevant policies or guidelines.

10.22 Risk management may require a sceptical response to behaviour, procedures, and positions that are sometimes presented as standard (especially if no substantive justification is offered), as well as a willingness to ask awkward but well-directed questions. A case study from a project financing (with identities concealed and facts somewhat simplified for obvious reasons) provides a good example of this in the context of **Situation D**.

10.23 During the course of negotiations with which the author had a degree of involvement, a bank was proposing to lend very large sums of money to A, a utility

---

[13] See para 11.15 et seq.

[14] See, eg *Triodos Bank NV v Ashley Charles Dobbs* [2005] EWCA Civ 630.

company in Ruritania, for the construction of a new industrial installation. A's credit was not strong enough to justify the bank taking the risk that there might be delays in completion of construction, although the bank was prepared to take more risk on A once the project had been built and was earning revenues. It was therefore proposed that, at least during the construction phase, the bank should have the benefit of a guarantee from the Ruritanian government. However, the guarantee was not to take the form of a conventional loan guarantee but an undertaking by the government, to A, that, provided certain conditions were satisfied, the government would meet any funding shortfalls that might otherwise cause A to default. This undertaking was to be assigned by A to the bank. It was to be governed by Ruritanian law. The bank's lawyers made extensive investigations of Ruritanian law (with Ruritanian lawyers) and, of course, spent a great deal of time considering the conditions in the government undertaking and the risk that they might not be satisfied. Eventually, it was decided that the risks implicit in such undertakings could be accepted. However, an unusual feature of the government undertaking was that it contained a large number of recitals (or 'whereas clauses') at the beginning. One of these stated: 'Whereas A has agreed to comply with all Ruritanian laws and regulations from time to time relevant to [industrial activity for which the plant was being commissioned].' The list of recitals was followed by a statement: 'Now therefore the government agrees as follows . . .'

The question arose as to whether the inclusion of such provisions would give the **10.24** Ruritanian government a defence to a claim under the undertaking if it was shown that A was not, or had not been, in compliance at all times with all the relevant laws and regulations. The question was one of Ruritanian law. The advice received was to the effect that although recitals do not generally have any substantive effect (in that they record the rationale for a transaction rather than contain contractual commitments) there was indeed a risk that a Ruritanian court might be sympathetic to such an argument. If the government had a defence to a claim by A, that defence would, of course, prevail also against any claim by the bank, as A's assignee. The bank was prepared to take a large number of risks associated with the project but it was not prepared to take the risk that its borrower, A, might in effect invalidate a crucial part of the bank's security by failing to comply with the law. Such a risk was completely outside the bank's control and, furthermore, there were a myriad relevant laws and regulations involving a relatively high risk of, at least, technical non-compliance. The Ruritanian government was asked to remove the offending provision, but refused to do so (or to waive its potential defence *vis-à-vis* the bank, as assignee), arguing that the provision was 'standard'.

After many unsuccessful attempts to find a compromise, the transaction was **10.25** abandoned. This was not a risk that the bank could take. The guarantee was of fundamental importance and had to be as 'cast-iron' as the law could make it. Although a breakdown in negotiations is never welcomed, it was, in this case, ultimately inevitable. The episode, from the identification of the risk at the outset to the various attempts to find solutions acceptable to the parties and the eventual parting of the ways, was an illustration of risk management in the context of negotiation.

10.26 **Situation E** also arises very frequently. There are times when the 'counsel of perfection', which involves little or no risk, is too expensive or otherwise commercially unacceptable. The perfection of security interests, for example, in certain countries may involve *ad valorem* taxes that are far too high to be tolerable. The service of notice of assignment, although conferring valuable benefits on an assignee bank, may be impracticable where the bank has acquired thousands of trade receivables payable by customers about whom there are insufficient records to enable the process to proceed with any confidence as to its accuracy or reliability. Some bank customers may in any case prefer to avoid troubling their own customers with (or allowing them to become aware of) matters which relate to the financing of their business. So the bank needs to: evaluate the risks involved in not serving notice; consider whether there are other steps that can be taken to make the risks more acceptable; and ultimately decide whether or not to proceed. If the risk is thought to be 'manageable' and is 'priced into' the transaction, it will generally go ahead.

10.27 **Situation F** is considered in Chapter 5.[15] It is an example of a phenomenon that is encountered very frequently; a failure to get the basics right. Nothing could be more basic than making sure that legal documentation is actually signed by all the parties. However, simple errors of this kind can creep into even the most sophisticated systems and procedures. They usually arise from a combination of human error and breakdowns in communication. Other examples in this category include: failure to register security where the law requires it; not realizing that a contractual commitment is being entered into (or that a particular formality is required for a certain kind of contract); and the so-called 'battle of the forms'. The latter occurs, typically, where one party offers to enter into a transaction, making reference in some way to its own standard terms which it wishes to apply, but the other party 'accepts' the offer making a reference to its own terms (or some other terms). This can happen because the forms used by each institution (for new transactions) attempt to get that institution's terms into the contract by cross reference ('this trade is subject to our standard terms as set out in [   ]') in a manner which may not be obvious to the non-lawyer. The risks arising include (a) that the other party's terms apply, not yours, with the result

---

[15] See 5.18–5.22 above.

that the protective provisions set out in your terms are not part of the contract, and (b) that there is no contract at all, because there was no clear offer and acceptance. Both these scenarios are potentially deeply unattractive.

The risk management response has to be on a number of levels. Because of the **10.28** human error element, emphasis, naturally, has to be placed on the quality of individuals employed in key positions. Secondly, attention must constantly be paid to training and supervision, so that key personnel are properly acquainted with the risks and understand the reason why certain procedures are to be followed, not just that certain procedures exist and are expected to be followed. Thirdly, since even the best-qualified will not be able to deliver if they are placed under intolerable pressure, either because of insufficient resources or undue influence from colleagues seeking a 'convenient' piece of advice, their ability to provide timely, independent advice needs to be properly safeguarded. As indicated in Chapter 5,[16] particular attention must be paid to the potential consequences of any outsourcing arrangements that affect procedures and risks of this kind. There will, of course, be a requirement that the consequences of any failures to deal with such risks are covered appropriately in the outsourcing contract.

Situation G is reminiscent of the *Hammersmith and Fulham* case.[17] One would **10.29** generally expect a well-managed institution to be sufficiently alert to a risk of this nature to render it very unlikely to occur. However, 'stress case' scenarios, such as transactions that have to be concluded quickly but which have a cross-border element or are with government entities (or have both features), can produce situations where the customary checks and due diligence are more likely to be overlooked or not carried out thoroughly enough. The risk of this tends to be increased where the transaction appears to be routine or standard in all respects except for the fact that the counterparty is different to the usual market participant. An individual trader or dealer, used to doing business rapidly and with minimal formality, might not readily appreciate the potential legal trap. The management of such risks will involve similar elements to those described for Situation F. There is no substitute for meticulous and constantly updated training, coupled with procedures that trigger awareness of the need for caution when a transaction has unusual structural elements.

How do we translate the lessons learned from examples such as those described **10.30** above into reliable and effective risk management systems and procedures? What are the key requirements for a risk management function? At its most basic, legal risk management for any institution can be broken down into

---

[16] See 5.18–5.22 above.
[17] *Hazell v Hammersmith and Fulham London Borough Council* [1992] 2 AC 1.

the component parts (suggested by BCBS) of identification, assessment, monitoring, and control/mitigation. For any of these functions to be effective, it is important that legal risk, as part of a firm-wide definition of operational risk, is appropriately defined (see BCBS Principle 1). Opinions may currently differ as to whether certain risks are properly to be regarded as 'legal' risk (for example, in relation to risks on the borderline with political risk or fraud),[18] but one would expect, over time, a consensus of opinion to develop as to what the term covers.[19] A flexible definition such as that proposed by the International Bar Association (IBA) may be applied in different ways to reflect the different businesses of different institutions. Some institutions, for example, may feel that certain kinds of legal risk are so unlikely to affect them that they feel it appropriate to discount them in their risk management procedures. This ultimately must be a matter of judgement for the management of the institution. Identification, assessment, monitoring, and control/mitigation are dealt with in turn below.

E. Identification of Risks

10.31 Identification of legal risks is partly a by-product of defining what the expression means and partly a result of the application of that definition to the day-to-day business of the institution. In practical terms, the institution needs to identify where it is most likely that legal risks will arise (given that it is impossible to prevent such risks arising entirely). The two broad categories of (a) claims against the institution, and (b) defective transactions (ie Type 1 risks and Type 2 risks) are likely to be relevant to most institutions. These categories need to be broken down further. For example, in relation to documentation, the institution needs to have a comprehensive analysis, which is kept up to date, of the kinds of documentation used in its business, how 'tried and tested' that documentation is (and what the process is for testing it), which documents are of particular financial significance in terms of both exposure and asset protection, who is responsible for the legal effectiveness of the documentation, and so on. In relation to claims being made against the institution, a similar analysis would involve examination of the different jurisdictions in which the institution does business and/or has potential liabilities, the nature of the potential legal exposures in those jurisdictions (whether for breach of contract, tort, statutory or regulatory liability, or otherwise), the litigation 'culture' of the jurisdiction and potential financial exposure, including the extent to which an adverse judgment might result in excessive or penal damages.

10.32 Such an analysis cannot take place in a vacuum. It needs to be conducted by reference to the products and services offered in each jurisdiction and the risk

---

[18] See para 4.42 et seq.   [19] See generally, Ch 4 above.

profile of those products and services, taking into account both objective and subjective criteria, including the institution's own experience in offering those products and services. It should also include amongst its reference points the 'claims experience' (insofar as it is publicly available) of competitors, especially those that have been subject to regulatory action. 'There, but for fortune' (coupled perhaps with a degree of smugness) is often the most apt (but strictly private) response when one reads of the calamities that have hit competitors, but much can be learnt from others' mistakes that may improve one's own risk management. For example, if we look again at the Abbey Life 'complaints procedures' case referred to in Ch 4,[20] we see that the FSA's 'final notice' not only sets out a detailed account of the 'mistakes' that led to the fine being imposed (against which any comparable firm in a similar line of business can make appropriate comparisons to check whether it might also have risk exposures with regard to how it handles complaints), we also see in the notice a fairly detailed description of revisions undertaken by Abbey to its complaints procedure—which in the current regulatory regime and climate has to be seen as one aspect of risk management. These include:

- establishment of a new single complaints handling centre which has been formed by drawing together Abbey's three central complaints handling teams;
- engaging additional resources to meet the demands of the new complaints handling process and the review of past mortgage endowment complaints;
- increase in the level of training provided to staff engaged in complaints handling . . .
- monitoring of quality assurance work on the new mortgage endowment complaints system by an independent firm of accountants.

10.33 Although the experience of direct competitors is likely to have particular relevance, it would be wrong for a firm in any given sector to ignore the experience of regulatory action of companies primarily active in other sectors, where the regulator is applying rules that might apply across a range of sectors. Comparable lessons to those in the Abbey case can, for example, be learnt from the information available in the FSA's final notice in the Shell 'market abuse' case referred to above.[21] The 'remedial action' taken by Shell, as detailed in the notice, included various restructurings of internal reserves audit functions and programmes that may raise comparable questions in companies that are not in the natural resources sector. Significantly, for the legal function, the new measures included: 'enhancement of the Group legal function to improve the ability of Group management to benefit from appropriate legal advice concerning potential corporate governance, reporting and disclosure issues'.[22] It is unfortunate that

---

[20] See para 5.61.   [21] See para 5.42.
[22] Specific roles of the legal department are considered in more detail in Ch 11 below.

more detail is not provided as to what the 'enhancement' involved. The general message, however, is reasonably clear.

10.34 It is possible that the identification process may result in a review of decisions as to whether or not particular products or services should be offered (which may in turn depend on the legal environment in particular jurisdictions). The institution might decide to refrain from a particular line of business (whether or not by reference to a particular jurisdiction) on the grounds of risk *avoidance* coupled with an assessment of the risk/reward ratio and other relevant factors.

10.35 Identification of risk is a function and objective to be established in conjunction with the use of risk indication, as described below. Identification ('these are the principal risks which we are concerned about') is the first step. Determining the situations which are indicators of a risk arising is the second.[22a]

F. Assessment of Risks

10.36 An earlier version of the BCBS Operational Risk Paper referred to risk measurement, but that concept has been dropped in favour of risk *assessment*. This change, amongst other things, recognizes the fact that it is impossible to ascribe rigid mathematical measurement formulae to operational and legal risks. Notoriously, they tend to have low probability/high impact characteristics. Low probability/high impact risks are arguably the most difficult of all to manage in that (a) they cannot be ignored, and (b) they do not conform to any pattern. Assessment is by its nature a somewhat vaguer concept than measurement. It is also more flexible and better suited to the objectives and realities of legal risk management. Senior management needs to develop an understanding, shared throughout the different businesses of any institution, of what assessment involves in the context of legal risk. Factors that could be taken into account include the following:

- the legal infrastructure of any particular jurisdiction where the institution conducts business, including the independence of judges, the sophistication of contract and corporate law concepts, enforcement of judgments and arbitration awards, and risks associated with transactional and contractual certainty (for example, the risk that courts may recharacterize important transactions to which the institution is commonly a party);

- whether relevant sources of law (typically, case law or legislation) together with market practice are reasonably firmly established with respect to the legal issues most likely to affect the institution's business in a given jurisdiction;

[22a] See para 10.45.

- to the extent there is any legal uncertainty, the 'worst case scenario' if the uncertainty was resolved in a manner adverse to the institution;
- the historical track record of other institutions in the same business in the same jurisdiction (so far as publicly available) in relation to adverse claims or defective transactions (taking account, of course, of the possibility that each institution may have particular reasons for its experience that may not be applicable to others);
- the institution's own knowledge and confidence in relation to the regulatory environment, especially in relation to the marketing of a new product;
- whether or not the market for any new product or service is a consumer market or a professionals market;
- the risk of 'collateral damage' if the risk materializes, for example, reputational issues and political implications—the Proposed Interagency Statement notes that 'when a financial institution provides advice on, arranges or actively participates in a complex structured finance transaction, it assumes the usual market, credit, and operational risks and also may assume substantial reputational and legal risk to the extent that an end-user enters into the transaction for improper purposes' (the FSA has, as mentioned above, registered similar concerns—the link between legal risk and reputational risk can in certain situations be very serious, threatening the continuing viability of the institution's business);
- whether the documentation (and legal and regulatory environment) is relatively easy to understand (or exceptionally difficult to understand) when viewed from the perspective of the individuals who will be involved in the marketing and selling, whether a trained sales force is readily available, and, if not, how it will be assembled and tested; and
- whether the activity is likely to increase the chances of conflict of interest allegations.

Who should be responsible for the assessment? It would seem that in the first **10.37** place this role would fall to the legal department. It is, however, a separate question as to who should take commercial decisions based upon the assessment (although one would expect some legal contribution to that process). Institutions might find it helpful to involve some form of 'scoring' process in the assessment exercise so that, as a track record is built up, it is easier to compare like with like when looking at a new decision and comparing it with decisions taken in similar circumstances in the past. Such methodology should not be confused with *measurement* or *valuation*, nor should it be regarded as being especially precise since the exercise inevitably involves a degree of subjective judgment. Nevertheless, a scoring system is likely to have some benefits, including the provision of a more detailed rationale for the more difficult risk assessment decisions. The BCBS Operational Risk Paper recommends score cards and scoring generally in the context of risk assessment (see BCBS Principle 4).

10.38 A model for (or at least an example of) legal risk assessment and scoring can be found in a recent publication of a multilateral development bank. In its 'Transition Report 2003', the European Bank for Reconstruction and Development (EBRD) included a 'legal indicator survey' which is intended to be 'a new way of measuring legal progress' in its countries of operation (principally Central and Eastern Europe, including the former Soviet Union). In the context of an analysis of various countries' laws regarding secured transactions, the Bank in effect assesses how successful these countries have been in reforming their laws and 'the extent to which legal rules comply with international standards'. Various charts are included in the survey, which develop a form of scoring system for different aspects of the laws. The scoring system is, in some respects, fairly basic, for example 'scores range from 1–3 where 1 indicates no significant problem, 2 indicates a relatively minor problem and 3 indicates a major problem'.

10.39 The survey is of interest in relation to legal risk since it not only identifies various countries that have 'legal infrastructure' problems of varying magnitudes, but it also sets out a number of concepts that financial institutions would generally regard as relevant to the effectiveness of law in almost any context. For example, in reviewing the effectiveness of laws relating to enforcement of security, the survey considers (in relation to twenty-six countries) how a country might be scored on issues such as the impact of corruption within the court system; the ability for the debtor to prevent, slow down, or otherwise obstruct enforcement proceedings; and the reliability of courts and 'other institutions necessary to support the enforcement process'. The results of the survey provide useful material for any general counsel concerned with the assessment of legal risk in the countries in question, especially in relation to transactions involving the provision of security. It is, amongst other things, a good example of a methodology for how legal risk can be assessed in a particular context. Rating agencies, in connection with projects in developing countries, use a comparable benchmark scoring system. Institutions may of course, in appropriate cases, choose to rely on surveys conducted by third parties rather than commission or carry out their own.

10.40 Parallels could also be drawn with the methodology used by the publisher, Euromoney, in connection with its 'global political risk map' (which scores the countries of the world for political risk by reference to five different grades). The document, amongst other things, identifies the industries which are considered to be most at risk from political interference and also draws distinctions between corruption risk, political violence risk, and convertibility risk. Use is made of the Transparency International Corruption Perceptions Index (in itself another example of scoring). The methodology involves the attribution of a weighting to nine separate categories, ie (1) Political Risk; (2) Economic Performance; (3) Debt Indicators; (4) Debt in Default or Rescheduled; (5) Credit Ratings; (6) Access to Bank Finance; (7) Access to Short-term Finance; (8) Access to Capital Markets; and (9) Discount on Forfeiting. The resulting map is, of course, intended as a guide to political/financial issues rather than legal issues but the relationship between political risk and legal risk is so close that its results should perhaps be taken into account when assessing the legal risk of doing business in particular countries.

G. Monitoring

Monitoring involves the regular reporting of material information to those who **10.41** can assess its significance, and ultimately to senior management. In relation to legal risk, it raises questions as to which departments should be responsible for the implementation of the monitoring procedures and which parts of management should receive and assess the information as and when it is produced. As with all aspects of risk management, it is important that the individuals and departments involved are able to perform the function in a manner which is not likely to result in distortions caused by conflicts of interest or other factors which might inhibit the free flow of clear factual information.

As regards the in-house lawyers themselves, it is particularly important that they **10.42** have sufficient independence within the organizational structure to allow a rigorous approach to the relevant procedures (whether or not this amounts to 'whistle blowing' in more extreme situations). It is also important that the lawyers have access to the necessary information. In this regard, it is interesting to note that the lead counsel to Parmalat's administrator (Bruno Cova) recently observed:

> . . . there was a legal department in Parmalat with perfectly good lawyers—but they were not given the opportunity to understand what was going on . . . before a general counsel accepts a job in any company, they must make sure that they report directly to the Chief Executive or the Chairman. All other lawyers within the company should report to the general counsel so that the general counsel can understand what is going on. Parmalat did not have those reporting lines. Lawyers only reported to the operation they were working for, and so the general counsel was not put in the situation where he could help.

It is not of course necessary (possibly not even desirable) that the monitoring **10.43** function be carried out entirely by in-house lawyers even though it may be primarily concerned with legal risk. Lawyers will obviously be needed in order to provide technical legal advice in a wide range of areas and, although it is likely to be advantageous that lawyers make some contribution to decision-making, it would be unlikely that lawyers would have sole control over all decisions that the monitoring process gives rise to. But the allocation of responsibilities and reporting lines has to be crystal clear (see generally BCBS Principle 6). Furthermore, the effectiveness of this function, as well as other aspects of the risk management framework, will need to be subject to comprehensive internal audit by operationally independent personnel (BCBS Principle 2). The fact that the procedure exists and that those involved in its implementation are guaranteed independence should itself be a substantive benefit in maintaining what the BCBS Operational Risk Paper describes as 'high standards of ethical behaviour at all levels of the bank'. These issues are considered in more detail in Chapter 11.

10.44 The Proposed Interagency Statement places great emphasis on the need to have the relevant control functions within the institution, including, independent risk management, subject to oversight by a senior management committee so that proper oversight of complex structured finance transactions is ensured. Both the board of directors and senior management should, according to the statement, send 'a strong message to others in the financial institution about the importance of integrity, compliance with the law, and overall good business ethics', which may be implemented through a Code of Professional Conduct.

> Such message should be accompanied by the creation of a 'firm-wide corporate culture that is sensitive to ethical issues as well as the potential risks to the financial institution'. In this regard, encouragement should be given to individuals to 'elevate ethical concerns' about complex structured finance transactions to 'appropriate levels of management' and in order to achieve this, it may be necessary to establish 'mechanisms to protect personnel by permitting confidential disclosure in appropriate circumstances'. Importantly, it should be ensured that 'incentive plans are not structured in a way that encourages transactors to cross ethical boundaries when executing complex structured finance transactions'.

10.45 In establishing monitoring procedures, institutions will need to think about the appropriate risk *indicators* in the context of legal risk. Entry into new markets and launching new financial products should always point to a rigorous risk assessment in any event. There are other, fairly obvious, indicators. Bill Lytton, the Senior Vice-President and General Counsel of Tyco recently said 'it is a warning sign if there is a meeting going on and as a lawyer, you are not allowed to go. There should be no meeting which a general counsel cannot go to—especially now, when general counsel are recognised as having more of a central part in management decisions than before.'[23] Notwithstanding some of the more obvious warning signs, the identification of legal risk indicators is likely to

---

[23] A more detailed consideration of the role of the in-house lawyer is contained in Ch 11 below.

vary significantly from institution to institution, depending on its range of businesses. The following are suggested as possible examples:

- new legislation (including proposals for new legislation);
- new case law;
- significant changes in market practice and related documentation;
- changes in key personnel;
- feedback from regulators or other market participants which indicates hitherto unidentified legal risks;
- legal actions brought against other market participants that could potentially be brought against one's own institution;
- legal actions or other circumstances affecting market participants that might have a direct or indirect impact on the institution (whether or not involving litigation);
- political changes which might be expected to result in a change in how laws or regulations are applied;
- a significant change in advice received from external legal advisers on a material point;
- the use of unfamiliar advisers;
- unusual qualifications or assumptions in formal legal opinions;
- significant changes to the availability, or cost, of insurance cover;
- the use of 'old' standard documentation;
- the erosion of rules concerning lawyer–client privilege; and
- unusual fee structures for advisers, especially if these could affect the delivery of objective advice (however reputable the firm of advisers might be).

The Proposed Interagency Statement also has a list of transaction characteristics **10.46** that (at least in the case of complex structured deals but possibly in other cases as well) might be regarded as risk indicators. These include the following:

(a) transactions with questionable economic substance or business purpose or designed primarily to exploit accounting, regulatory, or tax guidelines;
(b) transactions requiring an equity capital commitment from the financial institution;
(c) transactions using non-standard legal agreements;
(d) transactions with unusual profits or losses or transactions that give rise to compensation that appears disproportionate to the services provided or the risk assumed by the institution;
(e) transactions that raise concerns about how the client will report or disclose the transaction;
(f) transactions with unusually short time horizons or potentially circular transfers of risk;

(g) transactions with oral or undocumented agreements, which, if documented, could have material legal, reputational, financial accounting, financial disclosure, or tax implications; and

(h) transactions that cross multiple geographical or regulatory jurisdictions, making processing and oversight difficult.

It is, of course, virtually impossible to draw up an exhaustive list. It is likely that an understanding of the role of risk indicators and the development of a more finely tuned approach will evolve as institutions increase the level of sophistication applied to the risk management process.

H. Control and Mitigation

10.47 If a risk is accepted, an institution needs to consider how it can be controlled or limited. Commercial insurance is an obvious method of controlling or mitigating loss caused by legal risk. As many have pointed out, it is unlikely that commercial insurance will be available to cover all forms of legal risk and it is important that the limits and conditions of particular insurance policies are properly analysed and understood. Similar issues arise with other mitigation instruments in the form of hedging transactions, derivatives, etc. Such mitigation tools give rise to issues of their own and, as has often been said, may simply replace one risk with another risk. Nevertheless, they can have value.

10.48 In relation to control, institutions will wish to develop (and many will no doubt have done so already) advance strategies to deal with at least the more predictable risk scenarios. However, much of legal risk not only has the low probability/ high impact characteristics, but also a quality of unpredictability. Controlling the loss resulting from legal risk will involve, at the legal level, a review of impact on documentation, establishing resources to defend (or prosecute) claims, and an analysis of the likely financial impact. Decisions as to how to react to the financial impact will ultimately be the responsibility of management. The methodology will depend to a significant extent on the facts. It is important, however, that the control mechanism enables as swift a reaction as possible, given the extremely rapid means of deal execution now to be found in the financial markets. Depending on the nature of the transaction, the control/ response may also need to involve trade associations and other market participants. It may not be appropriate or practical for an institution to act in isolation in response to a risk scenario that affects a broad range of market participants (for example, a defect in market standard documentation or a new legal case that has implications for many participants).

10.49 Day-to-day control of legal risk will, amongst other things, involve periodic review and updating of documentation used by the institution. Sound practice would suggest that documentation should be reviewed both in response to specific events (for example, new case law or legislation) that might require amendment and also on a regular basis in order to ensure that the institution remains in step with market practice and legal developments that might otherwise have escaped attention. Depending on the resources of the in-house legal department, it may be appropriate to use external legal resources for all or part of such review.[24]

Documentation reviews should not, however, be carried out in isolation from the procedures and practices in which the documentation is used. The review procedure needs to have an appreciation of how transactions are typically concluded, when and how market standard documents (or master agreements) are used, telephone commitments made, and confirmation notes dispatched. The contractual significance of such events may vary from jurisdiction to jurisdiction. It may be appropriate for non-legal personnel involved in deal-making to be regularly updated as to any important legal issues that might flow from the manner in which they execute deals. Here, as in other procedural aspects, there will be close relationships with aspects of the compliance function.   **10.50**

Specific control procedures referred to in the Proposed Interagency Statement include the following: **10.51**

(1) ensure that staff approving each transaction fully understand the scope of the institution's relationship with the customer and have evaluated and documented the customer's business objectives, the economic substance of the transaction and the potential legal and reputational risks to the financial institution;

(2) ensure a thorough review and evaluation of whether credit exceptions, accounting issues, rating agency disclosures, law suits against the customer, or other factors expose the financial institution to unwarranted legal or reputational risks;

(3) develop procedures to ensure that all relevant personnel receive and document full information about the transaction, its purpose, and the materiality of it;

(4) ensure sufficient time is allowed for proper review of the transaction;

(5) ensure that transactions which are perceived to have 'heightened risks' receive thorough review by senior management; and

(6) ensure that transactions that present unacceptable risk are declined.

---

[24] See BCBS Operational Risk Paper, para 22.

10.52 Other procedures and policies that may be helpful to a bank's legal department in relation to risk management might include:

(a) a clear procedure for checking and establishing whether a conflict of interest might arise as a result of accepting a particular mandate and clear rules, that are kept up to date with the case law and other developments, for reaching a swift and 'transparent' decision on any conflicts question;

(b) A 'document retention' policy (with appropriate warnings and guidance notes) that, ideally, has been approved by external counsel, enabling decisions to be taken as to destruction or preservation of records that do not have implications for the honesty or good faith of either the institution or the individuals involved when sensitive questions arise;[25]

(c) control over selection of external counsel;

(d) control over the development, and use of, standard documentation and procedures, both for use in transactions and for use internally, where there may be legal risk implications (for example, as regards codes of conduct, complaints and disciplinary procedures, responses to claims from third parties, protocols on the use of e-mail etc);

(e) the establishment of transaction management programmes for non-routine deals where (as suggested by the C&I Group Paper referred to in Chapter 11 below) 'milestones at which critical legal or ethical issues will be re-addressed and/or escalated and action taken as necessary (e.g. sanity checks; independent advice; the involvement of external law firms)';

(f) the legal audit of new products or services;

(g) the training of legal and other employees in relation to the use of documents, contractual negotiations, codes of conduct, etc and other areas where legal risks might reasonably be expected to arise.

10.53 The bank's lawyers may also wish to consider standardization of the bank's position (or, at least, clarification of its preferred position) on particular contractual issues. As mentioned earlier,[26] risk management is usually a central part of document negotiation. This may occur in the context of ordinary market transactions or less standard scenarios, such as transactions for the sale or acquisition of a business or a complex project financing, where the bank is relying on documents such as construction contracts, operating agreements, or off-take contracts as part of its security. The negotiation of certain types of provision can, viewed from a risk management perspective, be characterized as a form of

---

[25] It has to be recognized, however, that if behaviour is dishonest, it cannot acquire the character of honesty merely because it happens to comply with a particular stated policy. Document retention policies are considered in more detail in Ch 11 below.

[26] See para 10.25.

risk mitigation or containment. The following are examples of provisions that tend to have this effect:

- clauses that limit liability under warranties or indemnities, for example, by reference to the nature of the loss for which a claim may be made (excluding, say, claims for 'consequential loss'), by reference to the quantum of the claim (placing overall 'caps' on liability and/or caps on liability under certain heads, as well as excluding *de minimis* claims), or by reference to the time for bringing a claim (requiring it to be brought within, say, three years of the agreement being entered into, or some other appropriate period);

- clauses that limit liability under warranties by reference to 'disclosure letters' and similar devices (such as the use of a 'data room') that, in effect, require the other party to examine the information disclosed (in either the letter or data room, or both) and then judge the acceptability of warranties that are given on a 'save as disclosed' basis (the selection of the individuals who are charged with the task of examining and reporting on documents made available in a data room is an important decision and, as discussed in Chapter 11 below,[27] the 'due diligence' reports that generally emerge from such exercises have to be handled with care from a risk management perspective);

- disclaimers of liability (for example, the standard disclaimers protecting the agent bank in a syndicated loan and exempting it from liability for practically anything except 'gross negligence or wilful default';

- 'changes in circumstances' clauses in euromarket loan documents, that excuse a bank performance of its obligations if such performance becomes illegal, enable it to restructure the pricing of the loan if the inter-bank deposit market ceases to function normally, and otherwise recover 'increased costs' in particular situations;

- *force majeure* provisions, that absolve a party from liability for failure to perform contractual obligations (providing for an extension of time for such performance or, in more severe cases, enabling it to cancel the contract) if that failure was due to certain phenomena outside its control (for example, political intervention, war, etc.);

- 'material adverse change' provisions, that enable a bank to decline to proceed with a transaction (or cancel an existing one) if unforeseen, major developments render its original decision to participate, in effect, unviable or no longer commercially justifiable;

- choice of law and jurisdiction clauses, that specify that, in the event of litigation, the matter will be heard by courts (or a tribunal) in which the bank

---

[27] See para 11.26.

has confidence as to impartiality and under a law that is modern and sufficiently sophisticated to provide answers to complex financial or commercial questions;

- 'conditions precedent' or similar provisions that entitle a bank to insist on, for example, the receipt of satisfactory legal opinions and/or clearances or consents from government agencies before its commitment to advance funds becomes unconditional.

10.54 Provisions of this nature should be reviewed on a periodic basis and in-house counsel should consider whether the array of risk mitigation/containment protections that they provide is being fully utilized across the bank's documentation; whether they need to be updated to take account of changes in law, market practice, and what the competition is doing; whether they are suitable for use in all relevant jurisdictions and markets, and so on. In reviewing contractual 'risk mitigators' it may also be advisable to consider the types of provision identified by the Contracts Working Group of the Bank of England's Task Force, set up (in the wake of the terrorist attacks in the US on 11 September 2001) to analyse the potential impact on the financial system of a major operational disruption. These are set out in the Task Force's Report (of December 2003) at paragraphs 8.9 to 8.21 of Annex 4, and include:

(a) business day provisions, that limit the requirement for the performance of various obligations (sometimes distinguishing payment from other obligations) to days that the financial markets are open in relevant centres;

(b) market convention override provisions, that temper performance requirements by reference to, for example, market conventions or rules of investment exchanges; 'these clauses provide a degree of flexibility in dealing with risks'; and

(c) grace periods, that provide time for a defaulting party to cure the default (similar in concept to the *force majeure* provisions referred to above, although not necessarily triggered by *force majeure* in the strict sense).

10.55 As the Working Group observes: 'Contractual treatment of risks varies among the agreements, reflecting differences in the relevant markets and differences in the parties' priorities, including with respect to the assumption of risk.'

10.56 Obviously, contractual provisions have their limitations in the context of risk management, not least because (a) not everything is negotiable, (b) risk transfer to the counterparty will generally come with a price, and (c) the effectiveness of the risk transfer may be limited by reference to the counterparty's creditworthiness (depending on the manner in which the provision operates). However, subject to these limitations, contractual risk allocation will, in certain situations, represent 'Route 1'.

11

LAWYERS' RESPONSIBILITY FOR THE MANAGEMENT OF LEGAL RISK

. . . the dicta to which I have referred all have in common the idea that it is necessary in our society, a society in which the restraining and controlling framework is built upon a belief in the rule of law, that communications between clients and lawyers, whereby the clients are hoping for the assistance of the lawyers' legal skills in the management of their (the clients') affairs, should be secure against the possibility of any scrutiny from others, whether the police, the executive, business competitors, inquisitive busy-bodies or anyone else . . . I, for my part, subscribe to this idea.[1]

A. The Need for Clear Methodology

Much of the content of this chapter concerns what many institutions (and their legal departments) would regard as sound risk management practice (or perhaps just good legal practice and common sense) as followed by them for decades. No claim is made that what follows represents novel or original insights. The substance of what has to be done to manage legal risk effectively has not changed a great deal over the years. But, as the modern regulatory regime evolves, changes are, nevertheless, likely to be necessary. They will affect the methodology used, how the processes and procedures are presented and recorded and, perhaps, the status and independence of individuals who are charged with the relevant responsibilities. To the extent that Basel II, the requirements of the Financial Services Authority (FSA) and other regulatory measures require innovation in this context, it is at least partly due to the need to formalize 'good habits' and provide evidence that such habits are followed in practice.[2]

11.01

---

[1] From the judgment of Lord Scott in *Three Rivers DC v Bank of England (No. 6)* [2004] 3 WLR 1274, para 34.

[2] According to the BCBS: 'Although compliance with laws, rules and standards has always been important, compliance risk management has become more formalised within the past

11.02 However, change is also required as a result of new laws, in the UK and else-where, that have, in a sense, put the role of the in-house lawyer under the spotlight. The Andersen Amicus Briefs, for example, contain powerful criti-cisms of US laws and court decisions that, apparently, placed in-house lawyers in an invidious position simply by virtue of performing relatively routine roles, such as suggesting amendments to draft internal memoranda.[3] The UK case of *Bowman v Fels*[4] also highlighted the dilemmas that confront lawyers of all kinds when faced with vaguely drafted, catch-all criminal legislation which, in effect, enlists banks and legal advisers in the fight against serious crime (but also, it would seem, petty crime).[5] If a bank's in-house lawyer is to fulfil his role in managing Type 1 risks, what guidelines should apply to his behaviour if there are laws that expose him or his colleagues to criminal prosecution when advising on how a bank's case can be best presented and managed or when dealing with customers (or others) who, at any time, might have been involved in question-able activity, 'however minor'?[6] The lawyer's traditional role is now threatened by laws that may implicate him personally for criminal liability, depending on the nature of the advice that he gives. As the brief prepared by the National Association of Criminal Defense Lawyers (in relation to the Andersen case) puts it: 'Any lawyer who must consider his or her own liability when revising a draft memorandum for a client is in an untenable position.'

B. The Role of Lawyers and the Legal Department in Legal Risk Management

11.03 Rules and procedures for risk management must address the role of the in-house legal department with as much clarity as possible. One of the most basic organ-izational issues concerns the relationship between 'legal' and 'compliance'. We have already seen[7] that the Basel Committee on Banking Supervision (BCBS) definition of the compliance function involves a significant overlap with legal advisory functions. This potential overlap is acknowledged by BCBS in the paper entitled 'The compliance function in banks', issued on 31 January 2004[8] where certain key functions of 'compliance' are listed as follows:

---

few years and has emerged as a distinct management discipline.' See BCBS document, 'The compliance function in banks', 31 January 2004, para 2.

[3] See, in particular, the Brief of Amicus Curiae of the National Association of Criminal Defense Lawyers, dated 22 February 2005, and the examples given at pp 11 and 12. The facts of the Andersen case are, however, somewhat unusual; see para 11.30.

[4] [2005] EWCA Civ 226; see chapter 8.   [5] See chapter 8.

[6] See the judgment of Brooke LJ in *Bowman v Fels*, para 8.   [7] See para 10.12 n. 9.

[8] At paras 26 and 27 of that paper (commenting on Principle 6, as set out in App 3, Part 3 below).

The responsibilities of the compliance function should include most if not all of the following. Any responsibilities which are not carried out by the compliance function should be carried out by another independent function.

- on a pro-active basis, identifying and assessing the compliance risks associated with the bank's business activities, including in relation to the development of new products and business practices, the proposed establishment of new business or customer relationships, or material changes in the nature of such relationships;

- advising management on the applicable laws, rules and standards, including keeping up-to-date with developments in the applicable laws, rules and standards and advising management accordingly;

- establishing written guidance to staff on the appropriate implementation of the laws, rules and standards through policies and procedures and other documents such as compliance manuals, internal codes of conduct and practice guidelines;

- assessing the appropriateness of internal procedures and guidelines, promptly following up any identified deficiencies in the policies and procedures and, where necessary, formulating proposals for amendments;

- monitoring compliance with the policy by performing regular and comprehensive compliance risk assessment and testing, and reporting on a regular basis to senior management, and, if necessary, the board or a committee of the board, on compliance matters; the reports should refer to the compliance risk assessment and testing which has taken place during the reporting period, and any identified breaches and/or deficiencies, and the corrective action taken; the reports should also contain information about compliance training provided to compliance function and other bank staff;

- exercising any specific statutory responsibilities (e.g. fulfilling role of anti-money laundering officer);

- educating staff with respect to compliance with the applicable laws, rules and standards, and acting as a contact point within the bank for compliance queries from staff members; and

- liaising with relevant external bodies, including regulators, standard setters and external legal counsel.

As noted above, not all these responsibilities are necessarily carried out by the compliance function. In some banks, for example, legal and compliance are separate functions; the legal function is responsible for advising management on the applicable laws, rules and standards and for preparing guidance for staff, while the compliance function is responsible for monitoring compliance with the policies and procedures and reporting to management. If there is a division of responsibilities between different functions, the allocation of responsibilities to each function should be clear.

Banks are thus allowed a degree of flexibility as to how responsibilities are **11.04** allocated between legal and compliance. To the extent a distinction is made, one might generally expect the advisory function to be placed with legal, especially as regards Type 2 risks, but the monitoring and, in effect, enforcement, of compliance by staff to be placed with compliance. However the allocation is made, the role of the legal department and in-house lawyers will be crucially important in relation to legal risk control. It is, perhaps, a curious omission that the BCBS has not apparently sought to lay down any general principles for the legal department's functions similar to those set out in Appendix 3, Part 3 below. Nevertheless, those principles would at least be a sensible starting point for any institution seeking to set out the legal department's 'constitution' in the post-Basel II world. For example, Principle 5, and issues associated with the independence of the function generally, would seem to apply equally to legal as to compliance. Hazards of the kind described in the Andersen Amicus Briefs would suggest that a degree of formalization in this area is now essential.

11.05 This also appears to be the view, at least provisionally, of the specialist in-house lawyer group, the Commerce & Industry (C&I) Group, which is recognized by the Law Society, as reported in its paper of 11 March 2005, 'Reconciling the Irreconcilable? Best Practice Guidelines for In-House Lawyers in England and Wales in the new corporate governance environment'. That paper looks at the role of in-house counsel generally, not just counsel employed by banks, but much of its content touches upon issues that bank lawyers would recognize. The following points are worth particular attention:

(1) It is remarked on that the many corporate governance reports and pronouncements that have been issued in recent years 'have tended to gloss over the in-house lawyer role'.

(2) 'We are beginning to see more attention being paid to the in-house legal function when things go wrong.'

(3) In the US, there is now legislation[9] requiring a public company's in-house lawyers to report to senior company officers if they hear of material violations of securities laws or fiduciary duties. There is no direct equivalent of this in the UK, as yet. However, it is noted that a solicitor's duty of confidentiality to the client, as laid down by the rules of the Law Society, does not apply to 'information acquired by a solicitor where he or she is being used by the client to facilitate the commission of a crime or fraud'.

(4) 'Even absent a formal whistleblowing system, an in-house lawyer may decide to escalate, within the company, concerns he or she has which are material and left persistently unaddressed' and 'in very exceptional cases' the lawyer may be left with no other option but to resign.

(5) 'The in-house legal community should . . . inform themselves as to their responsibilities under the Proceeds of Crime Act 2002, the Terrorism Act 2000 and the Money Laundering Regulations 2003.'

---

[9] Sarbanes-Oxley Act, s 307.

(6) '. . . for the senior in-house lawyer, even where board representation is not an option, access to the board is essential.'

(7) It can be very difficult in certain contexts to determine whether statements by in-house lawyers are genuine legal advice (which would qualify for legal professional privilege in line with the important recent case of *Three Rivers District Council and ors v The Governor and Company of the Bank of England*)[10] or business advice that just happens to emanate from a lawyer (some practical recommendations from the C&I Group Paper on this subject are reproduced in Appendix 4 below).

(8) 'To do your job to the best of your ability, as an in-house lawyer you need a thorough understanding of your client's objectives. This means close involvement with directors and other managers, with whom a constructive and collaborative relationship is also necessary. At the same time, the in-house lawyer must retain the professional detachment that allows him to recognise and point out issues of (for example) legal compliance, even at the risk of being perceived as unduly pessimistic or obstructive.'

The C&I Group Paper provides the following graphic example to illustrate some of the practical difficulties to be addressed: **11.06**

> When, at the coffee machine, Sheila asks you for your take on some issue or other, the capacity in which you are asked or in which you respond (friend, company lawyer, adviser, conscience of the company, a fellow-employee who happens to have a legal qualification) may be equally unclear. To make it explicit may appear to be defensive, rude, politically incorrect, counter-cultural and/or not in your best interests. When you propose a given course of action and Sheila appears satisfied and walks away, advice has been given. But is it legal advice or business advice? Advice which she expects you to stand by? If you prefaced your comments with a disclaimer or added one as she left, were those accepted? Recorded? Have you advised Sheila in her personal capacity and in so doing have you extended to her a personal duty of care?

There have been a number of suggestions from time to time regarding the desirability of a 'charter' for in-house counsel, and this appears to be the direction in which commentaries like the C&I Group Paper are taking us. In Australia and New Zealand, two professional lawyers' bodies have already produced a 'handbook' for in-house lawyers which contains a prominent ethical message as well as many practical pointers.[11] The handbook's advice includes the following: **11.07**

---

[10] [2004] UKHL 48. For a critique of certain aspects of this case, see Wallis and Dodwell, 'Three Rivers meet at the House of Lords: an opportunity missed' (2005) 02 JIBFL 53.

[11] See 'Ethics for In-house Counsel', produced by the Australian Corporate Lawyers Association (ACLA) and the Corporate Lawyers Association of New Zealand (CLANZ) in association with the St James Ethics Centre (now in its second edition).

- 'In-house counsel, when acting in relation to a transaction, must exercise caution, trading off legal risk against the desire to facilitate a successful consummation of the transaction.'

- 'In-house counsel should encourage an environment which permits whistle-blowers to come forward without fear of retribution.'

- In-house counsel should also protect their own interests as potential whistle-blowers by, amongst other things, ensuring that their contract of employment 'specifically recognises that the employee, as counsel, may be obliged to act as whistle-blower and requires that there will not be recriminations in that event'.

11.08 Further advice from the handbook regarding legal opinions is considered below.[12] The strong moral overtone of the handbook's approach is reflected in the section stating its ten 'ethical foundations'. These include:

- 'The profession of law is intrinsically tied to a noble ideal of justice as a cornerstone of any good society';
- 'Lawyers are their client's advisers and not merely their agents'; and
- 'The practise of law requires the exercise of moral courage.'

11.09 One can almost sense here a desire for the legal profession to 'go back to basics' and remind itself of what it really stands for. It is interesting that the dilemmas being faced by in-house lawyers (who at least do not have to cope with the competitive pressures affecting private legal practice) seem to be coaxing them to take a lead.

11.10 If we were to draw up a 'constitution' for an in-house legal department that responded to the issues that have been considered above, what would it contain? Questions that are likely to require consideration in the context of a legal department's terms of reference (or, as the BCBS might phrase it, 'charter or formal document')[13] include the following:

(1) Is the role of the lawyer merely to advise and notify, or are there situations where the lawyer has decision-making power?

(2) Can the lawyer overrule a decision of commercial colleagues and, if so, does this have 'final' effect or does it result in the question being taken to a higher level?

(3) Is the lawyer's advice or recommendation or any other related communication likely to be privileged in the event of any subsequent litigation?

(4) How can the lawyer ensure that he:
(a) receives full information to enable advice to be given,
(b) is kept properly informed as to whether or not any advice or recommendation has actually been followed,

---

[12] See para 11.23. [13] See Principle 4, in App 3, Part 3 below.

(c) is in a position to check whether any conditions or qualifications attached to any advice or recommendation are appropriately dealt with?

(5) What is the inference to be drawn from having lawyers made members of committees which are not in themselves specifically part of the legal function? Is the legal department to be deemed to have knowledge of everything that is discussed in such committees? If so, are there, in practice, procedures that have the effect of the necessary dissemination of information within the legal department?

(6) Should the general counsel be a member of the board of directors?[14] If he is, how should one distinguish the different 'hats' he might wear?

(7) Is the lawyer's professional independence protected and are his duties consistent with the professional obligations imposed on him by all relevant professional bodies?

(8) What is the lawyer's formal responsibility as regards corporate governance, reputational risk, and compliance with any codes of conduct or similar rules or guidelines that are imposed by regulators or other third parties?[15]

11.11   Formalization of such matters has its advantages but it may come at a price. One of the potential sacrifices (which astute drafting and common sense should, however, avoid being necessary) is the residual exercise of discretion in appropriate cases. For example, what advice should the lawyer give if he is aware that the institution is not strictly compliant with a particular requirement, but has good reason to believe that compliance will be achieved within a reasonably short time frame? Are there, in effect, 'discretionary areas', or must 'whistle-blowing' become automatic and immediate in all cases? To what extent is the lawyer

---

[14] At the time of the launch of the new organization 'General Counsel 100 Group' (March 2005) this question was raised in interviews reported in *The Lawyer* with Mark Harding, General Counsel of Barclays Bank, and Helen Mahy, Group General Counsel of National Grid Transco. According to the article, Harding was of the view that it is possible to combine the role of board member and general counsel but that general counsel 'should act as an adviser to the board and not take executive decisions', whereas Mahy was not in favour of being a board member, saying: 'Personally, I think there can be governance issues with the general counsel actually being a member of the board. However, it is essential for the FTSE 100 boards to have the general counsel present at all meetings as a trusted and important adviser.' Harding is also quoted as observing: 'With the change in the regulatory climate, there's a great deal more emphasis on the role of general counsel. The days when general counsel can simply react are gone. Now they have to be ahead of the game, which is difficult to do and requires a different mindset. People have realised that there are serious consequences of poor governance and risk management. A lot of those consequences can be mitigated by getting good legal advice.'

[15] The FSA's 'Final Notice', of 24 August 2004, imposing a record £17m fine on the Shell Group of companies for market abuse in connection with false or misleading statements about petroleum reserves noted that, amongst the remedial actions being undertaken by Shell, was the 'enhancement of the Group legal function to improve the ability of Group management to benefit from appropriate legal advice concerning potential corporate governance, reporting and disclosure issues'.

allowed to exercise a reasonable degree of judgment and discretion and to what extent is that ability being removed by legislation or regulation?

11.12 Determining the degree of discretion which is exercisable by the legal department is a difficult area. The issue arises, to some extent, as a result of the movement away from more traditional methods of regulation to a more formulaic and rules-based approach. Apart from the exercise of discretion in relation to infringements or non-compliance which are thought to be non-material and readily cured, questions arise in relation to judgement calls which lawyers might be expressly required to make. For example, the Proposed Interagency Statement expressly states that areas for 'legal review' in relation to complex structured products include 'suitability or appropriateness assessments'. Borderline questions on, say, legal (but 'aggressive') tax avoidance (as opposed to tax evasion) arrangements may resurface in this area. When is an 'aggressive' transaction to be regarded as permissible, cutting edge, innovative, etc and when is it to be regarded as 'too close to the wind'?

11.13 It is clear that the line is not drawn by reference only to compliance with the law. The close link with reputational risk implies that 'appropriateness' needs to take into account other factors. Using 'appropriateness' as a test in the context of risk management can give rise to a number of difficulties. Should all decisions be ad hoc or should they be based on precedent? Is it sensible, or even practical, to establish hard-and-fast criteria? If there is to be a test of 'appropriateness' in the context of complex structured transactions, is it likely to be relevant in other contexts? It is not entirely clear why this should just be a question for 'legal review' (if that is what is intended). The above issues as to the ability to overrule and the ability to take final decisions will apply in this context.

11.14 An overarching question concerns the extent to which 'good habits' that will have developed naturally in a legal department over generations may now need to be formalized by a 'rule book'. No one takes kindly to the imposition of rules requiring them to follow practices and procedures which they would have regarded as common sense and normal professional behaviour in any event— and lawyers are no exception here. Nevertheless, the new regime may require more formalization as we go forward and it seems likely that, to the extent that there might be any doubt, a written record of prescribed or approved procedure may be desirable. This should also provide at least some assistance for lawyers who may be understandably unsure of the correct procedure to be followed where their institution may be under threat of official investigation or criminal proceedings.[16] Many institutions will have done this either in anticipation of

---

[16] See the situations described in the Andersen Amicus Briefs.

Basel II or simply because they regard it as best practice in any event. Others may feel that it is somewhat counter-cultural but would be unlikely to risk being the 'odd man out'.

C. Opinions and Similar Documents

In appropriate circumstances, reliance will be placed on formal legal opinions **11.15** from external counsel. However, such opinions need to be treated with caution. They are usually directed towards very specific sets of circumstances (and documents). They also tend to be based on precisely crafted assumptions and qualifications, many of which are of a highly technical nature. If reliance is to be placed on the opinions, the assumptions need to be examined and, where appropriate, checked out.[17] (If the assumption is incorrect, the legal opinion may be valueless; similarly, unusual qualifications may mean that the institution does in fact have a significant risk exposure, notwithstanding the opinion.) Care needs to be taken also that the opinion is addressed to the institution that is relying on it or that it contains a clear statement that the institution may rely upon it. The fact that the opinion might be addressed to another company in the same group as the institution may not be sufficient.

As noted above, legal opinions are sometimes obtained by trade associations **11.16** and made available to their members in connection with standard form documents. Legal opinions may also be required by regulators. For example, the Financial Services Authority (FSA) is very specific as to its requirements for legal opinions in connection with close-out netting agreements.[18] The requirements, which are a good example of what one should generally look for in opinions on complex, cross-border transactions, include the following:

(1) The opinion should be written, reasoned and independent (see 4 below).
(2) It should be to the effect that if the netting agreement is terminated due to the default, liquidation or bankruptcy (or other similar circumstances) of either the counterparty or the bank, or the member of the bank's group which is party to the agreement, the relevant courts and administrative authorities would in such cases find that the bank's claims and obligations would be limited to the net sum under:
  (a) the law of the jurisdiction in which the counterparty is incorporated and, if a foreign branch of an undertaking is involved, also under the law of the jurisdiction in which the branch is located;

---

[17] See para 11.18 et seq. as regards specific qualifications and assumptions.
[18] See 'Interim Prudential Sourcebook: Banks' at NE: Section 1, para 6. As to close-out netting generally, see Ch 3 above.

     (b) the law that governs the individual transactions included; and

     (c) the law that governs any contract or agreement necessary to effect the contractual netting.

(3) The bank should review the validity of the opinion(s) annually and confirm the result to the FSA.

(4) By 'independent', the FSA means that the opinion(s) should be provided by 'an external independent source of advice of appropriate professional standing'.[19]

11.17 The FSA is also keen to ensure that banks check that the opinion really does cover the precise transaction. Banks are told to satisfy themselves that the agreement and opinion(s) 'are applicable to the counterparty, transaction type, product and jurisdictions involved', and if they are not so satisfied they should obtain additional opinions. The FSA even provides a list (which is not exhaustive) of issues to be covered by opinions. This is as follows:

    a) which are the central clauses in the documentation which provide for netting of transactions;

    b) that the unenforceability or illegality of any other clause in the documentation would be unlikely to undermine these central netting clauses;

    c) what are the factual circumstances in which the documentation may validly be used, including the type of counterparty. Banks should take particular care in obtaining opinions regarding counterparties governed by special rules relating to insolvency (e.g. local authorities, insurance companies etc.);

    d) whether the netting or other default provisions would be enforceable in non-liquidation events, such as administration, receivership, voluntary arrangements or schemes of arrangement;

    e) to what extent, if at all, the netting needs to be reflected in the records of the counterparties in order for it to be effective;

    f) whether a court or other relevant administrative authority in the jurisdiction covered by each legal opinion would uphold the rate chosen for the conversion of foreign currency obligations for the purpose of calculating the close-out amount; whether statutory or any other applicable rules applied by a court would detract from the enforceability of the agreement;

    g) if there is anything in the detail of the close-out methodology which might be held inconsistent with a view of the transactions as part of a single agreement insofar as the relevant law requires the same, and if so the effect of this on the enforceability of the netting (if a single agreement provision is not vital to the enforceability of netting in any jurisdiction the opinion should confirm this);

    h) though it might be difficult to state absolutely that enforceability would not be affected by the law of another jurisdiction, whether there is any reason to believe that the agreement would be unenforceable because of the law of another jurisdiction;

---

[19] The opinion(s) 'may be in the form of memoranda of law and addressed directly to the bank or to the sponsors of a particular agreement or may be the product of a number of banks pooling together to seek a collective opinion on a particular netting agreement'.

i)   whether there is a legal preference for automatic rather than optional close-out;

j)   if there would be legal problems in exercising any discretion or flexibility allowed under the netting agreement; and

k)   if other clauses are added to a standard form agreement, the FSA would expect lawyers, in giving their opinion, both to explain their effect in full and opine that these additional provisions do not throw any doubt upon the overall effectiveness of the netting agreement.

Examples of assumptions and qualifications in the context of legal opinions can be found in the formal legal opinion that relates to the ISLA standard document referred to in Chapter 3 above. As can be seen, there are a great number of them, but, evidently, the markets can live with them. The frequently heard protests about legal uncertainty should not blind us to the fact that market participants are, in reality, able to tolerate a fair amount of legal uncertainty, but they are more likely to be tolerant if: **11.18**

(1) they are familiar with the issues involved;

(2) the uncertainty is unavoidable;

(3) the uncertainty is not unique to English law (or, if it is, it is not material); and

(4) the risk represented by the uncertainty is manageable.

Two examples of qualifications from the opinion referred to above illustrate the point. There are express qualifications to the opinion in relation to indemnities for stamp duties and 'agreements to agree' as follows: **11.19**

• 'Any undertaking or indemnity given by a Party in respect of stamp duties or registration taxes payable in the United Kingdom may be void.'

• 'To the extent that any matter is expressly to be determined by future agreement or negotiation, the relevant provision may be unenforceable or void for uncertainty.'

The first qualification is not usually material in English law-governed finance transactions because it is very rarely the case that the documents involved attract any significant stamp duty. The second qualification is rarely material because legal advisers involved in the preparation of the documents would have alerted the parties to clauses that fall into this category (and, if clients wanted something enforceable, would have made appropriate amendments so that the qualification would not apply to an important provision, or, alternatively, clarified that the clients understood and were content with the risk implicit in the vagueness of the provision). The process of explanation, enquiry, amendment (if needed), and general risk analysis is, whether or not so named, all part of legal risk management.   **11.20**

Somewhat more complex is the 'standard' qualification found in opinions of this kind regarding provisions that require the performance of acts in countries where such acts would be illegal. English law will generally treat such provisions   **11.21** as unenforceable. More obviously, English law will also treat as unenforceable a provision that is illegal under the governing law of the document itself. Difficulties have arisen in the past where financing documents governed by English law have involved parties (usually borrowers or guarantors) located in countries which have fallen out of favour with the US (but not necessarily the UK) and US banks involved in the financing have been put under pressure (typically by virtue of a US legal requirement 'freezing' payments to and from such entities) to find a way to avoid compliance with their contractual obligations. If it can be found that the transaction requires an 'act' to be performed in, say, the US, where the 'freeze order' now renders it illegal, then the 'illegality in the place of performance' principle will apply and the obligations of the banks will not be enforceable. Because of this, a good deal of time has been spent in recent years analysing whether or not dollar payments between banks and customers require acts to be performed in the US.[20] It seems that, in the view of the English courts, ordinary payment obligations in US dollars do not so require, but, as ever, much will turn on the facts of any particular case, including the specific language used in the relevant documents. This qualification is a good example of how the market practice in opinion-giving has developed and, perhaps inevitably, resulted in longer and longer lists of qualifications. The qualification was rarely seen before the Iranian hostage crisis during the presidency of Jimmy Carter (and the subsequent 'freeze order' affecting Iranian assets) but that episode focused attention on the point and it would seem that the qualification is now here to stay. It does not, however, seem to cause the market any difficulty.

11.22 Assumptions in formal opinions can be at least as important as qualifications. They tend to describe the areas on which no legal opinion is being provided, but which may well merit further investigation by the client. For example, in relation to the opinion referred to above:

(1) It is clear from paragraphs 1.5 and 2 of that opinion that it is covering only certain very technical (but very important) matters; it is not a general opinion on the enforceability of the document. This is reflected in the assumption set out in paragraph 1(e) of Schedule 1 to the opinion.

(2) It is also apparent that the opinion-giver has not investigated whether or not the parties have followed appropriate corporate procedures (see paragraph 1 of Schedule 1 generally); the opinion is, after all, on a standard form, not a 'real' transaction.

(3) No opinion is given as to whether any party will actually have title to any assets to be transferred pursuant to the document (see paragraph 2(d) to

---

[20] See *Libyan Arab Bank v Bankers Trust* [1989] QB 728.

Schedule 1); again, an opinion on a standard form could not be expected to extend to such matters.

Sometimes, clients may raise legitimate questions as to the assumptions that **11.23** lawyers wish to make when giving opinions (especially where the lawyer makes assumptions about questions of law on which he is expected to advise!) but the above assumptions seem inescapable. In the context of legal risk management, they leave questions unanswered which, in any given transaction, probably should be answered. The in-house lawyer's job is therefore far from completed merely by virtue of the provision of this opinion or others like it. Further questions have to be considered and investigated. Beware of assumptions as to facts. It may be the most prudent course to interpret them as though they were questions: have you looked into this or that question (as to which an assumption has been made), and are you satisfied? Further advice on the use of legal opinions can be found in the ACLA/CLANZ Handbook referred to above (under the heading of 'Opinion Shopping'):[21]

> In-house counsel
> * must ensure that external counsel, when consulted, are appropriately briefed with all the relevant facts
> * must beware of in-house 'opinion shopping' and of clients who 'trade-off' in-house views against external views. Where practical, they should install appropriate controls to prevent this
> * must state their views unequivocally particularly where they have a contrary view to the one obtained
> * should record all advice given, particularly if that advice is ignored by the client
> * must endeavour to obtain the best available advice in the circumstances and inform the client of all advice obtained, at the same time as stating their own view.

Legal opinions, at least the more formal variety, are not a substitute for legal **11.24** advice. They are always confined to a relatively limited selection of important, but very narrow, points, typically regarding the 'valid, binding and enforceable' nature of obligations in particular documents and/or the capacity of particular parties and due execution.[22] They do not, for example, tell the recipient whether or not a document protects his interests (or exposes him to risks, and, if so, what risks) in accordance with instructions received; whether a document is in line with market practice; whether any of its terms seem unusual (or whether any terms one might have expected have been left out); or whether any terms seem

---

[21] See para 11.07 above.

[22] The opinions of 'local counsel' on cross-border transactions will generally go further, covering requirements for consents and government permits, whether or not any taxes are payable or any documents should be filed, whether a foreign judgment would be recognised in local courts, etc.

ambiguous. It should also be remembered that opinions only 'speak' as of the date they are given. An opinion can quickly become out of date (because the law changes) and care needs to be taken as to whether opinions 'on file' (or on a trade association's website) need to be brought up to date. They may have 'become' unreliable, incomplete, or just plain wrong.

11.25 In short, opinions do not really tell you very much at all, and they certainly do not provide advice. They are useful, but their use is limited. And unwarranted reliance on them can be dangerous. The following general points can be made by way of summary:

(1) A legal opinion is only as good as the firm or counsel who signs it; it is not the law, it is an opinion about the law, and opinions sometimes differ.

(2) A legal opinion may be out of date. The 'shelf life' tends to vary according to the kind of opinion. For example, an opinion that is confined to the interpretation of legislation (for example, the meaning of a given word or phrase) will generally stand until such time as either the legislation is repealed or amended or there is a court decision that affects its interpretation. An opinion that is on the application of the law to a given set of facts can cease to be relevant either because of changes to the law (including court decisions) or because the facts in question are not 'on all fours' with the relevant facts the next time the point has to be considered. An opinion on the effectiveness of provisions in a standard document should hold good as long as there are no subsequent changes to the law and as long as the document, when used, is used in circumstances contemplated, or 'assumed', by the opinion.

(3) Assumptions in opinions should always be checked. Qualifications and reservations should also be studied. Such provisions can prove to be risk 'warning lights', especially where they depart from the standard. The outcome of this may be that the assumption, qualification, or reservation is challenged, that a further opinion is required or that documentation is amended.

(4) Legal opinions are, usually, highly technical documents. Somewhat disappointingly, it is generally necessary for them to be reviewed by a lawyer rather than a layman. Lawyers can thus often find themselves giving advice about what another lawyer's opinion actually means.[23]

11.26 The practice of obtaining 'due diligence' reports in connection with major transactions also requires consideration in this context. The degree of protection

---

[23] For an excellent account of current best practice in relation to the provision of formal legal opinions, see Yeowart, 'Principles for Giving Opinion Letters on English law in Financing Transactions' (2003) 5 JIBFL 164.

such reports or similar documents provide against legal risk may be far from comprehensive. For example, the reports will, like legal opinions, usually have and, as with opinions, such [...]e diligence is to be of value. It [...]ce report, quite rightly, raises [...] in the institution should be [...]nsible for such investigation [...] itself monitored? These ques-[...]action may be proceeding at a [...]ce report might, wrongly, be [...]lways require some follow-up. [...] to this can result in risks being [...] if they have been contemplated

11.27 be contrasted with the use of [...]ormer is a sub-category of the [...] involves an exercise (the provi-[...]f the issues involved, the analy-[...] and, possibly, the provision of [...]ailored to the specific needs of a [...] expensive than reliance on an [...]ver, it may be the safer course to

[...]ention

11.28 [...]tages in the adoption of a clear [...]n) of documents and other (for [...]cent phenomena have brought [...]as brought with it an enormous [...]titutions of all kinds, in the form [...]randa, e-mails of various kinds [...]ormal and incautious language), [...]arties, diary notes, etc. Secondly, [...]ndals have involved instances of [...]ave tended to lead to 'no smoke [...]where and generally caused the

See para 1[...]2.

Roger McCormick *Legal Risk in the Financial Markets*

22 February 2006

CORRIGENDA SLIP

The following footnote should be inserted in Appendix 1 Part 1:

FOOTNOTE FOR APPENDIX 1 Part 1

"The effect of the amendment to Rule 4.90 of the Insolvency Rules 1986 (SI 1986/1925) introduced by the Insolvency (Amendment) Rules 2003, SI 2003/1730 (which was quickly superseded by the Insolvency (Amendment) Rules 2005, SI 2005/527) has been ignored."

mere fact of document destruction (whether by shredding or the more low-tech 'garden bonfire') to be a badge of guilt. The issues raised are closely linked to questions of legal professional privilege and the role of in-house counsel.

11.29 The management of legal and reputational risk will be assisted by some form of policy on document retention. At the most basic level, any business organization needs to be aware of any legal requirements affecting the retention of documents and records. Certain things have to be retained for a minimum period of time by law. More difficult questions arise in relation to documents that are not legally required to be kept, especially those that may be relevant in litigation. Here, some form of institutional policy is now virtually essential. The adoption of a policy, however, is not itself a cure-all. When delicate situations arise, such as when an official investigation is expected to be announced into a bank's affairs, decisions will be required which might have to override the policy if compliance with it would hinder, or give the impression that it was intended to hinder, that investigation. (The precise course to be followed will of course turn upon the requirements of the relevant laws, which may vary from country to country.) Further, compliance with a policy must be reasonably consistent. It will not impress anyone if the policy is generally ignored except when trouble seems to be around the corner.

11.30 As Rosenfeld has noted,[25] commenting on the US Supreme Court decision in *Arthur Andersen LLP v United States*[26] there are situations when certain kinds of behaviour are very difficult to justify, whatever the policy may be:

> The Government did not attack Andersen's document retention policy itself, but instead saw criminality in the firm's sudden interest in stressing compliance in light of the Enron investigation . . .
>
> . . . for five pages, the Court painstakingly details the actions that led Andersen to the obstruction charge. Without commenting on the prospects of a substantive charge, it is clear that the Court used these pages as a primer on what not to do when destroying documents. The Court cited the following facts:
>
> • Andersen had substantial issues with the SEC, including being enjoined from violating the securities laws.
>
> • Sometime soon after August 14th, 2001, Andersen was advised by a senior Enron accountant that the company could 'implode in a wave of accounting scandals and in early September it formed an emergency Enron team including Nancy Temple.'[27]

---

[25] 'Box of Sox Docs: Document Retention Policies and how the Andersen decision helps interpret Sarbanes-Oxley' (2005) 08 JIBFL 297.

[26] 544 US (2005). The Supreme Court reversed Arthur Andersen's conviction by lower courts, the reversal being based on an interpretation of the relevant US statute that the Court determined required a greater level of 'consciousness of wrongdoing' than the lower courts had thought appropriate.

[27] An in-house lawyer at Andersen.

- On October 8th, Andersen hired outside counsel to handle any Enron litigation and the next day Temple had a meeting where she wrote that an SEC investigation is 'highly probable'.

- On October 10th, an Andersen partner encouraged the Enron team to comply with the firm's document retention policy, stating, 'if [a document is] destroyed in the course of [the] normal policy and litigation is filed the next day, that's great . . . [W]e've followed our own policy, and whatever there was that might have been of interest to somebody is gone and irretrievable.'

- On October 12th, Temple e-mailed a fellow Andersen partner to 'remin[d] the engagement team to "[m]ake sure to follow the [document] policy." ' Again three days later several partners on the Enron engagement team were told to ensure that team members complied with the document retention policy. This was followed by the policy being hand distributed to all Enron team members with instructions to comply.

- On October 26th, an Andersen senior partner circulated an e-mail about Enron that said, 'the problems are just beginning and we will be in the cross hairs. The market place is going to keep the pressure on this and is going to force the SEC to be tough.'

- On that same day, an Andersen partner saw an Andersen senior partner shredding Enron documents and told him 'this wouldn't be the best time in the world for you guys to be shredding a bunch of stuff'.

- On October 31st, an Andersen forensics investigator met that same senior partner who, during the meeting, picked up a document with the words 'smoking gun' written on it, said 'we don't need this' and began to destroy it. The forensics investigator later informed Temple that the partner needed advice on Andersen's document retention policy.

- On November 8th, the SEC served Andersen with document subpoenas.

- On November 9th, Andersen informed its Enron staff by e-mail: 'No more shredding . . . We have been officially served for our documents.'

The court points out that throughout this time period until November 9th 2001, Andersen's Enron staff engaged in 'substantial destruction of paper and electronic documents.'

In its factual recitation, the Court couples Andersen's violations of the securities laws with the Enron team's repeated insistence on document destruction. The Court effectively showed that Andersen knew about the document destruction specifically because the Enron team ensured it took place. The Court also showed Andersen's knowledge of the contemplated proceeding.

Document retention policies should not be used to cover up 'dirty laundry'. **11.31** Leaving aside the legal and moral issues associated with such activity, at the purely practical level it is unlikely to work and will tend to suggest (and will be regarded by a court as suggesting) that the merits of any particular claim lie with the organization's opponent. Any such policy should operate in such a way that employees are alert to the fact that the policy requires, or may require, documents that in the ordinary course might have been destroyed, to be preserved if litigation is in prospect and that in such a situation guidance as to the right course of action should be sought from senior officers.

11.32 In-house counsel should be involved in the formulation and management of document retention policies and should, as indicated earlier,[28] take into account the developing case law on legal advice privilege and litigation privilege.[29] They should, for example, consider the extent to which their advice about the policy itself might qualify for privilege (which may depend on whether litigation has commenced, is reasonably in prospect, or is simply a possibility that 'comes with the territory') and, most importantly, whether their client in the organization has been sufficiently clearly identified. Whilst the destruction of documents in sensitive situations may be reprehensible, and even illegal, it is a different question as to the practice and policy to be adopted with regard to the creation of documents (including e-mail exchanges) which are neither strictly necessary nor likely to benefit from legal professional privilege.

11.33 The Proposed Interagency Statement (regarding complex structured finance products) suggests that procedures should be established for the generation, distribution, and retention of documents associated with individual transactions and that such documents would include (in addition to the standard legal documents and formal opinions) the following:

(1) a deal summary, including a list of deal terms;
(2) marketing materials;
(3) internal and external correspondence, including electronic communications;
(4) transaction and credit approvals, including any documentation of actions taken to mitigate initial concerns;
(5) minutes of critical meetings with the client;
(6) disclosures provided to the customer, including disclosures of all conflicts of interest and descriptions of the terms of any complex structured finance transactions; and
(7) acknowledgements received from the customer concerning accounting, tax, or regulatory implications associated with complex structured transactions.

E. Clarity of Lawyer Roles

11.34 Due diligence and the procedures associated with it are an example of legal risk issues that can arise as a result of, or at least be associated with, the relationship

---

[28] See para 11.05.
[29] See *Three Rivers DC v Bank of England (No 6)* [2004] UKHL 48 and *US v Philip Morris and BAT (Investments) Ltd* [2004] EWCA Civ 330.

between in-house lawyers and external lawyers. As with all advisory functions, the responsibility for advice and communication to and from the client needs to be absolutely clear. There is an inherent danger that responsibility for advice and the implementation of advice 'falls between the cracks'. The in-house function needs to be alert to this and take steps to minimize the risk of it happening. (The Proposed Statement also draws attention to a parallel problem that can arise where compliance functions are organized along product lines. 'This structure may prove challenging when offering complex structured finance transactions that cross product lines.') The problem is further accentuated where there is a multiplicity of external advisers (not uncommon in complex cross-border transactions) with no clear single point of responsibility to the institution.

Where in-house counsel assumes a more 'hands on' role in transaction man- **11.35** agement (even where external counsel has been appointed) this may have certain commercial advantages but it can increase the risk of confusion as to responsibility. This is particularly the case where there may be some risk of the 'true' client misunderstanding advice provided by external counsel or, for whatever reason, failing to implement it. These risks have, arguably, not been made easier to handle by the predominant use in recent years of electronic communication and the degree of informality and imprecision in language that such communication frequently involves. Traditional practices, such as the keeping of attendance notes in relation to the provision of advice and the confirmation of important advice in formal letters is, it would seem, less common. Given the pace and complexity of negotiations in major transactions this may be understandable, but it does have risk implications in that it can result in less effective record-keeping in relation to responsibility for advice. In this connection, it is important for the institution to appreciate that not only is the provision of correct legal advice a risk-sensitive issue, but so also is the record of responsibility for that advice.

Care needs to be taken as to the terms upon which external advisers are retained. **11.36** Formal documentation (whether in the form of letters or contracts) has become more common. This can have some benefits insofar as it clarifies the role of the external adviser. However, it is not unusual for the external adviser to take the opportunity to include limiting language in such documents which may not only affect the role and responsibility, but also the financial liability, of the adviser. Law firms may also, in certain cases, seek to disclaim responsibility for highly technical aspects of documentation, including the effectiveness of complex mathematical formulae.

It would be comforting to believe that external legal advisers would be in a **11.37** better position to provide a detached and objective view of an institution's position where legal risk issues arise. However, the in-house lawyer should not take objectivity and detachment for granted. The deregulation of the legal profession has had a number of effects, many of them positive, but it has not reinforced the ability of the external adviser to remain 'detached' (an attitude which is currently decidedly out of fashion). As noted in a recent article by David Gold and Adam Johnson (Herbert Smith) in *The European Lawyer*:

> Law firms routinely express their desire to get close to their clients, to understand the business better and to provide an improved service. While these sentiments may make sense, the risks of getting too close should not be ignored. Close involvement between a lawyer and the client company which fails or which is found to have been carrying on illicit business practices will inevitably result in closer scrutiny of the lawyer's role . . .

11.38 In the same article, Gold and Johnson draw attention to the dangers of lawyers accepting roles on the board of directors of clients and the potential conflict of interest that can result from this. They note that 'this practice, which has traditionally been seen as a vote of confidence in the company which hires a lawyer as director, but which is perceived by common law practitioners as a continental tolerance of an obvious source of conflict, should be a subject of careful review for firms who are concerned about managing risk in the post-Enron and Parmalat world'.

11.39 Parallel questions can arise in the context of in-house counsel and the relationship with specific business units of an institution. If, for example, the remuneration of in-house counsel is in some way dependent on the success of a business unit and the lawyer 'reports' to that unit, this may make it more difficult for the lawyer to be objective and independent when performing some of the functions that have been described.

11.40 Questions of conflicts and clarity of responsibility may be accentuated in transactions where the institution's legal adviser is appointed (and paid) by its customer. In such cases, the financial terms of the appointment (which might involve risk-sharing) merit scrutiny by the institution to whom the external lawyer is intended to owe a duty of care. The introduction of more open competition into the legal profession has brought many benefits to clients (or 'consumers of legal services') but it has increased pressures on lawyers to develop business more aggressively, and there may be dangers in situations where the lawyer owes his appointment in a major transaction (and the expectation of similar appointments in the future) to his banking client's customer rather than the client itself.

Part V

CONCLUSIONS

12

A 'RISK-BASED APPROACH' TO LAW

A book of this nature would not have been written thirty years ago. In those **12.01** days, books may have been produced about risks and risk management or about banking and financial law. But there would have been a lack of comprehension as to the significance of 'legal risk' as a distinct topic, and even greater puzzlement, and, no doubt, scepticism, over what legal risk management entailed or why anyone would need to know about it. Surely the combination of (a) obtaining sound legal advice, when needed, and (b) sensible business judgement results, inevitably, in legal risks being properly managed? Such a 'no nonsense' viewpoint would even now command a good deal of support. There is, however, a problem. If this is really all that is required, why do situations like those in the *Hammersmith and Fulham* case occur? (Why, for that matter, do bankers, accountants, and lawyers get into what we might loosely call 'Enron- or Parmalat-type' deals?) How confident can one be that the necessary advice will be sought, and that it will be heeded, when the biggest, most profitable deal of the year is apparently in prospect? Bonuses and success fees may be at stake! If we are to learn from some of the mistakes of the past two decades (and the regulators are insisting on this, whether we like it or not) we must accept that human weakness may undermine procedures that simply rely on honesty and common sense. Sadly, this means more rules and more rule books, for the legal function as well as other business units concerned with operational risk.

We live in a time when, for better or worse, awareness of, and concern about, **12.02** risk has reached extraordinary proportions in the financial markets as well as elsewhere. It could be said that what this book tries to do, to employ the jargon that has now become so popular, is explore the possibilty of a risk-based approach to the analysis of law and regulation, as they affect banks and other financial institutions. The apparent pretentiousness of such a statement may, it is hoped, be rebutted by consideration of the following:

• The regulators themselves purport to have a 'risk-based' approach to regulation; if regulation is itself risk-based, then the regulated should also attempt to respond in like manner.

- 'Risk-based' in this context must surely mean 'by reference to the relevant risks'—and legal risk is, as we have seen, one such, being a component part of operational risk.

- The legal adviser to a bank (whether internal or external) may, depending on the nature of the question asked, provide advice that is, implicitly or explicitly, linked to an appreciation of the legal risks involved in any given situation. However, under the new regulatory regime, the legal department of a financial institution, taken as a whole, is likely to be expected to deliver (using whatever resources may be available to it) regular analysis of, and proposals for (and possibly delivery of), the management of legal risk as it may be perceived to affect that institution. To do this, it will need to adopt a risk-based approach to the legal department function.

12.03 What is such an approach likely to involve? The management of risk is not a precise science. The management of legal risk is particularly difficult in this regard. For example, many have argued, and will no doubt continue to argue, that legal risk should not be perceived as a risk which is truly separate from other risks (whether operational risks, credit risks, or otherwise). There is something in this argument, in that legal risks rarely become a significant problem unless an associated risk (typically the risk of a counterparty being unwilling or unable to pay or the risk of an employee 'going off the rails') also manifests itself. However, the argument can also be made that at least certain kinds of risks (for example, defective documentation) may give rise to difficulties in their own right. A security interest which turns out to be invalid in the context of the customer's insolvency is almost certain to result in loss for an institution and the root cause of the loss is likely to be, essentially, a defect in procedure or behaviour which is in the nature of legal risk. In any event, it would be an extremely robust institution which, in the light of Basel II, decided to give no independent recognition to the management of legal risk as such.

12.04 The role of the in-house lawyer seems certain to become further involved with risk management rather than simply the provision of legal advice. The traditional legal training and experience acquired in the early years of practising law do not necessarily develop risk management skills of the kind that may be required. On the other hand, it is probably fair to say that expertise in risk management now 'comes with the territory' for most in-house lawyers. It would be foolish to err on the side of complacency but also unduly alarmist to assume that this represents a significant problem. It should, one might think, be seen more as an opportunity for lawyers to require that training in risk management skills and procedures become even more rigorous and professional than it is at present. It is notable that a number of the FSA's Final Notices issued in recent high profile cases refer to remedial measures being taken by the regulated firm that include an enhanced role for the legal department, in circumstances that suggest that the lawyers have more influence on risk management.

The following legal risk management objectives are suggested as a starting point **12.05** for a legal department that is to take a 'risk-based' approach to its function:

(1) The promotion of understanding of the responsibility of the department, and the individuals who work in it:
  (a) to the institution; and
  (b) under the law.
(2) The promotion of understanding of where, and in what circumstances, legal risks generally arise in the institution's business.
(3) The maintenance (and regular updating) of an accessible description of the key legal risks faced by the institution.
(4) Agreed procedures that facilitate the updating of the description referred to above (which, of course, requires factual and 'business' data as well as 'legal' data).
(5) Regular assessment of the impact of statements from regulators (including, for example 'Final Notices' issued by the Financial Services Authority (FSA) with respect to other regulated institutions) not only on relevant legal risks but also on the role of the department, and consideration of whether or not some modification of that role has become appropriate.
(6) With respect to any given 'risk situation', ensuring that the department has the ability to assess, and does assess:
  (a) whether it is peculiar to the institution or shared more widely;
  (b) whether there exists a reliable written description of the nature of the risk (for example, in a Financial Markets Law Committee (FMLC) or Law Society paper);
  (c) if there is some ambiguity or uncertainty as to the nature of the risk, what the scope of that is;
  (d) which parts of the institution's business are affected;
  (e) whether the appropriate individuals in the institution are fully apprised of the existence of the risk and what evidence there is of this;
  (f) whether or not the risk has been accepted and, if so, 'priced in';
  (g) if the risk has not been accepted, what steps have been taken to contain it or otherwise deal with it;
  (h) how frequently, and by whom, the situation is being monitored and updated information provided to those who need to have it.

12.06 From time to time, the carrying out of a legal 'stress testing' exercise should also be considered, in order to check how well systems and procedures for the implementation of the above are working.

12.07 The traditional position of the in-house lawyer as employee also needs further consideration. A degree of independence, perhaps quite a considerable degree, would seem to be essential if the in-house lawyer is to be able to perform the role effectively. It is not clear to what extent the financial world has adjusted to this requirement. It is obviously a sensitive area. Although perfection may not be achievable (and seeking to achieve it may be counter-productive if it results in lawyers losing the necessary 'feel' for the dynamics of the business that employs them) it seems prudent to adopt the habit of checking at regular intervals that the independence of the function (and the ability to give a 'detached view') is not being eroded. This should not be a mere box-ticking exercise. A suitable role for a committee of non-executive directors? One would hope that most institutions would find it an easy hurdle to clear.

12.08 It is clear, however, that dealing effectively with legal risk, when viewed as a social phenomenon, is not just a question for in-house lawyers. Others have responsibilities too. Questions remain as to the relationship between the role of the in-house lawyer as risk-manager, the traditional compliance function, and those who are charged with responsibility for risk generally (as opposed to legal risk alone). How will market practice in this area evolve? At present, there does not seem to be any consistent pattern, but perhaps there is too much variance amongst individual institutions' business models for there to be one right answer.

12.09 The role of regulators will be crucial, not merely as 'supervisor' and 'enforcer' in the traditional sense, but also as an effective cross-pollinator of ideas. This was traditionally one of the more valuable aspects of the 'old fashioned' approach to regulation and the now somewhat discredited 'light touch'. Financial institutions can learn a good deal from those who are able to see how the market as a whole is responding to new challenges. This does not necessarily involve the acceptance of unnecessary intrusiveness. It does, however, involve an acceptance of the possibility that other institutions might have even better ideas than one's own. It is in the nature of competitive endeavour that the best ideas are not always readily shared. However, enlightened self-interest would suggest that, at least in relation to technical legal risk issues, a degree of knowledge and experience pooling, perhaps through the informal medium of the regulator on occasions (although other fora may emerge as more appropriate), would in the long run benefit the market as a whole, and everyone who benefits from its smooth operation. It would be a pity if the FSA's role as rule-maker, 'policeman', and, in effect, judge (as regards the imposition of fines) was allowed to impede this.

Similarly, it is important that the FMLC (along with other similar bodies) **12.10**
continues to perform the valuable roles of:

(1) identifying concerns (through its 'radar function', etc);
(2) providing expert analysis of the relevant law in relation to specific concerns;
(3) acting as an informal 'bridge' to the judiciary; and
(4) being an authoritative voice for City lawyers when representations need
     to be made (although it, rightly, shrinks away from being perceived as a
     pressure group; there are other bodies who can fulfil that role).

If difficulties such as those considered in Part I of this book should recur, the **12.11**
essential elements appear to be in place to enable a concerted, market-wide,
risk management approach of the kind that was needed in certain of the
circumstances described at 3.30 to 3.36 above.

Legal risk management on both a unilateral and multilateral basis will evolve as **12.12**
the market and its regulatory regime evolves. What of the law itself? Part III of
this book sets out a series of examples of laws and situations that are commonly
regarded as involving a degree of legal risk at the present time. It is not intended
to be a comprehensive description of all current legal risk; that would be both
very lengthy and, unfortunately, quickly out of date. A visit to the FMLC's
website, and a perusal of past papers and reports produced by the Financial Law
Panel (FLP) shows that the range of issues that have given rise to concern over
the past fifteen years is remarkably broad, and includes (apart from those
covered elsewhere in this book) the following:

• the regulation of financial services on the internet;
• the implications of the introduction of the euro;
• the regulatory treatment of credit derivatives;
• the London Metal Exchange and LME warrants;
• agency dealing by intermediaries;
• financial dealings with trustees;
• insider dealing and chargee banks;
• shadow directorships;
• directors' duties; and
• emergency powers legislation.

Notwithstanding the number of issues mentioned above, the markets currently **12.13**
seem relatively relaxed about Type 2 risks and, as noted in Chapter 4, much
more worried by Type 1 risks. Perhaps those Type 2 risks which are known
about (for example, the risks considered in Chapter 7) are now so familiar that
we have learned, at least for the time being, to live with them? It is widely
acknowledged by market participants in the UK that the *existing* law, especially
the common law, is broadly satisfactory. It was perhaps regrettable that the

poorly drafted original version of Rule 4.90, so important to a wide range of basic market transactions, remained unamended for nearly twenty years, but during the period between the rule's coming into force and its amendment the markets did at least have the benefit of Lord Hoffmann's clarificatory interpretations of the law in the series of cases referred to in Chapter 6. There was a degree of uncertainty but it was manageable. For this, thanks are due to the courts.

12.14 What worries banking lawyers more in the current era is the endless and overwhelming production of *new* regulations and legislation, especially that which arises in the implementation of expansively drafted EU directives or in the name of 'protecting the consumer'. Much of the concern centres on the sometimes alarming potential that new laws have for 'surprise' and (generally unintended) side-effects. However, it is true that the concerns are sometimes overstated. One senses that in certain quarters it is felt that City lawyers might cry 'wolf' a little too often. However, bodies like the FMLC are not given to hyperbole and they do seem to identify areas that are genuinely troubling with remarkable frequency. Whatever may be the official target of some of this new legislation, poor drafting can lead to significant collateral damage.

12.15 If the lawyers and the law itself are in reasonable shape to facilitate legal risk management, how far have financial institutions as a whole progressed since the era under consideration in the first two chapters of this book? Politicians have in the past encouraged us all to 'move on' from the brashness and greed of the 1980s. The 1990s were supposed to be 'kinder and gentler'. A 'new financial architecture' was under construction. The horrors of '9/11' and the 'war on drugs' have also had repercussions for banks and what society expects of them in combating crime. But the same period has also witnessed a large number of appalling corporate frauds, some of which have severely damaged the reputation of major banks and the financial sector as a whole. Heavier regulation has resulted and, as yet, shows no signs of abating. The financial services sector is admired for its success and contribution to the economy, but our legal and regulatory system give the impression that it is still treated with a degree of suspicion.

12.16 Will banks in future be 'less aggressive' in response to this experience? And, if so, will that make it easier to deal with legal risk? It seems unlikely. (And it is not necessarily desirable.) We want banks to be risk-takers—but we also seek greater awareness of knowing where to draw the line. It is easy to say this, much harder to convey what we mean with any degree of precision. Such recent attempts as have been made at promulgating laws, rules, or regulation in this area illustrate the problem.

On the whole, the London markets have a good track record as regards the **12.17**
handling of legal risk, but it would be a brave man who would bet against there
being some event in the markets in, say, the next ten years that has overtones of
at least one of the Guinness, BCCI, Barings, Equitable Life, or Hammersmith
and Fulham affairs. The professionalism of our markets is exemplary, but legal
risk lurks just around the corner from human weakness—a factor that can never
be ruled out. Legal risk will therefore never disappear completely. We can only
strive to be as effective as possible in our management of it.

Recently, the *Financial Times* reported, *on the same day*,[1] that, 'Britain is good at **12.18**
banking (three of the world's top 10 banks are British); risk is not out of control;
and customers are protected by banks' desire not to make the wrong decisions
and through robust regulation', and also (drawing comparisons with Parmalat)
that, 'The [BPI][2] saga suggests some banks have learned little from the experience of the past few years'. Admittedly, the first comments were contained in an
article by the chief executive of the British Bankers Association, so there may
have been an element of PR in it—but the facts quoted are still impressive. On
the other hand, the second article strikes a critical chord that seems terribly
familiar. Good news stories and bad news stories seem to walk hand in hand.
Some of the bad news stories are indeed regrettable, but if they suddenly
stopped appearing, it would probably be an indication that banks were losing
their appetite for risk. We do not want that to happen. A market-based economy needs its risk takers. The policy questions are, inevitably, difficult. Like
most difficult questions, they are, essentially, questions of degree.

---

[1] 8 August 2005.
[2] BPI is an Italian bank, reported to be in financial difficulties. It had recently raised a large
loan from a consortium of lenders, including two major British banks, to fund a take-over that
went badly wrong.

Appendices

APPENDIX 1

Part 1

Rule 4.90 of the Insolvency Rules 1986 (as in effect until amended by the Insolvency (Amendment) Rules 2005)[1]

Rule 4.90   Mutual credit and set-off

(1) This Rule applies where, before the company goes into liquidation, there have been mutual credits, mutual debts or other mutual dealings between the company and any creditor of the company proving or claiming to prove for a debt in the liquidation.

(2) An account shall be taken of what is due from each party to the other in respect of the mutual dealings, and the sums due from one party shall be set off against the sums due from the other.

(3) Sums due from the company to another party shall not be included in the account taken under paragraph (2) if that other party had notice at the time they became due that a meeting of creditors had been summoned under section 98 or (as the case may be) a petition for the winding up of the company was pending.

(4) Only the balance (if any) of the account is provable in the liquidation. Alternatively (as the case may be) the amount shall be paid to the liquidator as part of the assets.

Part 2

Rule 4.90 of the Insolvency Rules 1986, as amended by the Insolvency (Amendment) Rules 2005

Mutual credits and set-off
4.90

(2) This Rule applies where, before the company goes into liquidation there have been mutual credits, mutual debts or other mutual dealings between the company and any creditor of the company proving or claiming to prove for a debt in the liquidation

(3) The reference in paragraph (1) to mutual credits does not include—

   (a) any debt arising out of an obligation incurred at a time when the creditor had notice that—

      (i) a meeting of creditors had been summoned under section 98; or

      (ii) a petition for the winding up of the company was pending;

   (b) any debt arising out of an obligation where—

      (i) the liquidation was immediately preceded by an administration; and

      (ii) at the time the obligation was incurred the creditor had notice that an application for an administration order was pending or a person had given notice of intention to appoint an administrator;

---

[1] Rule 4.90, as amended by the Insolvency (Amendment) Rules 2005, is set out in Part 2 of this Appendix. The amendments came into effect on 1 April 2005.

(c) any debt arising out of an obligation incurred during an administration which immediately preceded the liquidation; or

(d) any debt which has been acquired by a creditor by assignment or otherwise, pursuant to an agreement between the creditor and any other party where that agreement was entered into—

(i) after the company went into liquidation;

(ii) at a time when the creditor had notice that a meeting of creditors had been summoned under section 98;

(iii) at a time when the creditor had notice that a winding up petition was pending;

(iv) where the liquidation was immediately preceded by an administration, at a time when the creditor had notice that an application for an administration order was pending or a person had given notice of intention to appoint an administrator; or

(v) during an administration which immediately preceded the liquidation.

(4) An account shall be taken of what is due from each party to the other in respect of the mutual dealings, and the sums due from one party shall be set off against the sums due from the other.

(5) A sum shall be regarded as being due to or from the company for the purposes of paragraph (3) whether—

(a) it is payable at present or in the future;

(b) the obligation by virtue of which it is payable is certain or contingent; or

(c) its amount is fixed or liquidated, or is capable of being ascertained by fixed rules or as a matter of opinion.

(6) Rule 4.86 shall also apply for the purposes of this Rule to any obligation to or from the company which, by reason of its being subject to any contingency or for any other reason, does not bear a certain value.

(7) Rules 4.91 to 4.93 shall apply for the purposes of this Rule in relation to any sums due to the company which—

(a) are payable in a currency other than sterling;

(b) are of a periodical nature; or

(c) bear interest.

(8) Rule 11.13 shall apply for the purpose of this Rule to any sum due to or from the company which is payable in the future.

(9) Only the balance (if any) of the account owed to the creditor is provable in the liquidation. Alternatively the balance (if any) owed to the company shall be paid to the liquidator as part of the assets except where all or part of the balance results from a contingent or prospective debt owed by the creditor and in such case the balance (or that part of it which results from the contingent or prospective debt) shall be paid if and when that debt becomes due and payable.

(10) In this Rule 'obligation' means an obligation however arising, whether by virtue of an agreement, rule of law or otherwise.

APPENDIX 2

Extract from the Turnbull Report

The following text is reproduced from the Appendix to the Turnbull Report

Assessing the effectiveness of the company's risk and control processes

Some questions which the board may wish to consider and discuss with management when regularly reviewing reports on internal control and carrying out its annual assessment are set out below. The questions are not intended to be exhaustive and will need to be tailored to the particular circumstances of the company.

The Appendix should be read in conjunction with the guidance set out in [the Turnbull Report].

1. Risk assessment

— Does the company have clear objectives and have they been communicated so as to provide effective direction to employees on risk assessment and control issues? For example, do objectives and related plans include measurable performance targets and indicators?

— Are there significant internal and external operational, financial, compliance and other risks identified and assessed on an ongoing basis? (Significant risks may, for example, include those related to market, credit, liquidity, technological, legal, health, safety and environmental, reputation and business probity issues).

— Is there a clear understanding by management and others within the company of what risks are acceptable to the board?

2. Control environment and control activities

— Does the board have clear strategies for dealing with the significant risks that have been identified? Is there a policy on how to manage these risks?

— Do the company's culture, code of conduct, human resource policies and performance reward systems support the business objectives and risk management and internal control system?

— Does senior management demonstrate, through its actions as well as its policies, the necessary commitment to competence, integrity and fostering a climate of trust within the company?

— Are authority, responsibility and accountability defined clearly such that decisions are made and actions taken by the appropriate people? Are the decisions and actions of different parts of the company appropriately co-ordinated?

— Does the company communicate to its employees what is expected of them and the scope of their freedom to act? This may apply to areas such as customer relations; service levels for both internal and outsourced activities; health, safety and environmental protection; security of tangible and intangible assets; business continuity issues; expenditure matters; accounting; and financial and other reporting.

— Do people in the company (and its providers of outsourced services) have the knowledge, skills and tools to support the achievement of the company's objectives and to manage effectively risks to their achievement?

— How are processes/controls adjusted to reflect new or changing risks, or operational deficiencies?

3. Information and communication

— Do management and the board receive timely, relevant and reliable reports on progress against business objectives and the related risks that provide them with the information, from inside and outside the company, needed for decision-making and management review purposes? This could include performance reports and indicators of change, together with qualitative information such as on customer satisfaction, employee attitudes etc.

— Are information needs and related information systems reassessed as objectives and related risks change or as reporting deficiencies are identified?

— Are periodic reporting procedures, including half-yearly and annual reporting, effective in communicating a balanced and understandable account of the company's position and prospects?

— Are there established channels of communication for individuals to report suspected breaches of laws or regulations or other improprieties?

4. Monitoring

— Are there ongoing processes embedded within the company's overall business operations, and addressed by senior management, which monitor the effective application of the policies, processes and activities related to internal control and risk management? (Such processes may include control self-assessment, confirmation by personnel of compliance with policies and codes of conduct, internal audit reviews or other management reviews).

— Do these processes monitor the company's ability to re-evaluate risks and adjust controls effectively in response to changes in its objectives, its business, and its external environment?

— Are there effective follow-up procedures to ensure that appropriate change or action occurs in response to changes in risk and control assessments?

— Is there effective communication to the board (or board committees) on the effectiveness of the ongoing monitoring processes on risk and control matters? This should include reporting any significant failings or weaknesses on a timely basis.

— Are there specific arrangements for managing monitoring and reporting to the board on risk and control matters of particular importance? These could include, for example, actual or suspected fraud and other illegal or irregular acts or matters that could adversely affect the company's reputation or financial position.

APPENDIX 3

Part 1
BCBS Principles

Developing an Appropriate Risk Management Environment

Principle 1: The board of directors should be aware of the major aspects of the bank's operational risks as a distinct risk category that should be managed, and it should approve and periodically review the bank's operational risk management framework. The framework should provide a firm-wide definition of operational risk and lay down the principles of how operational risk is to be identified, assessed, monitored, and controlled/mitigated.

Principle 2: The board of directors should ensure that the bank's operational risk management framework is subject to effective and comprehensive internal audit by operationally independent, appropriately trained and competent staff. The internal audit function should not be directly responsible for operational risk management.

Principle 3: Senior management should have responsibility for implementing the operational risk management framework approved by the board of directors. The framework should be consistently implemented throughout the whole banking organisation, and all levels of staff should understand their responsibilities with respect to operational risk management. Senior management should also have responsibility for developing policies, processes and procedures for managing operational risk in all of the bank's material products, activities, processes and systems.

Risk Management: Identification, Assessment, Monitoring, and Mitigation/Control

Principle 4: Banks should identify and assess the operational risk inherent in all material products, activities, processes and systems. Banks should also ensure that before new products, activities, processes and systems are introduced or undertaken, the operational risk inherent in them is subject to adequate assessment procedures.

Principle 5: Banks should implement a process to regularly monitor operational risk profiles and material exposures to losses. There should be regular reporting of pertinent information to senior management and the board of directors that supports the proactive management of operational risk.

Principle 6: Banks should have policies, processes and procedures to control and/or mitigate material operational risks. Banks should periodically review their risk limitation and control strategies and should adjust their operational risk profile accordingly using appropriate strategies, in light of their overall risk appetite and profile.

Principle 7: Banks should have in place contingency and business continuity plans to ensure their ability to operate on an ongoing basis and limit losses in the event of severe business disruption.

Role of Supervisors

Principle 8: Banking supervisors should require that all banks, regardless of size, have an effective framework in place to identify, assess, monitor and control/mitigate material operational risks as part of an overall approach to risk management.

Principle 9: Supervisors should conduct, directly or indirectly, regular independent evaluation of a bank's policies, procedures and practices related to operational risks. Supervisors should ensure that there are appropriate mechanisms in place which allow them to remain apprised of developments at banks.

Role of Disclosure

Principle 10: Banks should make sufficient public disclosure to allow market participants to assess their approach to operational risk management.

Part 2
Risk Management Principles for Electronic Banking[1]

Principle 1: The Board of Directors and senior management should establish effective management oversight over the risks associated with e-banking activities, including the establishment of specific accountability, policies and controls to manage these risks.

Principle 2: The Board of Directors and senior management should review and approve the key aspects of the bank's security control process.

Principle 3: The Board of Directors and senior management should establish a comprehensive and ongoing due diligence and oversight process for managing the bank's outsourcing relationships and other third party dependencies supporting e-banking.

Principle 4: Banks should take appropriate measures to authenticate the identity and authorization of customers with whom they conduct business over the Internet.

Principle 5: Banks should use transaction authentication methods that promote non-repudiation and establish accountability for e-banking transactions.

Principle 6: Banks should ensure that appropriate measures are in place to promote adequate segregation of duties within e-banking systems, databases and applications.

Principle 7: Banks should ensure that proper authorization controls and access privileges are in place for e-banking systems, databases and applications.

Principle 8: Banks should ensure that appropriate measures are in place to protect the data integrity of e-banking transactions, records and information.

Principle 9: Banks should ensure that clear audit trails exist for all e-banking transactions.

Principle 10: Banks should take appropriate measures to preserve the confidentiality of key e-banking information. Measures taken to preserve confidentiality should be commensurate with the sensitivity of the information being transmitted and/or being stored in data bases.

Principle 11: Banks should ensure that adequate information is provided on their websites to allow potential customers to make an informed conclusion about the bank's identity and regulatory status of the bank prior to entering into e-banking transactions.

Principle 12: Banks should take appropriate measures to ensure adherence to customer privacy requirements applicable to the jurisdiction to which the bank is providing e-banking products and services.

Principle 13: Banks should have effective capacity, business continuity and contingency planning processes to help ensure the availability of e-banking systems and services.

---

[1] These principles are reproduced from the BCBS paper, 'Risk Management Principles for Electronic Banking' of July 2003. Principles 11–14 are described as having particular relevance to legal and reputational risk management (banks being encouraged to ensure e-banking services are 'delivered on a consistent and timely basis in accordance with high customer expectations for constant and rapid availability and potentially high transaction demand'. However, other principles listed here, eg Principle 6, also have some bearing on legal risk management.

Principle 14: Banks should develop appropriate incident response plans to manage, contain and minimise problems arising from unexpected events, including internal and external attacks, that may hamper the provision of e-banking systems and services.

Part 3
Principles Applicable to the Compliance Function in Banks

Principle 1: The bank's board of directors has the responsibility for overseeing the management of the bank's compliance risk. The board should approve the bank's compliance policy, including a charter or other formal document establishing a permanent compliance function. At least once a year, the board or a committee of the board should review the bank's compliance policy and its ongoing implementation to assess the extent to which the bank is managing its compliance risk effectively.

Principle 2: The bank's senior management is responsible for establishing a compliance policy, ensuring that it is observed and reporting to the board of directors on its ongoing implementation. Senior management is also responsible for assessing whether the compliance policy is still appropriate.

Principle 3: The bank's senior management is responsible for establishing a permanent and effective compliance function within the bank as part of the bank's compliance policy.

Principle 4: The bank's compliance function should have a format status within the bank. This is best achieved by a charter or other formal document approved by the board of directors that sets out the function's standing, authority and independence.

Principle 5: The bank's compliance function should be independent from the business activities of the bank.

Principle 6: The role of the bank's compliance function should be to identify, assess and monitor the compliance risks faced by the bank, and advise and report to senior management and the board of directors about these risks.

Principle 7: The head of compliance is responsible for the day-to-day management of the activities of the compliance function in accordance with the principles set out in this paper.

Principle 8: Staff exercising compliance responsibilities should have the necessary qualifications, experience and professional and personal qualities to enable them to carry out their duties effectively.

Principle 9: The compliance function for banks that conduct business in other jurisdictions should be structured to ensure that local compliance issues are satisfactorily addressed within the framework of the compliance policy for the bank as a whole.

Principle 10: The scope and breadth of the activities of the compliance function should be subject to periodic review by the internal audit function.

Principle 11: Specific tasks of the compliance function may be outsourced, subject to appropriate oversight by the head of compliance, who should remain an employee of the bank.

APPENDIX 4

Recommendations from the C&I Group Paper regarding legal advice privilege

Three Rivers is a very recent decision, with very significant implications for in-house lawyers in many areas including governance. Organizations must continue to be very wary as to how, and through whom, they seek legal advice. This applies just as much when advice is being sourced internally as externally. Consider the following to help ensure that legal advice privilege does attach:

- Identify at the outset who the internal client is for the purpose of seeking the legal advice in question. It is likely that this will be the person or persons who actually communicate with the lawyer and who make decisions upon the advice to be sought and received. If the communicator with the lawyer is not the same person as the relevant decision maker, then you could have a problem.
- Once the client is identified, do not allow the provision or receipt of information to, or from, legal advisers to be delegated to others.
- Be careful how information is disseminated internally and externally. If it is disseminated widely there is again a possibility that legal advice privilege will be lost.
- Consider the greater use of 'litigation privilege' when litigation is reasonably in prospect. It can cover communications with a third party so long as the dominant purpose of the communication is that there is an intention it be put before the lawyer.
- Avoid making manuscript amendments in the margin of documents or correspondence, as these may not be privileged.
- Where legal advice is obtained, any internal assessment of that advice may not be privileged, so consider how it is recorded. It may be sensible for all initial assessments and summaries to be conducted by an in-house lawyer before circulation to internal clients.

. . .

All communications relating to legal advice between a client and its lawyer, whether in-house or external should be clearly marked 'Legally Privileged'. This practice could be devalued however if used indiscriminately, and the courts will consider the dominant purpose of the communication when determining whether privilege does in fact attach . . . In select cases, cautionary language should be considered putting it beyond doubt:

- who you are advising and in what capacity;
- that you are advising the recipient in his or her capacity as an executive of the organization and in no other capacity;
- the facts on which your advice is based;
- the limitations to which your advice is subject; and
- if you are copying your advice to colleagues, the reasons why, in order to deflect any argument that by doing so you are waiving privilege.

INDEX